975
.C9

JURISPRUDENCE

THE PHILOSOPHY AND
METHOD OF THE LAW

JURISPRUDENCE

THE PHILOSOPHY AND
METHOD OF THE LAW

Edgar Bodenheimer

HARVARD UNIVERSITY PRESS
Cambridge, Massachusetts · 1967

TO MY FATHER AND
TO THE MEMORY OF MY MOTHER

PREFACE

My early work (*Jurisprudence*, 1940) which forms the nucleus for parts of the present volume, stated as its purpose "to give aid to the student of law and politics who is interested in the general aspects of the law as an instrument of social policy." The purpose of the present book remains essentially the same, although large portions of the material have been completely rewritten and the scope of coverage has been substantially enlarged. Attention has here been given to a number of jurisprudential problems which were not mentioned in the early work, and an entirely new part, entitled "The Sources and Techniques of the Law," has been included. This last part of the book is addressed primarily, but by no means exclusively, to law students and members of the legal profession interested in the methodology of the law and in the characteristic features and instrumentalities of the adjudicatory process.

The historical materials dealing with the development of jurisprudential thought, which were dispersed through the 1940 volume, have been concentrated in the first part of the present book and have been reorganized along essentially chronological lines. The reader will soon discover that this historical introduction is largely descriptive in character and, with the exception of the concluding section, contains almost no critical appraisal of the schools of thought therein discussed from the point of view of my own legal philosophy. I felt that inasmuch as the use of the book for instructional purposes was included within the objectives for which it was published, an evaluation of the contributions of the great legal thinkers might appropriately be reserved for class discussion.

The treatment of the substantive problems of general legal theory in the second and third parts of this book, on the other hand, is based on certain philosophical and methodological assumptions which are implicit in my approach to the domain of jurisprudence. Perhaps the most basic one among these assumptions is the firm conviction that no jurisprudential treatise should bypass or ignore the burning questions connected with the achievement of justice in human relations, notwithstanding the difficulties encountered in any attempt to apply objective criteria in dealing with this subject. It is submitted that the theory and philosophy of the law must remain sterile and arid if they fail to pay attention to the human values which it is the function of the law to promote. This does not mean, of course, that the jurisprudential scholar should be encouraged to let his imagination and emotional predispositions run amok in his treatment of the fundamental problems of the legal order. On the contrary, he should be held to a standard of detachment and objectivity which enjoins him to separate, to the best of his ability and within realizable limits, objective phenomena or data verifiable by reason or experience from subjective opinion or purely speculative thought. Furthermore, the jurist must be aware that conclusions with respect to axiological questions are necessarily tentative in character and subject to reconsideration in the light of new findings and new experiences. But although scholarly modesty and restraint is mandatory for those who attempt to seek the truth in the realm of human values, no a priori reason can be shown to exist which compels us to ban all scientific effort from this important sphere of human existence.

The subject matter of jurisprudence is a very broad one, encompassing the philosophical, sociological, historical, as well as analytical components of legal theory. It is impossible within the limits of a one-volume introductory treatise to pursue all the various objectives of this discipline at the same time. Inasmuch as a considerable number of jurisprudential works have been published in this century in English-speaking countries which have concentrated upon an analytical elucidation of basic legal concepts (such as the concepts of right, duty, liability, or corporate personality), no attempt has been made in this volume to provide definitions or explanations of such technical terms of the law or to develop a general theory of contract, property, or criminal responsibility. Furthermore, there has been undertaken only a cursory treatment of the historical, sociological, and economic forces which in the past and present have helped to shape the evolution of the law. Much valuable insight into this field of jurisprudence can be gained from the works of Ehrlich, Pound, Fechner, Friedmann, and others. Since I feel that the philosophical analysis of the essential nature of the law and of the basic goals and values to be served by the legal order is an aspect of jurisprudential theory which has been somewhat neglected in the nineteenth and twentieth centuries, a substantial part of the present volume has been devoted to this critical area of legal thought.

I wish to thank the Rockefeller Foundation for facilitating the completion of this volume by a generous research grant. Gratitude is also expressed to the Yale Law School, which afforded me not only the use of its excellent research facilities but also the benefit of great intellectual stimulation. Invaluable help has been given by my wife, Brigitte M. Bodenheimer, who assisted in my research and contributed much constructive criticism. She also prepared the Index. Last but not least, appreciation is expressed to Miss Dorothy Alice Cox and Mrs. Mar Dean Leslie for their painstaking assistance in the preparation of the manuscript.

Salt Lake City   Edgar Bodenheimer
February 1962

CONTENTS

PART II

THE NATURE AND
FUNCTIONS OF THE LAW

PART III

THE SOURCES AND
TECHNIQUES OF THE LAW

PART I

HISTORICAL

INTRODUCTION TO

THE PHILOSOPHY

OF LAW

I

GREEK AND ROMAN LEGAL THEORY

Section 1. *Early Greek Theory*

All peoples and nations of this world, beginning with the early stages of their history, have formed certain ideas and conceptions—of varying concreteness and articulateness perhaps—about the nature of justice and law. If we start our survey of the evolution of legal philosophy with an account of the legal theory of the Greeks rather than that of some other nation, it is because the gift of philosophical penetration of natural and social phenomena was possessed to an unusual degree by the intellectual leaders of ancient Greece. By subjecting nature as well as society and its institutions to a searching, fundamental analysis, the Greeks became the philosophical teachers of the Western world and Greek philosophy a microcosm of world philosophy as a whole. While some of the presuppositions and conclusions stated by Greek thinkers have not been able, of course, to stand the test of time because of the discoveries and experience of later epochs, the way these thinkers posed and discussed the basic problems of life in philosophical terminology and explored various possible approaches to their solution may claim enduring validity. In this sense, the words of Friedrich Nietzsche still hold true today: "When we speak of the Greeks, we unwittingly speak of today and yesterday." [1]

The legal conceptions of the archaic age of the Greeks are known to us through the epic works of Homer and the poetry of Hesiod. Law at that time was regarded as issuing from the gods and known to mankind through revelation of the divine will. Hesiod pointed out that wild animals, fish, and birds devoured each other because law was unknown to them: but Zeus, the chief of the Olympian gods, gave law to mankind as his greatest present.[2] Hesiod thus contrasted the *nomos* (ordering principle) of nonrational nature with that of the rational (or at least potentially rational) world of human beings. Foreign to his thought was the skepticism of some of the Sophists of a later age, who sought to derive a right of the strong to oppress the weak from the fact that in nature the big fish eat the little ones.[3] To him law was an order of peace founded on fairness, obliging men to refrain from violence and to submit their disputes to an arbiter.

Law and religion remained largely undifferentiated in the early period. The famous oracle of Delphi, considered an authoritative voice for the enunciation of the divine will, was frequently consulted in matters of law and legislation. The forms of lawmaking and adjudication were permeated with religious ceremonials, and the priests played an important role in the administration of justice. The king, as the supreme judge, was believed to have been invested with his office and authority by Zeus himself.[4]

The burial of the dead was regarded by the Greeks as a command of the sacral law, whose violation would be avenged by divine curse and punishment. A famous scene in Sophocles' tragedy *Antigone* graphically depicts a situation where this religious duty came into irreconcilable conflict with the command of a secular ruler. King Creon forbade the burial of Polyneikes, brother of Antigone, because he had offended against the laws of the state. Antigone, convinced that her action would expose her to certain death, heroically defied this command and buried her brother in accordance with the prescribed rites

---

[1] *Human, All-Too-Human*, vol. 7 of *Complete Works*, ed. O. Levy (New York, 1924), pt. II, p. 111.

[2] Hesiod, *Erga* (Works and Days), transl. A. W. Mair (Oxford, 1908), pp. 273–285 (verses 274 ff.).

[3] Felix Flückiger, *Geschichte des Naturrechts*, I (Zürich, 1954), 10; Alfred Verdross-Drossberg, *Grundlinien der antiken Rechts- und Staatsphilosophie* (Vienna, 1948), p. 17.

[4] See Flückiger, pp. 12–13.

of the Greek religion. When the king called her to account, she pleaded that in burying her brother she had broken Creon's law, but not the unwritten law:

> "Not of today or yesterday they are,
> But live eternal: (none can date their birth)
> Not I would fear the wrath of any man
> (And brave God's vengeance) for defying these." [5]

Here, in a famous dramatic work, we find one of the earliest illustrations of a problem which has occupied the attention of the legal thinkers of all ages: namely, the problem of the conflict between two orders of law, both of which seek to claim the exclusive allegiance of man.

An incisive change in Greek philosophy and thought took place in the fifth century B.C. Philosophy became divorced from religion, and the ancient, traditional forms of Greek life were subjected to searching criticism. Law came to be regarded not as an unchanging command of a divine being, but as a purely human invention, born of expediency and alterable at will. The concept of justice was likewise stripped of its metaphysical attributes and analyzed in terms of human psychological traits or social interests.

The thinkers who performed this "transvaluation of values" were called the Sophists, and they may be regarded as the first representatives of philosophical relativism and skepticism. Protagoras, for instance, one of the leading figures among the earlier Sophists, denied that man could have any knowledge about the existence or nonexistence of the gods and asserted that man as an individual was the measure of all things; "being" to him was nothing but subjectively colored "appearance." He also took the view that there exist at least two opinions on every question, and that it is the function of rhetoric to transform the weaker line of argumentation into the stronger one. [6]

A sharp distinction between nature (*physis*) and law (*nomos*) was drawn by the Sophist Antiphon. The commands of *physis* are necessary and inexorable, he taught, but those of the *nomos* stem from human arbitrariness and are nothing but casual, artificial arrangements changing with the times, men, and circumstances. According to him, nobody can violate the laws of nature with impunity; but one who violates a law of the state does not suffer either punishment or dishonor if the violation remains undetected. Implicit in this argument

---

[5] *Antigone* 450.
[6] The text of the preserved fragments of Protagoras (in Greek and German) is found in Hermann Diels, *Die Fragmente der Vorsokratiker*, 6th ed. by W. Kranz (Berlin, 1952), II, 263 ff.

is the assumption that human conventions are in reality nothing but fetters of natural "right." [7]

Proceeding from similar premises, the Sophist Callicles proclaimed the "right of the strong" as a basic postulate of "natural" as contrasted with "conventional" law. Nature in animal as well as human life, he argued, rests on the innate superiority of the strong over the weak; human legal enactments, on the other hand, are made by the weak and the many, because they are always in the majority. The laws attempt to make men equal, while in nature they are fundamentally unequal. The strong man, therefore, acts merely in accordance with *physis* if he flouts the conventions of the herd and throws off the unnatural restrictions of the law.[8]

The "right of might" was likewise taught by Thrasymachus, who, though he did not perhaps share Callicles' love of the self-sufficient superman, was convinced that laws were created by the men and groups in power to promote their own advantage. In a famous passage in the *Republic*, Plato puts into his mouth the following definition of justice: "I declare that justice is nothing else than that which is advantageous to the stronger." [9] It follows that the just man is he who obeys the laws serving the interest of the governing groups; the unjust man is he who disregards them. But since the subject who obeys the commands of the ruler is in reality promoting the good of another and inflicting injury on himself, Thrasymachus submitted, the just man is always worse off than the unjust man; it pays therefore to act unjustly, if one can get away with it. "Injustice, when great enough, is mightier and freer and more masterly than justice." [10]

Section 2. *Plato's View of the Law*

Socrates, in discussing the meaning of justice with Thrasymachus in Plato's *Republic*, is able to convince the listeners to the argument that the definition of justice had been turned "upside down" by Thrasymachus.[1] This indeed was the considered opinion of Socrates and his great pupil, Plato (429–348 B.C.), of most of the teachings of the Sophists: that the meaning of truth had been turned "upside down" by them, and that their skepticism and agnosticism posed a danger to the

---

[7] Diels, II, 346. See also J. Walter Jones, *The Law and Legal Theory of the Greeks* (Oxford, 1956), p. 38.

[8] See Callicles in Plato, *Gorgias*, transl. W. R. M. Lamb (Loeb Classical Library ed., 1932), 483–484.

[9] *The Republic*, transl. A. D. Lindsay (Everyman's Library ed., 1950), Bk. I. 338.

[10] *Id.*, Bk. I. 344.

[1] *The Republic*, transl. A. D. Lindsay, Bk. I. 343. On Thrasymachus' view of justice see the preceding section.

well-being of society and harmony within the commonwealth. Socrates set himself the task of overcoming the subjectivism and relativism of the Sophists and of establishing a substantive system of ethics based on an objectively verified theory of values. But he developed his ideas solely in oral disputation with his Athenian fellow citizens; as far as we know, he never reduced his teachings to written form. His philosophical views are known to us exclusively through the dialogues of Plato, who used Socrates—with whose ideas he was in basic agreement —as the mouthpiece through which he enunciated his own philosophy.[2]

In Plato's philosophy, a clear-cut distinction must be made between his thinking about justice and his ideas about law. His theory of justice was elaborate and forms a cornerstone of his philosophical edifice; it also remained largely unchanged throughout his life. His ideas on law, on the other hand, were peripheral in his scheme of thought and underwent a substantial change in the latter part of his life.

Justice meant in Plato's eyes that "a man should do his work in the station of life to which he was called by his capacities."[3] Every member of society, according to him, has his specific functions and should confine his activity to the proper discharge of these functions. Some people have the power of command, the capacity to govern. Others are capable of helping those in power to achieve their ends, as subordinate members of the government. Others are fit to be tradesmen, or artisans, or soldiers.

Plato was deeply convinced of the natural inequality of men, which he considered a justification for the establishment of a class system in his commonwealth. He exclaimed:

You in this city are all brothers, but God as he was fashioning you, put gold in those of you who are capable of ruling; hence, they are deserving of most reverence. He put silver in the auxiliaries, and iron and copper in the farmers and the other craftsmen. For the most part your children are of the same nature as yourselves, but because you are all akin, sometimes from gold will come a silver offspring, or from silver a gold, and so on all round. Therefore the first and weightiest command of God to the rulers is this— that more than aught else they be good guardians of and watch zealously over the offspring, seeing which of those metals is mixed in their souls; if their own offspring has an admixture of copper or iron, they must show no pity, but giving it the place proper to its nature, set it among the artisans or the farmers; and if on the other hand in these classes children are born with an admixture of gold and silver, they shall do them honour and appoint the

---

[2] On Socrates see Ernest Barker, *Greek Political Theory: Plato and His Predecessors*, 4th ed. (London, 1951), pp. 86–99.
[3] This able definition of Platonic justice is found in Barker, p. 149.

first to be guardians, the second to be auxiliaries. For there is an oracle that the city shall perish when it is guarded by iron or copper.[4]

The men of gold are to become the rulers in Plato's ideal commonwealth; they must be philosophers (for until philosophy and governmental power coalesce, there will be no end to evil in the state in Plato's opinion),[5] and they will be endowed with absolute power, to be exercised rationally and unselfishly for the good of the state. The men of silver are to be the military guardians of the state and are to assist the rulers in the discharge of their governmental duties. The men of iron and copper will form the producing classes. The first two classes, in order to be able to devote their full energy to public duties, must renounce family life and private property; all unions between men and women in these two classes are to be temporary and to be regulated by the state for eugenic ends—the production of the fittest stock. The members of the third and largest class, on the other hand, will be permitted to found families and to own private property under the strict supervision of the government.

Each class, says Plato, must strictly confine its activity to the performance of its own specific functions. A rigorous division of labor among the three classes is to prevail within his commonwealth. Each citizen must fully discharge the duties which have been assigned to him by the government, according to his special capabilities and qualifications. The ruler, the auxiliary, the farmer, the craftsman—each of them must keep to his own calling and not interfere with the business of anyone else. "To mind one's own business and not to be meddlesome is justice." [6]

Plato realized that even in his ideal commonwealth disputes will arise which must be decided by the public authorities. It is the theory of *The Republic* that in deciding such controversies, the judges of the state should have a large amount of discretion. Plato does not wish them to be bound by fixed and rigid rules embodied in a code of laws.[7] The state of *The Republic* is an executive state, governed by the free intelligence of the best men rather than by the rule of law. Justice is to be administered "without law." [8]

[4] *The Republic*, Bk. III. 415.
[5] *Id.*, Bk. V. 473.
[6] *Id.*, Bk. IV. 433. A further discussion and analysis of Plato's views on justice will be found *infra* Sec. 44.
[7] *Id.*, Bk. IV. 425, 427.
[8] See Roscoe Pound, "Justice According to Law," 13 *Columbia Law Review* 696–713 (1913); 14 *Col. L. Rev.* 1–26, 103–121 (1914). Karl R. Popper, in *The Open Society and Its Enemies* (Princeton, 1950), chs. 6–8, depicts Plato as the philosopher of racialist totalitarianism. A different view is taken by John Wild, *Plato's Modern Enemies and the Theory of Natural Law* (Chicago, 1953). See also Jerome

The reasons for Plato's unfavorable attitude toward law are stated in his dialogue, *The Statesman.* "Law," he says there, "can never issue an injunction binding on all which really embodies what is best for each; it cannot prescribe with perfect accuracy what is good and right for each member of the community at any one time. The differences of human personality, the variety of men's activities, and the restless inconstancy of all human affairs make it impossible for any art whatsoever to issue unqualified rules holding good on all questions at all times." [9] Principles of law, he believed, consist of abstractions and oversimplifications; a simple principle, however, can never be applied to a state of things which is the reverse of simple. Hence, "the best thing of all is not full authority for laws but rather full authority for a man who understands the art of Kingship and has wisdom." [10]

In the last decade of his life, however—perhaps under the impact of the negative experiences which an attempt to set up the ideal Platonic commonwealth in the city of Syracuse in Sicily had produced — [11] Plato contrasted the picture of the state governed by the free and untrammeled rule of personal intelligence with that of another type of state, in which the discretion of the rulers was limited by law. While the "non-law" state was still upheld by him as the highest and most perfect type of government, he admitted that its effective operation required men of the highest wisdom and infallibility of judgment. Since such men could only rarely be found, he proposed the "law state" as the second best alternative for the governance of man. The blueprint of such a state is drawn in great detail in his last work, *The Laws.* No longer are the governing authorities of the state free to administer justice without written codes and legal enactments; they are to become the servants of the law, bound to take their directions from the general enactments which are to guide the conduct of the citizens without respect of persons.[12]

Hall, "Plato's Legal Philosophy," in *Studies in Jurisprudence and Criminal Theory* (New York, 1958), pp. 48–82; Carl J. Friedrich, *The Philosophy of Law in Historical Perspective* (Chicago, 1958), pp. 13–19; Huntington Cairns, *Legal Philosophy from Plato to Hegel* (Baltimore, 1949), pp. 29–76.

[9] *The Statesman,* transl. J. B. Skemp (New York, 1957), 294b. In a later passage, Plato says in a similar vein: "The legislator . . . will never be able, in the laws he prescribes for the whole group, to give every individual his due with absolute accuracy." *Id.,* 295a.

[10] *Id.,* 294a.

[11] The Sicilian experiment is described in Barker, pp. 113–116.

[12] See Plato, *The Laws,* transl. R. G. Bury (Loeb Classical Library ed., 1926), Bk. IV. 715. D. The communism of the ruling classes advocated in *The Republic* is also abandoned in this work. The rulers of the state and their auxiliaries, like the members of the producing class, are allowed to possess a family and private property.

Section 3. *The Aristotelian Theory of Law*

Aristotle (384–322 B.C.) received his philosophical education at Plato's Academy in Athens and was strongly influenced by the ideas of his teacher. He departed from them in many respects, however, in his own philosophy and tempered the Platonic idealism and rationalism by paying greater deference than his teacher to the actual conditions of social reality and the imperfections of men and institutions.

Aristotle's realism permitted him to see that a state organized in the image of Plato's ideal republic would necessarily founder on the rocks of average human nature. As Plato himself had come to realize after the bitter experiences of the Sicilian adventure,[1] "no human being . . . is capable of having irresponsible control of all human affairs without becoming filled with pride and injustice."[2] Aristotle, avoiding the Platonic route of drawing blueprints for the "perfect" as well as the "second-best" state, postulated a state based on law as the only practicable means of achieving the "good life," which, according to him, was the chief goal of political organization.[3] "Man," he exclaimed, "when perfected is the best of animals, but if he be isolated from law and justice he is the worst of all."[4]

Rightly constituted laws, said Aristotle, should be the final sovereign; these laws should be sovereign on every issue, except that personal (that is, executive) rule should be permitted to prevail in those matters on which the law was unable to make a general pronouncement.[5] In general, Aristotle held, "the rule of law is preferable . . . to that of a single citizen."[6] Even though he agreed with Plato that, if there was a man of outstanding eminence in virtue and political capacity in the state, such a man should become the permanent ruler,[7] he insisted that even such a "godlike" man must be a lawgiver, and that there must be a body of laws even in a state governed by such a man.[8]

[1] See *supra* Sec. 2, n. 11.

[2] Plato, *The Laws*, transl. R. G. Bury, Bk. IV. 713. C.

[3] Aristotle, *The Politics*, transl. E. Barker (Oxford, 1946), Bk. I. 1252b. See also Ernest Barker's introduction to this volume and Friedrich, *The Philosophy of Law in Historical Perspective*, pp. 19–26.

[4] *The Politics*, Bk. I. 1253a.

[5] *Id.*, Bk. III. 1282b; Bk. IV. 1292a.

[6] *Id.*, Bk. III. 1287a. This is probably the first historical formulation of Harrington's conception of an "empire of laws and not of men."

[7] *Id.*, Bk. III. 1284a and b. In the absence of such a "God among men," Aristotle regarded a democracy based on the strength of the middle classes as the best form of government. Bk. IV. 1295b and 1296a.

[8] *Id.*, Bk. III. 1286a. This view seems to be contradicted by an earlier passage, according to which "there can be no law which runs against men who are utterly superior to others. They are a law in themselves." *Id.*, 1284a. The context suggests,

"He who commands that law should rule may thus be regarded as commanding that God and reason alone should rule; he who commands that a man should rule adds the character of the beast. Appetite has that character; and high spirit, too, perverts the holders of office, even when they are the best of men. Law . . . may thus be defined as 'reason free from all passion.' " [9]

Aristotle, however, was conscious of the fact that in the administration of a system of law situations may arise where the universality and rigidity of legal rules may cause hardship in an individual case.[10] Aristotle proposes to cure such hardships by means of equity (*epieikeia*). In his definition, equity is "a rectification of law where law is defective because of its generality." [11] The law takes into consideration the majority of cases, the typical and average situation, but it cannot condescend upon particulars; it is frequently unable to do justice in the unique case. When such a case arises, the judge may depart from the letter of the law and decide the case as the lawgiver himself would presumably have disposed of the matter had he foreseen the possibility of its occurrence.[12]

The famous Aristotelian distinction between distributive and corrective justice will be discussed elsewhere.[13] Aristotle makes a further important distinction between that part of justice which is *natural* and that which must be regarded as *conventional*. "A rule of justice is natural that has the same validity everywhere, and does not depend on our accepting it or not. A rule is conventional that in the first instance may be settled in one way or the other indifferently, though after having once been settled it is not indifferent: for example, that the ransom for a prisoner shall be a mina, that a sacrifice shall consist of a goat and not of two sheep." [14]

While the meaning of the term "conventional justice" is quite clear

---

however, that Aristotle is speaking here of election laws and laws relating to the distribution and terms of political office, which, in his opinion, should not be applied to men who are "utterly superior to others."

[9] *Id.*, Bk. III. 1287a.

[10] "Law is always a general statement, yet there are cases which it is not possible to cover in a general statement." Aristotle, *The Nicomachean Ethics*, transl. H. Rackham (Loeb Classical Library ed., 1934), Bk. V. x. 4.

[11] *Id.*, Bk. V. x. 6. The early English system of equity, in accordance with Aristotle's idea, was conceived as a correction of the rigid, inflexible system of the common law.

[12] *Id.*, Bk. V. x. 4–6. On the Aristotelian conception of *epieikeia* see also *infra* Sec. 50.

[13] See *infra* Sec. 44.

[14] *Nicomachean Ethics*, Bk. V. vii. 1. In *The Politics*, Aristotle took the view that the state belongs to the class of things that exist by nature, and that man is by nature an animal intended to live in a state. See Bk. I. 1253a.

—the rule of the road being a typical example of it—the Aristotelian notion of natural justice has been obscured by the passages immediately following the sentence quoted above, where Aristotle seems to recognize a changeable part of natural law as well as an immutable one. He even seems to suggest that permanent justice exists perhaps only among the gods, and that within the range of our human world, although there is such a thing as natural justice, all rules of justice are variable. What Aristotle may have had in mind—although the text has perhaps been transmitted to us in a garbled form—is that what might be regarded by man as "naturally just" in a primitive society might offend the common sense of justice in a highly developed civilization. As men advance in controlling the blind forces of nature, in developing a stronger moral sense, and in gaining a greater capacity for mutual understanding, their feeling of justice becomes more refined; it may dictate to them certain forms of social conduct and intercourse which, unlike the rules of conventional justice, are considered imperative rather than accidental or morally indifferent.[15] He may also have meant that natural law is variable in the sense that human effort can, to some extent, interfere with its operation. Thus he tells us that "the right hand is naturally stronger than the left, yet is it possible for any man to make himself ambidextrous." [16] The cryptic way in which the thought is formulated by Aristotle makes any attempt at genuine interpretation a hazardous guess.

The question as to the legal consequences of a collision between a rule of natural justice and a positive enactment of the state is left unanswered by Aristotle. He clearly admits the possibility of an "unjust" law, giving as an example an enactment by a majority dividing among its members the possessions of a minority.[17] He also points out that other acts of oppression, whether committed by the people, the tyrant, or the wealthy, are "mean and unjust." [18] Aristotle also taught, as was stated earlier, that *rightly constituted* laws (rather than laws *per se*) should be the final sovereign.[19] But he does not give us his opinion on whether bad laws must under all circumstances be enforced by the judiciary and observed by the people.[20]

[15] The author's own views on this question are stated in Sec. 46.
[16] *Nicomachean Ethics*, Bk. V. vii. 4.
[17] *The Politics*, Bk. III. 1281a.
[18] *Ibid.*
[19] See *supra* n. 5.
[20] Plato, on the other hand, to some extent recognized a right—or even a duty—of resistance to unconscionable commands of the state in *The Laws*, Bk. VI. 770 E. On the question of the validity of unjust laws see *infra* Sec. 53.

Section 4. *The Stoic Law of Nature*

The Stoic school of philosophy was founded by a thinker of Semitic origin by the name of Zeno (350–260 B.C.). Zeno and his followers placed the concept of "nature" in the center of their philosophical system. By nature they understood the ruling principle which pervades the whole universe and which, in a pantheistic manner, they identified with God. This ruling principle was of an essentially rational character; to Zeno the whole universe consisted of one substance, and this substance was reason. The law of nature was to him identical with the law of reason. Man, as a part of cosmic nature, was an essentially rational creature. In following the dictates of reason, he was conducting his life in accordance with the laws of his own nature.[1] The Stoics taught that man should live free from emotions and passions, that he should make himself independent of the outside world and of worldly goods, and that he should order all his faculties in a rational manner. He should be fearless, bear his ineluctable fate with equanimity, and strive to attain a complete inner tranquillity and harmony.

Reason, as a universal force pervading the whole cosmos, was considered by the Stoics as the basis of law and justice. Divine reason, they held, dwells in all men everywhere, irrespective of nationality or race. There is one common law of nature, based on reason, which is valid universally throughout the cosmos. Its postulates are binding upon all men in every part of the world. The Stoic philosophers taught that there should not be different city-states, each distinguished from the rest by its own peculiar system of justice. They developed a cosmopolitan philosophy, founded on the principle of the equality of all men and the universality of natural law. Their ultimate ideal was a world-state in which all men would live together harmoniously under the guidance of divine reason.

Cicero (106–43 B.C.), the great Roman lawyer and statesman, was strongly influenced by the ideas of the Stoic philosophers. Like them, he was inclined to identify nature and reason and to assume that reason was the dominating force in the universe.

True law is right reason in agreement with nature; it is of universal application, unchanging and everlasting; it summons to duty by its commands, and averts from wrongdoing by its prohibitions. And it does not lay its commands or prohibitions upon good men in vain, though neither have any

---

[1] "What then is peculiar to man? Reason. When this is right and has reached perfection, man's felicity is complete." Seneca, "Ad Lucilium," in *Epistulae Morales*, transl. R. M. Gummere (Loeb Classical Library ed., 1930), Epistle 76. 10.

effect on the wicked. It is a sin to try to alter this law, nor is it allowable to attempt to repeal any part of it, and it is impossible to abolish it entirely. . . . And there will not be different laws at Rome and at Athens, or different laws now and in the future, but one eternal and unchangeable law will be valid for all nations and all times and there will be one master and ruler, that is God, over us all, for he is the author of this law, its promulgator, and its enforcing judge.[2]

In ascribing "natural force" to the law, Cicero made it clear that the mind and reason of the intelligent man was the standard by which justice and injustice were to be measured.[3] Characteristic of the reasonable man was the disposition of his mind to give everyone his due, and this attitude was equated with justice by Cicero.[4] Being perhaps first confined to the family, relatives, and friends of a man, he pointed out, this attitude was with the unfolding of civilization bound to spread to fellow citizens, then to political allies, and would finally embrace the whole of the human race.[5] To Cicero, the sense of justice, though capable of growth and refinement, was a universal possession of all reasonable men. "For since an intelligence common to us all makes things known to us and formulates them in our minds, honourable actions are ascribed by us to virtue and dishonourable actions to vice; and only a madman would conclude that these judgments are matters of opinion, and not fixed by Nature." [6] Justice is therefore inherent in nature (understood as human nature), and as a necessary condition of human collective well-being it can never be separated from utility (as some Sophists had attempted to do).[7]

Cicero regarded as "the most foolish notion of all" the belief that everything was just which was found in the customs or laws of nations. Would this be true, he asked, even if these laws had been enacted by tyrants? Could, for instance, a law be considered just which provided that a dictator might put to death with impunity any citizen he wished, even without a trial? Could theft and adultery and forgery

[2] *De Re Publica*, transl. C. W. Keyes (Loeb Classical Library ed., 1928), Bk. III. xxii. Examples of "natural law" given by Cicero are the rule permitting self-help against aggression (*De Inventione*, transl. H. M. Hubbell, Loeb Classical Library ed., 1913, Bk. II. liii. 61); prohibitions against insidious and fraudulent acts (*De Officiis*, transl. W. Miller, Loeb Classical Library ed., 1913, Bk. III. xvii); and in general the principle that one should not do harm to anybody (Bk. III. v). Cf. Ernst Levy, "Natural Law in the Roman Period," 2 *University of Notre Dame Natural Law Institute Proceedings* 43, at 44–51 (1949).

[3] *De Legibus*, Bk. I. vi. 20.

[4] *De Finibus Bonorum et Malorum*, transl. H. Rackham (Loeb Classical Library ed., 1951), Bk. V. xxiii.

[5] *Ibid.*

[6] *De Legibus*, Bk. I. xvi. 45.

[7] *Id.*, Bk. I. xii. 33–34.

of wills be sanctioned by the edict of a ruler or a law passed by a legislature? To Cicero the answer was clear.[8] "Pestilential" statutes put into effect by nations, he emphasized, no more deserved to be called laws than the rules a band of robbers might pass in their assembly.[9] Cicero thus appeared to favor the position that an utterly unjust law lacks the quality of law.

Many of the famous Roman jurists of the classical epoch of Roman law (which lasted from the first century B.C. to the middle of the third century A.D.) were likewise under the influence of the Stoic philosophy. However, the work of these men was largely of a practical nature, and they had little occasion to engage in abstract theoretical discussions about the nature of law and justice. Although the legal texts of the classical epoch abound with references to *jus naturale*, *naturalis ratio*, and *natura rerum*, the "natural law" envisaged in these texts is usually not the universal and supratemporal law discussed by Cicero, but rather represents a proposed solution of a case which is in accord with the expected conduct of men in Roman society or with the inherent justice of a particular factual situation. As Ernst Levy points out, " 'Natural' was to them not only what followed from physical qualities of men or things, but also what, within the framework of [the legal] system, seemed to square with a normal and reasonable order of human interests and, for this reason, need not be in need of any further evidence." [10]

Sometimes the concept of natural law was employed by the classical Roman jurists in a sense more closely akin to Cicero's use of the term. The classical jurist Gaius, for instance, declares in his *Institutes:* "All nations who are ruled by law and customs make use partly of their own law, and partly of that which is common to all men. For whatever law any people has established for itself is peculiar to that State and is called the *jus civile*, as being the particular law of that state. But whatever natural reason has established among all men is equally observed by all mankind, and is called *jus gentium*, because it is the law which all nations employ." [11]

The *jus civile* referred to by Gaius was a law that was applicable to Roman citizens only. *Jus gentium*, on the other hand, was a body of

---

[8] *Id.*, Bk. I. xvi. 43–44.

[9] *Id.*, Bk. II. v. 13. On Cicero see also Cairns, *Legal Philosophy from Plato to Hegel*, pp. 127–162; Friedrich, *Philosophy of Law in Historical Perspective*, pp. 27–34.

[10] Levy, *op. cit. supra.* n. 2, p. 51. Many examples are given on pp. 51–54. See also Max Kaser, "*Mores maiorum und Gewohnheitsrecht,*" 59 *Zeitschrift der Savigny-Stiftung (Roman. Abt.)* 59 (1939).

[11] Gaius, *Inst.* I. 1. 1; *Justinian's Digest* I. 1. 9.

rules which were applied in controversies involving non-citizens of Rome. It was composed of usages, rules, and principles which represented the common ingredients in the legal systems of the people with which Rome came into contact.[12] Whenever a particular rule or usage was observed by the Romans to be practiced by a large number of other nations, it was incorporated into the *jus gentium*.[13] As a body of universal or well-nigh universal principles, Gaius equated it with *jus naturale*.

However, another and less meaningful definition of natural law also appears in the Roman sources. According to Ulpian, a Roman jurist of the third century A.D., "The law of nature is that which nature has taught all animals. This law is not peculiar to the human race, but belongs to all creatures living on the land or in the sea and also to birds. Hence arises the union of male and female which we call marriage, hence the procreation of children, hence their rearing; for we see that all animals, even wild beasts, appear to take part in this knowledge of the laws." [14] This community of law among men and animals is foreign to the thinking of Cicero and the Stoics, and the passage is also not considered by modern scholars to be representative of the views of the classical jurists.[15]

An important element in the Stoic concept of natural law was the principle of equality. The Stoic philosophers were convinced that men were essentially equal and that discriminations between them on account of sex, class, race, or nationality were unjust and contrary to the law of nature. This Stoic idea of human equality gained some ground in the political philosophy and jurisprudence of the Roman Empire. Naturally, the influence of Stoic philosophy was merely one element among others that contributed to the tendency toward a somewhat greater social equality, which was noticeable in the post-Augustan period. But since some of the great emperors of that period, like Antoninus Pius and Marcus Aurelius, as well as some of the jurists, like Papinian and Paul, were under the sway of Stoicism, the causal connection between this philosophy and the growth of humanitarian and equalitarian ideas in the Roman Empire should not be underestimated. Various attempts were made to adapt the positive law to the

[12] See Henry Maine, *Ancient Law,* ed. Frederick Pollock (London, 1930), pp. 52–60.

[13] Common observances of this type were, among others, the right of self-defense; the right to appropriate chattels that had been abandoned by their owner; the prohibition of incest between ascendants and descendants; the determination of the status of an illegitimate child according to the status of the mother.

[14] *Dig.* I. 1. 1. 3.

[15] Levy, *op. cit. supra* n. 2, p. 66.

assuming more humane forms, although this was accomplished very slowly and gradually. The autocratic power which the Roman family father held over the person and property of his children was never abolished as such, but it was gradually mitigated through a series of specific legal measures. Caracalla forbade the sale of children except in case of extreme poverty. Hadrian punished abuses of the right of the *pater familias* to kill his child. The right of the father to force his grown-up son or daughter to divorce a spouse with whom he or she lived in free marriage was taken away by the emperors Antoninus Pius and Marcus Aurelius. A duty of the father to support his children was recognized in the late imperial period. The father's absolute power of disposition over the property of his grown-up sons was gradually restricted. Under Augustus, soldiers who stood under *patria potestas* gained the independent use of property which they had acquired during their service in the army (*peculium castrense*). Other restrictions on the father's power of disposition were introduced in the course of time.[22]

It shall by no means be contended that in this whole development the influence of Stoic natural-law concepts was the primary factor. Every historical development is determined by a great number of concurring and intertwining causes, and it is often very difficult to measure the exact weight of one particular factor. All that may be said is that many of the leading men of Roman political and legal life in the late republic and the imperial period stood under the influence of Stoic philosophy, and that it is very likely that this humanitarian philosophy played some part in the legal and social reforms which took place in this period of Roman history. Among the sociological reasons which may perhaps explain why the Stoic philosophy fell on such fertile soil in Rome must be counted the trend toward a universal empire, which was very marked in the last period of antiquity and which led to the creation of the *Imperium Romanum*. The Stoic concept of a world-state with a common citizenship and a common law, based on natural reason, acquired a very real and nonutopian meaning under these circumstances. With the granting of citizenship rights to most of the Roman provincial subjects in 212 A.D., the idea of a community of civilized mankind (*civitas maxima*), as opposed to the parochialism of

---

[22] On the development of family relations in Roman law see Schulz, pp. 192–202; W. W. Buckland, *The Main Institutions of Roman Private Law* (Cambridge, Eng., 1931), pp. 56–72; H. F. Jolowicz, *Historical Introduction to the Study of Roman Law* (Cambridge, Eng., 1932), pp. 112–120, 238–245; Jörs, Kunkel, and Wenger, pp. 271–296; James Bryce, "Marriage and Divorce," in *Studies in History and Jurisprudence* (New York, 1901), pp. 782–811.

the small city-states of earlier periods, had found an approximate realization. It was no wonder that under these conditions the philosophical concepts of Stoicism, which found additional support in the rise and spreading of Christian ideas, had a significant impact on the political and legal developments of the Roman Empire.

II

LEGAL PHILOSOPHY
IN THE MIDDLE AGES

Section 5. *Early Christian Doctrine*

In the Middle Ages all Christians shared one common concept of the universe: that which had been laid down in the New Testament and in the teachings of the Fathers of the Church. Legal philosophy, like all other branches of sciences and thinking, was dominated by the church and its doctrines. But the heritage of antiquity was not lost; Plato, Aristotle, and the Stoics exercised an influence upon the minds of many ancient and medieval Christian thinkers, even though the concepts and ideas which the philosophy of antiquity had produced were reinterpreted or revised in the light of the theology and doctrines of the Christian church.

The early foundations of Christian legal philosophy were laid several centuries before the beginning of the Middle Ages. A reference to "natural law" can be found in the Epistle of Paul to the Romans, in which he speaks of a "law written in [men's] hearts" and contemplates the possibility of Gentiles, who do not have the law of the sacred books, doing "by nature the things contained in the law." [1] This passage may be interpreted as a recognition of an innate moral sense in man which, if properly developed, directs him toward the good even in the absence of a written law known to him.

Perhaps the most important and influential among the Fathers of the Church was St. Augustine (354–430 A.D.). He was born in North Africa and lived and died as a citizen of the late Roman empire. It was Augustine's conviction that in a golden age of mankind, prior to man's fall, an absolute ideal of the "law of nature" had been realized. Men lived in a state of holiness, innocence and justice; they were free and equal; slavery and other forms of dominion of men over other men were unknown. All men enjoyed their possessions and goods in common and lived as true brothers under the guidance of reason. Not even death existed at this period.

At the time of man's fall, Augustine taught, his nature was vitiated by original sin. The good elements in man's nature were not eradicated, but they became vulnerable and easily thwarted by evil predispositions.[2] The former order of love gave way to a condition of existence in which concupiscence, greed, passion, and lust for power came to play a conspicuous part, and the curse of mortality befell mankind as a punishment for its corruption. The absolute law of nature which had mirrored the perfection and unqualified goodness of the human soul was no longer capable of realization. Reason had to devise practical means and institutions to meet the new conditions. Government, law, property, and the state appeared on the scene; although products of sin in their roots, they were justified by Augustine in the light of the deteriorated condition of mankind. Augustine believed that the church, as the guardian of the eternal law of God (*lex aeterna*), may interfere at will with these sinful institutions. It has unconditional sovereignty over the state. The state is justified only as a means of keeping peace on earth. It must defend the church, execute its commands, and preserve order among men by enforcing the worldly law (*lex temporalis*).[3]

The worldly law, in Augustine's opinion, must strive to fulfill the demands of the eternal law. If it contains provisions which are clearly contrary to the law of God, these provisions are of no force and should be disregarded. "Justice being taken away then, what are King-

---

[1] Rom. ii:14–15.

[2] See *Basic Writings of Saint Augustine*, ed. W. J. Oates (New York, 1948), I, 432–433, 643–644. Augustine believed that "the entire mass of our nature was ruined beyond doubt, and fell into the possession of its destroyer. And from him no one—no, not one—has been delivered, or is being delivered, or ever will be delivered, except by the grace of the Redeemer." *Id.*, p. 644.

[3] *Id.*, II, 468 ff.

doms but great robberies?"[4] Even if the worldly law attempts to comply with the postulates of the *lex aeterna* and to accomplish justice in the relations of men, it will never attain the perfection of the eternal law. At some time in the remote future, Augustine hoped, the *civitas terrena*, the mundane commonwealth, would be replaced by the *civitas dei*, the commonwealth of God. In that commonwealth, envisioned as a community of all the faithful and believing, the eternal law of God would reign forever, and man's original nature, contaminated by Adam's transgression, would be restored to full glory.

Isidore of Seville (who died in 636) taught, like Augustine, that the institution of the state owed its origin to man's corrupted nature. Government became necessary to restrain bad men from evil-doing through fear of punishment. He maintained, however, that only just rulers deserve to be respected as genuine bearers of authority, while tyrants are not entitled to such reverend homage.

Isidore, following the Roman jurists, distinguished between *jus naturale*, *jus civile*, and *jus gentium*. His conception of natural law was formulated as follows: "Natural law is common to all peoples in that it is possessed by an instinct of nature, not by any human agreement, as the marriage of man and woman, the begetting and rearing of children, the common possession of all things, the universal freedom of all, the acquisition of those things that are taken in the air or sea or on land, likewise the restoring of property entrusted or lent, the repairing of violence by force. For this, or whatever is like this, could never constitute an injustice but must be considered in accord with natural equity."[5] Obviously the definition, insofar as it speaks of a "common possession of all" and of universal liberty, contemplates partly the supposed "absolute natural law" of mankind's early period, since at the time when Isidore of Seville wrote, neither communism nor the equal liberty of all men were realized either in his country or in others.

Section 6. *The Thomist Philosophy of Law*

The theology and philosophy of medieval Catholicism reached its culmination in the monumental system of Thomism. St. Thomas Aquinas (1226–1274) was the greatest of the Scholastic philosophers

---

[4] *Id.*, p. 51. On St. Augustine see also Carl J. Friedrich, *The Philosophy of Law in Historical Perspective* (Chicago, 1958), pp. 35–41; Alfred Verdross, *Abendländische Rechtsphilosophie* (Vienna, 1958), pp. 60–65.

[5] Isidore, *Etymologia* (in Migne, *Patrologia Latina*, vol. 82), Bk. V, ch. 4; see also the *Decretum Gratiani*, dist. prima, ch. vii, in *Corpus Juris Canonici*, ed. A. Friedberg (Leipzig, 1879), p. 1.

A different conception of natural law is found in the Preamble to the *Decretum Gratiani*, where we read that the law of nature is nothing other than the golden rule, comprised in the law and the gospel, which bids us to do as we would have done to us, and forbids the contrary.

of the Middle Ages,[1] and his teachings may still be regarded as an authoritative expression of the theological, philosophical, and ethical convictions of Roman Catholicism. His system represented an ingenious synthesis of Christian scriptural dogma and Aristotelian philosophy. The influence of Aristotle reveals itself particularly in Aquinas' thinking on law and justice, but is adapted by him to the doctrines of the gospel and integrated into an imposing system of thought.

Thomas Aquinas distinguished between four different kinds of law: the eternal, the natural, the divine, and the human law.

The eternal law (*lex aeterna*) is the "plan of government in the Chief Governor." [2] It is the divine reason and wisdom directing all movements and actions in the universe. All things subject to divine providence are ruled and measured by the eternal law. In its entirety it is known only to God. No human being is capable of knowing it as it is, except perhaps "the blessed who see God in His essence." [3]

But though no ordinary mortal can know the eternal law in its whole truth, he can have a partial notion of it by means of the faculty of reason, with which God has endowed him. This participation of the rational creature in the cosmic law is called natural law (*lex naturalis*) by St. Thomas. The natural law is merely an incomplete and imperfect reflection of the dictates of divine reason, but it enables man to know at least some of the principles of the *lex aeterna*.[4]

Natural law directs the activities of man by means of certain general precepts. The most fundamental of these precepts is that good is to be done and evil to be avoided.[5] But what are the criteria of that which is to be regarded as good and that which must be apprehended as evil? St. Thomas is convinced that the voice of reason in us (which enables us to obtain a glimpse of the eternal law) makes it possible for us to distinguish between morally good and bad actions. According to his theory, those things for which man has a natural inclination must be apprehended as good and must be regarded as forming part of the natural law. First, there is the natural human instinct of self-preservation, of which the law must take cognizance. Second, there exists the attraction between the sexes and the desire to rear and educate children. Third, man has a natural desire to know the truth about God, an inclination which drives him to shun ignorance. Fourth, man wishes to

---

[1] By Scholasticism we designate a system of medieval thinking under which an attempt was made to bring secular philosophy, especially Aristotelianism, into harmony with religious dogma.

[2] St. Thomas Aquinas, *Summa Theologica*, transl. Fathers of the English Dominican Province (London, 1913–1925), pt. II, 1st pt., qu. 93, art. 3.

[3] *Id.*, qu. 93, art. 2.

[4] *Id.*, qu. 91, arts. 2 and 3.

[5] *Id.*, qu. 94, art. 2.

live in society, and it is therefore natural for him to avoid harming those among whom he has to live.[6] While the basic precepts of natural law are considered immutable by St. Thomas, he admits the possibility of changing the secondary precepts (which are certain detailed conclusions derived from the first principles) under certain circumstances.[7]

It is obvious that natural law according to the Thomistic conception consists of certain physical and psychological traits of human beings and, in addition, of some dictates of reason which direct man toward the achievement of the good. The latter are regarded by Aquinas as "natural" in the same sense that the instinct of self–preservation or the sex instinct are natural. "There is in every man a natural inclination," he says, "to act according to reason: and this is to act according to virtue. Consequently, considered thus, all acts of virtue are prescribed by the natural law: since each one's reason naturally dictates to him to act virtuously." [8] Under this view, irrational, antisocial, and criminal acts are interpreted as morbid deviations from our normal nature, just as the innate instinct of self-preservation may in some people and under certain circumstances be blotted out by an urge to destroy one's own life.

Natural law, as a body of rather general and abstract principles, is supplemented in Thomist philosophy by more particular directions from God as to how men should conduct their lives. This function is performed by the divine law (lex divina). It is the law revealed by God through the Holy Scriptures and recorded in the Old and New Testaments.

The last kind of law is the human law (lex humana). It is defined by Aquinas as "an ordinance of reason for the common good, made by him who has care of the community, and promulgated." [9] Thus Aquinas, like Aristotle, incorporates the concept of reason into his definition of law.[10] In order that a governmental mandate may have the quality of law, it needs to comply with some postulate of reason. An unjust and unreasonable law, and one which is repugnant to the law of nature, is not a law, but a perversion of law.[11] In St. Thomas' view, an enactment which is arbitrary, oppressive, or blasphemous does not bind in conscience, "except perhaps in order to avoid scandal or disturbance, for which cause a man should even yield his right." [12] In other words, the appropriateness of exercising a right of resistance

[6] Ibid.
[7] Id., qu. 94, art. 5.
[8] Id., qu. 94, art. 3. Cf. also art. 6.
[9] Id., qu. 90, art. 4.
[10] Cf. qu. 90, art. 1: "Law is something pertaining to reason."
[11] Id., qu. 92, art. 1; qu. 95, art. 2.
[12] Id., qu. 96, art. 4.

must be weighed against the inconvenience of disturbing the public peace and order, a disturbance from which the community may suffer great harm. St. Thomas believed, however, that the right of resistance becomes transformed into a genuine duty of disobedience in the case of laws promulgated by tyrants which induce to idolatry or prescribe anything else contrary to the divine law. "Laws of this kind must nowise be observed, because . . . we ought to obey God rather than men." [13]

The Thomistic conception of justice, as distinguished from his theory of law, strongly shows the influence of Cicero and Aristotle. Justice is defined as "a habit whereby a man renders to each one his due by a constant and perpetual will." [14] It consists of two parts: *distributive* justice, which "allots various things to various persons in proportion to their personal dignity," [15] and *commutative* (corrective) justice, which concerns the dealings of individuals with one another and the adjustments to be made in case of the performance of improper or illegal acts. Like Aristotle, he holds that the equality implicit in the concept of distributive justice is not a mechanical, but a proportional, equality.[16] "In distributive justice something is given to a private individual, insofar as what belongs to the whole is due to the part, in a quantity that is proportionate to the importance of the position of that part in respect of the whole. Consequently in distributive justice a person receives all the more of the common goods, according as he holds a more prominent position in the community." [17] In corrective justice, on the other hand, it is necessary to equalize thing with thing in an arithmetical fashion, so that losses suffered by someone as a result of a harmful act can be restored and unjust enrichments of one party at the expense of another can be rectified.

Section 7. *The Medieval Nominalists*

One of the recurrent themes of medieval philosophy was the celebrated dispute about "universals," which had as its subject matter the question as to the character of our general ideas and their relationship to the particular objects existing in reality. Two chief schools of

---

[13] *Ibid.*

[14] *Id.,* pt. II, 2d pt., qu. 58, art. 1. Cf. Cicero's definition *supra* Sec. 4.

[15] *Id.,* qu. 63. art. 1.

[16] See *infra* Sec. 44.

[17] *Id.,* qu. 61, art. 2; see *infra* Sec. 44. On St. Thomas Aquinas see also Friedrich, *Philosophy of Law in Historical Perspective,* pp. 43–50; Huntington Cairns, *Legal Philosophy from Plato to Hegel* (Baltimore, 1949), pp. 163–204; Wolfgang Friedmann, *Legal Theory,* 4th ed. (Toronto, 1960), pp. 58–62; Thomas E. Davitt, "Law as Means to End—Thomas Aquinas," 14 *Vanderbilt Law Review* 65 (1960).

thought emerged with respect to the solution of this question, although within these schools radical as well as moderate viewpoints were advanced and attempts were sometimes made to bridge the gulf between the most extreme positions on each side.

The great contestants in this dispute were the "realists" and the "nominalists." According to the view of the medieval realists, there exists a strict parallelism between the world of our thought and the world of external reality. To the general conceptions that we form, the mental representations that we make to ourselves of external objects and phenomena, there corresponds an extramental, objective counterpart in the real world. Such universal ideas as truth, virtue, justice, and humanity are therefore not merely constructions of the human mind but are real substances and things in themselves, existing independently of their concrete manifestations in the empirical world.

The medieval nominalists, on the other hand, denied the reality of universals. To them, the only real substances in nature were the individual things apprehended by us through observation and the perception of our senses. The generalizations and classifications which we use to describe the outside world are merely *nomina*, that is, names, which have no direct and faithful copies and counterparts in external nature. There can be in the real world no justice apart from just acts, no mankind apart from concrete living human beings. No universal, abstract representation, in their opinion, can adequately reflect a world in which individuation is the dominating principle.[1]

This dispute—which raises basic questions as to the genesis and objective validity of our intellectual knowledge—has an important bearing on the problem of natural law. The realist (or rationalist) who believes that human beings have the possibility of knowing things as they really are and to detect the uniformities and laws operative in nature by the use of their reasoning faculties will be much more inclined to recognize the existence of a law of nature than the nominalist, who is skeptical with respect to our power to ascertain the essential nature of things and prone to close his eyes to propositions which cannot be validated by immediate sense perception and concrete observation of individual facts.

A train of thought away from Thomist realism toward nominalism and positivism in theology and social ethics is clearly noticeable in the

[1] On the dispute over universals see Maurice de Wulf, *History of Medieval Philosophy*, transl. P. Coffey, 3d ed. (London, 1909), pp. 149 ff.; Henry Adams, *Mont-Saint-Michel and Chartres* (Boston, 1905), pp. 294–300; Glanville Williams, "Language and the Law," 61 *Law Quarterly Review* 71, at 81–82 (1945). The author's views on this dispute appear in Sec. 74.

writings of the Scotch Franciscan monk John Duns Scotus (1270–
1308).[2] Scotus taught that the individual alone possesses full and complete substantiality in nature and that universal conceptions and abstractions are merely the product of thought. From these premises
Scotus arrived at a philosophy in which the determination of individuals by universal laws (such as laws of reason) plays a subordinate
role, while the decisions brought about by free individual volition assume a place of paramount importance. The main intention of the
Creator, said Scotus, was to produce individuals.[3] That which is singular and unique, however, cannot be derived from general conceptions
and laws: it can only be experienced spontaneously by human souls.
The individual acts by means of concrete decisions which flow from
his will rather than from his intellect; and it is impossible, according
to Scotus, to explain the vagaries of the individual will fully by in-
voking general notions of reasonableness. If will were subordinate to
reason, as St. Thomas assumed, a truly free decision and genuinely
moral act would be impossible in the view of Scotus, for every act of
reason is necessarily determined by a sufficient cause and thus is not
free. Scotus teaches that it is wrong to say that the intellect dictates
to the will; on the contrary, it is the will that governs the intellect.[4]
Even from the point of view of a hierarchy of values, will must be
rated more highly than intellect, for the will is the only unfettered
agency of human conduct.

This primacy of the will is characteristic, according to Duns Scotus,
not only for human beings but also for God. God is not subjected to
paramount immutable laws of the cosmos. His own will is the sole
source of all law, and his justice merely an efflux of his power. All laws
are merely contingent edicts of the maker. "The rules of divine world
government are shaped by divine will rather than by divine wisdom." [5]
All emanations of divine volition are to be accepted as just, and it is
improper to ask why God has decreed a certain order of things and
not an entirely different one. There exists only one principle of natural
law, according to Scotus: that is, to love God, however harshly and
incomprehensively he may deal with mankind. A natural law such as
the one conceived by Thomas Aquinas, distinguishing between things
that are in their essential nature good or bad, is unknown to Scotus.

---

[2] The ensuing discussion follows closely the thorough study of medieval nominalism and its impact on legal philosophy made by Hans Welzel, *Naturrecht und Materiale Gerechtigkeit* (Göttingen, 1951), pp. 67–89.
[3] Duns Scotus, *Opus Oxoniense* II d. 3 qu. 7 n. 10. On Scotus see also Thomas E.
Davitt, *The Nature of Law* (St. Louis, 1951), pp. 24–38.
[4] *Opus Oxoniense* IV d. 49 qu. 4 n. 16.
[5] *Id.*, II d. 7 qu. un. n. 18.

He was not, however, afraid that by his theses he was in danger of supplanting divine law by divine arbitrariness. This danger was obviated by his conviction that God was always benevolent and benign.

An even more radical version of theological voluntarism and nominalism is found in the philosophy of William of Occam (ca. 1290–1349). Any attempt of human reason to comprehend the divine government in terms of human rational postulates is sharply rejected by him. God might have taken the shape of a stone, a piece of wood, or a donkey, he said, and this possibility need not tax our religious faith.[6] Instead of ordering man to refrain from murder, theft, and adultery, he might some day decide to command the commission of these acts, in which case we would have to regard them as good and meritorious.[7] Under his view, the concepts of the criminal law do not relate to substantive ethical qualities of our actions, but merely reflect the existence of a prohibitory command; if this command were changed, the quality of the act itself would be transformed. In other words, moral injunctions are valid only under the premises of a particular given order.[8] Occam maintained that as God had revealed his present will to us in the sacred books of the Bible, these laws constituted the only genuine source for the ascertainment of the divine will. There is no natural law, discoverable by human reason, apart from the positively revealed divine law.

The close relation of these views to the ethical relativism and positivism of a later age is obvious. As in the case of Scotus, however, the potential nihilism of these theories was mitigated by Occam's conviction that God was by his nature a benevolent ruler, not an arbitrary tyrant. Occam was also convinced that there existed a basis for true morality in the subjectively good or evil intentions of human beings, guided by the dictates of the individual conscience.

A return to rationalism and the Thomistic view of natural law took place in the writings of the late Catholic scholastics, such as the Spaniards Francisco de Vitoria (d. 1546) and Francisco Suarez (1548–1617). In the writings of these men, the dispute over whether will or reason represented the nobler faculty was again resolved in favor of reason, and the possibility of an objectively existing *lex naturalis* was reasserted. "Natural law," said Suarez, "embraces all precepts or moral principles which are plainly characterized by the goodness necessary to rectitude of conduct, just as the opposite precepts clearly involve

---

[6] William of Occam, *Centilog.* 6 f. On Occam see also Davitt, *Nature of Law*, pp. 39–54.
[7] Occam, *Sententiae* II qu. 19. o.
[8] *Id.*, III qu. 12 CCC.

moral irregularity or wickedness." [9] He pointed out that the promulgation of law and its enforcement by means of sanctions clearly required an exercise of will on the part of the governing authorities. However, the will of the prince does not suffice to make law unless "it be a just and upright will." [10] This rationalistic strain in Roman Catholic legal philosophy can, on the whole, be said to conform to the official position of the Catholic Church up to our own day.

[9] Francisco Suarez, *Selections from Three Works,* The Classics of International Law, ed. J. B. Scott (Oxford, 1944), p. 210. See also *id.,* p. 42: "Natural law is that form of law which dwells within the human mind, in order that the righteous may be distinguished from the evil."
[10] *Id.,* p. 58.

III

THE CLASSICAL ERA
OF NATURAL LAW

Section 8. *Introduction*

During the Middle Ages, the Church was the center of life in Europe. It controlled education and science, and theology occupied the first place among the sciences. All knowledge emanated from the mainsprings of Christian belief, as interpreted by the Church of Rome. Access to truth about ultimate things could be obtained only through the interposition of the Church and its dignitaries.

The domination of the spiritual life by the Church was attacked by Protestantism in the sixteenth century. The Protestant religion reinterpreted the statement of the Bible that all souls have equal value before God to mean that everybody had the right of communion with the Deity without mediation through a priest. It was therefore willing to allow the individual a larger degree of autonomy to form an opinion about God's intentions and the guiding principles of life than had been accorded to him in the preceding centuries.

The attack against hierarchy which was waged in a number of countries in Europe in the sixteenth century was directed against the spiritual order of Catholicism as well as against the worldly order of feudalism. In the economic field, its chief target was the feudal system of economics, with its concomitant institutions of serfdom and vocational guilds. In the political field, the new orientation found expression in the fight against the feudal nobility and its privileges. Its ultimate effect in the countries in which the rebellion was successful was a strengthening of secular, individualistic, and liberalistic forces in the political, economic, and intellectual life.

In the legal field, the early centuries of the modern age were dominated by a new form of natural-law philosophy, which we have designated as the natural law of the classical era. This classical natural-law philosophy which, in various and often-discrepant manifestations dominated Europe in the seventeenth and eighteenth centuries, was a legal by-product of the forces which transformed Europe as a result of the Protestant revolution. It cannot be said, however, as has sometimes been asserted, that the classical natural law constituted a complete break with medieval and scholastic legal theory. There are many links and influences connecting Aristotelian and scholastic thinking with the doctrines of the classical law-of-nature philosophers, especially those of the seventeenth century. On the other hand, the new law of nature, in spite of the notable diversity of views expressed by its representatives, possessed certain distinct characteristics which make it necessary to set it apart from medieval and scholastic natural law. First, it completed and intensified the divorce of law from theology for which the Thomistic distinction between a divinely revealed law and a natural law discernible by human reason had already prepared the ground. Second, while the medieval scholastic philosophers were strongly inclined to restrict the scope of natural law to a few first principles and elementary postulates, the classical law-of-nature jurists tended to favor the elaboration of systems of concrete and detailed rules which were believed to be directly deducible from human reason. The legal thinkers of the new age were convinced that the power of reason was universal for all men, nations, and ages, and that a complete and satisfactory system of law could be erected on the foundation of a rational analysis of human social life. Third, the postmedieval law of nature, by a process of gradual development, shifted the emphasis from a law of reason objectively grounded in the social nature of human beings to a doctrine in which the "natural rights" of man and his individual aspirations and happiness played a dominant role. That version of the postmedieval natural law which gained wide acceptance in the United States of America was strongly tinged with individualistic tendencies and postulates.[1] Fourth and last, the classical natural-law philosophy by gradual steps accomplished a shift in its mode of approach from a

[1] See *infra* Sec. 12.

teleological to a causal and empirical view of the nature of man. Aristotle and St. Thomas Aquinas had grounded their natural-law doctrine on a picture of man according to which the human being strives for perfection and has in himself the potentialities for a full and complete development as a rational and social being; this development, unless interrupted by morbid or "unnatural" impediment, will result in a full maturing of his true "nature." Thus "nature" is, under this theory, more or less identified with the highest potential of a human being.[2] With Hobbes, Locke, Spinoza, Montesquieu, and other representatives of the classical natural law, a conception of man emerges which is based on mere observation of his characteristic traits and a study of the causal laws that determine or influence human behavior. Thus, the rise of modern natural and psychological science did not fail to exert an impact on the history of natural law theory.

From its early beginnings in the modern age, the classical law-of-nature doctrine found a rival in another doctrine which in some respects was a product of the same political, social, and economic forces that helped shape the rationalistic and individualistic natural law philosophy. This rival was the doctrine of *raison d'état* (reason of state), which received its most influential formulation in the writings of the Italian political philosopher Niccolo Machiavelli (1469–1527). Machiavelli glorified the omnipotence of the state and subordinated ethical principles in public life entirely to the political necessities of statecraft. Drawing an uncomplimentary picture of the passions, weaknesses, and vices of men, he counseled the rulers to be hard-boiled and cynical in using their subjects as instruments for the building up of powerful, unified, national states. This end, in his opinion, justified the employment of means which might easily be considered reprehensible from a purely moral point of view.

In order to understand the doctrine of *raison d'état* in its historical significance, it must be kept in mind that the emancipation of the individual which took place in Europe in the postmedieval period went hand in hand with the rise of sovereign, independent, and national states, which sought to emancipate themselves from the universal medieval empire which was still in existence in large parts of Europe. This national emancipation was part of the struggle against feudalism and the "ultramontane" claims of the Church. The rising national states were for the most part governed by absolute monarchs who claimed freedom of political action in order to establish and strengthen the

[2] For a modern version of the teleological concept of man see John Wild, *Plato's Modern Enemies and the Theory of Natural Law* (Chicago, 1953), pp. 64–76. *Contra:* Hans Kelsen, "Plato and the Doctrine of Natural Law," 14 *Vanderbilt Law Review* 23, at 27–33 (1960).

power and prestige of their countries. A weapon against the claims of the universal Holy Empire as well as against possible interventions by other states was offered to them in the doctrine of national sovereignty, which received its first elaboration at the hands of the French political philosopher Jean Bodin (1530–1597). A weapon against their own nationals was available to them in the doctrine of *raison d'état*, which sought to subordinate the individual citizen to the needs of the state. Every European political thinker of this era attempted in some way to reconcile the claims of the law-of-nature doctrine (which assumed the existence of a law superior to political force and independent of it) with the postulates of *raison d'état* (which sought to protect the rights of the states and their rulers). In general it can be said that in western Europe, and later in the United States, the law-of-nature philosophy gained the upper hand, while in central Europe the doctrine of *raison d'état* tended to prevail, although it did not completely defeat the claims of the law-of-nature school. The differences in the views of the political and legal thinkers of the seventeenth and eighteenth centuries can often be explained by reference to the manner in which they sought to combine and reconcile the conflicting doctrines of *raison d'état* and natural law.

Three periods may be distinguished in the evolution of the classical law-of-nature philosophy. These periods correspond roughly to three successive stages in the social, economic, and intellectual development of this epoch. The first stage in the process of emancipation from medieval theology and feudalism which took place after the Renaissance and Reformation was marked by the rise of Protestantism in religion, of enlightened absolutism in politics, of mercantilism in economics. To this epoch, which lasted longer in Germany than in the western countries of Europe, belong the theories of Grotius, Hobbes, Spinoza, Pufendorf, and Wolff.[3] It is a characteristic feature of the theories of these men that the ultimate guaranty for the enforcement of natural law is to be found largely in the wisdom and self-restraint of the ruler. The second epoch, which started approximately with the English Puritan Revolution of 1649, was marked by a tendency toward free capitalism in economics and liberalism in politics and philosophy. The views of Locke and Montesquieu were characteristic expressions of this epoch, which sought to guarantee by means of a separation of powers the natural rights of individuals against undue encroachments by the government.[4] The third epoch was marked by a strong belief in popular sovereignty and democracy. Natural law was entrusted to

[3] See *infra* Secs. 9 and 10.
[4] See *infra* Sec. 11.

the "general will" and the majority decision of the people. The most outstanding representative of this stage was the French political thinker Jean-Jacques Rousseau.[5] The third stage in the development of the law-of-nature school had a profound impact on the political and constitutional development of France, while the second form of the law-of-nature school gained the upper hand in the United States of America.[6]

Section 9. *Grotius and Pufendorf*

Hugo Grotius (1583–1645), a great Dutch jurist and thinker, was not only one of the fathers—if not *the* father—of modern international law, but also the author of an influential natural law philosophy. In detaching the science of law from theology and religion, he prepared the ground for the secular, rationalistic version of modern natural law. Among the traits characteristic of man, he pointed out, was an impelling desire for society, that is, for the social life—"not of any and every sort, but peaceful, and organized according to the measure of his intelligence, with those who are of his own kind." [1] He refuted the assumption of the Greek Skeptic Carneades that man was actuated by nature to seek only his own advantage, believing that there was an inborn sociability in human beings which enabled them to live peacefully together in society. Whatever conformed to this social impulse and to the nature of man as a rational social being was right and just; whatever opposed it by disturbing the social harmony was wrong and unjust. Grotius defined natural law as "a dictate of right reason which points out that an act, according as it is or is not in conformity with rational nature, has in it a quality of moral baseness or moral necessity." [2] This law of nature would obtain "even if we should concede that which cannot be conceded without the utmost wickedness, that there is no God, or that the affairs of men are of no concern to Him." [3] Grotius thereby grounded the natural law on an eternal reason pervading the cosmos, although he admitted the alternative possibility of a theist foundation.[4]

[5] See *infra* Sec. 13.
[6] See *infra* Sec. 12.
[1] *De Jure Belli ac Pacis*, transl. F. W. Kelsey, The Classics of International Law (Oxford, 1925), proleg. 6. On Grotius see also F. J. C. Hearnshaw, "Hugo Grotius," in *The Social and Political Ideas of Some Great Thinkers of the Sixteenth and Seventeenth Centuries*, ed. F. J. C. Hearnshaw (London, 1926), pp. 130–152.
[2] *De Jure Belli ac Pacis*, Bk. I, ch. i. x. 1.
[3] *Id.*, proleg. 11; see also Bk. I, ch. i. x. 5: "The law of nature . . . is unchangeable—even in the sense that it cannot be changed by God."
[4] *Id.*, proleg. 12–13.

Grotius pointed out that two methods existed for proving whether something was or was not in accordance with the law of nature. "Proof *a priori* consists in demonstrating the necessary agreement or disagreement of anything with a rational or social nature; proof *a posteriori*, in concluding if not with absolute assurance, at least with every probability, that that is according to the law of nature which is believed to be such among all nations, or among all those that are more advanced in civilization." [5] Grotius added that no conclusions unfavorable to human nature needed to be drawn from the practices of nations that were savage or inhuman. He agreed with Aristotle that in order to find out what was natural, we must look to those things which are in a sound condition, not to those that are corrupted.[6]

Among the chief axioms of natural law enumerated by Grotius are the following: to abstain from that which belongs to other persons; to restore to another any goods of his which we may have; to abide by pacts and to fulfill promises made to other persons; to repay any damage done to another through fault; and to inflict punishment upon men who deserve it.[7] Many of the more detailed and special rules of the law, in his opinion, represented merely necessary derivations from these general precepts.

To the law of nature Grotius opposed the "volitional law," whose rules could not be deduced from immutable principles by a clear process of reasoning and which had their sole source in the will of man. A combination of both forms of law, in his opinion, existed in the law of nations. Grotius devoted the main part of his lifework to investigating this combination. To him the law of nations consisted of those rules which had been accepted as obligatory by many or all nations, but he sought its deeper roots in the natural principles of social life which followed from man's social impulse, namely in the principles of the law of nature.

The state was defined by Grotius as "a complete association of free men, joined together for the enjoyment of rights and for their common interest." [8] It originated in a contract, but usually the people had transferred their sovereign power to a ruler who acquired it as his private right and whose actions were ordinarily not subject to legal control.[9] The ruler is bound, however, to observe the principles of natural law and of the law of nations. If he misuses his power, his sub-

---

[5] *Id.*, Bk. I, ch. i. xii. 1.
[6] *Id.*, Bk. I, ch. i. xii. 2. Quoting Andronicus of Rhodes, Grotius makes the point that "He who says that honey is sweet does not lie, just because to sick people it may seem otherwise." *Ibid.*
[7] *Id.*, proleg. 8.
[8] *Id.*, Bk. I, ch. i. xiv. 1.
[9] *Id.*, Bk. I, ch. iii. vii–xii.

jects, as a general rule, have no right to revolt against him. But in some clear cases of usurpation or flagrant abuse of power Grotius was willing to recognize a right of resistance.[10]

A system of natural law even more elaborate than that of Grotius was worked out by Samuel Pufendorf (1632–1694), a German law professor. Pufendorf was in accord with Thomas Hobbes [11] that man is strongly motivated by self-love and egotism and that there is a certain amount of malice and aggressiveness inherent in his nature. But at the same time he believed, like Grotius, that there is in man also a strong inclination to seek association with other men and to live a peaceful and sociable life in society. These inclinations, according to Pufendorf, coexist in man's soul, and both are implanted in man by nature. The law of nature is an expression of this dual character of human existence. It acknowledges the fact that nature has commended self-love to man, but it also takes cognizance of the fact that self-love is tempered by man's social impulse. In accordance with these two sides of human nature, there are two fundamental principles of natural law. The first of these principles tells man to protect life and limb as far as he can, and to save himself and his property. The second axiom demands that he not disturb human society, or, in his words, that he not do anything whereby society among men may be less tranquil. These two principles of natural law were combined and integrated by Pufendorf into one single fundamental precept, which he formulated as follows: "That each should be zealous so to preserve himself that society among men be not disturbed." [12]

From the second axiom of natural law Pufendorf derived the following important legal postulate: "Let no one bear himself towards a second person so that the latter can properly complain that his equality of right has been violated in his case." [13] This rule of natural law, which breaks up into a number of special rules,[14] expresses the principle of legal equality which is often emphasized by Pufendorf. It is

[10] For instance, if a ruler who under the constitution is responsible to the people transgresses against the law and the state (*Id.*, Bk. I, ch. iv. viii), or if the king has abdicated or lost his sovereign power (Bk. I, ch. iv. ix), if he alienates his kingdom (Bk. I, ch. iv. x), if he shows himself to be the enemy of the whole people (Bk. I, ch. iv. xi), or in certain cases, if he has usurped his power (Bk. I, ch. iv. xv–xix).

[11] See *infra* Sec. 10.

[12] *Elementa jurisprudentiae*, transl. W. A. Oldfather (Oxford, 1931), Bk. II, observ. iv, 4.

[13] *Id.*, Bk. II, observ. iv, 23; cf. also Pufendorf, *De officio*, transl. F. G. Moore (Oxford, 1927), Bk. I, ch. 7, 1.

[14] For instance, the rule not to do harm to the body of another; not to violate the chastity of a woman against her will; not to usurp the property of a second person; not to break a promise; to make good the damage caused by one's own fault, etc. Pufendorf, *Elementa jurisprudentiae*, Bk. II, observ. iv, 24–34.

essential, he says, that everybody should himself practice the law which he has set up for others. The obligation to maintain and cultivate sociability binds all men equally, and one man should no more be permitted than another to violate the dictates of the law of nature.

Two fundamental compacts are necessary, in the view of Pufendorf, to maintain society and to guarantee the enforcement of natural and civil law. By the first, men agree among themselves to abandon the state of natural liberty and to enter into a permanent community for the purpose of guaranteeing their mutual safety. Following this agreement, a decree must be made stating what form of government is to be introduced. After this decree, a second contract is needed, this time made between the citizens and the government. By this compact the ruler binds himself to take care of the common security and safety, while the citizens promise obedience to him and subject their wills to the authority of the ruler in all things that make for the safety of the state.[15] The sovereign power is bound by the principles of natural law, which, in Pufendorf's view, is true law and not merely a moral guide for the sovereign. But the obligation of the ruler to observe the law of nature is merely an imperfect obligation, because there exists no court in which an action can be brought against the prince. God alone is the "avenger of the law of nature"; the citizens under normal circumstances have no right of resistance against the sovereign for a breach of the law of nature. Only in the extreme case when the prince has become a real enemy of the country, and in the face of actual danger, does there belong to individuals or the people the right to defend their safety against him.[16]

A follower of Pufendorf was the Genevese jurist Jean Jacques Burlamaqui (1694–1748), whose works, Les Principes du droit naturel (1747), and Les Principes du droit politique (1751), exercised a considerable influence on natural-law jurists, especially in the United States.[17] Reason, he pointed out, was the only means that man had at his disposal to attain happiness. Law was to him nothing else but what reason prescribes as a reliable road to happiness. Burlamaqui defined the law of nature as a law "that God imposes on all men, and which they are able to discover and know by the sole light of reason, and by

[15] De officio, Bk. I, ch. 6, 8–9.

[16] Pufendorf, Elementa jurisprudentiae, Bk. I, def. xii, 6; Pufendorf, De jure naturae et gentium, transl. C. H. and W. A. Oldfather (Oxford, 1934), Bk. VII, ch. 8. 5. Later, in De officio, Pufendorf goes further in restricting the right of resistance, confining it to obvious violations of a divine command. Bk. II, ch. 9, 4. For a detailed study of Pufendorf's natural-law philosophy see Hans Welzel, Die Naturrechtslehre Samuel Pufendorfs (Berlin, 1958).

[17] On Burlamaqui see Ray F. Harvey, Jean Jacques Burlamaqui (New York, 1938).

attentively considering their state and nature"; [18] like Pufendorf, he viewed the principle of sociability as the basis of this law.

Mention should also be made of another great teacher of law who made valuable contributions to the interpretation and systematization of the law of nature: the German jurist Christian Wolff (1679–1754), who may be regarded as the legal theorist of the enlightened absolutism of the Prussian king Frederick the Great. A follower of the philosophical doctrines of Leibniz, he taught that the highest duty of human beings was to strive after perfection. This moral duty of self-perfection, combined with an effort to further the perfection of others, was to him the basis of justice and natural law. The law of nature commands one to do that which makes for the improvement of oneself and one's condition. From this first principle Wolff rigidly deduced a vast system of positive law designed to effectuate the basic purpose of the natural law. It was one of Wolff's chief convictions, linking his theory to the political philosophy of his age, that the self-perfection of man cannot be achieved in a state of complete liberty. In order that men may live together harmoniously, they must be governed by a paternalistic and benevolent sovereign, whose task it is to promote peace, security, and self-sufficiency for the purpose of guaranteeing a contented life to the citizens of the state.

Section 10. *Hobbes and Spinoza*

It has been pointed out above [1] that the efforts of seventeenth- and eighteenth-century thinkers were directed toward maintaining some form of balance or adjustment between the claims of the law of nature and the needs of state policy (*raison d'état*). We find that in the philosophical systems of Thomas Hobbes, an English thinker, and Benedict Spinoza, a Dutch philosopher, the scales of the conflicting demands of natural law and governmental power were tipped in favor of the latter.

Thomas Hobbes (1588–1679) proceeded from anthropological and psychological assumptions quite different from those of Grotius. While Grotius believed that man is an essentially social and gregarious being, Hobbes pictured him as intrinsically selfish, malicious, brutal, and aggressive.[2] In the state of nature—a theoretical construct used by

---

[18] *The Principles of Natural and Politic Law*, transl. T. Nugent, 7th ed. (Philadelphia, 1859), p. 87.

[1] See *supra* Sec. 8.

[2] Hobbes's gloomy view of human nature must be accounted for by his experiences in observing the English civil war, in which the fabric of English society had broken down and violence had become the order of the day. Cf. Leo Strauss, *Natural Right and History* (Chicago, 1953), p. 196.

Hobbes to denote the absence of organized government—each man is a wolf to every other man (*homo homini lupus*) and, in an atmosphere of hate, fear, and mutual distrust, everybody is at war with everybody else (*bellum omnium contra omnes*); in this war all men were considered by Hobbes to be of equal strength, since even the weakest is able to kill the strongest.[3] According to Hobbes, there exists no right or wrong in the moral or legal sense in this state of nature. Everybody has a right to all things, and profit is the only measure of lawfulness. Furthermore, every individual in this state possesses the "natural right" to preserve his life and limbs with all the power he has against the aggressions of others.[4]

Hobbes pointed out, however, that men have certain passions that incline them to prefer peace to the warlike state of nature. These are, first, a strong fear of death; second, the desire for things necessary to commodious living; and third, the hope of obtaining these things by industry. Since these passions cannot be satisfied in the state of nature, reason suggests to mankind certain convenient articles of peace termed by Hobbes the "laws of nature."[5]

It is the first and most fundamental law of nature, according to Hobbes, that peace is to be sought wherever it can be found. From this law, a number of more specific precepts are derived: Everybody must divest himself of the right he has to do all things by nature; every man must stand by and perform his covenants; all men should help and accommodate each other as far as may be done without danger to their persons; no man should reproach, revile, or slander another man; there must be an impartial arbiter in controversies; and, above all, men should not do to others what they would not wish others to do to them.[6] These laws are declared to be eternal and immutable.[7]

These mandates of nature cannot be safely carried out as long as the state of nature and the war of all against all continues. In order to secure peace and to enforce the law of nature, Hobbes argued, it is

[3] Hobbes, *Elements of Law*, ed. F. Tönnies (Cambridge, Eng., 1928), pt. I, ch. xiv. 2–5; *De Cive*, ed. S. P. Lamprecht (New York, 1949), Preface, p. 13; pt. I, ch. i. 3–6. Hobbes contends that "though the wicked were fewer than the righteous, yet because we cannot distinguish them, there is a necessity of suspecting, heeding, anticipating, subjugating, self-defending." *De Cive*, Preface, p. 12.

[4] *Elements of Law*, pt. I, ch. xiv. 6–11; *De Cive*, ch. i. 7–10.

[5] *Leviathan*, ed. M. Oakeshott (Oxford, 1946), pt. I, ch. xiii; see also *Elements of Law*, pt. I, ch. xv. 1.

[6] See *Elements of Law*, pt. I, chs. xv–xvii; *De Cive*, ch. iii. Among the other "laws of nature" are (1) avoiding ingratitude; (2) using things in common that cannot be divided; (3) allowing commerce and traffic indifferently to everybody; (4) insuring safety to the messengers of peace.

[7] *De Cive*, ch. iii. 29.

necessary for men to enter into a compact mutually among themselves by which everyone agrees to transfer all his power and strength upon one man, or upon an assembly of men, on condition that everybody else does the same. The sovereign power thus constituted, called "Leviathan" or the "Mortal God" by Hobbes, should use the combined power and strength of the citizens for the purpose of promoting the peace, safety, and convenience of all.[8]

Hobbes was convinced that the sovereign, in order to perform its functions adequately, should be omnipotent and not subject to legal restraints. This view was a necessary consequence of his pessimistic estimate of human beings as selfish, uncooperative, and pugnacious creatures;[9] only an indivisible and extremely strong power can keep peace and order among such an intractable crowd.

The chief instrument by which Hobbes' sovereign imposes its will on the people are the "civil laws" (as distinguished from "laws of nature" which are laws only in a nontechnical sense).[10] Civil laws are "to every subject, those rules which the commonwealth hath commanded him, by word, writing, or other sufficient sign of the will, to make use of, for the distinction of right and wrong." [11] It appears from this definition that the contents of "right" and "wrong" are determined solely by the imperatives of the civil laws: there can be no right or wrong, justice or injustice, apart from the commands of the sovereign power. "No law can be unjust." [12] The people themselves, by having transferred their powers to the sovereign, are the authors of all laws, and nobody can do an injustice to himself.[13]

But while laws cannot be unjust in the view of Hobbes, they can be iniquitous.[14] They are iniquitous if they depart from the precepts of the "law of nature" as defined by him. Sovereign dominion is established for the sake of peace, and it is the highest duty of the rulers to promote the safety and well-being of the people. In order to be faithful to their trust, the rulers must defend the people against their enemies, permit them to enrich themselves, and see to it that they enjoy a "harmless" liberty.[15] There should be "infinite cases which are neither

[8] *Leviathan*, ch. xvii.
[9] "All society . . . is either for gain, or for glory; that is, not so much for love of our fellows as for the love of ourselves." *De Cive*, ch. i. 2.
[10] *Leviathan*, ch. xv.
[11] *Id.*, ch. xxvi.
[12] *Id.*, ch. xxx; see also *De Cive*, ch. xii. 5.
[13] *Leviathan*, ch. xviii.
[14] *Ibid.*
[15] *De Cive*, ch. xiii. 2 and 6. This liberty may not be extended so far as to permit the teaching of heretical opinions dangerous to the safety of the state. *Elements of Law*, pt. II, ch. ix. 8.

commanded, nor prohibited, but every man may either do, or not do them, as he lists himself." [16] A certain amount of property should be conceded to each man. Men should be allowed to buy and sell and otherwise contract with each other, and to choose their own trade. There should be no penalties imposed upon citizens which they cannot foresee, and every man should without fear be able to enjoy the rights accorded to him by the laws.[17]

If the government enacts iniquitous or tyrannical laws, this does not entitle the people to resist their enforcement; the only sanction for governmental wrong is that the rulers, instead of enjoying a happy afterlife, will suffer "the pain of eternal death." [18] There is one situation, however, in which the subjects are absolved from their duty of loyalty toward their rulers: when the sovereign has lost the power to preserve the peace in society and to protect the safety of the citizens.[19]

Hobbes in his political and legal doctrines advocated a form of government which may be described as "enlightened absolutism" and which was to prevail in the eighteenth century in many countries of Europe.[20] The sociological basis for his philosophy was a commonwealth consisting of equal individuals who were endowed with private property, lived by their own industry, and regulated their mutual relations by way of contract, being protected in their life and possessions by a strong government. Life, liberty, and property were not yet recognized as "inalienable rights," immune from governmental interference; they were subject to benevolent regulation by the state. In spite of this fact, certain distinct elements of individualism and liberalism are discernible in Hobbes' theory of natural law and in his philosophy of governmental duties.[21] It is a liberalism whose enforcement is entrusted to an "enlightened" absolute monarch. He is to be the faithful guardian of natural law. He is to secure the life, property, and happi-

---

[16] *De Cive*, ch. xiii. 15.

[17] *Id.*, ch. xiii. 16–17; *Elements of Law*, pt. II, ch. ix. 4–5.

[18] *Elements of Law*, pt. II, ch. i. 7; ch. ix. 1.

[19] *Leviathan*, ch. xxi. Hobbes also points out that the sovereign cannot force a citizen to kill, maim, or accuse himself so as to destroy his right of self-preservation; such a command would not be binding. *Id.*, ch. xxi. According to Hobbes, the right of self-preservation must be protected at all costs. Cf. Strauss *op. cit. supra* n. 2, p. 181.

[20] See Ferdinand Tönnies, *Thomas Hobbes*, 3d ed. (Stuttgart, 1925), p. 222; Friedrich Meinecke, *Idee der Staatsräson* (Munich, 1925), p. 265.

[21] René Capitant is right when he denies that Hobbes is the spiritual father of the collectivist totalitarian state of the twentieth century. Cf. Capitant, "Hobbes et l'état totalitaire," *Archives de philosophie du droit et de sociologie juridique*, nos. 1–2 (1936), p. 46. Hobbes's *Leviathan* is the state of Frederick the Great or Napoleon, not of Hitler or Mussolini. For the same view see Carl J. Friedrich, *The Philosophy of Law in Historical Perspective* (Chicago, 1958), p. 87.

ness of his subjects; their welfare (not his own self-aggrandizement) is to be his highest concern. But in executing his functions he is not bound by any legal curbs on his power. Thus in its practical effect Hobbes's law of nature is nothing more than a moral guide for the sovereign, while law in its proper sense consists of the commands of the sovereign.[22] On this ground it has not unjustly been said that Hobbes is a precursor of modern positivism and analytical jurisprudence.[23]

Hobbes's theories of law and government have often been compared to those of the great philosopher Benedict Spinoza (1632–1677). Indeed, there are some striking resemblances, although divergences also exist between the two philosophies. Spinoza believed, like Hobbes, that man in his natural state is ruled less by reason than by desire and the will to power. According to Spinoza, the right of an individual in the state of nature extends as far as his power. "Every individual has sovereign right to do all that he can; in other words, the rights of an individual extend to the utmost limits of his power, as it has been conditioned. Now it is the sovereign law and right of nature that each individual should endeavour to preserve itself as it is, without regard to anything but itself. . . . Whatsoever an individual does by the laws of its nature, it has a sovereign right to do inasmuch as it was conditioned by nature, and cannot act otherwise." [24]

There is no sin, no justice or injustice, Spinoza declares, so long as men live under the sway of nature alone. But this condition must lead to strife and disorder, because men, in the desire to increase their individual power and to satisfy their passions, will necessarily clash. In the state of nature, hatred, jealousy, and warfare will always exist. Men will attempt to overcome this miserable condition. They will discover that if they combine, they will possess much more power, even as individuals, because it will no longer be necessary for each individual to be in constant fear of his neighbor and on perpetual guard against enemies. Thus, the power of reason inherent in men drives them to give up the state of nature and to order their lives in a peaceful and rational manner. They will combine in the state and set up a govern-

[22] See *Leviathan*, ch. xxvi; *De Cive*, pt. II, ch. xiv. 1. In the view of Hobbes, the law of nature becomes a part of the civil law of all countries. It is the moral philosophy underlying the legislative enactments of the state. But the binding force of these enactments upon the citizens is derived from the will of the sovereign power. Bentham and Austin, who recognized the command of the sovereign as the sole source of all law, built upon this doctrine. See *infra* Secs. 22 and 25.

[23] On positivism see *infra* Sec. 24.

[24] *Tractatus theologico-politicus*, transl. R. H. M. Elwes (London, 1895), ch. 16. On Hobbes and Spinoza see also Huntington Cairns, *Legal Philosophy from Plato to Hegel* (Baltimore, 1949), pp. 246–294.

ment whose primary function will consist in the preservation of peace and security of life for those who have submitted to its authority.

So far Spinoza's doctrine largely conforms to that of Hobbes, but their ways separate when they express their views on the scope of governmental functions and the best form of government. For Hobbes, the function of government exhausts itself in preserving peace and security, and in granting to the citizens a "harmless liberty" which does not include the right of free speech or even free thought.[25] Spinoza, on the other hand, considered liberty to be the highest aim of government.[26] "The object of government is not to change men from rational beings into beasts or puppets, but to enable them to develop their minds and bodies in security, and to employ their reason unshackled; neither showing hatred, anger, or deceit, nor watched with the eyes of jealousy and injustice." [27]

A good government, in his opinion, will grant freedom of speech to its citizens and will not attempt to control their opinions and thoughts. It will rule according to the dictates of reason and refrain from oppressing its subjects. If no higher motive guides it, the mere desire for self-preservation will induce the government to follow such a course. The right of the sovereign, just as the right of an individual in the state of nature, does not extend farther than its power, and this power will be short-lived if it is not supported by moderation, sound reason, and the consent of the citizens. "No one can long retain a tyrant's sway." [28] The limits to sovereign power, in Spinoza's view, are set, not by any superior legal rules by which it is restrained, but by the power of the many or by the government's own well-conceived self-interest. In this sense, it might be said that Spinoza's sovereign is limited by natural law; by disregarding a dictate of reason, the government violates a law of nature, namely, the law of its own self-preservation. In other words, natural law, in Spinoza's doctrine, is coextensive with those limitations on sovereign might which result from the power of the multitude, or from the government's reasonable realization of its own interests.[29]

As far as the best form of government is concerned, Spinoza believed, contrary to Hobbes, that democracy or a moderate form of constitutional aristocracy was preferable to monarchy. His discussions

---

[25] See *supra* n. 15.
[26] *Tractatus theologico-politicus,* ch. 20.
[27] *Ibid.*
[28] *Id.,* ch. 16 (quoting Seneca).
[29] Cf. Spinoza, *Tractatus politicus,* transl. R. H. M. Elwes (London, 1895), ch. 4, 4; ch. 3, 7 and 9; *Tractatus theologico-politicus,* ch. 17. (Both of these works are found in the same volume.)

on the nature of democracy, begun in the last chapter of his *Tractatus Politicus*, unfortunately remained unfinished because of his early death.

Section 11. *Locke and Montesquieu*

The second period in the history of the classical law-of-nature school is marked by an attempt to erect effective safeguards against violations of natural law by the government. Law in this period was conceived primarily as an instrument for the prevention of autocracy and despotism. The rise of absolute rulers throughout Europe made it evident that a shield of individual liberty against governmental encroachments was strongly needed. Thus, the emphasis was shifted to those elements in law which render the institution capable of functioning as a guarantor of individual rights. In this period legal theory placed the main emphasis on liberty, while the first period had favored security more than liberty.

In the political theory of John Locke (1632–1704), this new tendency became very obvious. Locke assumed that the natural state of man was a state of perfect freedom, in which men were in a position to determine their actions and dispose of their persons and possessions as they saw fit, and that it was, furthermore, a state of equality, in the sense that no man in this state was subjected to the will or authority of any other man. This state of nature was governed by a law of nature which, looking toward the peace and preservation of mankind, taught men that, all persons being equal and independent, no one ought to harm another in his life, health, liberty, or possessions.[1] As long as the state of nature existed, everybody had the power to execute the law of nature and punish offenses against it with his own hand.

This situation was fraught with disadvantages, inconveniences, and dangers. In the first place, the enjoyment of the natural rights of life, liberty, and property was uncertain and constantly exposed to the invasions of others. Second, in punishing infractions of the law of nature, each man was a judge in his own cause and liable to exceed the rule of reason in avenging transgressions.[2] In order to end the confusion and disorder incident to the state of nature, men entered into a compact by which they mutually agreed to form a community and set up a body politic. In contrast to Hobbes, who construed the social contract as a pact of complete subjection to an absolute sovereign, Locke as-

---

[1] Locke, *Of Civil Government* (Everyman's Library ed., 1924), Bk. II, ch. ii, secs. 4 and 6. On Locke see Frederick Pollock, "Locke's Theory of the State," in his *Essays in the Law* (London, 1922), pp. 80–102; Cairns, *Legal Philosophy from Plato to Hegel*, pp. 335–361.

[2] Locke, *Of Civil Government*, Bk. II, ch. ix, sec. 123; ch. ii, secs. 12–13.

serted that men in establishing a political authority *retain* those natural rights of life, liberty, and property (often grouped by Locke under the single concept of property [3]) which were their own in the pre-political stage. "The law of nature," said Locke, "stands as an eternal rule to all men, legislators as well as others." [4] Only the right to *enforce* the law of nature was given up to the organs of the body politic. In consequence of this view, Locke—again in opposition to Hobbes—rejected absolute monarchy as a form of government and favored a government with limited powers. "The great and chief end . . . of men uniting into commonwealths, and putting themselves under governments, is the preservation of their property; to which in the state of Nature there are many things wanting." [5] The preservation of property, in the broad sense in which Locke used the term, was declared by him to be coincident with "the common good," and he pointed out that "the power of the society or legislative constituted by them can never be supposed to extend farther than the common good." [6] The supreme power cannot take away from any man any part of his property without his own consent. If it deals arbitrarily and improperly with the lives and fortunes of the people, it violates the essential conditions of the social compact and the trust relationship under which it holds its power.

What authority, asked Locke, should decide whether or not the government has transgressed the bounds which are set to its power? In other words, what organ of the community is the ultimate guarantor of the law of nature? On this question, Locke does not seem to have reached a clear-cut conclusion. At one point he drops a somewhat obscure hint to the effect that the judicial power might have to be the ultimate arbiter to decide whether the law of nature had been violated by a legislative act.[7] On the other hand, in his discussion of separation of powers within the state, the judicial power is not mentioned, the chief emphasis being placed on the divorce of the legislative from the

---

[3] *Id.,* ch. vii, sec. 87; ch. ix, sec. 123. It is obvious that in Locke's contemplation the right to property was not created by the community or state, but existed already in the state of nature.

[4] *Id.,* ch. xi, sec. 135.

[5] *Id.,* ch. ix, sec. 124.

[6] *Id.,* ch. ix, sec. 131.

[7] "The legislative or supreme authority cannot assume to itself a power to rule by extemporary arbitrary decrees, but is bound to dispense justice and decide the rights of the subject by promulgated standing laws, and known authorised judges. For the law of Nature being unwritten, and so nowhere to be found but in the minds of men, they who, through passion or interest, shall miscite or misapply it, cannot so easily be convinced of their mistake where there is no established judge." *Id.,* ch. xi, sec. 136.

executive power.[8] The legislative power, being but a delegated power from the people, cannot be transferred to any other hands.[9] It must be exercised through the promulgation of laws, "not to be varied in particular cases, but to have one rule for rich and poor, for the favourite at Court, and the countryman at plough." [10] The end of these laws, in the opinion of Locke, is "not to abolish or restrain, but to preserve and enlarge freedom." [11]

The execution and enforcement of the laws passed by the legislators is placed by Locke in the hands of the executive branch of the government. In a well-framed political order, he said, the legislative and executive powers must be in distinct hands. He pointed out, however, that for the good of society certain things must be left to the discretion of the executive authorities. They may, for instance, use their prerogative for the public advantage in instances where the municipal law has given them no direction, until the legislature can conveniently be assembled; in times of stress, even the laws themselves may have to give way to executive prerogative.[12]

While the separation of the legislative from the executive power of government will accomplish a great deal in the way of preventing governmental tyranny and arbitrariness, it does not in itself constitute a full and complete safeguard against the violation of individual rights. Locke was aware of this fact, and therefore was willing to recognize one additional and final guarantor of the law of nature: the people as a whole. They may remove and replace a legislature forgetful of its trust.[13] When the executive or the legislative power attempts to make its rule absolute and to enslave or destroy the people, the last resort of an "appeal to Heaven" is open to the people. By the exercise of the right of resistance or revolution, the natural law may then be revindicated against an oppressive positive law which negates and denies it.[14]

A necessary complement to the legal philosophy of John Locke was offered by the teachings of the French nobleman Baron Charles Louis de Montesquieu (1689–1755). Locke had presented a clear and con-

---

[8] See *id.*, ch. xii. Locke also mentions a third power, called "federative power," whose function it is to conclude treaties and other arrangements with foreign nations or their subjects. This power, as Locke himself recognized, is in reality a special department of the executive power. See ch. xii, secs. 146–148.

[9] *Id.*, ch. xi, sec. 141. See also *infra* Sec. 65.

[10] *Id.*, ch. xi, sec. 142.

[11] *Id.*, ch. vi, sec. 57. See also ch. xviii, sec. 202: "Wherever law ends, tyranny begins."

[12] *Id.*, ch. xiv, sec. 159. On Locke's conception of the executive prerogative see also *infra* Sec. 70.

[13] *Id.*, ch. xiii, sec. 149.

[14] See *id.*, ch. xiv, sec. 168; ch. xix, secs. 203–204, 222, and 242; cf. also Giorgio Del Vecchio, *Justice,* transl. L. Guthrie (New York, 1953), p. 158.

sistent theory of natural law, but he had neglected to elaborate a political system by which the observance of his law of nature would be effectively guaranteed. Montesquieu agreed with Locke that human liberty was the highest goal to be achieved by a nation, but his concern for liberty found its expression not so much in his natural-law philosophy as in his attempt to devise a system of government under which liberty could be obtained and secured in the most practicable and efficient way.

Montesquieu's natural-law philosophy can be dealt with rather briefly. He proceeded from the assumption that laws are "the necessary relations arising from the nature of things." [15] The "nature of things," according to him, manifests itself partly in universal and partly in variable tendencies and traits of human nature. Among the universal conditions of man's existence in society, he mentions the desire for peace (without which no social group life would be possible), the satisfaction of certain primary needs such as food, clothing, and shelter, the attraction arising from the difference of the sexes, and man's inherent sociability.[16] The other "necessary relations" which form the basis of laws are described as relative and contingent by him. They depend on geographical, especially climatic, conditions, on religious factors, on the political structure of a particular country. In tracing and describing the multifarious natural and cultural factors responsible for the genesis of laws, Montesquieu became in fact the precursor of the sociological jurisprudence of a later age.[17] And yet his affinity with the classical natural-law philosophers is clearly attested by the fact that he viewed law in general as "human reason" [18] (although he was aware that human reason may demand different legal solutions under different circumstances), as well as by his acknowledgment that there existed relations of justice antecedent to the positive laws by which they were established. "To say that there is nothing just or unjust but what is commanded or forbidden by positive laws, is the same as saying that before the describing of a circle all the radii were not equal." [19]

[15] *The Spirit of the Laws*, transl. T. Nugent (New York, 1900), Bk. I, ch. i. On Locke and Montesquieu see Friedrich, *Philosophy of Law in Historical Perspective*, pp. 101–109.

[16] *The Spirit of the Laws*, Bk. I, ch. ii. In some of the later chapters of the book he gives concrete examples of laws which would violate the law of nature: for example, laws authorizing incest (Bk. XXVI, ch. xii), laws forbidding self-defense (Bk. XXVI, ch. iii), laws permitting a father to dissolve the marriage of his daughter (Bk. XXVI, ch. iii), laws dispensing the father from the duty to care for his children (Bk. XXVI, ch. v).

[17] See Eugen Ehrlich, "Montesquieu and Sociological Jurisprudence," 29 *Harvard Law Review* 582 (1916).

[18] *The Spirit of the Laws*, Bk. I, ch. iii.

[19] *Id.*, Bk. I, ch. i.

Montesquieu's fame rests above everything else on his political theory of the separation of powers. "Constant experience shows us," he said, "that every man invested with power is apt to abuse it, and to carry his authority as far as it will go." [20] To prevent such abuses it is necessary that power should be checked by power. In Montesquieu's opinion, that form of government will be safest in which the three powers—legislative, executive, and judicial—are separated; that is, made independent of each other and entrusted to different persons or groups of persons. Furthermore, according to him, they should be so constituted that they hold one another in check.[21] By this device he hoped to prevent an undue extension and arbitrary use of governmental authority in general.

Montesquieu believed that his scheme for a division and mutual balancing of governmental powers had been observed and carried out by the unwritten constitution of England. In reality, however, the executive and judicial powers, under the British system of government, are inferior in strength to the legislative power, which for all practical purposes is regarded as omnipotent. As Professor Hanbury has pointed out, "By a curious irony Montesquieu, searching, like the children in Maeterlinck's play, for the Blue Bird of Happiness, imagined that it had already taken tangible form in the neighbouring wood, whereas his thought had really called it into being in the Country of the Future. That is to say, abandoning the language of metaphor, the system, whose existence he wrongly ascribed to contemporary England, was destined to see the light for the first time in the United States of America." [22]

Section 12. *The Philosophy of Natural Rights in the United States*
The combination of Locke's theory of natural law with Montesquieu's doctrine of separation of powers forms the philosophical basis of the American system of government. The constitutional division of government into three independent branches, accompanied by an intricate system of checks and balances to forestall a decisive supremacy of any one of these three branches, owes its inspiration to Montesquieu. Among other details, the grant of the veto power to the chief executive, the vesting in the legislature of the power to impeach and try high officials, and the delegation to the legislative branch of the prerogative to make appropriations of money may be traced back to Montesquieu's renowned treatise.[1] The Lockian theory of natural rights, on the other

[20] *Id.*, Bk. XI, ch. iii (the chapter numbers vary in different editions).
[21] See particularly *id.*, Bk. XI, ch. v.
[22] H. G. Hanbury, *English Courts of Law*, 2d ed. (London, 1953), p. 26.
[1] *The Spirit of the Laws*, transl. T. Nugent (New York, 1900), Bk. XI, ch. v.

hand, together with Locke's doctrine of justified resistance against governmental oppression, formed the philosophical background of the Declaration of Independence. It also influenced the interpretation of certain clauses of the Bill of Rights, especially the due-process clauses, by the United States Supreme Court during certain periods of its history.[2] Typical in this respect is the language used by the court in the case of *Savings and Loan Association v. Topeka:*

There are . . . rights in every free government beyond the control of the state. A government which recognized no such rights, which held the lives, the liberty, and the property of its citizens subject at all times to the absolute disposition and unlimited control of even the most democratic depository of power, is after all but a despotism. . . . There are limitations on such power which grow out of the essential nature of all free governments, implied reservations of individual rights, without which the social compact could not exist, and which are respected by all governments entitled to the name.[3]

Locke, it can be assumed, would have thoroughly agreed with this statement. Furthermore, the right of private property, which he held very high among the natural rights of man, has received an exceedingly strong protection at the hands of the Supreme Court in the nineteenth and early twentieth centuries.[4]

The link between Montesquieu and Locke in the system of American government was forged chiefly by the doctrine of judicial review. The United States Supreme Court has taken the position that, in order to guarantee the enforcement of natural rights, the power to make the laws must be separated not only from the power to execute the laws, but also from the power to review the laws with regard to their conformity with higher-law principles, as recognized by the United States Constitution. Thus, in the United States the courts, and especially the Supreme Court, have assumed guardianship over natural law.

A typical representative of American natural-law philosophy was

[2] See J. A. C. Grant, "The Natural Law Background of Due Process," 31 *Columbia Law Review* 56 (1931); Lowell J. Howe, "The Meaning of Due Process of Law," 18 *California Law Review* 583, 588–589 (1930); Wolfgang Friedmann, *Legal Theory*, 4th ed. (Toronto, 1960), pp. 87–98.

Cf. also the Constitution of Virginia of June 12, 1776, which says that "all men are by nature equally free and independent, and have certain inherent rights, of which, when they enter into a state of society, they cannot, by any compact, deprive or divest their posterity; namely, the enjoyment of life and liberty, with the means of acquiring and possessing property, and pursuing and obtaining happiness and safety."

[3] 20 Wall. 655, at 662-663, 22 L.Ed. 455, at 461 (1875).

[4] See Edward S. Corwin, *Liberty against Government* (Baton Rouge, La., 1948), pp. 47–48, 171 ff.; Charles G. Haines, *The American Doctrine of Judicial Supremacy*, 2d ed. (Berkeley, 1932), pp. 216–217; Walton H. Hamilton, "Property—According to Locke," 41 *Yale Law Journal* 864, at 873–874 (1932).

James Wilson (1742–1798), an associate justice of the United States Supreme Court and a professor of law in the College of Philadelphia. He believed strongly in the existence of a law of nature emanating from God and "manifesting itself to the universal conscience of mankind in simple, eternal, and self-evident principles." [5] One chapter in his lectures on law, which he delivered in Philadelphia during the winters of 1790 and 1791, begins with the following statement: "Order, proportion, and fitness pervade the universe. Around us we see; within us we feel; above us, we admire a rule from which a deviation cannot, or should not, or will not be made." [6] Human law, Wilson believed, must depend for its ultimate sanction on this immutable law of nature. He rejected Blackstone's assumption that human law involved the command of a superior to an inferior; in his view human law was grounded on the consent of those whose obedience the law required.[7] He thus linked the doctrine of natural law with the theory of popular sovereignty, believing that the natural law had its foundation in the character, strivings, and mutual relations of men and, therefore, "had an essential fitness for all mankind." [8]

The state, in Wilson's opinion, was founded by a compact of its members, who united together for their common benefit in order to enjoy peaceably what was their own and to do justice to others.[9] Each man, he said, has a natural right to his property, to his character, to liberty, and to safety.[10] It is the function of the law to guarantee these natural rights against any encroachment by the government. Law and liberty are thus closely connected in Wilson's philosophy. "Without liberty, law loses its nature and its name, and becomes oppression. Without law, liberty also loses its nature and its name, and becomes licentiousness." [11] In order to safeguard the rule of law, a system of checks and controls must be introduced into the system of government, so "as to make it advantageous even for bad men to act for the public good." [12] The legislative power should not only be separated from the executive power, but it should be divided in itself, by instituting two branches of the legislature. If one of them should depart, or attempt to depart, from the principles of the constitution, so Wilson

---

[5] Morris R. Cohen, "A Critical Sketch of Legal Philosophy in America," in *Law—A Century of Progress* (New York, 1937), II, 272.

[6] James Wilson, *Works,* ed. J. D. Andrews (Chicago, 1896), I, 49.

[7] *Id.,* I, 88.

[8] *Id.,* I, 124.

[9] *Id.,* I, 271.

[10] *Id.,* II, 309. By "character" Wilson means the reputation, integrity, and honor of a person, which should be protected by the law. *Id.,* p. 310.

[11] *Id.,* I, 7.

[12] *Id.,* I, 352.

argued, it would probably be drawn back by the other.[13] If, however, the legislature as a whole should do violence to the commands of the constitution, it should be curbed by the judicial branch of the government, to which falls the duty of declaring void all statutes which are repugnant to the supreme law of the land.[14]

The philosophy of James Wilson is perhaps the most consistent expression of the classical American philosophy of law and government. It was shared by most of the fathers of the United States Constitution. John Adams, Thomas Paine, and Thomas Jefferson were convinced that there existed natural rights which could not be restrained or repealed by human laws. And the view that it was the function of the courts to defend human rights, as recognized and sanctioned by the Constitution, against any violations by the legislature, was held not only by Wilson, but also by Hamilton and Jefferson.[15] Men like Chancellor James Kent (1763–1847) and Justice Joseph Story (1779–1845) likewise were firm believers in the existence of a natural law.[16] It can safely be stated that there is no country in the world where the idea of a law of nature, understood as a safeguard of liberty and property against governmental encroachments, gained a higher significance for the political and social development and the molding of all political and legal institutions than in the United States of America.

[13] *Id.*, I, 355.

[14] *Id.*, I, 415–417.

[15] Hamilton said in the *Federalist*, essay no. 78, "The interpretation of the laws is the proper and peculiar province of the courts. A constitution is, in fact, and must be regarded by the judges, as a fundamental law. It therefore belongs to them to ascertain its meaning, as well as the meaning of any particular act proceeding from the legislative body. If there should happen to be an irreconcilable variance between the two, that which has the superior obligation and validity ought, of course, to be preferred; or, in other words, the Constitution ought to be preferred to the statute; the intention of the people to the intention of their agents."

Jefferson said: "What I disapproved from the first moment, also, was the want of a bill of rights to guard liberty against the legislative as well as executive branches of the government." "In the arguments in favor of a declaration of rights, you omit one which has great weight with me, the legal check which it puts into the hands of the judiciary." Letters to F. Hopkinson, March 13, 1789, and to J. Madison, March 15, 1789, in the *Papers of Thomas Jefferson*, ed. J. P. Boyd (Princeton, 1958), XIV, 650, 659. After Jefferson's party was in command of the legislative and executive branches, Jefferson occasionally attacked "judicial usurpation."

[16] See particularly Joseph Story's "Essay on Natural Law," reprinted in 34 *Oregon Law Review* 88 (1955), where natural law is defined as "that system of principles which human reason has discovered to regulate the conduct of man in his various relations." The essay contains an interesting attempt to prove that the institution of polygamy violates the law of nature. *Id.*, pp. 95–96. On Wilson, Kent, and Story see also Harold G. Reuschlein, *Jurisprudence—Its American Prophets* (Indianapolis, 1951), pp. 38–44, 46–55.

Section 13. *Rousseau and His Influence*

Jean Jacques Rousseau (1712–1778), a native of the Swiss city of Geneva, may be said to belong to the classical tradition of natural law in the sense that he firmly believed in the existence of "natural rights" of the individual. But it has been asserted that, at least in some parts of his teaching, he deserted this classical tradition by seeking the ultimate norm of social life, not in the protection of indestructible personal rights, but in the supremacy of a sovereign and collective "general will." [1]

It is not altogether easy to follow the rather complex deductions of Rousseau. To him the fundamental political problem was "to find a form of association which will defend and protect with the whole common force the person and goods of each associate, and in which each, while uniting himself with all, may still obey himself alone, and remain as free as before." [2] In order to achieve this goal, each individual must by a social contract alienate all his natural rights without reservation to the whole community.[3]

One would expect that by alienating all of their natural rights to the community the citizens of the state would deprive themselves of their liberty. Rousseau, however, strongly denied this consequence. "Each man," he said, "in giving himself to all, gives himself to nobody; and as there is no associate over whom he does not acquire the same right as he yields others over himself, he gains an equivalent for everything he loses, and an increase of force for the preservation of what he has." [4] In the words of Sir Ernest Barker, "All are thus, at one and the same time, a passive body of subjects and an active body of sovereigns." [5] This sovereign body of citizens will see to it that what the individual has lost by the surrender of his natural rights he will regain in the form of civil liberty and in the guaranteed security of his possessions.[6]

In civil society, the individual is subject to no other individual, but merely "to the general will" (*volonté générale*), that is, the will of the

---

[1] See in this connection the Introduction by Sir Ernest Barker, ed., to *Social Contract: Essays by Locke, Hume, and Rousseau* (London, 1947), pp. xxxvii ff.; Friedmann, *Legal Theory*, pp. 75–77.

[2] *The Social Contract*, transl. G. D. H. Cole (Everyman's Library ed., 1913), Bk. I, ch. vi.

[3] As Barker points out, Rousseau agrees with Hobbes that each individual, by the social contract, surrenders all his natural rights; he differs from Hobbes in that the individual, according to him, surrenders his right to no man or group of men, but to the community as a whole. See Barker, p. xlvi.

[4] *Social Contract*, Bk. I, ch. vi.

[5] *Op. cit. supra* n. 1, p. xlvi.

[6] *Social Contract*, Bk. I, ch. viii.

community. Sovereignty, to Rousseau, meant the exercise of the general will. The sovereign, he argued, being formed wholly of the individuals who compose the state, can never have any interests contrary to theirs. The sovereign therefore need not give any guarantees to his subjects. Each individual, in obeying the general will, merely obeys himself; his individual will is merged in the general will. When the state is formed by means of the social contract, the general will is expressed by a unanimous consent of all citizens; all subsequent manifestations of the general will, however, are to take place in the form of majority decisions.[7]

The general will is the central concept in Rousseau's philosophy, but the full meaning of the term is far from clear and has been the subject of a great deal of argument and controversy.[8] Rousseau asserted that the general will is "always in the right," although the judgment which guides it may not always be enlightened.[9] Did he mean to say that the majority entrusted with the execution of the general will could make no mistakes, that it would be incapable of violating the rights of a minority? The answer must be sought in part in Rousseau's identification of the general will with the common good.[10] At least in a well-governed state, the general will operates to promote the welfare of all, although Rousseau conceded the possibility of a weak state in which the particular interests outweigh or smother the common good.[11] Rousseau's conclusions can also in part be explained by his optimistic appraisal of man's original nature and of the chances for perfecting this nature through moral teaching and political education.[12] This optimism led him to the belief that the majority would be prone to exercise its judgment in an enlightened and rational way, and that those opposing its opinion must be deemed to have acted in error.[13]

Rousseau, in contrast to Montesquieu, did not provide for a system of government under which the three powers of government are separate, independent, and equal. In the political scheme advocated by him, the legislative power is superior to the other two powers. It is vested in the people as a whole, not in a representative organ like a

[7] *Id.*, Bk. I, ch. vii; Bk. IV, ch. ii.
[8] See the discussion of the concept by Friedrich, *Philosophy of Law in Historical Perspective*, pp. 123–125.
[9] *Social Contract*, Bk. II, ch. vi; cf. also Bk. II, ch. iii, and Bk. IV, ch. i.
[10] *Id.*, Bk. II, ch. iii. This chapter seems to indicate that there is a definite *ideal* element in Rousseau's concept of the general will.
[11] See *id.*, Bk. IV, ch. i.
[12] His appraisal of man's uncorrupted nature in early primitive society is found in his *Dissertation on the Origin and the Foundation of the Inequality of Mankind*, reprinted in the edition cited in n. 2. On man's perfectibility through education and religion, see *Social Contract*, Bk. II, chs. vi and xii, and Bk. IV, ch. viii.
[13] *Id.*, Bk. IV, ch. ii.

parliament. "The moment a people allows itself to be represented, it is no longer free." [14] Rousseau went so far as to contend that a law not ratified by the people as a whole was null and void. In consequence of these views, he came to the conclusion that the English nation, with its representative system of government, was not a free nation. "It is free only during the election of members of parliament. As soon as they are elected, slavery overtakes it, and it is nothing." [15]

Law, according to Rousseau, must be general in character and equally applicable to all within the purview of its mandates. It cannot be directed to a particular man or a particular object.[16] For particular acts of authority the community institutes a government, a commission for the execution of the general will. There is no contract of subjection between the people and the government, such as had been construed by Hobbes.[17] Expressed in legal language, government is nothing but an agency which may be revoked, limited, or modified at the will of the sovereign people. The depositaries of public power are not the masters of the people, but merely their officers. The government exists by grace of the sovereign and does not itself possess any attributes of sovereignty.[18]

There can be no doubt that Rousseau's theory may easily lead to an absolute democracy, in which the will of the majority is not subject to any limitations. He leaves no safeguard against the omnipotence of the sovereign and no guaranty of natural law except the wisdom and self-restraint of the majority.[19] Rousseau himself was convinced that there would be no conflict between individual liberty and collective authority in a well-governed state, but it is highly doubtful whether he was justified in this assumption. A social system based on the om-

[14] *Id.*, Bk. III, ch. xv.

[15] *Ibid.* In Rousseau's native land, Switzerland, the system of direct legislation by the people is in force in a few cantons. Other cantons have representative legislative bodies but submit many important issues to the populace as a whole for decision.

[16] "Thus the law may indeed decree that there shall be privileges but cannot confer them on anybody by name. It may set up several classes of citizens, and even lay down the qualifications for membership of these classes, but it cannot nominate such and such persons as belonging to them." *Id.*, Bk. II, ch. vi.

[17] Rousseau said: "There is only one contract in the State, and that is the act of association, and it excludes all others." *Id.*, Bk. III, ch. xvi. (The translation has been slightly modified.)

[18] See Bk. III, ch. xviii.

[19] Roscoe Pound's statement that "to Rousseau, the law is an expression not of natural law or of eternal principles of right and justice but simply of the general will" ("Theories of Law," 22 *Yale L.J.* 129, 1912) seems to go too far. Rousseau, because of his optimistic view of man's propensity to act for the common good, merely thought that the protection of natural rights, especially the rights of freedom and equality, was generally safe in the hands of the sovereign people.

nipotence of the general will contains some danger of a form of despotism which Tocqueville has described as the "tyranny of the majority." [20]

Rousseau's ideas exercised a strong influence upon the political doctrines of the French Revolution. Furthermore, Rousseau's concept of the general will affected the constitutional structure of the French Republic during the nineteenth century and the first half of the twentieth. Even though Rousseau's idea of a pure democracy, in which the people themselves exercise the legislative function, did not prevail in the French political system, his postulate of a sovereign *volonté générale* finding its expression through majority vote was accepted as the basic premise of a parliamentary democracy. This meant that the protection of the natural rights of men was entrusted to the legislature rather than to an organ of government set up as a brake upon majority rule.

In England, too, the will of the majority as expressed through the elected representatives of the people is deemed to have unlimited sway. There had been an epoch in English legal history in which a different theory prevailed. Sir Edward Coke (1552–1634), a great English judge, took the view that there existed an immutable law of nature which no parliament could change. As Chief Justice of the Court of King's Bench, he enunciated the doctrine that in many cases the common law, considered as an embodiment of certain unchangeable principles of natural reason, will control an act of Parliament, and that a parliamentary law contravening "common right and reason" must be adjudged null and void.[21]

The political development of the following centuries worked, however, against this theory. When Sir William Blackstone (1723–1780) wrote his famous *Commentaries on the Laws of England*, the doctrine of parliamentary supremacy had already defeated Coke's theory of judicial supremacy. Like most legal authors in the eighteenth century, Blackstone assumed that there was an eternal law of nature from which all human laws derived their force of authority. He even contended that "no human laws are of any validity, if contrary to this [law of

---

[20] Alexis de Tocqueville, *Democracy in America,* transl. H. Reeve (New York, 1899), pp. 263–274.

[21] Dr. Bonham's Case, 77 Eng. Rep. 646 (1610). For comments on this case see Charles H. McIlwain, *The High Court of Parliament and Its Supremacy* (New Haven, 1910), pp. 286 ff.; Haines, *American Doctrine of Judicial Supremacy,* pp. 32–36; Edward S. Corwin, "The Higher Law Background of American Constitutional Law," 42 *Harv. L.R.* 365, at 367 ff. (1928); Samuel E. Thorne, "Dr. Bonham's Case," 54 *Law Quarterly Review* 543 (1938).

nature]." [22] But it has been rightly said that these statements are but "ornamental phrases." [23] In another passage in his *Commentaries,* Blackstone clearly admitted that no authority could prevent Parliament from enacting laws contrary to the law of nature. "The power of Parliament," he said, "is absolute and without control." [24] This doctrine has prevailed in England to the present day. Its implications are clear: it entrusts the enforcement of man's natural rights to the wisdom of a parliamentary majority, in the expectation that the commands of reason and justice will act as moral restraints on the omnipotence of the legislature.

Section 14. *Practical Achievements*
of the Classical Law-of-Nature School

The classical natural-law jurists prepared the ground for the legal order of modern civilization by elaborating certain elements and principles of legal regulation which constitute the basic prerequisites of a mature system of law. The classical law-of-nature school detected that there is some connection between law and the values of freedom and equality, at least in the sense that a wholly oppressive and arbitrary rule over human beings is incompatible with the concept of law.[1] All of the philosophers of natural law, including Hobbes, would probably have agreed with Rousseau's statement that "force does not create right." [2] Furthermore, the classical philosophers found out, by successive steps, that law must be a bulwark against anarchy as well as against despotism. Even those authors who, like Hobbes and Spinoza, put the antianarchical features of the law into the foreground, demanded that the strong government which they desired should grant, of its own free will, certain liberties to the citizens. Those authors who, like Locke and Montesquieu, emphasized above all the antidespotic features of the law, recognized the necessity of governmental authority to prevent the spread of anarchy. The methodical approaches of these philosophers to the problem of law were often characterized by unhistorical simplicity and arbitrary assumptions such as, for example, the

[22] *Commentaries on the Laws of England,* ed. W. C. Jones (San Francisco, 1916), vol. I, intro. sec. 2, par. 39.
[23] H. D. Hazeltine, "Blackstone," *Encyclopedia of the Social Sciences,* II, 580.
[24] *Commentaries,* Bk. I, ch. 2, sec. 222. Blackstone did state that Parliament could not do things that are "naturally impossible." But his idea of a law of nature embodying "the relations of justice" (*Id.,* intro. sec. 2, par. 39) would appear to encompass more than absolute natural necessity.
[1] This thought will be developed in Part II of this book.
[2] *The Social Contract,* transl. G. D. H. Cole, Bk. I, ch. iii.

unfounded belief that reason had the capacity to devise universally valid legal systems in all their details. Even in this respect the classical natural-law jurists do not deserve an excessive blame. By disregarding history and concentrating their efforts upon the discovery of an ideal system of law and justice, they performed a task superior in social significance to the efforts of the pure historians of the law. Through the collective efforts of several generations of thinkers, the classical law-of-nature philosophers laid the foundation stones which were used in erecting the legal edifice of modern Western civilization.

Even though the doctrines of the classical law-of-nature school have undergone needed revisions and modifications in the twentieth century, this does not detract from the great historical accomplishments of this school. In the practical politics of their own day, the teachers of natural law furnished valuable aids to progress. They created the legal instruments by which the liberation of the individual from medieval ties was achieved. The law of nature contributed to the abolishment of villeinage and serfdom. It helped to destroy the medieval guilds and medieval restrictions upon trade and industry. It aided in freeing landed property from feudal burdens. It created freedom of movement and of vocational choice. It inaugurated an era of religious and spiritual freedom. It purged criminal law and procedure of its most serious shortcomings by abolishing torture and humanizing punishment. It did away with witchcraft trials.[3] It sought to achieve legal security for everybody and sponsored the principle of equality before the law. It elaborated the general principles of international law. All these achievements were not due exclusively to the immediate influence and pressure of the natural-law philosophers. Many factors were at work in the process of the liberation of the individual, which started in the sixteenth century, and the vigor and speed of this process were different in the various countries of the Western world. But there can be no doubt that the classical law-of-nature movement was one of the creative and invigorating forces in the rise of liberalism and in the legal reforms which liberalism achieved.

Another practical result of the philosophy of natural law was a strong movement for legislation. The advocates of a law of nature believed that by the mere use of their rational powers men would be able to discover an ideal legal system. It was only natural that they should endeavor to work out in a systematic form all the various rules and principles of natural law and to embody them in a code. Accordingly, about the middle of the eighteenth century a movement for

[3] It was a teacher of natural law, Christian Thomasius, who led the attack upon witchcraft trials in Germany.

legislation set in. Its first fruit was the Code of Frederick the Great of Prussia (*Allgemeines Landrecht*, promulgated in 1794 under Frederick's successor), which contained important elements of the benevolent and paternalistic legal philosophy of Christian Wolff.[4] One of the highest achievements of the movement for legislation was the Code Napoléon of 1804, which is still law in France. Austria enacted a code in 1811. Later milestones on the road to codification were the German Civil Code of 1896 and the Swiss Civil Code of 1907. All of these codes, by granting a certain amount of freedom, equality, and security to all persons within their sphere of operation, realized and put into effect some of the elementary postulates of the classical law-of-nature school.

[4] See *supra* Sec. 9.

IV

GERMAN
TRANSCENDENTAL
IDEALISM

Section 15. *The Legal Philosophy of Kant*

Transcendental idealism is a philosophical attitude which attributes an autonomous existence to ideas and concepts formed by the human mind and denies that such ideas and concepts are merely human reactions to the empirical world of flux. It is characteristic of this philosophical approach that it ascribes great force and strength to the human intellect and considers that empirical reality is to a great extent shaped by the ideas conceived or produced by human thinking. Transcendental idealism also inclines to the belief that either knowledge of reality itself, or at least the forms, ways, and categories by which the human mind attempts to gain knowledge of reality, are not given a posteriori, through sense experience, but a priori, independently of empirical sense data. In the most radical manifestations of this philosophy, human thought becomes converted into "the exclusive pillar of the universe." [1] It was in the Germany of the eighteenth and nine-

[1] Guido de Ruggiero, "Idealism," *Encyclopedia of the Social Sciences*, VII, 568.

teenth century that the idealistic strain in Western philosophy was carried to its highest pitch.

Whether the great German philosopher Immanuel Kant (1724–1804) should properly be classified as a transcendental idealist has been the subject of debate and doubt. Kant's philosophy, at least in certain of its aspects, lends itself to the interpretation that its primary objective was to attempt a reconciliation between an idealistic rationalism, characterized by a belief in the primacy of thinking over experience, and an empirical sensualism, guided by the assumption of the dependence of all human knowledge upon sense perception. Kant took the position that "sensations" are the only source of our knowledge of objects in the empirical world. However, he viewed sense experience as conditioned by the constitution of the human mind, which, in his opinion, contained certain forms of cognition or understanding by which the fleeting impressions of the senses are absorbed, coordinated, and integrated. Among these forms and categories of cognition indigenous to the human mind he listed the concepts of space, time, and causality, as well as the propositions of mathematics. All of these he considered not as products of experience but as a priori categories brought by the knowing observer to the data of the senses.[2]

While Kant's scientific philosophy, as outlined in his *Critique of Pure Reason*, is susceptible of being interpreted as a compromise between empirical sensualism and transcendental idealism, his idealistic bent becomes very strong in his philosophy of morality and freedom. Insofar as man is part of the world of empirical phenomena, he taught, his will and actions are subject to the iron laws of causality as expounded in Newton's theory of the physical universe; they are therefore unfree and determined. Man's inner experience and practical reason, on the other hand, tell him that he is a free moral agent who can choose between good and evil. In order to solve this contradiction between the theoretical reason of natural science and the practical reason of the human moral life, Kant assumed that man belongs not only to the "sensible" world (that is, the world of sense perception), but also to a world he called "intelligible" or "noumenal."[3] In this world freedom, self-determination, and moral choice are possible and real. To Kant, law as well as morality must be assigned to the intelligible world. In con-

[2] See F. S. C. Northrop, *The Meeting of East and West* (New York, 1946), pp. 196–199; B. A. G. Fuller and Sterling McMurrin, *A History of Modern Philosophy*, 3d ed. (New York, 1955), II, 219.

[3] Kant did not believe that these two worlds were separate and independent from each other, although he distinguished them for purposes of philosophical inquiry. He seems to have assumed that the noumenal world was the ground or cause of the empirical world.

trast to the philosophers of the natural law, he rejected all attempts to predicate general principles of morality and law on the empirical nature of man; instead he sought to find their basis in an a priori world of "oughts" founded on the dictates of reason. A close study of Kant's philosophy as a whole strongly conveys the impression that he considered the noumenal world, the world of freedom and human reason, as the *real* world, as the "thing-in-itself," while the empirical world of physical nature and causality was to him a shadow world, a world of appearances, viewed by us through colored and defective spectacles. If this interpretation is correct, then it is entirely proper to classify Kant as a transcendental idealist.[4]

The concept of freedom is central in Kant's moral and legal philosophy.[5] He makes a distinction, however, between ethical and juridical freedom. Ethical or moral freedom meant to him the autonomy and self-determination of the human will; we are morally free insofar as we are capable of obeying a moral law which is engraved in the hearts of all of us.[6] This moral law, formulated by Kant in the form of the Categorical Imperative, demands that we act according to a maxim which we could wish to become a universal law.[7] Juridical freedom, on the other hand, he defines as independence of an individual from the arbitrary will and control of another. This freedom he considered as the only original and inborn right belonging to man by virtue of his humanness.[8] This basic right, he pointed out, comprises in itself the ideas of a formal equality, because it implies that each man is independent and his own master. Kant had a strong belief in the inherent dignity of the human personality, and he taught that no man had the right to use another person merely as a means to attain his own subjective purposes; each human individual was always to be treated as an end in itself.[9]

Law was defined by Kant as "the totality of the conditions under which the arbitrary will of one can coexist with the arbitrary will of

---

[4] On Kant's philosophy of morality and freedom see H. J. Paton, *The Categorical Imperative* (London, 1946).

[5] The line drawn by Kant between morality and law is discussed elsewhere. See *infra* Sec. 57. On Kant's legal philosophy see also Huntington Cairns, *Legal Philosophy from Plato to Hegel* (Baltimore, 1949), pp. 390–463; Giorgio Del Vecchio, *Philosophy of Law*, transl. T. O. Martin (Washington, 1953), pp. 102–115.

[6] In Kant's own words: "A free will and a will subject to moral laws are one and the same." *Fundamental Principles of the Metaphysic of Morals*, transl. J. K. Abbot (New York, 1949), p. 64. A free will, under this concept, is not one which freely and without inhibitions satisfies desires, inclinations, and appetites but, on the contrary, one which is in full control of irrational impulse.

[7] *Id.*, p. 38.

[8] "The Science of Right," transl. W. Hastie, in *Great Books of the Western World*, ed. R. M. Hutchins (Chicago, 1952), XLII, 401.

[9] *Metaphysic of Morals*, p. 46.

another according to a general law of freedom." [10] This means: if my action or my condition can coexist with the freedom of everybody else, according to a general law, then whoever hinders me in the performance of this act or in the maintenance of this condition is doing me a wrong. From this it follows that the law may use coercive force against a person who improperly and unnecessarily interferes with the freedom of another individual. As Roscoe Pound has pointed out, this conception of law "seems to be the final form of an ideal of the social order which governed from the sixteenth to the nineteenth century: an ideal of the maximum of individual self-assertion as the end for which the legal order exists." [11]

Kant's theory of the state corresponded to that of Rousseau. Kant recognized the social contract, not as a historical fact, but as a postulate of reason and "a criterion whereby to evaluate the legitimacy of a State." [12] Kant also adopted Rousseau's theory of the general will by proclaiming that the legislative power can only belong to the united will of the people. The will of the legislator with regard to what constitutes the external Mine and Thine is irreproachable, for it is the joint will of all, and this will cannot do any wrong to an individual citizen (*Volenti non fit injuria*).[13]

In Kant's opinion, it is the sole function of the state to guarantee the enforcement of law. Consequently, he defined the state as a "union of a number of men under juridical laws." [14] The state must not needlessly interfere with the activity of its citizens or paternalistically look after

[10] *Metaphysik der Sitten*, ed. K. Vorländer (Leipzig, 1922), pp. 34-35. (Translations from publications in foreign languages are mine unless otherwise indicated.) The term "arbitrary will" (*Willkür*) is identified by Kant with the capacity to act or not to act according to one's pleasure. *Id.*, p. 13.

It is of interest to observe that the term "law" connoted to Kant a set of invariable, inflexible principles from which, in the words of James Wilson (*supra* Sec. 12), "a deviation cannot, or should not, or will not be made." This conception had its source in Newton's view of the physical universe as an entity governed by immutable, never-failing causal laws. As a result of this conception, Kant rejected the Aristotelian idea that the general rules of the positive law might be corrected or mitigated, in harsh cases, by individual equity; he also was unwilling to recognize the maxim "Necessity knows no law" except as a justification for mitigating or abating punishment; and he wished to limit the executive's right of pardon to cases of *lesé-majesté*. See Kant, "Science of Right," pp. 399-400, 449.

[11] *Interpretations of Legal History* (Cambridge, Mass., 1930), p. 29. On Kant's concept of law see also Pound, *The Spirit of the Common Law* (Boston, 1921), pp. 147-148, 151-154; Carl J. Friedrich, *The Philosophy of Law in Historical Perspective* (Chicago, 1958), pp. 125-130.

[12] Del Vecchio, p. 113.

[13] Kant, "Science of Right," p. 436. In view of the fact that Kant excluded large classes of people, such as women, servants, and day laborers from active participation in the formation of the political will, this argument appears to lack conviction.

[14] *Id.*, p. 436.

their interests and personal happiness; it ought to confine itself to the protection of their rights. In order to prevent the establishment of a despotic regime, Kant demanded a separation of powers. The legislative power must belong to the people; if it is entrusted to the executive arm of the government, tyranny will result. The judicial power will award to each person that which is due to him under the law. The Kantian judiciary does not, however, possess the right to pass upon the validity of legislation. Thus, freedom and the rights of men are, in Kant's view, guaranteed solely by the will of a legislative majority. This will, Kant said, cannot be resisted under any circumstances; nor does a right of rebellion against executive tryanny exist under his political scheme. "The Supreme Power in the State has only Rights, and no (compulsory) Duties towards the subject." [15] It is the duty of the people to bear the abuses and the iniquities of the supreme power even though they may become unbearable; for the sovereign, being the source of all law, can himself do no wrong.[16] By thus attributing obligatory force to positive law alone, Kant prepared the ground for the rise of positivism in legal theory.[17]

Section 16. *The Legal Philosophy of Fichte*
Transcendental idealism presented itself in a pure and uncompromising form in the philosophy of Johann Gottlieb Fichte (1762–1814). To him, the starting point and center of all philosophical thinking is and must be the intelligent human ego. Not only the *forms* of our cognition, as Kant had taught, but also the *content* of our perceptions and sensations, were regarded by Fichte as the product of our consciousness. "All being, that of the ego as well as that of the non-ego, is a certain modality of consciousness; and without consciousness there is no being." [1] The nonego, that is, the world of objects, is in Fichte's view, nothing but a target for human action, a domain for the exertion of the human will, which is able to shape and transform this world.[2] Fichte's philosophy is one of human activism without bounds, and it represents an enthusiastic affirmation of the sovereign power of human intelligence.

The rational human ego is viewed as free by Fichte in the sense that it sets its own goals and is capable of attaining them; in other words,

---

[15] *Id.*, p. 439.
[16] *Id.*, p. 440.
[17] On legal positivism see *infra* Sec. 24.
[1] "Grundlage des Naturrechts nach Prinzipien der Wissenschaftslehre," in *Sämtliche Werke* (Berlin, 1845), p. 2 (translation mine).
[2] Although we may be disinclined today to accept this form of subjective idealism as a true philosophy, it gave strong impetus in its day to man's attempts to become the master of nature and use his creative powers to the fullest extent.

the actions of human beings are determined solely by their own will.[3] Since, however, human egos stand in relations of interaction with other human egos, their respective spheres of freedom must be adjusted and harmonized. Thus Fichte, like Kant, considered law as a device for securing the coexistence of free individuals. Every man must respect the freedom of every other man. No one may claim a freedom which he would not concede to others in the same way. Differently expressed, each individual must exercise his freedom within certain limits determined by the equal freedom of every other person.[4] Fichte emphasized that limitations upon the freedom of the individual ego should be decreed by general laws, not by the individual pronouncements of judges.[5] For the individual must be deemed to have consented to the promulgation of general laws guaranteeing the freedom of all; he cannot be deemed to have subjected himself to the arbitrary decision of a particular judge.

Fichte's philosophy of law was laid down in a complete and systematic form in a relatively early period of his academic activity. It underwent certain important modifications, however, in the course of his life.[6] While Fichte had emphasized the freedom, independence, and natural rights of the individual in his early period, his later writings stressed the importance of the national state and justified an extension of its activities beyond the protection of universal freedom. In the economic field, for example, he rejected free trade and laissez-faire policies, demanding governmental regulation of production and the establishment of a foreign trade monopoly by the state. In the political domain, too, he gradually and increasingly moved away from the individualism of his younger years and came to see the chief destiny and duty of the individual in his submergence in the national state, conceived as an indivisible and organic collective entity. His cult of the spirit ended with his surrendering the political life of the state to Machiavellian policies.

Section 17. *Hegel's Philosophy of Law and the State*
In the philosophy of Georg Wilhelm Friedrich Hegel (1770–1831), German transcendental idealism took a turn from a subjective to an

---

[3] "Grundlage des Naturrechts," pp. 8, 59, 85.

[4] *Id.*, pp. 10, 92.

[5] *Id.*, p. 103. Like Kant, Fichte held that human laws should be categorical and invariable, i.e., not subject to equitable exceptions in cases where they would work severe hardship. *Id.*, p. 104.

[6] A good brief account of the evolution in Fichte's thought is given by Alfred Verdross, *Abendländische Rechtsphilosophie* (Vienna, 1958), pp. 147–149; see also Cairns, *Legal Philosophy from Plato to Hegel*, pp. 464–502; Wolfgang Friedmann, *Legal Theory*, 4th ed. (Toronto, 1960), pp. 111–114.

objective form of rationalism. While Fichte had placed the seat of rationality chiefly in the mind of the human individual, Hegel declared the "objective spirit" manifesting itself in the unfolding of history and civilization to be the principal standard bearer of reason. He taught that reason revealed itself in different ways in the various epochs of history and that its content was constantly changing. Hegel saw in history an "evermoving stream which throws up unique individualities as it moves, and is always shaping individual structures on the basis of a law which is always new." [1] The new idea which he developed and which was to become of far-reaching importance in the history of legal philosophy was the idea of *evolution*. All the various manifestations of social life, including the law, taught Hegel, are the product of an evolutionary, dynamic process. This process takes on a dialectic form: it reveals itself in thesis, antithesis, and synthesis. The human spirit sets a thesis which becomes the leading idea of a particular epoch. Against this thesis an antithesis is set up, and from the struggle of both a synthesis develops which absorbs elements of both and reconciles them on a higher plane. This process repeats itself again and again in history.

What is the meaning and ultimate goal of this dynamic process? According to Hegel, the great ideal which lies back of the colorful and often perplexing pageant of history is the realization of *freedom*. History, said Hegel, did not realize this ideal once and for all. The achievement of freedom is a long and complicated process, in which the working of reason, although always present, cannot be easily discerned; it is the "ruse of reason" to let even the forces of evil work in its service. In this evolutionary process a specific task has been assigned to each nation in history. After its fulfillment this nation loses its significance in history: the "world spirit" has surpassed its ideas and institutions, and it is compelled by fate to hand the torch to a younger and more vigorous nation. It is in this fashion that the world spirit, according to Hegel, accomplishes its ultimate goal of universal freedom. In the old oriental monarchies only one person, the king, was really free. In the Greek and Roman world some were free, but the majority of the population were slaves. The Germanic peoples were the first to recognize that every individual is free, and that freedom of the spirit is man's most peculiar characteristic.[2]

In this historical process, law and the state play a vital role, according to Hegel. The system of law, he asserted, is designed to realize the

[1] Ernst Troeltsch, "The Ideas of Natural Law and Humanity in World Politics," in Otto Gierke, *Natural Law and the Theory of Society*, transl. E. Barker (Cambridge, Eng., 1934), I, 204.
[2] See Hegel, *Lectures on the Philosophy of History*, transl. J. Sibree (London, 1890), Introduction.

ideal of freedom in its external manifestations.[3] It bears emphasis, however, that for Hegel freedom did not signify the right of a person to do as he pleased. A free person, in his view, is one whose mind is in control of his body, one who subordinates his natural passions, irrational desires, and purely material interests to the superior demands of his rational and spiritual self.[4] Hegel admonished men to lead a life governed by reason and pointed out that one of the cardinal postulates of reason was to accord respect to the personality and rights of other human beings.[5] The law was considered by him as one of the chief instruments devised to reinforce and secure such respect.

The state was defined by Hegel as the "ethical universe" and the "actuality of the ethical ideal." [6] This definition demonstrates that Hegel, unlike Kant, viewed the state not merely as an institution for the enactment and execution of laws but, in a much broader use of the term, as an organism within which the ethical life of a people unfolds itself. This ethical life finds its expression in the mores, customs, common beliefs, art, religion, and political institutions of a nation; in short, in the pattern of its community values. Hegel taught that, since the individual is embedded in the entire culture of his country and epoch, since he is a "Son of his Nation" as well as a "Son of his Age," he possesses his worth and reality as a rational being only through the state, conceived as the total embodiment of the spirit and social ethics of the people. It is the highest privilege of an individual to be a member of the state, Hegel said.[7] In his singularity the individual is often not capable of discerning clearly the specific content of his ethical duties; their content must be determined in an objective fashion by the mores and ways of life of the organized community.[8]

The contention has often been made that Hegel was a panegyrist of the power state and the philosophical progenitor of modern fascist totalitarianism. Undoubtedly, legal theorists of fascist persuasion have sometimes tended to rely extensively on Hegel's philosophy of the state,[9] and passages can be found in Hegel's writings which would seem to give countenance to such reliance. This is particularly true

[3] Hegel, The Philosophy of Right, transl. T. M. Knox (Oxford, 1942), pp. 20, 33 (secs. 4 and 29). Knox in his translation erroneously uses the word "right" where he should have used the term "law."
[4] Philosophy of History, p. 43; Philosophy of Right, p. 231 (addition to sec. 18).
[5] Id., p. 37 (sec. 36).
[6] Id., p. 11 (Preface) and p. 155 (sec. 257).
[7] Philosophy of History, pp. 40-41, 55 (Introduction).
[8] Philosophy of Right, p. 156 (sec. 258).
[9] See, for example, Karl Larenz, Rechts- und Staatsphilosophie der Gegenwart, 2d ed. (Berlin, 1935). On other authors who call themselves neo-Hegelians see Friedmann, Legal Theory, pp. 125-127. Friedmann is inclined to blame Hegel himself for the deification of the national state found in many of the neo-Hegelian writings.

for Hegel's discussion of the external relations of states. Hegel believed that the sovereignty of individual states in the conduct of their foreign affairs was absolute and unrestrained. Disputes between states not susceptible of being settled by mutual agreement could be decided only by war, an institution which Hegel regarded at the same time as necessary and beneficial for the preservation of the internal health and vigor of the nation.[10] But it would be incorrect to assert that Hegel advocated totalitarian methods of government in the internal relations of the state or, more particularly, in the treatment of the citizens or subjects. He did not believe that the highest aim to be pursued by the state was aggrandizement of the power of its rulers.[11] This would be contrary to Hegel's basic conviction that the state should serve the interests of the human mind, and that, in its innermost essence, it was an embodiment of spiritual forces. He viewed that type of state as the ideal commonwealth in which art, science, and other forms of cultural life were developed to the highest degree. Such a state, he thought, would at the same time be a powerful state.

Hegel made it quite clear that the state should grant its citizens the right to own private property, and he expressed a general dislike for public ownership.[12] He wished to give individuals the right to enter into contracts of their own choice, and he assigned a very high value to the institution of the family. Furthermore, he demanded that the rights and duties of the citizens, as well as the rights and duties of the state, be fixed and determined by law. He conceded to individuals the right to live a private life, to foster their personality, and to promote their particular interests as long as they did not in so doing lose sight of the interests of the community as a whole.[13]

The following famous aphorism is found in the preface to Hegel's *Philosophy of Law:* "That which is rational is real and that which is real is rational." Some writers have attempted to deduce Hegel's supposed approval of modern totalitarian governments from this statement. A close study of Hegel's philosophical disquisitions will reveal, however, that for Hegel only *ideas* had genuine reality.[14] History was real and rational to him to the extent that its events demonstrated and

[10] *Philosophy of Right,* pp. 209–210 (sec. 324), 213–214 (secs. 333–334), 295 (addition to sec. 324).

[11] *Id.,* pp. 158–160 (note to sec. 258). See also the excellent exposition of Hegel's philosophy of law and the state by Friedrich, *Philosophy of Law in Historical Perspective,* pp. 131–138.

[12] *Philosophy of Right,* p. 42 (sec. 46), and p. 236 (addition to sec. 46).

[13] *Id.,* p. 160 (sec. 260). Cf. also p. 280 (additions to secs. 260 and 261), and *The Philosophy of Hegel,* ed. C. J. Friedrich (New York, 1953), p. xlvii.

[14] See Hegel, "The Phenomenology of the Spirit," in *The Philosophy of Hegel,* pp. 411–412.

symbolized the forward march of the idea of freedom in its gradual and relentless progress toward its goal, even though in particular and perhaps inessential happenings a considerable degree of irrationality might manifest itself. It must not be forgotten that Hegel was a thoroughgoing idealist who believed in the sovereignty of the spirit over the material and the essential dignity of the human being. The state he glorified was the ethical state, not the state which degraded and enslaved the individual and was oblivious of his justified claims.[15] Hegel's philosophy contained, therefore, a substantial amount of individualistic liberalism, although this aspect of his thought is sometimes obscured by statements which, taken in isolation, might appear to exalt the state at the expense of the individual.

[15] This is emphasized by Friedrich, *op. cit. supra* n. 11, pp. 131-132. On Hegel's philosophy of law see also Cairns, *Legal Philosophy from Plato to Hegel*, pp. 503-550.

V

HISTORICAL
AND EVOLUTIONARY
THEORIES OF LAW

Section 18. *Savigny and the Historical School in Germany*
The natural-law philosophers of the seventeenth and eighteenth centuries had looked to reason as a guide for discerning the ideal and most perfect form of law. They were interested in the aims and purposes of the law, not in its history and growth. They sought to construct a new legal order based on certain principles of liberty and equality, which they proclaimed to be eternal postulates of reason and justice.

The age of rationalism and natural law in Europe culminated in the French Revolution of 1789. When this revolution failed to reach its objectives in the doctrinaire way in which it had set about to achieve them, and had to be content with partial results, a certain reaction against its rationalistic premises set in throughout Europe. In Germany and England especially, those two countries which had resisted and to some extent thwarted the attempts to spread the ideas of the French Revolution across the whole continent of Europe, the movement against the unhistorical rationalism of the forerunners of the revolution became quite powerful. Conservative ideas, based on history and tradition, were emphasized and propagated. In the sphere of law and legal philosophy, this meant the accentuation of legal history and legal tradition as against the speculative attempts to establish a law of nature. The history of law was investigated thoroughly and brakes were put on the zeal of law reformers. This was the period in which scientific research into the law-shaping forces began to replace the rationalistic inquiries into the ideal nature, purposes, and social objectives of the law.

In England, it was Edmund Burke who, in his *Reflections on the Revolution in France* (1790), denounced the excesses of this revolution and emphasized the values of tradition and gradual growth. He protested against what he considered a reckless reshuffling of the political and legal order of the French people and pointed to history, habit, and religion as the true guides to social action. An even stronger reaction against the rationalistic and cosmopolitan principles of the French Revolution took place in Germany. There arose in that country a powerful movement which was romantic, irrational, and vehemently nationalistic in character and found its expression in literature, art, and political theory. In the domain of law, this movement was represented by the historical school of law. The most eminent exponent of this school was Friedrich Carl von Savigny (1779–1861), whose most distinguished pupil was Georg Friedrich Puchta (1798–1846).

Savigny's view of the law was first presented in his famous pamphlet "Of the Vocation of Our Age for Legislation and Jurisprudence" (1814). This pamphlet was an answer to a proposal made by a professor of civil law, A. F. J. Thibaut of Heidelberg University, to the effect that a codification of the laws and customs of the various German states be undertaken in a coherent arrangement, on the basis of Roman law and the Napoleonic code. Savigny vehemently attacked this suggestion. In his view, the law was not something that should be made arbitrarily and deliberately by a lawmaker. Law, he said, was a product of "internal, silently-operating forces."[1] It was deeply rooted in the past of a nation, and its true sources were popular faith, custom, and "the common consciousness of the people." Like the language, the constitution, and the manners of a people, law was determined above all by the peculiar character of a nation, by its "national spirit" (*Volksgeist*).[2] In every people, Savigny pointed out, certain

[1] *Of the Vocation of Our Age for Legislation and Jurisprudence,* transl. A. Hayward (London, 1831), p. 30.
[2] Savigny, *System des Heutigen Römischen Rechts* (Berlin, 1840), I, 14.

traditions and customs grow up which by their continuous exercise evolve into legal rules.[3] Only by a careful study of these traditions and customs can the true content of law be found. Law in its proper sense is identical with the opinion of the people in matters of right and justice. In the words of Savigny,

In the earliest times to which authentic history extends the law will be found to have already attained a fixed character, peculiar to the people, like their language, manners, and constitution. Nay, these phenomena have no separate existence, they are but the particular faculties and tendencies of an individual people, inseparably united in nature, and only wearing the semblance of distinct attributes to our view. That which binds them into one whole is the common conviction of the people, the kindred consciousness of an inward necessity, excluding all notion of an accidental and arbitrary origin.[4]

Thus in the view of Savigny, law, like language, is a product not of an arbitrary and deliberate will but of a slow, gradual, and organic growth.[5] The law has no separate existence, but is simply a function of the whole life of a nation. "Law grows with the growth, and strengthens with the strength of the people, and finally dies away as the nation loses its individuality." [6]

What role was assigned by Savigny to the legal profession in this evolutionary process? Savigny was well aware of the fact that in an advanced system of law, legal scholars, judges, and lawyers play an active part in the shaping of legal institutions. He knew that the popular spirit does not fashion codes of procedure, rules of evidence, or bankruptcy laws. But he viewed the technical jurists less as members of a closed profession than as trustees of the people and as "representatives of the community spirit . . . authorized to carry on the law in its technical aspects." [7]

Puchta agreed with his teacher that the genesis and unfolding of law out of the spirit of the people was an invisible process. "What is

[3] On the role of custom in law see *infra* Sec. 58.
[4] *Legislation and Jurisprudence*, p. 24.
[5] Hermann Kantorowicz, "Savigny and the Historical School of Law," 53 *Law Quarterly Review* 326, at 340 (1937), gives an excellent summary of the chief doctrine of this school: "Law, like civilization in general, is the emanation of unconscious, anonymous, gradual, and irrational forces in the individual life of a particular nation."
[6] *Legislation and Jurisprudence*, p. 27. Hayward translates *Eigentümlichkeit* as "nationality." I have substituted "individuality," which seems preferable in the context of this sentence.
[7] Edwin W. Patterson, *Jurisprudence* (Brooklyn, 1953), p. 412. On Savigny see also Roscoe Pound, *Interpretations of Legal History* (Cambridge, Mass., 1930), pp. 12–21.

visible to us is only the product, law, as it has emerged from the dark laboratory in which it was prepared and by which it became real." [8] His investigations on the popular origin of law convinced him that customary law was the most genuine expression of the common conviction of the people, and for this reason, far superior to legislation. He considered explicit legislation useful only insofar as it embodied the prevailing national customs and usages.

It will easily be seen that the doctrines of the historical jurists stood in sharp contrast to the teachings of the classical natural-law philosophers. The thinkers of the age of enlightenment believed that the legal rules could be discovered and laid down in a code by consulting human reason alone. The historical school detested legislation and placed the emphasis on the irrational, almost mystical concept of a "national spirit" rooted in the traditions of a remote past.[9] The law-of-nature school taught that the fundamental principles of law were everywhere and at all times the same. The historical jurists believed in the predominantly national character of legal institutions. The classical law of nature, as an essentially revolutionary doctrine, looked to the future. The historical school, as a reaction to it, looked to the past. The historical school was, in fact, a legal counterpart to the epoch of political reaction in Europe which followed the defeat of Napoleon and the Congress of Vienna and found its expression in the "Holy Alliance" of imperial dynasties. In evaluating the historical school of law it should not be forgotten that Savigny was a conservative nobleman who detested the equalitarian rationalism of the French Revolution. Furthermore, he was a German nationalist who was opposed to the cosmopolitan implications of the French doctrine. He was very critical of the Code Napoléon and sought to prevent the enactment of similar codes in Germany. These facts explain his dislike of legislation and his emphasis upon silent, anonymous, and unconscious forces as the true elements of legal growth, with which no legislator should be allowed to interfere.

The historical school of law was perhaps the strongest stimulating factor for the revival of historical interest which was typical of nine-

[8] Georg Friedrich Puchta, *Outlines of Jurisprudence as the Science of Right,* transl. W. Hastie (Edinburgh, 1887), p. 38. (The word "right" in the translation has been replaced by the term "law.")

[9] Even though Hegel (see *supra* Sec. 17) had to some extent inspired the ideas of the historical school by his emphasis on the "spirit of the people" as the chief vehicle through which reason unfolds itself in history in a gradual, dynamic, and evolutionary process, he sharply denounced the antilegislative attitude of this school as disgraceful and insulting to the intelligence of the peoples of this world. Hegel, *The Philosophy of Right,* transl. T. M. Knox (Oxford, 1942), sec. 211.

teenth-century jurisprudence. Everywhere, but above all in Germany, detailed investigations into the primitive and early periods of legal history were undertaken. Elaborate volumes were frequently written on some minor details in a remote legal system. In some cases the labor expended on these historical studies was out of proportion to the result achieved, but in many instances it led to a great and indispensable enrichment of our knowledge of the early development of legal institutions.

Section 19. *The Historical School in England and the United States*
The founder and chief exponent of the English historical school of law was Sir Henry Maine (1822–1888).[1] He was strongly influenced by Savigny's historical approach to the problems of jurisprudence, but he went beyond Savigny in undertaking broad comparative studies of the unfolding of legal institutions in primitive as well as progressive societies. These studies led him to the conviction that the legal history of peoples shows patterns of evolution which recur in different social orders and in similar historical circumstances. There do not exist infinite possibilities for building and managing human societies; certain political, social, and legal forms reappear in seemingly different garb, and if they reappear, they manifest themselves in certain typical ways. Roman feudalism produced legal rules and legal institutions strikingly similar to English feudalism, although differences and divergences can also be demonstrated.

One of the general laws of legal evolution which Maine believed to have discovered is set forth in his classical treatise *Ancient Law:*

The movement of the progressive societies has been uniform in one respect. Through all its course it has been distinguished by the gradual dissolution of family dependency, and the growth of individual obligation in its place. The Individual is steadily substituted for the Family, as the unit of which civil laws take account. The advance has been accomplished at varying rates of celerity, and there are societies not absolutely stationary in which the collapse of the ancient organization can only be perceived by careful study of the phenomena they present. But, whatever its pace, the change has not been subject to reaction or recoil, and apparent retardations will be found to have been occasioned through the absorption of archaic ideas and customs

---

[1] His chief works are: *Ancient Law* (London, 1861); new ed. with notes by Frederick Pollock (London, 1930); *Village Communities in the East and West* (London, 1871); *Lectures on the Early History of Institutions* (London, 1874); *Dissertations on Early Law and Custom* (London, 1883).

On Maine see Pound, *Interpretations of Legal History*, pp. 53–61; Paul Vinogradoff, "The Teaching of Sir Henry Maine," in *Collected Papers* (Oxford, 1928), II, 173–189; Patterson, *Jurisprudence*, pp. 414–418; Wolfgang Friedmann, *Legal Theory*, 4th ed. (Toronto, 1960), pp. 164–170.

from some entirely foreign source. Nor is it difficult to see what is the tie between man and man which replaces by degrees those forms of reciprocity in rights and duties which have their origin in the Family. It is Contract. Starting, as from one terminus of history, from a condition of society in which all the relations of Persons are summed up in the relation of Family, we seem to have steadily moved towards a phase of social order in which all these relations arise from the free agreement of Individuals.[2]

Thus Maine arrived at his often-quoted conclusion that "the movement of the progressive societies has hitherto been a movement from Status to Contract."[3] Status is a fixed condition in which an individual finds himself without reference to his will and of which he cannot divest himself by his own efforts. It is indicative of a social order in which the group, not the individual, is the primary unit of social life; every individual is enmeshed in a network of family and group ties. With the progress of civilization this condition gradually gives way to a social system based on contract. This system is characterized by individual freedom, in that "the rights, duties, and liabilities flow from voluntary action and are consequences of exertion of the human will."[4] A progressive civilization, in the view of Maine, is manifested by the emergence of the independent, free, and self-determining individual as the primary unit of social life.

Maine's "status to contract" doctrine is by no means his only outstanding contribution to jurisprudence. He has enriched our knowledge and understanding of legal history in several respects. Very interesting, for example, is his theory regarding the sequence of phenomena in the general development of law and lawmaking. He believed that in the earliest period law was created by the personal commands of patriarchal rulers, who were considered by their subjects to act under divine inspiration. Then followed a period of customary law, expounded and applied by an aristocracy or small privileged class which claimed a monopoly of legal knowledge. The third stage was marked by a codification of these customs as the result of social conflicts (the Law of the Twelve Tables in Rome, for example). The fourth stage, according to Maine, consists in the modification of strict archaic law by the help of fiction, equity, and legislation; these instrumentalities are designed to bring the law into harmony with a progressing society. Finally, scientific jurisprudence weaves all these various forms of law into a consistent and systematic whole. Not all

[2] New ed., p. 180.
[3] Id., p. 182.
[4] Roscoe Pound, "The End of Law as Developed in Juristic Thought," 30 *Harvard Law Review* 201, at 210 (1917).

societies, said Maine, succeed in passing through all these stages, and their legal development in its particular aspects does not show a uniform line. Maine merely wished to indicate certain general directions and trends of development in the evolution of law. Modern research has shown that, on the whole, he has succeeded remarkably well in tracing some of the fundamental lines of a "natural history" of the law.

Maine's comparative analysis of legal evolution was supplemented in the early twentieth century by the historical studies of Sir Paul Vinogradoff.[5] English historical research also produced such ripe fruits as Pollock and Maitland's *History of English Law Before the Time of Edward I*[6] and Holdsworth's *History of English Law*,[7] as well as a host of specialized treatises and monographs. What is lacking up to this day is a history of English law which closely correlates legal developments with the general political, social, and cultural history of England.

We shall now turn to the United States of America. In 1849, Luther S. Cushing gave a course of lectures at Harvard Law School, in which he sympathetically expounded the doctrines of the German historical school, especially those of Savigny. One of the students in this course was James Coolidge Carter (1827–1903), who subsequently became a prominent New York attorney and leader of the American bar.[8] The lectures left a deep imprint on Carter's mind, and in the course of his life he became a devoted American apostle of Savigny's legal creed.

It was a basic thesis of Carter that habit and custom furnish the rules which govern human conduct, and that a judicial precedent is nothing but "authenticated custom."[9] It is essentially custom which determines whether an act is right or wrong, and a judicial decision which settles a problem of right or wrong merely puts the stamp of public approval on a societal custom and evidences its genuineness. Thus, in Carter's opinion, the courts do not make law, but discover and find it in an existing body of facts, that is, the customs recognized by so-

---

[5] *Outlines of Historical Jurisprudence*, 2 vols. (Oxford, 1922); *Essays in Legal History* (London, 1913); *Villeinage in England* (London, 1892); *Custom and Right* (Oslo, 1925).

[6] 2d ed., 2 vols. (London, 1909).

[7] 3rd ed., 13 vols. (London, 1922–1938).

[8] See Roscoe Pound, *The Spirit of the Common Law* (Boston, 1921), p. 154.

[9] James C. Carter, *Law: Its Origin, Growth, and Function* (New York, 1907), pp. 59, 65, 84–86, 119–120. Carter argued that, while all law is custom, all custom is not necessarily law, since there is a large range of conduct of which the law takes no notice and which is controlled by rules of morality, fashion, and etiquette. *Id.*, p. 120. See also Carter, "The Ideal and the Actual in Law," 24 *American Law Review* 752 (1890). For a full account of Carter's views see Moses J. Aronson, "The Juridical Evolutionism of James Coolidge Carter," 10 *University of Toronto Law Journal* 1 (1953).

ciety.[10] Even the great codes of continental Europe he considered restatements of pre-existing law rooted in the popular consciousness. "The creation of new law was but a small part of the object." [11]

Like his great predecessor, Savigny, Carter became involved in an acrimonious controversy over codification. In the second half of the nineteenth century, David Dudley Field proposed the adoption of a comprehensive civil code for the state of New York. He argued that judges should not be lawmakers, as in his opinion they necessarily were under the common law system; that a code would give definiteness and certainty to the law, so that people could know beforehand what their rights, duties, and obligations consisted of; and that a code would make the law systematic and accessible and thus reduce the load of legal research. Carter opposed the proposal vigorously, asserting, among other things, that code law, requiring interpretation and implementation, would still be judge-made law; that laymen would not consult a codified law any more than they had hitherto studied and consulted case law; and that a code would impede the growth of law, since amendments could come only after the mischief caused by a bad rule had been done.[12] Just as Savigny's crusade against legislation had been successful in preventing the adoption of a German civil code, at least during his lifetime,[13] Carter's arguments against the Field Code had considerable influence in defeating the enactment of this piece of legislation in the state of New York.

Section 20. *Spencer's Evolutionary Theory of Law*
Herbert Spencer (1820–1903) was an English philosopher and sociologist who became the author of a theory of law, justice, and society strongly influenced by Charles Darwin's *Origin of Species*. Spencer considered civilization and law as products of biological, organic evolution, with the struggle for existence, natural selection, and the "survival of the fittest" as the principal determining factors. Evolution revealed itself to him in differentiation, individuation, and increasing division of labor. Civilization, according to his teaching, was a gradual progress of social life from simple to more complex forms, from primitive homogeneity to ultimate heterogeneity. He distinguished two main stages in this development of civilization: a primitive or military

[10] Carter, *Law: Its Origin, Growth, and Function,* p. 85.
[11] *Id.,* p. 118.
[12] This condensation of the arguments is based on the excellent summary in Jerome Hall, *Readings in Jurisprudence* (Indianapolis, 1938), pp. 119–121; see also the account of the Field-Carter controversy in Patterson, *Jurisprudence,* pp. 421–425.
[13] See *supra* Sec. 18.

form of society, with war, compulsion, and status as regulatory devices, and a higher or industrial form of society, with peace, freedom,
and contract as the controlling elements.[1]

The second stage of development, Spencer wrote, was marked by
an increasing delimitation of the functions of government in favor of
individual liberty. Government gradually comes to confine its field of
action to the enforcement of contracts and a guaranty of mutual protection. Spencer rejected all forms of social legislation and collective
regulation as an unjustified interference with the law of natural selection which, in the most developed stage of civilization, should have
unlimited sway. He abhorred any social activity by the state and was
opposed to public education, public communications, public hospitals,
a national currency, a government-operated postal system, and poor
laws.[2]

Spencer's concept of justice was shaped by the idea of liberty and
composed of two elements. The egoistic element of justice, he argued,
demands that each man derive the utmost benefit from his nature and
capabilities. The altruistic sentiment of justice is conscious of the limits
which the existence of other men having like claims necessarily imposes upon the exercise of freedom. A combination of both elements
yields the law of "equal freedom," formulated by Spencer as follows:
"Every man is free to do that which he wills, provided he infringes not
the equal freedom of any other man." [3] Differently expressed, justice is
the liberty of each limited only by the like liberties of all.

This "law of equal freedom" clearly and unequivocally expressed a
notion of justice adapted to a period of individualism and *laissez faire*.
The corollaries of this notion were a number of particular determinations of freedom which Spencer denominated by the term "rights."
Among these he counted the right of physical integrity, the right of
free motion, the right to use the natural media (light and air), the
right of property, the right of free exchange and free contract, the
right of free belief and worship, the right of free speech and publication. It is interesting to note that his strong individualism prompted
him to deny the attribute of right to social "rights," which only the
state could guarantee and implement, such as the right to work and the
right to public maintenance in the case of indigence.[4] He was even
reluctant to recognize a political "right" of every citizen to vote.

[1] The analogies to Maine's doctrine should be noted. See *supra* Sec. 19.
[2] See particularly his work *Social Statics*, first published in 1850.
[3] *Justice* (New York, 1891), p. 46. The formula is strongly reminiscent of Kant's
definition of law. See *supra* Sec. 15. Spencer points out, however, that he arrived
at his definition independently of Kant. *Id.*, p. 263.
[4] *Id.*, p. 63.

"With a universal distribution of votes," he said, "the larger class will inevitably profit at the expense of the smaller class." [5] The best constitution for an industrial society seemed to him one in which there was a representation of interests rather than a representation of individuals. His zeal for *laissez faire* made him fearful of the political consequences of majority rule.

Section 21. *The Marxian Doctrine of Law*
The theory that law is in the first place a product of evolving economic forces was put forward by Karl Marx (1818–1883) and his friend Friedrich Engels (1820–1895). These two founders of so-called scientific socialism took over from the German philosopher Hegel the dialectical method of interpreting social phenomena. Like Hegel, Marx believed that history was a struggle of opposing forces, revealing itself in the logical form of thesis, antithesis, and synthesis.[1] But while for Hegel spiritual forces and ideas were the moving factors in history, to Marx and Engels history was determined by material forces. Marx pointed out that an idea "is nothing else than the material world reflected by the human mind and translated into forms of thought." [2] The political, social, religious, and cultural order of any given epoch, according to Marx and Engels, is determined by the existing material system of production and exchange of commodities; in other words, all manifestations of social life are basically caused by economic phenomena.

In its application to the law, Marxian dialectical materialism contains three leading doctrines. The first is the doctrine of the economic determination of law. Law is merely a superstructure erected above an economic basis. "Legal relations as well as forms of the State could neither be understood by themselves, nor explained by the so-called general progress of the human mind, but they are rooted in the material conditions of life. . . . With the change of the economic foundation the entire immense superstructure is more or less rapidly transformed." [3] Thus the form and content of the law are shaped by eco-

---

[5] *Id.*, p. 192. On Spencer see also Friedmann, *Legal Theory*, pp. 175–178.
[1] Cf. *infra* Sec. 17.
[2] *Capital*, transl. S. Moore and E. Aveling from 3d German ed. (Chicago, 1906), I, 25. On Marx and Engels' views on the law see also Carl J. Friedrich, *Legal Philosophy in Historical Perspective* (Chicago, 1958), pp. 143–153.
[3] Marx, *A Contribution to the Critique of Political Economy*, transl. N. I. Stone (Chicago, 1904), p. 11. Cf. also Friedrich Engels, *Ludwig Feuerbach*, ed. C. P. Dutt (New York, 1934), p. 63: "If the State and public law are determined by economic relations, so too, of course, is private law, which indeed in essence sanctions only the existing economic relations between individuals which are normal in the given circumstances."

nomic factors, and the concepts and a priori principles which the jurists use are nothing but reflexes of economic conditions.

According to this view, law seems to be nothing more than a function of the economy without any independent existence. Engels, however, in some letters written in his later years, admitted that to some degree he and Marx had overestimated the importance of economic factors. "The economic situation is the basis, but the various elements of the superstructure . . . are in many cases influential upon the course of historical struggle." [4] Engels counts the law among the elements which may exercise a reciprocal effect upon the economic basis. Likewise Bukharin, a Russian Marxist, conceded that "the superstructure, growing out of the economic conditions and the productive forces determining these conditions, in its turn, exerts an influence on the latter, favoring or retarding their growth." [5] These reservations do not, however, mean an abandonment of the basic doctrine of dialectical materialism. Though it is conceded that the prevailing system of economic production is not the exclusive cause in the development of history and law, still it is held that the economic system is in the last instance the determining and by far the most important factor of historical and legal evolution.[6]

The second important doctrine of the Marxian theory of law is the doctrine of the class character of law. In the view of Marx and Engels, all legal systems from the beginning of history to the present time have been created by an economically ruling class. According to them, law is merely an instrument used by this class to perpetuate its power and to keep an oppressed class in subjection. Through the establishment of legal institutions the victorious and dominant class seeks to give a firm foundation to its economic interests and a formal sanction to the exploitation and oppression of other classes. Even after the establishment of a proletarian dictatorship the class character of law would not cease to exist, because the proletariat would need the law in order to suppress and eliminate hostile elements and groups. Not until the complete victory of communism and the establishment of a classless society will

On the economic interpretation of history see Henri Sée, *The Economic Interpretation of History*, transl. M. M. Knight (New York, 1929); E. R. A. Seligman, *The Economic Interpretation of History* (New York, 1903); Pound, *Interpretations of Legal History*, pp. 92–115; Pound, "The Economic Interpretation and the Law of Torts," 53 *Harv. L. Rev.* 365 (1940).

[4] Friedrich Engels, Letter to J. Bloch. Sept. 21, 1890, in Marx and Engels, *Correspondence 1846–1895: A Selection*, transl. and ed. Dona Torr (New York, 1936), p. 475.

[5] Nikolai Bukharin, *Historical Materialism*, transl. from 3d Russian ed. (New York, 1925), p. 228.

[6] Cf. Engels, Letter to Bloch, *Correspondence*, p. 475.

law and the state as instruments of oppression disappear and be replaced by a mere "administration of things." [7]

This prophecy of the disappearance of law in a communistic society is the third leading doctrine of the Marxian philosophy of law. It is this doctrine which gives a certain metaphysical aspect to the Marxian interpretation of law. Marx was convinced that the world was traveling from lower to higher forms of social life. He believed that communism, which he considered to be the next stage in the evolution of mankind, would be a social system superior to the capitalistic system that preceded it, and that a socialist or communist order would be able to dispense with instruments of compulsion like law and the state. He as well as Engels was convinced that, after the establishment of communism, the inexorable, deterministic laws of development that had hitherto governed the history of mankind would cease to be controlling, and that mankind would leap from the "realm of necessity into the realm of freedom." [8] The realization of material abundance, social justice, and full cultural bloom would be the great accomplishments of the new social order.

After the Russian Revolution of 1917, the Marxian interpretation of law was accepted in the Soviet Union as an official creed. The doctrine, however, went through a number of substantial transformations in the decades following the revolution, and there is no indication that the process of reinterpretation and readaptation of the doctrine to the changing political scene has come to a halt. No attempt will be made to trace this complex development, whose end is not as yet in sight.[9]

[7] Engels, *Anti-Dühring*, transl. E. Burns (New York, 1934), p. 309.
[8] *Id.*, p. 312.
[9] For a sketch of the development up to approximately 1945 see Edgar Bodenheimer, "The Impasse of Soviet Legal Philosophy," 38 *Cornell Law Quarterly* 51 (1952). See also Lon L. Fuller, "Pashukanis and Vyshinski," 47 *Michigan Law Review* 1157 (1949).

VI

UTILITARIANISM

Section 22. *Bentham and Mill*

Utilitarianism was a philosophical movement which flourished in nineteenth-century England and, although it made converts in other countries, always retained a distinctly English flavor. Some of its roots can be found in the writings of the Scottish eighteenth-century philosopher David Hume (1711–1776), who became the founder of an empirical theory of value grounded on the value experiences of the common man.[1] Hume cannot, however, be regarded as a typical and thoroughgoing exponent of utilitarianism.[2] We must look to the writings of Jeremy Bentham (1748–1832) and John Stuart Mill (1806–1873) in order to obtain a fully elaborated and systematic view of utilitarian doctrine.

Bentham proceeded from the axiom that nature has placed mankind under the governance of two sovereign masters, pleasure and pain. They alone point out to us what we ought to do, and what we should refrain from doing.[3] The good or evil of an action, according to him,

[1] See particularly Hume's two essays *Inquiry concerning Human Understanding* (1748) and *Inquiry concerning the Principles of Morals* (1752).

[2] See the Introduction by Charles Hendel to Hume, *An Inquiry concerning the Principles of Morals* (New York, 1957), pp. xxxv–xxxvi.

[3] Bentham, *An Introduction to the Principles of Morals and Legislation* (Oxford, 1823), p. 1. On Bentham see Elie Halévy, *The Growth of Philosophical Radicalism*,

should be measured by the quantity of pain or pleasure resulting from it.

Utility was defined by Bentham as "that principle which approves or disapproves of every action whatsoever, according to the tendency which it appears to have to augment or diminish the happiness of the party whose interest is in question." [4] If that party should be a particular individual, then the principle of utility is designed to promote his happiness; if it should be the community, then the principle contemplates the happiness of the community. Bentham emphasized, however, that the community can have no interests independent of or antagonistic to the interests of the individual; community interest meant to him nothing but "the sum of the interests of the several members who compose it." [5]

The business of government, according to Bentham, was to promote the happiness of the society by furthering the enjoyment of pleasure and affording security against pain.[6] "It is the greatest happiness of the greatest number that is the measure of right and wrong." [7] He was convinced that if the individuals composing the society were happy and contented, the whole body politic would enjoy happiness and prosperity.

The Benthamite legislator who wishes to insure happiness for the community must strive to attain the four goals of *subsistence, abundance, equality,* and *security* for the citizens. "All the functions of law," said Bentham, "may be referred to these four heads: to provide subsistence; to produce abundance; to favour equality; to maintain security." [8] Of these four ends of legal regulation, security was to him the principal and paramount one. Security, he pointed out, demands that a man's person, his honor, his property, and his status be protected, and that his expectations, insofar as the law itself had produced them, be maintained. Liberty, although a highly important branch of security in his view, must sometimes yield to a consideration of the gen-

transl. M. Morris (New York, 1928), pp. 35–87; John Plamenatz, *The English Utilitarians* (Oxford, 1949), pp. 59–84; Edwin W. Patterson, *Jurisprudence* (Brooklyn, 1953), pp. 439–459; Wolfgang Friedmann, *Legal Theory*, 4th ed. (Toronto, 1960), pp. 267–275.
[4] *Morals and Legislation*, p. 2.
[5] *Id.*, p. 3.
[6] *Id.*, p. 70. The pleasures of which human nature is susceptible are analyzed by Bentham as pleasures of sense, wealth, skill, amity, good name, power, piety, benevolence, malevolence, memory, imagination, expectation, association, and relief from pain. *Id.*, p. 33. They are defined further on pp. 34–37. Bentham believed that pleasure and pain could be treated as mathematical quantities and weighed against each other through the application of a "hedonistic calculus."
[7] *A Fragment of Government*, ed. F. C. Montague (Oxford, 1891), p. 93.
[8] *The Theory of Legislation*, ed. C. K. Ogden (London, 1931), p. 96.

eral security, since laws cannot be made except at the expense of liberty.[9]

Next to security, the legislator must try to foster equality, Bentham demanded. Equality, he maintained, "ought not to be favoured except in the cases in which it does not interfere with security; in which it does not thwart the expectations which the law itself has produced, in which it does not derange the order already established." [10] The equality which Bentham had in mind was not an equality of condition, but merely an equality of opportunity. It was an equality that allows every individual to seek his own happiness, strive after wealth, and live his own life.

Bentham never questioned the desirability of economic individualism and private property.[11] A state, he said, can become rich in no other wise than by maintaining an inviolable respect for the rights of property. Society should encourage private initiative and private enterprise.[12] The laws of the state, he argued, can do nothing to provide directly for the subsistence of the citizens; all they can do is to create motives, that is, punishments and rewards, by whose force men may be led to provide subsistence for themselves. Nor should the laws direct individuals to seek abundance; all they are capable of doing is to create conditions that will stimulate and reward man's efforts toward making new acquisitions.[13]

In spite of Bentham's preference for economic liberalism, there exists a link between his theory of legislation and the ideas of modern social reformers. This connection was shown by A. V. Dicey, who pointed out that the greatest-happiness principle may be adopted by the advocates of the welfare state as well as by believers in *laissez faire*.[14] It is not without significance in this respect that in Bentham's view it is not liberty, but security and equality that form the main objective

[9] *Id.*, p. 98.

[10] *Id.*, p. 99. See also *id.*, p. 120: "The establishment of perfect equality is a chimera; all we can do is to diminish inequality."

[11] Property was defined by Bentham as "a basis of expectation; of deriving certain advantages from a thing which we are said to possess, in consequence of the relation in which we stand towards it." *Id.*, pp. 111–112.

[12] Bentham believed that if the laws do nothing to combat private economic effort, do not maintain certain monopolies, put no shackles upon industry and trade, great properties would be divided little by little without shock and revolution, and a much greater number of men would come to participate in the moderate favors of fortune. *Id.*, p. 123. On Bentham's advocacy of *laissez faire* see Friedrich Kessler, "Natural Law, Justice, and Democracy," 19 *Tulane Law Review* 32, at 44–46 (1944).

[13] *Theory of Legislation*, pp. 100–102.

[14] A. V. Dicey, *Law and Public Opinion in England,* 2d ed. (London, 1914), pp. 303 ff.

of legal regulation. Bentham rejected natural rights and recognized no limitations whatsoever on parliamentary sovereignty. His theory of legislation therefore opened the door to state intervention and social reform, and certain pieces of legislation which were favored by Bentham or his disciples (like the Poor Act of 1834, the creation of authorities for the enforcement of public health laws, and other measures) constituted first steps in that direction.[15]

John Stuart Mill agreed with Bentham that "actions are right in proportion as they tend to promote happiness; wrong as they tend to produce the reverse of happiness." [16] He attempted, on the other hand, to defend utilitarianism against the reproach of coarse hedonism by pointing out that human beings have faculties more elevated than the animal appetites and do not regard anything as happiness which does not include their gratification. The conclusion at which he arrived was that the pleasures of the intellect (such as the enjoyment of art, poetry, literature, and music), the pleasures of the feelings and imagination, as well as those of the moral sentiments, must be assigned a much higher value than those of mere sensations.[17] He also insisted that the utilitarian doctrine of happiness was altruistic rather than egoistic, since its ideal was "the happiness of all concerned." [18]

One of the chief issues of legal philosophy to which Mill suggested an approach different from that of Bentham was the significance that should be attributed to the concept of justice. Bentham had spoken of justice in a deprecatory fashion and had subordinated it completely to the dictates of utility.[19] Mill, although taking the position that the *standard* of justice should be grounded on utility, believed that the *origin* of the sense of justice must be sought in two sentiments other than utility: namely, the impulse of self-defense and the feeling of

---

[15] *Id.*, pp. 306–307.

[16] *Utilitarianism*, ed. O. Piest (New York, 1957), p. 10. Mill is also known for his essay *On Liberty* (1859), in which he made an eloquent plea on behalf of freedom of speech, assembly, and religion. On Mill see Plamenatz, *op. cit. supra* n. 3, pp. 122–144.

[17] *Utilitarianism*, pp. 11–12, 18–19.

[18] *Id.*, p. 22. Mill added: "In the golden rule of Jesus of Nazareth, we read the complete spirit of the ethics of utility." Cf. also *id.*, pp. 15–16.

[19] "Sometimes in order the better to conceal the cheat (from their own eyes doubtless as well as from others) they set up a phantom of their own, which they call Justice: whose dictates are to modify (which being explained, means to oppose) the dictates of benevolence. But justice, in the only sense in which it has a meaning, is an imaginary personage, feigned for the convenience of discourse, whose dictates are the dictates of utility applied to certain particular cases." *Morals and Legislation*, pp. 125–126.

Bentham was also opposed to all doctrines of natural law. He defined law as "the will or command of a legislator." *Theory of Legislation*, p. 82. Bentham thereby became a precursor of legal positivism. See *infra* Sec. 24.

sympathy.[20] Justice appeared to him to be "the animal desire to repel or retaliate a hurt or damage to oneself or to those with whom one sympathizes, widened so as to include all persons, by the human capacity of enlarged sympathy and the human conception of intelligent self-interest." [21] Differently expressed, the feeling of justice is the urge to retaliate for a wrong, placed on a generalized basis. This feeling rebels against an injury, not solely for personal reasons, but also because it hurts other members of society with whom we sympathize and identify ourselves. The sense of justice, Mill pointed out, encompasses all those moral requirements, which are most essential for the well-being of mankind, and which human beings therefore regard as sacred and obligatory.[22]

Section 23. *Jhering*

In his well-known essay "On Liberty," John Stuart Mill had set forth a principle which, in his opinion, should guide the actions of the state in delimiting and curbing the freedom of the individual. That principle was "that the sole end for which mankind are warranted, individually or collectively, in interfering with the liberty of action of any of their number, is self-protection. That the only purpose for which power can be rightfully exercised over any member of a civilized community, against his will, is to prevent harm to others. His own good, either physical or moral, is not a sufficient warrant." [1]

The German jurist Rudolph von Jhering (1818–1892), in his influential work *Law as a Means to an End*, subjected this formula to a detailed criticism. He pointed out, for example, that under this formula the Chinese government could not prohibit the importation of opium into China because this would constitute an unwarranted infringement on the liberty of the buyer. "So the Chinese government," he asked, "has not the right to prohibit the opium trade? It must stand idly by with folded arms and look on while the nation is ruining itself physically and morally, simply out of academic respect for liberty, in order not to violate the inherent right of every Chinaman to buy whatever he pleases?" [2]

In the opinion of Jhering, it is not the sole purpose of the law to pro-

---

[20] *Utilitarianism*, p. 63.
[21] *Id.*, p. 65.
[22] *Id.*, pp. 73, 78.
[1] In *The English Philosophers from Bacon to Mill*, ed. E. A. Burtt (New York, 1939), p. 956.
[2] Jhering, *Law as a Means to an End*, transl. I. Husik (New York, 1924), pp. 408–409. On Jhering see Patterson, *Jurisprudence*, pp. 459–464; Friedmann, *Legal Theory*, pp. 277–281; Iredell Jenkins, "Rudolf von Jhering," 14 *Vanderbilt Law Review* 169 (1960).

tect individual liberty; Jhering rejected all attempts to solve the problem of control of personal liberty by the use of an abstract, all-embracing formula. To him the goal of the law was to bring about an equilibrium between the individual principle and the social principle. An individual exists for himself as well as for society, he argued, and the law should be viewed as the "realized partnership of the individual and society." [3] He saw the principal aim of this partnership in the accomplishment of a common cultural purpose. "To make the work of the individual, whether it be of the hand or the brain, as useful as possible for others, and thereby indirectly also for himself, to effectuate every force in the service of humanity—this is the problem which every civilized people must solve, and with regard to which it must regulate all its economies." [4] In the light of this basic philosophic attitude, Roscoe Pound has characterized Jhering as a "social utilitarian." [5]

The central notion in Jhering's philosophy of law was the concept of *purpose*. In the preface to his chief jurisprudential work, he pointed out that "the fundamental idea of the present work consists in the thought that *Purpose* is the creator of the entire law; that there is no legal rule which does not owe its origin to a purpose, i.e., to a practical motive." [6] Law, he declared, was consciously set by the human will to achieve certain desired results. He admitted that the institution had part of its roots in history; but he rejected the contention of the historical jurists that law was nothing but the product of unintended, unconscious, purely historical forces.[7] In his opinion, law was to a great extent shaped by an action of the state intentionally directed to a certain end.

The end or purpose of legal regulation was indicated by Jhering in his often-quoted definition of law: "Law is the sum of the conditions of social life in the widest sense of the term, as secured by the power of the State through the means of external compulsion." [8] This definition contains a substantive and a formal element. Jhering viewed the securing of the conditions of social life as the substantive aim of the law. In the conditions or foundations of social life he included not only physical existence and self-preservation of society and its members, but "all those goods and pleasures which in the judgment of the subject give life its true value"—among them honor, love, activity, education,

[3] *Op. cit. supra* n. 2, p. 397.
[4] *Id.*, pp. 68–69. The value of the individual life, Jhering said, must be measured in terms of the benefits which society derives from it. *Id.*, p. 63.
[5] Pound, *Jurisprudence* (St. Paul, Minn., 1959), I, 130.
[6] *Op. cit. supra* n. 2, p. liv.
[7] Jhering, *The Struggle for Law,* transl. J. Lalor (Chicago, 1915), pp. 8–9.
[8] *Op. cit. supra* n. 2, p. 380.

religion, art, and science.[9] He believed that the means and instrumentalities used by the law to secure these values cannot be uniform and unvarying; they must be adapted to the needs of the period and the state of civilization reached by a nation.

The formal element in Jhering's definition is found in the concept of *compulsion*. The state exercises compulsion and force for the purpose of ensuring compliance with the norms of the law. A legal rule without compulsion, Jhering declared, was "a fire which does not burn, a light that does not shine." [10] International law, in which the element of coercion is weakly developed, was described by him as a merely incomplete form of law.

A theory which looks upon law as a means for the accomplishment of utilitarian purposes will have a tendency to place great faith in the conscious and systematic activity of legislators. "It is not mere chance, but a necessity," said Jhering, "deeply rooted in the nature of the law, that all thorough reforms of the mode of procedure and of positive law may be traced back to legislation." [11] If purpose is the creator of law, a purposeful formulation of rules by statute appears to be the best way of producing a legal system which conforms to the demands of the time. It is, therefore, no accident that Bentham, the English utilitarian reformer, insisted upon a complete codification of the law. His efforts at achieving a codified law were at least partly successful. In the very year of his death, 1832, some of his proposals for improvement of the law were realized in the English reform legislation of that date. In Germany, a civil code was adopted four years after Jhering's death. Although Jhering had no decisive share in its enactment, his general attitude toward the law and his insistence upon "purpose" as the motivating force in legal control had prepared the ground and created the atmosphere for a legislative effort of this kind.

[9] *Id.*, p. 331.
[10] *Id.*, p. 241.
[11] *Op. cit. supra* n. 7, pp. 9-10.

VII

ANALYTICAL POSITIVISM

Section 24. *What Is Positivism?*

The French mathematician and philosopher Auguste Comte (1798–1857), who may be regarded as the philosophical founder of modern positivism, distinguished three great stages in the evolution of human thinking. The first stage, in his system, is the theological stage, in which all phenomena are explained by reference to supernatural causes and the intervention of a divine being. The second is the metaphysical stage, in which thought has recourse to ultimate principles and ideas, which are conceived as existing beneath the surface of things and as constituting the real moving forces in the evolution of mankind. The third and last stage is the positivistic stage, which rejects all hypothetical constructions in philosophy, history, and science and confines itself to the empirical observation and connection of facts under the guidance of methods used in the natural sciences.[1]

This celebrated "law of the three stages," insofar as it characterizes positivism as the last and final stage in the development of human thought, is open to grave objections.[2] It serves, however, a useful pur-

---

[1] Comte, *The Positive Philosophy*, transl. and condensed by H. Martineau (London, 1875), I, 2.

[2] In our own day, interpretations of human life and society have arisen in opposition to positivism which, according to the terminology of the movement, should

pose in describing the movement and general direction of Western philosophy from the early Middle Ages to the beginning of the twentieth century. As far as the philosophy of law is concerned, we have seen that the interpretation of law during the Middle Ages was strongly influenced by theological considerations: law was brought into close connection with divine revelation and the will of God. The period from the Renaissance to about the middle of the nineteenth century, on the other hand, may be described as the metaphysical era in legal philosophy. The classical law-of-nature doctrine as well as the evolutionary philosophies of law advocated by Savigny, Hegel, and Marx were characterized by certain metaphysical elements. These theories sought to explain the nature of law by reference to certain ideas or ultimate principles, which were conceived as working beneath the empirical surface of things. Neither the eternal reason of the natural-law philosophers, nor Savigny's "national spirit" and "silently operating forces" shaping the law, nor Hegel's "world spirit" handing the torch of evolution from one nation to another, nor Marx's "withering away of the law" in a communist society, can be judged and measured in terms of the empirical world. All these constructions are "metaphysical" in a broad sense, inasmuch as they go beyond the physical appearance of things and proceed from the assumption of invisible forces and ultimate causes that are to be sought behind the facts of immediate observation.[3]

In the middle of the nineteenth century a strong countermovement against the metaphysical tendencies of the preceding centuries set in. This movement may be described by the loose but comprehensive term positivism. Positivism as a scientific attitude rejects a priori speculations and seeks to confine itself to the data of experience. It turns away from the lofty heights of the spirit and restricts the task of scholarship to

---

be denominated "metaphysical." It should also be noted that Comte's law itself, by making untested and categorical assertions about the evolution of human thought, should be described as "metaphysical."

[3] The following are good definitions of the concept of metaphysics:

"Metaphysics is the systematic study of the fundamental problems relating to the ultimate nature of reality and of human knowledge." *Encyclopaedia Britannica,* 14th ed., XV, 332.

"One calls 'metaphysical' every inquiry which claims to go beyond the sphere of the empirical and seeks either hidden essences behind phenomenal appearances, or ultimate efficient and final causes behind things." Guido de Ruggiero, "Positivism," *Encyclopedia of the Social Sciences,* XII, 260.

"The metaphysical view of the world contemplates the whole (the totality) and the absolute (the ultimate reality)." Karl Jaspers, *Psychologie der Weltanschauungen* (Berlin, 1925), p. 189 (translation mine).

"Metaphysics is philosophical search going beyond the existing world in order to regain it for our comprehension as a whole." Martin Heidegger, *Was ist Metaphysik?* (Bonn, 1929), p. 24 (translation mine).

the analysis of the "given." It refuses to go beyond the phenomena of perception and denies the possibility of a comprehension of nature in its "essence." The basis for positivism had been prepared by the immense success achieved in the domain of the natural sciences during the first half of the nineteenth century. This success brought about a strong temptation to apply the methods used in the natural sciences to the realm of the social sciences. A careful observation of empirical facts and sense data was one of the principal methods used in the natural sciences. It was expected that in the social sciences this same method would prove to be highly fruitful and valuable.

In the twentieth century, positivism assumed a new and radical shape in the logical positivism of the so-called Vienna Circle. This circle was formed after World War I around Moritz Schlick and Rudolf Carnap and found a considerable number of adherents in England, the United States, and the Scandinavian countries.[4] The epithet logical was annexed to the term positivism by the members of the Circle because they wished to use the discoveries of modern logic, especially symbolic logic, in their analytical work. Although neither all of the original members of the Circle nor the later converts adhered to an identical set of philosophical convictions, certain basic ideas and postulates are typical for logical positivism as such. In the first place, it rejects all dogmatic and speculative assertions in philosophy. Statements about reality (or more precisely, about phenomena which appear to us as reality) are considered valid only on the basis of tested and verified sensory experience.[5] Second, a deprecatory and almost contemptuous attitude is taken by the adherents of this creed toward the development of philosophy from Plato to the modern era. The majority of the great philosophers of Western civilization are regarded by them as metaphysicians and purveyors of nonsense.[6] Third, while the logical

---

[4] The best introduction to the work of the Circle is Victor Kraft, *The Vienna Circle*, transl. A. Pap (New York, 1953). The Circle was dissolved in 1938.

[5] "Nothing is in the intellect which was not previously in the senses." Hans Hahn, "Logics, Mathematics, and Knowledge of Nature," in *Logical Positivism*, ed. Alfred J. Ayer (Glencoe, Ill., 1959), p. 149.

Schlick, in one of his last papers, modified the requirement of verifiability by demanding only a "logical" and not necessarily an empirical possibility of verification. Thus he stated that the proposition "Man is immortal" is meaningful because it possesses logical verifiability; it could be verified by following the prescription "Wait until you die." See Arnold Brecht, *Political Theory* (Princeton, 1959), pp. 177–178.

[6] The famous "book burning" statement by David Hume was described by the logical positivist Alfred J. Ayer as an "excellent statement of the positivist's position." *Logical Positivism*, p. 10. Hume's words are as follows: "If we take in our hand any volume, of divinity or school metaphysics, for instance; let us ask, *Does it contain any abstract reasoning concerning quantity or number?* No. *Does it contain any experimental reasoning concerning matter of fact and existence?* No. Com-

positivists assign to science the task of description and analysis of phenomena, they limit the task of philosophy to the logical classification
of ideas. In the words of Schlick, "it is the peculiar business of philosophy to ascertain and make clear the meaning of statements and questions." [7] Only logical questions are regarded as philosophical questions,
and the building of a logical syntax is described as one of the highest
tasks of philosophy. Fourth, the logical positivists hold that ethical
imperatives are merely "ejaculations" or "emotive" utterances which
are cognitively worthless. Inasmuch as the objective validity of a value
or ethical norm cannot be empirically verified, it cannot be meaning-
fully asserted.[8] It is not, according to this view, the task of ethics to
provide guidance to people as to how they ought to live. At best, its
task can be to explain causatively why people hold, accept, or reject
certain ethical views.

Beginning with the second half of the nineteenth century, positivism
invaded all branches of the social sciences, including legal science.
Legal positivism shared with positivistic theory in general the aversion
to metaphysical speculation and to the search for ultimate principles.
It rejected any attempt by jurisprudential scholars to discern and articulate an idea of law transcending the empirical realities of existing
legal systems. It sought to exclude value considerations from the science of jurisprudence and to confine the task of this science to an
analysis and dissection of positive legal orders. The legal positivist
holds that only positive law is law; and by positive law he means those
juridical norms which have been established by the authority of the
state.[9] In the words of the Hungarian jurist Julius Moór, "Legal positivism is a view according to which law is produced by the ruling

---

mit it then to the flames: for it can contain nothing but sophistry and illusion."
Hume, "An Enquiry concerning Human Understanding," in *The English Philosophers from Bacon to Mill*, ed. E. A. Burtt (New York, 1939), p. 689. Ayer added
that the Vienna positivists had not gone so far as to say that all metaphysical works
deserved to be committed to the flames; they allowed that some of them might
have poetic merit or might express an exciting attitude toward life.
  [7] Moritz Schlick, "Positivism and Realism," in *Logical Positivism*, p. 86; see also
Rudolf Carnap, "The Elimination of Metaphysics," *id.*, p. 68.
  A. J. Ayer says: "The philosopher, as an analyst, is not directly concerned with
the physical properties of things. He is concerned only with the way in which we
speak about them." *Language, Truth, and Logic* (London, 1950), p. 57.
  [8] "From the statement 'Killing is evil' we cannot deduce any proposition about
future experiences. Thus this statement is not verifiable and has no theoretical sense,
and the same is true of all other value statements." Rudolf Carnap, "Philosophy
and Logical Syntax," in Morton White, *The Age of Analysis* (Boston, 1955), p.
217. The view that this approach to ethics leads to the "self-destruction of civilization" was developed by Albert Schweitzer in his *Verfall und Wiederaufbau der
Kultur* (Munich, 1923), pp. 2-5. See also *infra* Sec. 38.
  [9] See Reginald Parker, "Legal Positivism," 32 *Notre Dame Lawyer* 31 (1956);
Brecht, *op. cit. supra* n. 5, p. 183.

power in society in a historical process. In this view law is only that which the ruling power has commanded, and anything which it has commanded is law by virtue of this very circumstance." [10] The legal positivist also insists on a strict separation of positive law from ethics and social policy, and he tends to identify justice with legality, that is, observance of the rules laid down by the state.[11]

Legal positivism has manifested itself most conspicuously in a jurisprudence of an analytical type, here designated as analytical positivism. Analytical positivism takes as its starting point a given legal order and distills from it by a predominantly inductive method certain fundamental notions, concepts, and distinctions, comparing them perhaps with the fundamental notions, concepts, and distinctions of other legal orders in order to ascertain some common elements. As Julius Stone has pointed out, analytical positivism is primarily interested in "an analysis of legal terms, and an inquiry into the *logical* interrelations of legal propositions." [12] In this fashion it provides the science of law with an anatomy of a legal system. Legal positivism, however, may also take on a sociological form. Sociological positivism undertakes to investigate and describe the various social forces which exercise an influence upon the making of positive law. It is concerned with analyzing not the legal rules produced by the state, but the sociological factors responsible for their enactment. It shares with analytical positivism a purely empirical attitude toward the law and a disinclination to search for and postulate ultimate values in the legal order.[13]

Section 25. *John Austin and the Analytical School of Law*

The view of analytical positivism that law is essentially a command or normative pronouncement by the state was foreshadowed by Bentham and Jhering.[1] Yet the jurisprudence of these two thinkers was so thoroughly permeated with philosophical deductions concerning the ends of the law and the values which the institution should serve to effectuate that they cannot be counted among the analytical positivists proper.

---

[10] "Das Problem des Naturrechts," 28 *Archiv für Rechts- und Wirtschaftsphilosophie* 331 (1935).

[11] See in this connection Friedrich Kessler, "Natural Law, Justice, and Democracy," 19 *Tulane Law Review* 32, at 53 (1944) and "Theoretic Bases of Law," 9 *University of Chicago Law Review* 98, at 105–108 (1941); F. S. C. Northrop, "Ethical Relativism in the Light of Recent Legal Science," 52 *Journal of Philosophy* 649–650 (1955), reprinted in Northrop, *The Complexity of Legal and Ethical Experience* (Boston, 1959), pp. 247–248.

[12] *The Province and Function of Law* (Cambridge, Mass., 1961), p. 31.

[13] An example of sociological positivism is Gumplowicz' theory of law, described *infra* Sec. 27.

[1] See Jeremy Bentham, *The Theory of Legislation*, ed. C. K. Ogden (London, 1931), p. 82; Rudolf von Jhering, *Law as a Means to an End*, transl. I. Husik (New York, 1924), pp. 240, 252.

It was John Austin (1790–1859), an English jurist, who became the founder of the analytical school of law.[2]

Like Bentham, Austin was an adherent of the utilitarian philosophy of life. The principle of utility appeared to him to be the ultimate test of law. "The proper purpose or end of a sovereign political government," he said, "is the greatest possible advancement of human happiness."[3] Since the principle of utility is a principle of ethics, and since the analytical method in legal science which Austin advocated rejects the infusion of ethics into law, it has been argued that Austin was not consistent in his method of approach to the problems of law.[4] It would seem that this reproach is unjustified. In contrast to Bentham, Austin drew a sharp theoretical line between jurisprudence and the science of ethics. He regarded jurisprudence as the autonomous and self-sufficient theory of positive law. "The science of jurisprudence (or, simply and briefly, jurisprudence) is concerned with positive laws, or with laws strictly so called, as considered without regard to their goodness or badness."[5] The science of legislation, on the other hand, which to Austin was a branch of ethics, was to perform the function of determining the tests by which positive law was to be measured and the principles upon which it must be based in order to merit approbation.[6] This separation of jurisprudence from ethics which Austin advocated is one of the most important characteristics of analytical positivism. According to this attitude, the jurist is merely concerned with the law as it is; the legislator or ethical philosopher alone should be interested in the law as it ought to be. Positive law, in the view of the analytical jurist, has nothing to do with ideal or just law.[7]

The function of jurisprudence, in the view of Austin, is the exposition of general notions and principles abstracted from positive systems

[2] For a sketch of the life of John Austin see Sarah Austin's Preface to Austin, *Lectures on Jurisprudence*, 5th ed. by R. Campbell (London, 1885). On Austin and the analytical school of law see also Wolfgang Friedmann, *Legal Theory*, 4th ed. (Toronto, 1960), pp. 221–227; Roscoe Pound, *Jurisprudence* (St. Paul, Minn., 1959), II, 68–79, 132–163.

[3] Austin, *The Province of Jurisprudence Determined*, ed. H. L. A. Hart (London, 1954), p. 294

[4] See James Bryce, "The Methods of Legal Science," in *Studies in History and Jurisprudence* (New York, 1901), II, 613–614.

[5] *Province of Jurisprudence*, p. 126.

[6] *Id.*, p. 127. Austin admitted, however, that it was impossible to consider jurisprudence quite apart from legislation, "since the inducements or considerations of expediency which lead to the establishment of laws must be adverted to in explaining their origin and mechanism." "The Uses of the Study of Jurisprudence," *id.*, p. 373.

[7] Samuel E. Stumpf is correct in pointing out that "Austin did not deny that moral influences were at work in the creation of law, but he allowed nowhere in his *theory* any place for the moral element when defining the nature of law." See his "Austin's Theory of the Separation of Law and Morals," 14 *Vanderbilt Law Review* 117, at 119 (1960).

of law. The more mature systems of law, Austin pointed out, are allied by numerous uniformities and analogies in their conceptual structure; and it was the objective of general jurisprudence (as distinguished from national or particular jurisprudence) to elucidate these uniformities and analogies. "I mean, then, by General Jurisprudence, the science concerned with the exposition of the principles, notions, and distinctions which are common to systems of law: understanding by systems of law, the ampler and maturer systems which, by reason of their amplitude and maturity, are pre-eminently pregnant with instruction." [8] This task would involve an exposition of the leading terms of the law, such as Right, Obligation, Injury, Sanction, Punishment, and Redress. It would also entail, among other things, the categorization of rights, the classification of obligations, and the elaboration of various distinctions indigenous to legal systems.[9]

The most essential characteristic of positive law, according to the Austinian doctrine, consists in its imperative character. Law is conceived as a command of the sovereign. "Every positive law is set by a given sovereign to a person or persons in a state of subjection to its author." [10] Not every type of command, however, was considered a law by Austin. Only *general* commands, obliging a person or persons to acts or forbearances of a class, merited the attribute of law in his opinion.[11]

It was not necessary, in Austin's view, that a command qualifying as a law must issue directly from a legislative body of the state, such as Parliament in England. It may proceed from an official organ to which lawmaking authority has been delegated by the sovereign. Judge-made law, according to Austin, was positive law in the true sense of the term, since the rules which the judges make derive their legal force from authority given by the state. Such authority the state may have conferred expressly; ordinarily, however, it imparts it by way of acquiescence.[12] "For, since the state may reverse the rules which he [the judge] makes, and yet permits him to enforce them by the power of the political community, its sovereign will 'that his rules shall obtain as law' is clearly evinced by its conduct, though not by its express declaration." [13] The norms enunciated by the judges comply with the prerequisite most essential to positive law in the Austinian sense,

---

[8] "The Uses of the Study of Jurisprudence," p. 367.
[9] *Id.*, pp. 367–368.
[10] *Province of Jurisprudence*, p. 201. Cf. also id., p. 350.
[11] *Id.*, pp. 22–24. See also *infra* Sec. 42.
[12] *Id.*, pp. 31–32. On Austin's position toward judicial legislation see W. L. Morison, "Some Myths about Positivism," 68 *Yale Law Journal* 212 (1958); Edgar Bodenheimer, "Analytical Positivism, Legal Realism, and the Future of Legal Method," 44 *Virginia Law Review* 365 (1958).
[13] *Province of Jurisprudence*, p. 32.

namely, that law be set by a political superior for the guidance of political inferiors. This prerequisite is not fulfilled, on the other hand, in that branch of the law which is called international law. True to his own premises, Austin therefore denied the character of law to the rules and principles of international law. In his view, they should be looked upon merely as rules of "positive morality," a branch of norms regarded by Austin as "rules set or imposed by opinion." [14]

A few words might be said about the Austinian conception of justice. He did not deny that a positive law could be "unjust" in a loose sense of the term if measured by a standard extraneous to it, as for instance the law of God.[15] This did not mean, in his opinion, that a human law conflicting with the law of God was not obligatory or binding. The positive law, he argued, carries its standard in itself, and a deviation from, or disobedience to, positive law "is unjust with reference to that law, though it may be just with reference to another law of superior authority. The terms just and unjust imply a standard, and a conformity to that standard and a deviation from it; else they signify a mere dislike, which it would be far better to signify by a grunt or a groan than by a mischievous and detestable abuse of articulate language." [16] According to this view, a law which actually exists is a law, disregard of which can never be legally justified, though it might be excusable from a purely moral point of view.[17]

Austin's theory of law, although it remained almost unnoticed during his lifetime, later gained a great influence on the development of English jurisprudence. The well-known treatises on jurisprudence by Thomas Erskine Holland,[18] William Markby,[19] and Sheldon Amos [20]

---

[14] *Id.*, pp. 1, 142, 201. The norms of customary law were likewise considered by Austin to be mere rules of positive morality. See *infra* Sec. 73.

[15] *Id.*, p. 184.

[16] *Id.*, p. 190.

[17] The following passages seem to suggest that Austin was willing to recognize a *moral* right of resistance in case of a conflict between the divine law and the human law: "The evils which we are exposed to suffer from the hands of God as a consequence of disobeying His commands are the greatest evils to which we are obnoxious; the obligations which they impose are consequently paramount to those imposed by any other laws, and if human commands conflict with the Divine law, we ought to disobey the command which is enforced by the less powerful sanction." *Id.*, p. 184.

[18] *The Elements of Jurisprudence*, 13th ed. (Oxford, 1924). Holland defined law as "a general rule of human action, taking cognizance only of external acts, enforced by a determinate authority, which authority is human and, among human authorities, is that which is paramount in a political society." *Id.*, p. 41. More briefly, "law is a general rule of external human action enforced by a sovereign political authority." *Id.*, p. 42.

[19] *Elements of Law*, 6th ed., (Oxford, 1905). Markby defined law as "the general body of rules which are addressed by the rulers of a political society to the members of that society, and which are generally obeyed." *Id.*, p. 3.

[20] *The Science of Law* (London, 1874).

were based on the analytical method which Austin advocated in legal science. George W. Paton in Australia and Sir John Salmond in New Zealand published texts which, although making concessions to non-analytical theories of jurisprudence, bear the earmarks of the Austinian approach.[21] In recent years, Professor Herbert L. A. Hart at Oxford has made himself the spokesman for a modernized form of analytical positivism.[22] Hart concedes that a positive legal system is not a self-contained whole, and that legal rules are often vague at their periphery, in which case they must be interpreted or implemented by recourse to considerations of social aim and policy. Yet it is his opinion that "the close and careful analysis of fundamental legal notions and those lying on the boundary of a legal system" rather than the interpenetration of law (in the technical, positivistic sense of the term) and the nonlegal forces of social life should remain the chief concern of jurisprudence.[23]

In the United States, John Chipman Gray, Wesley N. Hohfeld, and Albert Kocourek made contributions to analytical jurisprudence. Gray, in an influential work, modified the Austinian theory by shifting the seat of sovereignty in lawmaking from the legislative assemblies to the members of the judiciary. "The law of the State or of any organized body of men," he maintained, "is composed of the rules which the courts, that is the judicial organs of that body, lay down for the determination of legal rights and duties." [24] It was his opinion that the body of rules the judges lay down was not the expression of pre-

---

[21] Paton, *A Textbook of Jurisprudence*, 2d ed. (Oxford, 1951); Salmond, *On Jurisprudence*, 11th ed., partly rewritten by G. Williams (London, 1957).

[22] See the following contributions by H. L. A. Hart: "Definition and Theory in Jurisprudence," 70 *Law Quarterly Review* 37 (1954); "The Ascription of Responsibility and Rights," in *Essays on Logic and Language*, ed. A. Flew (New York, 1951), pp. 145 ff.; "Analytical Jurisprudence in Mid-Twentieth Century," 105 *University of Pennsylvania Law Review* 953 (1957); "Legal and Moral Obligation," in *Essays in Moral Philosophy*, ed. A. I. Melden (Seattle, 1958), pp. 82 ff.; "Positivism and the Separation of Law and Morals," 71 *Harvard Law Review* 593 (1958); *The Concept of Law* (London, 1961).
See also Carl A. Auerbach, "On Professor H. L. A. Hart's Definition and Theory in Jurisprudence," 9 *Journal of Legal Education* 39 (1956).

[23] See particularly Hart, "Analytical Jurisprudence in Mid-Twentieth Century," pp. 955, 957, and "Positivism and the Separation of Law and Morals," pp. 608, 614. In his inaugural lecture, "Definition and Theory in Jurisprudence," Hart argued that the older analytic approach consisting in the attempt to supply dictionary-like definitions of fundamental legal conceptions should be abandoned in favor of an elucidation and explanation of legal terms in the light of the specific context in which these terms are used. For a criticism of this view see Edgar Bodenheimer, "Modern Analytical Jurisprudence and the Limits of Its Usefulness," 104 *U. Pa. L. Rev.* (1956); see also Hart's answer to this criticism in "Analytical Jurisprudence in Mid-Twentieth Century."

[24] John C. Gray, *The Nature and Sources of the Law*, 2d ed. (New York, 1931), p. 84. See also p. 103: "To determine rights and duties, the judges settle what facts exist, and also lay down rules according to which they deduce legal consequences from facts. These rules are the law."

existing law but the law itself, that the judges were the creators rather than the discoverers of the law, and that the fact must be faced that they are constantly making law ex post facto.[25] Even the statutory law laid down by a legislature gains meaning and precision, in his view, only after it has been interpreted by a court and applied in a concrete case.[26] Although the judges, according to Gray, seek the rules laid down by them not in their own whims, but derive them from sources of a general character (such as statutes, judicial precedents, opinions of experts, customs, public policies, and principles of morality),[27] the law becomes concrete and positive only in the pronouncements of the courts. Judge-made law thus was to Gray the final and most authoritative form of law, and this conviction led him to the sweeping declaration that "it is true, in the Civil as well as in the Common Law, that the rules laid down by the courts of a country state the present Law correctly." [28]

Section 26. *The Pure Theory of Law*

Austin believed that the proper purpose or end of government was "the greatest possible advancement of human happiness," and he insisted that the principle of utility, as thus formulated, was to be the

[25] *Id.*, pp. 100, 121.

[26] "The shape in which a statute is imposed on the community as a guide for conduct is that statute as interpreted by the courts. The courts put life into the dead words of the statute." *Id.*, p. 125.

[27] *Id.*, p. 124.

[28] *Id.*, p. 94. See the comments on Gray's views by Hans Kelsen, *General Theory of Law and State*, transl. A. Wedberg (Cambridge, Mass., 1949), pp. 150-155.

Hohfeld's attempt at a systematic classification and arrangement of basic legal relations is briefly described *infra* Sec. 74. Albert Kocourek, dissatisfied with the attempt, tried to improve and refine the system. See his *Jural Relations*, 2d ed. (New York, 1928); *Introduction to the Science of Law* (Boston, 1930).

In recent years, under the influence of the doctrines of logical positivism, the searchlight has been turned in England and the United States on the semantic aspects of jurisprudence. See, for example, Glanville Williams, "Language and the Law," 16 *L. Q. Rev.* 71, 179, 293, 384 (1945), 62 *L. Q. Rev.* 387 (1946); R. W. M. Dias and G. B. J. Hughes, *Jurisprudence* (London, 1957), pp. 16-19; "The Language of Law: A Symposium," 9 *Western Reserve Law Review* 115 (1958); Walter Probert, "Law and Persuasion: The Language Behavior of Lawyers," 108 *U. Pa. L. Rev.* 35 (1959). Probert goes so far as to define justice in semantic terms as "the search for some verbal guide to aid in selecting among competing premises." *Id.*, p. 57. See also Richard von Mises, *Positivism* (Cambridge, Mass., 1951), p. 331: "An essential task of jurisprudence can be characterized as the establishing of transitions between the artificial language of the law to the currently used everyday language." This view has its foundation in the doctrine (propagated particularly by Ludwig Wittgenstein) that analysis and critique of language must be the sole function of philosophy. See Introduction to *Logic and Language*, ed. by A. Flew (Oxford, 1955), p. 6. On the philosophy of semantics and its relation to logical positivism see also George Nakhnikian, "Contemporary Ethical Theories and Jurisprudence," 2 *Natural Law Forum* 4, at 16-36 (1957). See also *supra* Sec. 24.

guiding rationale in the making of law by legislatures and judges.[1] By raising the principle of utility to the level of an authoritative test to control the "science of legislation," Austin imparted an evaluative element to a scientific endeavor. In this sense, it might be said that a remnant of "natural-law" thinking remained inherent in Austin's theory of law.

It is the objective of Hans Kelsen (b. 1881) in his Pure Theory of Law [2] to divest the science of law of all elements considered by Kelsen as "ideological." [3] Justice, for example, is viewed by Kelsen as an ideological concept. He sees in justice an "irrational ideal" representing the subjective predilection or value preference of a particular person or group.[4] "The usual assertion," he writes, "that there is indeed such a thing as justice, but that it cannot clearly be defined, is in itself a contradiction. However indispensable it may be for volition and action of men, it is not subject to cognition. Regarded from the point of view of rational cognition, there are only interests, and hence conflicts of interests." [5] The Pure Theory of Law, Kelsen maintains, cannot answer the question of what constitutes justice because this question cannot be answered scientifically at all. If justice is to be given any scientifically meaningful denotation, it must be identified with legality. Justice, in this restricted sense, means "the maintenance of a positive order by conscientious application of it." [6]

The Pure Theory of Law, according to Kelsen, is a theory of the positive law. It endeavors to answer the question "What is the law?" but not the question "What ought it to be?" It concerns itself with law exclusively, and seeks to free the science of law from the intrusion of foreign and extraneous sciences, such as psychology, sociology, and ethics.[7] Kelsen admits that law can be made the object of sociological research; but such a sociological study of law, in his opinion, has nothing whatever to do with jurisprudence in the true sense of the term.[8]

---

[1] *Province of Jurisprudence*, pp. 59, 294.

[2] See in general: William Ebenstein, *The Pure Theory of Law* (Madison, 1945); Hersch Lauterpacht, "Kelsen's Pure Science of Law," in *Modern Theories of Law* (London, 1933), pp. 105–138; Edwin W. Patterson, "Hans Kelsen and His Pure Theory of Law," 40 *California Law Review* 5 (1952).

[3] See Kelsen, "The Pure Theory of Law," 50 *L. Q. Rev.* 474, at 483 (1934).

[4] *Id.*, p. 482. See also Kelsen, *General Theory of Law and State*, p. 13.

[5] Kelsen, "The Pure Theory of Law and Analytical Jurisprudence," 55 *Harv. L. Rev.* 44, at 48–49 (1941).

[6] *General Theory of Law and State*, p. 14. See also his *What Is Justice* (Berkeley, 1957).

[7] *Op. cit. supra* n. 3, p. 477.

[8] *Id.*, p. 480. Kelsen defines legal sociology as "a science which sets itself the task of examining the causes and effects of these natural processes which, receiving their designation from legal norms, appear as legal acts." *Ibid.*

Kelsen defines jurisprudence as "the knowledge of norms." [9] By the term "norm" he understands a hypothetical judgment which declares that the doing or nondoing of a specified act will be followed by a coercive measure of the state. "Whoever unlawfully appropriates a chattel belonging to another, shall be punished by fine or imprisonment." In other words, a norm signifies that under certain circumstances the state will exercise compulsion in order to enforce a certain behavior. The law is a graduated system of such norms of compulsion; it is in its essence "an external, compulsive order." [10]

The legal order as conceived by Kelsen receives its unity from the fact that all the manifold norms of which the legal system is composed can be traced back to a final source. This final source is the basic norm. The basic norm of a legal order is defined by Kelsen as "the postulated ultimate rule according to which the norms of this order are established and annulled, receive or lose their validity." [11] This fundamental condition of lawmaking may be a written constitution embodied in a formal document or an unwritten constitution resting on custom. Compulsion is to be exercised according to the method and procedures prescribed by the fundamental law. [12]

The next stage in the order of law descending from the basic norm are those general rules which have been established through legislation. It is the function of legislation to determine the content of general norms and to provide organs and procedure (courts and administrative tribunals) for the execution of these norms. These general norms need to be made concrete if they are to have any meaning, since the general norm links an abstract condition of fact to an equally abstract consequence. The agent in this process of making general norms concrete is the judicial power, exercised by the courts and administrative tribunals. The adjudicating authority decides whether and in what way a general norm is to be applied to a concrete case. This process is partly declaratory, partly creative, and it results in the laying down of what Kelsen calls an "individual norm," that is, a concrete application of an abstract, general norm. [13] Kelsen points out, however, that in certain spheres of the law, especially in private law, making the general norm concrete is not always accomplished by an official state

---

[9] *Ibid.*

[10] *Id.*, p. 488. See also *General Theory*, p. 19, n. 6: "Law is a coercive order."

[11] *Id.*, p. 113, n. 6.

[12] See Kelsen, "The Pure Theory of Law," 51 *L. Q. Rev.* 513, at 518 (1935); Kelsen, *General Theory*, pp. 115–117, 124–128.

[13] "The judicial decision is itself an individual legal norm." Kelsen, *op. cit. supra* n. 12, p. 521. On the character of the judicial act see also *General Theory*, p. 135, n. 6.

organ, such as a court. There is often interposed between the statute and the judicial decision a legal transaction between private parties, such as a contract. Directed or authorized by statute, the parties set up concrete norms regulating their mutual behavior; the violation of these norms results in a compulsive act decreed by means of a judicial decision. The final stage in the graduated process which began with the formation of the constitution is the execution, the carrying out, of the compulsive act.[14]

Law, according to Kelsen, is a specific technique of social organization. "Law is characterized not as an end but as a specific means, as an apparatus of compulsion to which, as such, there adheres no political or ethical value, an apparatus whose value derives rather from some end which transcends the law." [15] Any social goal whatsoever may be pursued through the instrumentality of the law. "Any content whatsoever can be legal; there is no human behavior which could not function as the content of a legal norm." [16] The possibility of natural law is categorically denied by Kelsen. Law is "not an eternal, sacred order, but a compromise of battling social forces," [17] and the concept of law has "no moral connotations whatsoever." [18] It is a purely mechanical apparatus, capable of protecting and sanctioning any political, social, or economic setup. "The law of the Soviet Republic should be considered every bit as much a legal order as that of Fascist Italy or that of democratic capitalist France." [19] A term like "government of laws" is considered devoid of meaning by Kelsen. "Every State is a government of laws," he says.[20] To him, law and the state are synonymous concepts. The state is nothing but the sum total of norms ordering compulsion, and it is thus coextensive with the law. "The law, the positive law (not justice) is precisely that compulsive order which is the State." [21]

Kelsen's doctrine is perhaps the most consistent expression of positivism in legal theory. For it is characteristic of legal positivism that it contemplates the form of law rather than its moral and social content, confines itself to the law as it is without regard to its justness or unjustness, and endeavors to free legal theory from all qualifications or value

[14] Op. cit. supra n. 12, pp. 521–522.
[15] Op. cit. supra n. 3, p. 488.
[16] Op. cit. supra n. 12, pp. 517–518.
[17] Erich Voegelin, "Kelsen's Pure Theory of Law," 42 Political Science Quarterly 268, at 276 (1927).
[18] General Theory, p. 5, n. 6.
[19] Op. cit. supra n. 3, p. 486.
[20] Der Soziologische und der Juristische Staatsbegriff, 2d ed. (Tübingen, 1928), p. 191.
[21] Op. sit. supra n. 12, p. 535.

judgments of a moral, political, social, or economic nature. Rarely has the complete segregation of jurisprudence from all other branches of social science been carried to such an extreme as in the Pure Theory of Law.[22]

[22] See the author's critical comments on Kelsen *infra* Sec. 38.

It was not possible to take into consideration in the above account the second German edition of Kelsen's *Reine Rechtslehre* (Vienna, 1960).

VIII

SOCIOLOGICAL
JURISPRUDENCE
AND LEGAL REALISM

Section 27. *Sociological and Psychological Theories of Law*
            in Europe

It was pointed out earlier [1] that positivism in jurisprudence may manifest itself in a sociological as well as in an analytical form. A good example of a sociological-positivistic interpretation of law is furnished by the doctrines of the Austrian sociologist Ludwig Gumplowicz (1838–1909). Gumplowicz erected a sociological foundation for the positivistic theory that law is essentially an exercise of state power. He taught that the chief moving force in history was the struggle of different races for supremacy and power.[2] In this struggle the stronger race subjugates the weaker race and sets up an organization for the stabilization and perpetuation of its dominion. This organization is the

[1] See *supra* Sec. 24.
[2] Ludwig Gumplowicz, *Der Rassenkampf*, 2d ed. (Innsbruck, 1909), pp. 218–219.

state, and the law is one of the most important instruments for the attainment of governmental objectives. Law, Gumplowicz wrote, is a form of social life arising from the conflict of heterogeneous social groups of unequal power.[3] Its aim is to establish and uphold the dominion of the stronger group over the weaker through the use of state power. The guiding idea of law, according to Gumplowicz, is the maintenance and perpetuation of political, social, and economic inequality. There exists no law which is not an expression of inequality. In this respect, law is a true reflection of state power, which also aims only at the regulation of the coexistence of unequal racial and social groups through the sovereignty of the stronger group over the weaker.[4] Law cannot arise outside the state, because it is essentially an exercise of state power. The notions of "natural law" and of "inalienable rights" are preposterous products of pure imagination, said Gumplowicz, as meaningless as the concepts of "free will" or "reason." [5] The assumption that law is concerned with the creation of freedom and equality among men is a manifestation of spiritual delusion. Exactly the opposite is true. Law is "universally the very contrary of freedom and equality and indeed naturally must be." [6]

Gumplowicz did not assert, however, that the relation between the dominant and subjugated groups within the state remained static throughout the life of a society. There takes place in human history, he pointed out, an emancipatory struggle of classes and groups that have been excluded from a share in political, social, and economic power. In this struggle for a greater amount of freedom and equality, the suppressed classes use ideal notions of law as an important weapon. This weapon has been forged by the ruling class, but it is employed by the lower classes in order to attack and destroy the dominion of the ruling class. For instance, the bourgeoisie in its struggle with the feudal class appealed to universal human rights, freedom, and equality.[7] In more recent times, the working class has made use of a similar ideology in its struggle for increased rights and economic power. Gumplowicz maintained that in their campaign for emancipation the lower classes are apt to obtain certain successes, but that their ultimate goal of complete freedom and total equality is never reached.

[3] Gumplowicz, *The Outlines of Sociology*, transl. F. W. Moore (Philadelphia, 1899), p. 178.
[4] *Id.*, p. 179.
[5] *Id.*, p. 180.
[6] *Id.*, p. 182. See also Gumplowicz, *Rechtsstaat und Sozialismus* (Innsbruck, 1881), p. 135.
[7] *Id.*, p. 149.

A pioneer of legal sociology in Germany was Max Weber (1864–1920), whose monumental work on the subject, covering a great variety of problems, is not easily summarized.[8] One of his most interesting contributions to legal theory is his elaboration of the distinction between irrational and rational methods of lawmaking and his detailed analysis of these two methods from a historical and sociological point of view.

A theory of law which contains components of a sociological character but which may also be explained as an attempt to revive some of the ideas of Hegel was advanced by the German jurist Joseph Kohler (1849–1919). Kohler taught that human activity was cultural activity, and that man's task was "to create and develop culture, to obtain permanent cultural values, thus producing a new abundance of forms which shall be as a second creation, in juxtaposition to divine creation."[9] The law, he pointed out, plays an important part in the evolution of the cultural life of mankind by taking care that existing values are protected and new ones furthered. Each form of civilization, Kohler said, must find the law which best suits its purposes and aims. There exists no eternal law; the law that is adequate for one period is not so for another. Law must adapt itself to the constantly changing conditions of civilization, and it is the duty of society, from time to time, to shape the law in conformity to new conditions.[10]

Kohler advocated a synthesis and reconciliation of individualism and collectivism in legal control. Egoism, he maintained, "stimulates human activity, urges man on to constant effort, sharpens his wit, and causes him to be unremitting in his search for new resources."[11] An attempt by the legal order to uproot or combat egoism would therefore be foolish. He pointed out, on the other hand, that social cohesion is also necessary, in order that humanity may not fall apart, turning into a collection of individuals, and the community lose control over its members. Nothing great can be accomplished, in his view, except

[8] His "Rechtssoziologie," in *Wirtschaft und Gesellschaft* (Tübingen, 1925), II, 387–513, has been published in English under the title *Max Weber on Law In Economy and Society*, transl. E. Shils and M. Rheinstein, with an excellent introduction by M. Rheinstein (Cambridge, 1954). On Weber see also Wolfgang Friedmann, *Legal Theory*, 4th ed. (Toronto, 1960), pp. 196–199 and Norman S. Marsh, "Principle and Discretion in the Judicial Process," 68 *Law Quarterly Review* 226 (1952).

[9] *Philosophy of Law*, transl. A. Albrecht (New York, 1921), p. 4. Culture meant to Kohler "the culture of knowledge on the one hand, and that of new production and new activity on the other; which again is divided into esthetic culture, and the culture that controls nature." *Id.*, p. 22.

[10] *Id.*, pp. 4–5, 58.

[11] *Id.*, pp. 60–61.

by devoted cooperative effort. "The individual should develop independently but the tremendous advantage of collectivism should not therefore be lost." [12]

While Kohler's philosophy of law moved on the borderline between sociological jurisprudence and legal idealism, a thoroughly sociological type of legal theory was propounded by the Austrian thinker Eugen Ehrlich (1862–1922). Genuine sociological jurisprudence teaches, in the words of Northrop, that the "positive law cannot be understood apart from the social norms of the 'living law.'" [13] The "living law" as conceived by Ehrlich is "the inner order of associations," that is, the law practiced by society, as opposed to the law enforced by the state.[14] He identified the living law with the law which dominates societal life, even though it has not been posited in legal propositions. "At the present as well as at any other time, the center of gravity of legal development lies not in legislation, nor in juristic science, nor in judicial decision, but in society itself." [15]

In the view of Ehrlich, a court trial is an exceptional occurrence in comparison with the innumerable contracts and transactions which are consummated in the daily life of the community. Only small morsels of real life come before the officials charged with the adjudication of disputes. To study the living body of law, one must turn to marriage contracts, leases, contracts of purchase, wills, the actual order of succession, partnership articles, and the bylaws of corporations.[16]

Ehrlich contrasted the "norms of decision," laid down for the adjudication of disputes, with the "norms of organization," which originate in society and determine the actual behavior of the average man. An individual, said Ehrlich, finds himself enmeshed in innumerable legal relations and, with some exceptions, he quite voluntarily performs the duties incumbent upon him by virtue of these relations. One performs one's duties as father and son or as husband or wife, one pays one's debts, delivers that which one has sold, and renders to one's employer the performance due to him. It is not, in the view of Ehrlich, the threat of compulsion by the state that normally induces a man to perform these duties. His conduct is usually determined by quite different motives: he might otherwise have quarrels with his relatives,

---

[12] *Id.*, p. 51. Cf. also pp. 60–61. On Kohler's philosophy of law see Roscoe Pound, *Jurisprudence* (St. Paul, Minn., 1959), I, 158–169.

[13] F. S. C. Northrop, "Ethical Relativism in the Light of Recent Legal Science," 52 *Journal of Philosophy* 649, at 651 (1955).

[14] Eugen Ehrlich, *Fundamental Principles of the Sociology of Law*, transl. W. L. Moll (Cambridge, Mass., 1936), p. 37.

[15] *Id.*, Foreword.

[16] *Id.*, p. 495.

lose customers, be dismissed from his job, or get the reputation of being dishonest or irresponsible.[17] His performance of legal duties is less a matter of conscious thinking than of unconsciously habituating himself to the emotions and thoughts of his environment. "The most important norms function only through suggestion. They come to man in the form of commands or of prohibitions; they are addressed to him without a statement of the reason on which they are based; and he obeys them without a moment's reflection." [18] Thus there is a psychological component in Ehrlich's theory of law: he attributes great weight to the power of habit in the life of the law.

The psychological element in law was more fully elaborated by Leon Petrazycki (1867–1931), a Russian philosopher of law. It was his opinion that legal phenomena consist of unique psychic processes which may be observed only through the use of the introspective method.[19] "In everyday life, we ascribe to ourselves and to others various rights at every step and act in conformity therewith—not at all because it is so stated in the Code or the like, but simply because our independent conviction is that it should be so." [20] Petrazycki developed a theory of "intuitive law," in which the individual juridical conscience and the inward experiences of human beings figure large in the explanation of legal and social phenomena. Petrazycki also put forward an interesting analysis of the relationship between law and morality, which will be discussed elsewhere.[21]

Section 28. *The Jurisprudence of Interests and the Free-Law Movement*

The jurisprudence of interests, a movement in legal theory which arose on the continent of Europe, was an offspring of sociological jurisprudence and gained a large following, particularly in Germany and France. In Germany, the movement was founded by Philipp Heck and was carried on by Heinrich Stoll, Rudolf Müller-Erzbach, and others.[1] The jurisprudence of interests arose as a protest against the conceptualism and formalism which had dominated German juridical thinking around the turn of the century. Conceptualistic jurisprudence

---

[17] *Id.,* p. 21.

[18] *Id.,* p. 78.

[19] Petrazycki, *Law and Morality,* transl. H. W. Babb (Cambridge, Mass., 1955), pp. 8, 12. On Petrazycki see F. S. C. Northrop, *The Complexity of Legal and Ethical Experience* (Boston, 1959), pp. 79–92.

[20] *Id.,* p. 57.

[21] See *infra* Sec. 57.

[1] A collection of important writings by the representatives of this school is presented in *The Jurisprudence of Interests,* transl. and ed. M. M. Schoch (Cambridge, Mass., 1948).

had proceeded from the assumption that the positive legal order was "gapless," and that by proper logical operations a correct decision could always be derived from the existing body of positive law.

Heck and his followers challenged this contention of the conceptualistic jurists, which they considered unfounded and contrary to fact. They pointed out that every positive legal order was necessarily fragmentary and full of lacunae, and that satisfactory decisions could not always be gained on the basis of existing legal norms by a process of logical deduction.

The method of judicial adjudication proposed by the jurisprudence of interests rests on the premise that the norms of the law constitute principles and maxims fashioned by the legislator for the solution of conflicts of interests. In this sense they must be regarded as value judgments, "pronouncements which one of the interests of conflicting social groups shall prevail over the other, or whether perhaps the interests of both have to yield to the interests of third groups or the community as a whole." [2] In order to arrive at a just decision, the judge must ascertain the interests which the legislator intended to protect by a particular statutory rule. Among conflicting interests, that which is favored and preferred by the law itself should be held to prevail. Thus Heck and his followers preached the subordination of the judge to the written and enacted law. They refused to provide the judge with a scale of values not contained in the positive law, and left him without much guidance in cases where the system of law, even if taken as an integrated whole, does not offer any clues to the solution of a conflict of interests.[3]

In France, François Gény (1861–1944) was the proponent of a system of legal methodology which had a number of points in common with the jurisprudence of interests. In a famous treatise,[4] he pointed out that the formal sources of the law were incapable of covering the whole field of judicial action. He showed that there is always a certain sphere of free discretion left to the judge within which he must exercise a creative mental activity. This discretion, Gény said, should not be exercised according to the uncontrolled and arbitrary personal feelings of the judge, but should be based upon objective principles. The judge should attempt to give the greatest possible satisfaction to the wishes of the litigants insofar as they are consistent with the general purposes of society. The method of accom-

[2] Max Rheinstein, "Sociology of Law," 48 *Ethics* 233 (1938).
[3] On the balancing of interests see also *infra* Sec. 61.
[4] *Méthode d'interprétation et sources en droit privé positif*, 2d rev. ed. (Paris, 1954). Portions of this work have been translated by E. Bruncken under the title "Judicial Freedom of Decision" in *The Science of Legal Method* (New York, 1921), pp. 1–46.

plishing this task should be "to recognize all the conflicting interests involved, to estimate their respective force, to weigh them, as it were, in the scales of justice, so as to give the preponderance to the most important of them tested by some social standard, and finally to bring about that equilibrium between them which is so greatly to be desired." [5]

In order to produce a just equilibrium of interests the judge, according to Gény, must carefully scrutinize the prevailing moral sentiments and inquire into the social and economic conditions of the time and place. He should respect, as far as possible, the autonomous will of the parties, as expressed in contracts, wills, and other transactions, but he should see to it that this autonomous will of the parties does not conflict with basic principles of public order.[6]

An approach to jurisprudential method substantially more radical than that of the jurisprudence of interests and of Gény was advocated by the adherents of the free-law movement, which originated in Germany at the beginning of the twentieth century. The pioneers of the movement were Ernst Fuchs (1859–1929) and Hermann Kantorowicz (1877–1940).[7] The free-law movement stressed the intuitive and emotional element in the judicial process and demanded that the judge should find the law in accordance with justice and equity. The free-law jurists did not want to go so far as to relieve the judge of a general duty of fidelity to the statutory law. When, however, the positive law was unclear or ambiguous, or when it was unlikely that the contemporary legislator would decide the case as required by the statute, then the judge was to decide the case according to the dominant conceptions of justice or, if such were absent, according to his subjective legal conscience.[8] With this far-reaching extension of judicial discretion by the adherents of the free-law movement, the representatives of the jurisprudence of interests expressed strong disagreement.

[5] Gény, "Freedom of Judicial Decision," in *The Science of Legal Method*, pp. 35–36.

[6] *Id.*, pp. 42–43. Gény is not only known for his methodological studies but also for his legal-philosophical work *Science et technique en droit privé positif* (Paris, 1913), a work belonging to the neo-Scholastic school of thought. See *infra* Sec. 35. On Gény see Pound, *Jurisprudence*, I, 181–184; Thomas J. O'Toole, "The Jurisprudence of Gény, 3 *Villanova Law Review* 455 (1958); B. A. Wortley, "François Gény," in *Modern Theories of Law* (London, 1933), pp. 139–159.

[7] Gnaeus Flavius (Kantorowicz), *Der Kampf um die Rechtswissenschaft* (Heidelberg, 1906); Hermann Kantorowicz, *Aus der Vorgeschichte der Freirechtslehre* (Mannheim, 1925); Ernst Fuchs, *Die Gemeinschädlichkeit der Konstruktiven Jurisprudenz* (Karlsruhe, 1909); Fuchs, *Juristischer Kulturkampf* (Karlsruhe, 1912).

[8] See particularly *Der Kampf um die Rechtswissenschaft*, p. 41. In his later years, Kantorowicz formulated the free-law doctrine in a more conservative way. See Kantorowicz, "Some Rationalism about Realism," 43 *Yale Law Journal* 1240, at 1241 (1934).

Section 29. *Pound's Sociological Jurisprudence*
In his essay "The Moral Philosopher and the Moral Life," the American philosopher William James, in attempting to determine the essence of the ethical "good," arrived at the following conclusion: "In seeking for a universal principle we inevitably are carried onward to the most universal principle,—that *the essence of good is simply to satisfy demand.*" [1] He expressed the view that all demands were prima facie respectable, and that the best imaginary world would be one in which every demand was gratified as soon as made. Since, however, there is always in reality a gap between the ideal and the actual, he asked: "Must not the guiding principle for ethical philosophy (since all demands conjointly cannot be satisfied in this poor world) be simply to satisfy at all times as many demands as we can?" [2]

Roscoe Pound (b. 1870), the founder of American sociological jurisprudence, was strongly influenced by James's pragmatic philosophy, although in his later years a certain sympathy with the idealism of natural-law philosophies has become noticeable in his writings. [3] A concise statement of the quintessence of his basic attitude toward law can be found in his *Introduction to the Philosophy of Law:*

For the purpose of understanding the law of today I am content with a picture of satisfying as much of the whole body of human wants as we may with the least sacrifice. I am content to think of law as a social institution to satisfy social wants—the claims and demands and expectations involved in the existence of civilized society—by giving effect to as much as we may with the least sacrifice, so far as such wants may be satisfied or such claims given effect by an ordering of human conduct through politically organized society. For present purposes I am content to see in legal history the record of a continually wider recognizing and satisfying of human wants or claims or desires through social control; a more embracing and more effective securing of social interests; a continually more complete and effective elimination of waste and precluding of friction in human enjoyment of the goods of existence—in short, a continually more efficacious social engineering. [4]

Unlike Kant and Spencer, Pound thinks of the end of law not primarily in terms of a maximum of self-assertion, but principally in terms

---

[1] *Essays on Faith and Morals* (New York, 1943), p. 201. On James see Edwin W. Patterson, *Jurisprudence* (Brooklyn, 1953), pp. 477–486.

[2] *Id.*, p. 205.

[3] See, for example, his *Social Control through Law* (New Haven, 1942), pp. 28–29, 38–39, 66, 97–101, 108–109, and *Justice According to Law* (New Haven, 1951), pp. 6, 19, 22–23.

[4] Rev. ed. (New Haven, 1954), p. 47.

of a maximum of satisfaction of wants.[5] During the nineteenth century, he points out, the history of the law was written largely as a record of a continually increasing recognition of individual rights, often regarded as "natural" and absolute. In the twentieth century, he proposed, this history should be rewritten in terms of a continually wider recognition of human wants, human demands, and social interests.

The interests to be secured and protected by the legal order were catalogued and classified by Pound in an ambitious project.[6] He distinguished between *individual interests* ("claims or demands or desires involved immediately in the individual life and asserted in title of that life"), *public interests* ("claims or demands or desires involved in life in a politically organized society and asserted in title of that organization"), and *social interests* ("claims or demands or desires involved in social life in civilized society and asserted in title of that life").[7] In the last category he included, among others, the interests in the general security, the individual life, the protection of morals, the conservation of social resources (physical as well as human), and the interest in economic, political, and cultural progress.

Pound declines to commit himself to a rigid canon of evaluation of these interests. He feels that certain interests may have priority at a certain time and that others should be given preferred treatment in other periods. "I do not believe the jurist has to do more than recognize the problem and perceive that it is presented to him as one of securing all social interests so far as he may, of maintaining a balance or harmony among them that is compatible with the securing of all of them." [8] This leaves the jurist with an indefinite commission, but in Pound's opinion jurisprudence cannot provide him with more absolute and authentic standards.

Justice, Pound writes, may be administered with or without law. Justice according to law means "administration according to authoritative precepts or norms (patterns) or guides, developed and applied by

---

[5] *Id.*, p. 42. This does not mean, however, that Pound wished to deny the protection of the law to the self-regarding impulses. "Free individual self-assertion," he said, "—spontaneous free activity—on the one hand, and ordered, even regimented cooperation, are both agencies of civilization." Pound, *The Task of the Law* (Lancaster, Pa., 1944), p. 36.

[6] See his "A Theory of Social Interests," 15 *Papers and Proceedings of the American Sociological Society* 16 (1921); "A Survey of Social Interests," 57 *Harvard Law Review* 1 (1943); cf. Patterson, *Jurisprudence*, pp. 518–527.

On Pound see also George W. Paton, "Pound and Contemporary Juristic Theory," 22 *Canadian Bar Review* 479 (1944); Friedmann, *Legal Theory*, pp. 293–299; Stone, *Province and Function of Law*, pp. 355–360.

[7] "A Survey of Social Interests," pp. 1–2. See also *infra* Sec. 61.

[8] *Op. cit. supra* n. 4, p. 46.

an authoritative technique, which individuals may ascertain in advance of controversy and by which all are reasonably assured of receiving like treatment. It means an impersonal, equal, certain administration of justice so far as these may be secured by means of precepts of general application." [9] Justice without law, on the other hand, is administered according to the will or intuition of an individual who in making his decision has a wide amount of free discretion and is not bound to observe any fixed and general rules. [10] The first form of justice is of a judicial, the second of an administrative character. According to Pound, elements of both of these forms of justice are to be found in all legal systems. The history of law, he points out, shows a constant swinging back and forth between wide discretion and strict detailed rule. For instance, the nineteenth century abhorred judicial discretion and sought to exclude the administrative element from the domain of the law, relying instead upon a systematic dispensing of justice according to fixed, uniform, and technical concepts. The twentieth century, on the other hand, has witnessed a revival of executive justice, as demonstrated by the growth of administrative boards and commissions. A demand for individualization of justice has arisen, which must be interpreted as a reaction against the overrigid application of the law in the preceding epoch of legal stability. The problem of the future, says Pound, is the achievement of a workable balance between the judicial and the administrative element in justice. "A legal system succeeds as it succeeds in attaining and maintaining a balance between extreme of arbitrary authority and extreme of limited and hampered authority. This balance cannot remain constant. The progress of civilization continually throws the system out of balance. The balance is restored by the application of reason to experience, and it is only in this way that politically organized societies have been able to maintain themselves enduringly." [11]

Section 30. *Cardozo and Holmes*

American sociological jurisprudence has arisen not merely as a protest against traditional concepts of natural rights, but also as a reaction to the formalistic attitude of analytical jurisprudence. American sociological jurisprudence denies that the law can be understood without regard for the realities of human social life. To the analytical cry for self-sufficiency of legal science it opposes the demand for teamwork

---

[9] Pound, *Jurisprudence*, II, 374–375.

[10] Pound, "Justice According to Law," 13 *Columbia Law Review* 696 (1913); see also *Jurisprudence*, II, 352 ff.

[11] "Individualization of Justice," 7 *Fordham Law Review* 153, at 166 (1938).

with the other social sciences.[1] Sociological jurists urge that a judge who wishes to fulfill his functions in a satisfactory way must have an intimate knowledge of the social and economic factors which shape and influence the law.

One of the greatest of American judges, Benjamin N. Cardozo (1870–1938), stressed the necessity of judicial alertness to social realities. Influenced by the theorems of sociological jurisprudence, he gave a keen and comprehensive analysis of the judicial process.[2] Without belittling the role of logical deduction in the interpretation and application of the law, Cardozo came to the conclusion that considerations of social policy loom large in the art of adjudication. The judge seeks to interpret the social conscience and to give effect to it in the law, but in so doing he sometimes helps to form and modify the conscience he is called upon to interpret.[3] Thus, there is an element of creation as well as an element of discovery contained in the judicial process. The judge must often weigh conflicting interests and make a choice between two or more logically admissible alternatives of decision. In making this choice, the judge will necessarily be influenced by inherited instincts, traditional beliefs, acquired convictions, and conceptions of social need. "He must balance all his ingredients, his philosophy, his logic, his analogies, his history, his customs, his sense of right, and all the rest, and adding a little here and taking out a little there, must determine, as wisely as he can, which weight shall tip the scales." [4]

Cardozo believed that adherence to precedent should be the rule and not the exception in the administration of justice. But he was willing to relax the rule in situations where faithfulness to precedent would clearly be inconsistent with the sense of justice or the social welfare. The need for certainty, he argued, must in some measure be reconciled with the need for progress, and the doctrine of precedent can therefore not be treated as an eternal and absolute verity. "Somewhere between worship of the past and exaltation of the present, the path of safety will be found." [5]

---

[1] Roscoe Pound, "Fifty Years of Jurisprudence," 51 *Harv. L. Rev.* 777, at 812 (1938); Pound, "How Far Are We Attaining a New Measure of Values in Twentieth-Century Juristic Thought?" 42 *West Virginia Law Review* 81, at 94 (1936).

[2] *The Nature of the Judicial Process* (New Haven, 1921); *The Growth of the Law* (New Haven, 1924); *The Paradoxes of Legal Science* (New York, 1928). These writings, together with other essays, were reprinted in *Selected Writings of Benjamin Nathan Cardozo*, ed. M. E. Hall (New York, 1947).

[3] *Selected Writings*, p. 228.

[4] *Id.*, p. 176.

[5] *Id.*, p. 175. See also pp. 170–172, 246, and *infra* Sec. 80.

Law, in Cardozo's view, constitutes "the expression of a principle of order to which men must conform in their conduct and relations as members of society, if friction and waste are to be avoided among the units of the aggregate, the atoms of the mass." [6] He was convinced that many social forces were instrumental in shaping the aggregate of norms called the law: logic, history, custom, utility, accepted standards of right and wrong.[7] Cardozo vigorously rejected the view that law was an institution lacking generality and coherence, that it consisted merely of a more or less fortuitous and haphazardous sequence of "isolated dooms." [8] He was certain that the existence of accepted community standards and objective value patterns imparted a measure of unity and consistency to the law, even though the personal and subjective decision of the judge could not be avoided in all cases.[9] In Cardozo's own words, "The traditions of our jurisprudence commit us to the objective standard. I do not mean, of course, that this ideal of objective vision is ever perfectly attained. We cannot transcend the limitations of the *ego* and see anything as it really is. None the less, the ideal is one to be striven for within the limits of our capacity. This truth, when clearly perceived, tends to unify the judge's function." [10]

When we compare the views of Cardozo with those of another distinguished American judge, Oliver Wendell Holmes (1841–1935), we shall find that the two men were in substantial agreement with regard to some of the major facets of the judicial decision-making process. We shall also note, however, that Holmes's judicial philosophy was less imbued with ethical idealism than that of his colleague Cardozo.

Holmes, like Cardozo, emphasized the limits that are set to the use of deductive logic in the solution of legal problems. But he went further than Cardozo in discounting the role of logical reasoning in adjudication:

> The life of the law has not been logic: it has been experience. The felt necessities of the time, the prevalent moral and political theories, intuitions of public policy, avowed or unconscious, even the prejudices which judges share with their fellow-men, have had a good deal more to do than the syllogism in determining the rules by which men should be governed. The law embodies the story of a nation's development through many centuries, and

[6] *Id.*, p. 248. This conception of the law was obviously influenced by Roscoe Pound's ideas. See *supra* Sec. 29.

[7] *Id.*, p. 153.

[8] *Id.*, p. 159.

[9] *Id.*, pp. 151–153.

[10] *Id.*, p. 151. On Cardozo see also Patterson, *Jurisprudence*, pp. 528–537, and "Cardozo's Philosophy of Law," 88 *University of Pennsylvania Law Review* 71–91, 156–176 (1939).

it cannot be dealt with as if it contained only the axioms and corollaries of a book of mathematics.[11]

Only a judge or lawyer who is acquainted with the historical, social, and economic aspects of the law will be in a position to fulfill his functions properly.[12]

While history and social forces were assigned a large role in the life of the law by Holmes, the ethical or ideal element in law was de-emphasized by him. As an ethical skeptic, he regarded law largely as a body of edicts representing the will of the dominant interests in society, backed by force. "When it comes to the development of a *corpus juris*, the ultimate question is what do the dominant forces of the community want and do they want it hard enough to disregard whatever inhibitions may stand in the way." [13] Although Holmes admitted that moral principles were influential in the initial formulation of rules of law, he was inclined to identify morality with the taste and value preferences of shifting power groups in society. Furthermore, he thought it would probably be a gain for the interpretation of the existing positive law if "every word of moral significance could be banished from the law altogether." [14] His basic philosophy was that life meant essentially a Darwinian struggle for existence, with survival of the fittest as the prize, and that the goal of social effort was "to build a race" rather than to strive for the attainment of humanitarian ethical objectives.[15]

Holmes's ethical agnosticism also influenced his general attitude toward the institution of law. A pragmatic approach to the law, he declared, must view the law from the point of view of the "bad man."

If you want to know the law and nothing else, you must look at it as a bad man, who cares only for the material consequences which such knowledge enables him to predict, not as a good one, who finds his reasons for conduct,

---

[11] *The Common Law* (Boston, 1923), p. 1.

[12] See Holmes, "The Path of the Law," in *Collected Legal Papers* (New York, 1920), pp. 180, 184, 187, 202.

[13] Letter to John Wu, in *Holmes' Book Notices and Uncollected Letters and Papers*, ed. H. C. Shriver (New York, 1936), p. 187. On Holmes's ethical skepticism see Francis E. Lucey, "Holmes—Liberal—Humanitarian—Believer in Democracy?" 39 *Georgetown Law Journal* 523 (1951). Cf. also Thomas Broden, Jr., "The Straw Man of Legal Positivism," 34 *Notre Dame Lawyer* 530, at 539–543 (1959); Friedmann, *Legal Theory*, pp. 307–309.

[14] "The Path of the Law," p. 179. On the relation between law and morals in Holmes's thought see Mark De Wolfe Howe, "The Positivism of Mr. Justice Holmes," 64 *Harv. L. Rev.* 529 (1951); reply by Henry M. Hart, Jr., "Holmes' Positivism—An Addendum," *id.*, p. 929; rejoinder by Howe, *id.*, p. 937.

[15] Holmes, "Ideals and Doubts," in *Collected Legal Papers*, p. 306. See his rejection of the Kantian injunction that human beings should never be treated as means, *id.*, p. 304.

whether inside the law or outside of it, in the vaguer sanctions of conscience. . . . If we take the view of our friend the bad man we shall find that he does not care two straws for the axioms or deductions, but that he does want to know what the Massachusetts or English courts are likely to do in fact. I am much of his mind. The prophecies of what the courts will do in fact, and nothing more pretentious are what I mean by the law.[16]

This epigrammatic definition of law became a basic tenet in the credo of some American legal realists, whose views will be discussed in the next section.

Section 31. *American Legal Realism*

The realist movement in American jurisprudence may be characterized as a radical wing of the sociological school of law. This movement does not constitute a school of law in itself, because it is not composed of a group of men with an identical creed and a unified program. It is a peculiar method of approach, a specific way of thinking about law which is typical of those writers who describe themselves as legal realists.

It is perhaps the most characteristic facet of the realist movement in jurisprudence that its representatives tend to minimize the normative or prescriptive element in law. Law appears to the realist as a body of facts rather than a system of rules, a going institution rather than a set of norms. What judges, attorneys, police and prison officials actually do about law cases—essentially this, to the legal realists, appears to be the law itself.[1]

Karl Llewellyn (1893–1962), in his earlier writings, was a spokesman for orthodox realist theory. He argued that the rules of substantive law are of far less importance in the actual practice of law than had hitherto been assumed. "The theory that rules decide cases seems for a century to have fooled, not only library-ridden recluses, but judges." [2]

---

[16] "The Path of the Law," pp. 171, 173. On Holmes see also Patterson, pp. 500–508.
[1] Friedrich Kessler, "Theoretic Bases of Law," 9 *University of Chicago Law Review* 98, at 109 (1941), says: "Realism introduced a sharp distinction between what courts say and what they actually do. Only the latter counts. . . . Law became the behavior pattern of judges and similar officials. Fortunately, legal realism did not stop at this empiricism. It developed and perfected the functional approach."
The treatment of legal realism in this work does not include functional approaches to the law which view the law primarily as an institution for the promotion of justice or the furtherance of an identifiable ideal of the social good. For critical evaluations of American legal realism see Lon L. Fuller, "American Legal Realism," 82 *U. Pa. L. Rev.* 429 (1934); Hermann Kantorowicz, "Some Rationalism about Realism," 43 *Yale L. J.* 1240 (1934).
[2] "The Constitution as an Institution," 34 *Col. L. Rev.* 1, at 7 (1934).

He proposed that the focal point of legal research should be shifted from the study of rules to the observance of the real behavior of the law officials, particularly the judges. "What these officials do about disputes is, to my mind, the law itself." [3]

This last statement, however, was withdrawn by Llewellyn in 1950.[4] In his more recent writings, he has placed a somewhat greater stress on the importance of normative generalization in law, pointing out that the rule part of the law is "one hugely developed part" of the institution, but not the whole of it.[5] He has also, in keeping with the postulates of sociological jurisprudence, sought to explore the relations and contacts between the law and the other social sciences, coming to the conclusion that the lawyers as well as the social scientists have thus far failed to make an "effective effort at neighborliness." [6]

Jerome Frank (1889–1957) presented a realist view of the law which, at least in its earlier expressions, was characterized by a considerable radicalism. In an influential book, *Law and the Modern Mind*,[7] he described the American system of judicial administration as a more or less disguised system of oriental cadi justice. The rules of law, he argued, are not the basis of the judge's decision. Judicial decisions are conditioned by emotions, intuitive hunches, prejudices, tempers, and other irrational factors.[8] The knowledge of legal rules will therefore offer little help in predicting the decision of a particular judge. "No one knows the law about any case or with respect to any given situation, transaction, or event, until there has been a specific decision (judgment, order, or decree) with regard thereto." [9]

According to this view, a court decision is obviously something very uncertain and almost unpredictable. But this uncertainty of the law, said Frank, should not be deplored; he considered much of it as

---

[3] *The Bramble Bush* (New York, 1930), p. 3. Cf. also "A Realistic Jurisprudence —The Next Step," 30 *Col. L. Rev.* 431, at 442–443, 464 (1930) and "Some Realism about Realism," 44 *Harv. L. Rev.* 1222 (1931).

[4] *The Bramble Bush*, rev. ed. (New York, 1951), Foreword, pp. 8–9. Llewellyn stated there that his earlier description of law contained "unhappy words when not more fully developed, and they are plainly at best a very partial statement of the whole truth." *Id.*, p. 9.

[5] "Law and the Social Sciences, especially Sociology," 62 *Harv. L. Rev.* 1286, at 1291 (1949). See also his "The Normative, the Legal and the Law Jobs," 49 *Yale L. J.* 1355, at 1359, 1364 (1940). Llewellyn's analysis of the judicial process in appellate courts is found in his *The Common Law Tradition: Deciding Appeals* (Boston, 1960).

[6] "Law and the Social Sciences, Especially Sociology," p. 1287.

[7] New York, 1930. On Frank see Julius Paul, *The Legal Realism of Jerome N. Frank* (The Hague, 1959), with a full bibliography.

[8] *Law and the Modern Mind*, pp. 100–117. See also Frank, "Are Judges Human?" 80 *U. Pa. L. Rev.* 17, 233 (1931).

[9] "Are Judges Human?" p. 41.

of immense social value.[10] The view that law can be made stable, fixed, and settled was dismissed by him as the "basic legal myth" and an infantile survival from a "father complex." Why do men seek unrealizable certainty in law, he asked. "Because, we reply, they have not yet relinquished the childish need for an authoritative father and unconsciously have tried to find in the law a substitute for those attributes of firmness, sureness, certainty, and infallibility ascribed in childhood to the father." [11] If men would relinquish their desire for a father substitute, they would acquire a much sounder attitude toward the law. They would realize that until a court has passed on some particular question, no law on that subject is as yet in existence. Prior to such decision the only law available is the guess of the lawyers as to what the court might do. "Law, then, as to any given situation is either (a) actual law, i.e., a specific past decision, as to that situation, or (b) probable law, i.e., a guess as to a specific future decision." [12] Roscoe Pound has characterized this view as the "cult of the single decision." [13]

After Frank had ascended to the bench of a federal appellate court, he shifted his attention from the rule aspect of the law to the scrutiny of the fact-finding process in the trial courts. To use his own nomenclature, the former "rule sceptic" turned into a "fact sceptic." [14] Trial-court fact-finding, Frank declared, constituted the soft spot, the Achilles heel in the administration of justice. With unrelenting zest, he probed into the innumerable sources of error which may enter into a determination of the facts by a trial court. There may be "perjured witnesses, coached witnesses, biased witnesses, witnesses mistaken in their observation of the facts as to which they testify or in their memory of their observations, missing or dead witnesses, missing or destroyed documents, crooked lawyers, stupid lawyers, stupid jurors, prejudiced jurors, inattentive jurors, trial judges who are stupid or bigoted and biased or 'fixed' or inattentive to the testimony." [15] Many of these factors, he said, and above all the impenetrable and unique personality of the judge, make every lawsuit in which conflicting testi-

---

[10] *Law and the Modern Mind*, p. 7.

[11] *Id.*, p. 21.

[12] *Id.*, p. 46.

[13] Roscoe Pound, "How Far Are We Attaining a New Measure of Values in Twentieth-Century Juristic Thought," 42 *W. Va. L. Rev.* 81, at 89 (1936). The similarity of Frank's view and Holmes's "prophecy" definition of law should be noted. See *supra* Sec. 30.

[14] Frank, *Courts on Trial* (Princeton, 1949), pp. 73–74.

[15] Frank, "Modern and Ancient Legal Pragmatism," 25 *Notre Dame Lawyer* 207, at 254 (1950).

mony is presented a highly subjective affair. According to Frank, the judge (or jury) has a "virtually uncontrolled and virtually uncontrollable fact discretion" or "sovereignty," that is, the power to choose which witnesses' stories are to be accepted as correct.[16] Although Frank made a number of positive proposals for the rationalization and improvement of trial court procedures,[17] he was convinced that, notwithstanding such reforms, a large element of irrationality, chance, and guesswork would always inhere in judicial fact-finding, making predictability of the outcome of lawsuits well-nigh impossible.[18]

With lower-court fact-finding as the center of his legal universe, Frank took a new look at legal rules and precedents. He admitted that many legal rules are settled and certain and that the precedent system possesses considerable value.[19] He recognized the necessity of legal rules as general guideposts for making decisions and declared that the rules embody important policies and moral ideals.[20] But he maintained that the objective legal norms are in many instances frustrated by the "secret, unconscious, private, idiosyncratic norms" applied in the fact-finding process by trial judges or jurors.[21] He concluded that the judges often play havoc with the precedent system, with the consequence that the uniformity and stability which the rules may seem to supply at first are frequently rendered illusory and chimerical in practice.

Notwithstanding his skepticism concerning the reliability of trial procedures for the discovery of the truth, Judge Frank was deeply concerned with the problem of achieving justice in the adjustment of the relations of individual parties before the courts. In order that this goal might be obtained, Frank demanded an "unblindfolding of justice." [22] He called for a greater individualization of cases and wished to inject a large dose of judicial discretion into all or most rules, making them as flexible as possible. Each legal controversy is unique and singular, he argued, and the judge for this reason should not be fettered too much by rigid universals and abstract generalizations.[23]

While Judge Frank focuses his attention primarily on those aspects of the law which revolve around court trials and other adjudicatory

---

[16] Frank, " 'Short of Sickness and Death': A Study of Moral Responsibility in Legal Criticism," 26 *New York University Law Review* 545, at 584 (1951).
[17] *Op. cit. supra* n. 14, pp. 98, 100, 141–145, 183–185, 224, 248–251.
[18] *Id.*, ch. iii; cf. also *op. cit. supra* n. 16, p. 630.
[19] *Op. cit. supra* n. 14, ch. xix.
[20] *Id.*, p. 396, and *op. cit. supra* n. 15, p. 256.
[21] *Op. cit. supra* n. 16, p. 582.
[22] *Op. cit. supra* n. 14, pp. 378 ff.
[23] *Id.*, pp. 395 ff.

procedures,[24] Thurman Arnold (b. 1891) is concerned with a social-psychological analysis of the institution as such.[25] This analysis is permeated with a deep-seated skepticism and distrust in the power of human reason. Legal theories and principles signify to Arnold "methods of preaching rather than of practical advice." [26] Jurisprudence is regarded by him as "the shining but unfulfilled dream of a world governed by reason." [27] In its actual practice, he asserts, the law consists of a large number of emotionally colored and contradictory symbols and ideals. The efforts made by legal scholars to construct a logical heaven for the courts wherein contradictory ideals are made to seem consistent is viewed by him not only as futile but also as devoid of beneficial purpose. The rule of law is best preserved, in his opinion, by the coexistence of various and conflicting symbolisms and ideologies. "The judicial system loses in prestige and influence whenever great, popular, and single-minded ideals sweep a people off its feet." [28] Only value-skepticism and value-pluralism can prevent the rise of intolerant and totalitarian political regimes, Arnold believes.[29]

Section 32. *Scandinavian Legal Realism*
Scandinavian legal realism differs from American legal realism chiefly in two respects: first, it is more speculative in its approach to juris-

[24] See his study of administrative justice in *If Men Were Angels* (New York, 1942).

[25] See *The Symbols of Government* (New Haven, 1935); *The Folklore of Capitalism* (New Haven, 1937).

[26] *Symbols of Government*, p. 21. See also *Folklore of Capitalism*, p. 148: "Legal and economic theories are in reality nothing more than huge compound words with high emotional content."

[27] *Symbols of Government*, p. 58.

[28] *Id.*, p. 247. See also *id.*, p. 243: "Intolerance and cruelty follow when great people march in step to a single ideal."

[29] Other writings of legal-realist vintage include: Joseph W. Bingham, "What Is the Law," 11 *Michigan Law Review* 1, 109 (1912); Underhill Moore, "Rational Basis of Legal Institutions," 23 *Col. L. Rev.* 609 (1923); Underhill Moore and Theodore S. Hope, "An Institutional Approach to the Law of Commercial Banking," 38 *Yale L.J.* 703 (1929); Herman Oliphant, "Facts, Opinions, and Value-Judgments," 10 *Texas Law Review* 127 (1932); Walter W. Cook, "Scientific Method and the Law," 13 *American Bar Association Journal* 303 (1927); Edwin N. Garlan, *Legal Realism and Justice* (New York, 1941); Max Radin, *Law as Logic and Experience* (New Haven, 1940); Frederick K. Beutel, *Some Potentialities of Experimental Jurisprudence as a New Branch of Social Science* (Lincoln, Neb., 1957).

In Argentina, Carlos Cossio has developed a theory of law which exhibits some points of contact with legal realism in the United States. His "egological theory" considers that the subject matter of jurisprudence is not legal rules, but human conduct in its intersubjective interaction. He also places much emphasis on the creative powers of the judge. See Carlos Cossio, "Phenomenology of the Deci-

prudential problems,[1] and secondly, it devotes less attention to peculiarly judicial psychology than has been true for some outstanding American legal realists. It shares with American legal realism a radically empiricist attitude toward life and law, as well as a disinclination to discuss and determine the supreme values to be served by the legal order.

Axel Hägerström (1868–1939), a Swedish professor of philosophy, is regarded as the founder of the "Upsala school" of the modern legal-realist movement in Scandinavia.[2] His doctrines were cast into a more extremist mold by his disciple A. Vilhelm Lundstedt (1882–1955). Other representatives of the movement are Karl Olivecrona, a Swede, and Alf Ross, a Dane. The ideas of these men revolve around three basic problems: (1) the nature and validity of law, (2) the significance or nonsignificance of the basic conceptions of analytical jurisprudence (such as rights and duties), and (3) the meaningfulness of the notion of justice.

Concerning the nature of law, the Scandinavian realists (even more radically than their American brethren) tend to regard law as a body of facts rather than a body of norms or commands. "Law is nothing but a set of social facts," says Olivecrona.[3] It is, essentially, a huge machinery set up for the purpose of protecting the security of society.[4] The actual or potential exercise of force is viewed by all Scandinavian realists as an integral part of the concept of law. "We are justified," Olivecrona declares, "in defining law as rules about force, since everything turns upon the regular use of force." [5] In the words of Ross, "Law is an instrument of power, and the relation between those who decide what is to be the law and those who are subject to the law is one of power." [6] The Scandinavian realists admit that most people obey

---

sion," transl. G. Ireland, in *Latin-American Legal Philosophy* (Cambridge, Mass., 1948), pp. 345–400.

[1] This difference is emphasized by Barna Horvath, "Between Legal Realism and Idealism," 48 *Northwestern University Law Review* 693, at 704 (1954). See also the account of Scandinavian legal realism by Friedmann, *Legal Theory*, pp. 258–265.

[2] A sketch by Karl Olivecrona of Hägerström's life and teachings is found in the Preface to Axel Hägerström, *Inquiries into the Nature of Law and Morals* (Stockholm, 1953).

[3] *Law as Fact* (Copenhagen, 1939), p. 127.

[4] See, for example, Hägerström, p. 354: "The legal order is throughout nothing but a social machine, in which the cogs are men." See also A. Vilhelm Lundstedt, *Legal Thinking Revised* (Stockholm, 1956), p. 301.

[5] *Law as Fact*, p. 135.

[6] Alf Ross, *On Law and Justice* (Berkeley, 1959), p. 58. On p. 59, Ross declares that "the law consists of rules concerning the exercise of force." See also *id.*, p. 34.

the law out of habit and without the actual application of physical force. But they regard the ultimate threat of coercion as an important psychological factor ensuring compliance.[7]

A question which looms large in the writings of the Nordic realists is the question of the validity of the legal order. A consistent empiricism which negates the reality of concepts formed by the human mind must question the validity of a legal order conceived as a system of normative "oughts." This consequence is drawn by the Scandinavian realists. They deny that law is binding in any sense other than that of actually exercising a psychological impact on the population and the law-administering officials. According to Olivecrona, "The 'binding force' of the law is a reality merely as an idea in human minds. There is nothing in the outside world which corresponds to this idea." [8] What gives the law its force is "the fact that unpleasant consequences are likely to occur in case of unlawful behaviour." [9] It is evident that from this point of view no clearcut distinction can be drawn between an order of law and a regime of violence—a conclusion candidly admitted by Ross.[10]

It was Ross who turned his attention with particular emphasis to the problem of the validity of law.[11] Taking as his starting point the assumption that the law provides the norms for the behavior of the courts, and not of private individuals,[12] Ross reaches the conclusion that a norm of law is "valid" if the prediction can be made that a court will apply it in a future case.[13] In making this prediction, Ross declares, not only the past actual behavior of the judge, but also the set of normative ideas by which he is governed and motivated, must be taken into account.[14]

An attack on the traditional concepts of analytical jurisprudence, particularly the concepts of right and duty, was initiated by Hägerström. He argued that rights cannot be said to represent protection afforded by the state for our property or personal claims, for the state

---

[7] See, e.g., Olivecrona, *Law as Fact,* p. 125: "There is at hand an organised force of overwhelming strength in comparison to that of any possible opponents. . . . Resistance is therefore known to be useless." See also *id.,* pp. 141, 156.

[8] *Id.,* p. 17.

[9] *Id.,* p. 12. See also Lundstedt, pp. 322, 333.

[10] Ross, p. 56: "It is . . . impossible to differentiate between a 'legal order' and a 'regime of violence,' because the quality of validity which should distinguish the law is not an objective quality of the order itself but only an expression of the way in which it is experienced by an individual." See also *id.,* p. 31.

[11] See *id.,* pp. 11–18, 29–74.

[12] *Id.,* p. 35.

[13] *Id.,* pp. 49–50.

[14] *Id.,* pp. 18, 73–74.

moves into action only after these have been actually invaded. Further-more, unless we can successfully bring forward proof to support our claims, our rights become even more meaningless. It is therefore use-less, in Hägerström's opinion, to speak of rights in dissociation from remedies and enforcement measures. In the same vein, he branded the concept of duty as a metaphysical notion devoid of reality.[15]

The fight against traditional legal concepts was sharpened by Lund-stedt and extended to other fundamental legal notions, such as wrong-fulness, guilt, liability, and the like. Such concepts, Lundstedt main-tained, were operative only in the "subjective conscience" and could have no objective meaning. To say, for instance, that the defendant acted wrongfully was merely a semantic circumlocution for the fact that he may be adjudged to pay damages.[16] To contend that the de-fendant had violated a duty was a judgment of value and thus an ex-pression of a mere feeling.[17] The only objective signification that could be assigned to such terms was in connection with the coercive legal machinery of the state, called into action for the purpose of en-forcing a contract or punishing a wrongdoer.[18] Similar sentiments were echoed by Ross. The word "right," he declared, had "no semantic ref-erence whatever." [19] It was merely a tool in the technique of presenta-tion, not something that could be "hypostatized" into a substance.[20]

The endeavor to eliminate value judgments completely from the realm of legal science has led the Scandinavian realists to wage an un-relenting war against what they called "the method of justice." Value judgments, Hägerström taught, are judgments only with regard to their verbal form.[21] No science of the Ought is possible, he declared. Inquiries into the true principles of justice are therefore illusory.[22] In the opinion of the Scandinavian realists, law is not based on justice

---

[15] *Inquiries*, pp. 3–9, 316–324.

[16] Lundstedt, pp. 34–35, 38.

[17] *Id.*, p. 48. "The duty is only a person's *feeling* or *sentiment* that he *ought* to conduct himself in a certain manner, consequently, something quite *subjective*. This subjective element legal writers have been forced to turn into the exact opposite, into the monstrous contradiction: an *objective duty!*" *Id.*, p. 62.

[18] *Id.*, pp. 118, 120. See also Olivecrona, *Law as Fact*, pp. 75–76.

[19] Ross, p. 172.

[20] *Id.*, pp. 178–179. Ross reports the following experiment with his children, made apparently for the purpose of forestalling such a hypostatization: "Until my chil-dren reached the age of ten I was able, to our mutual satisfaction, to come to an arrangement with them that they should 'have' certain flowers in the garden, at the same time reserving for myself complete control over what should be done with them." *Id.*, p. 179.

[21] Hägerström, p. xi.

[22] Note the affinity of this view with the teachings of the logical positivists, *supra* Sec. 24.

but is brought about by social group pressures or inescapable societal needs.[23] Justice is merely the feeling of the addressees of the law, engendered by habit and by the ruling ideology, that the legal order is satisfactory.[24] If the concept has any meaning, it might possibly have meaning for the judge in the limited sense that he should apply the positive law correctly and without arbitrary discrimination.[25]

To the method of justice described by Lundstedt as "completely useless," he opposed the "method of social welfare." [26] He insisted that this method was free of all ethical evaluation, and that the notion of social welfare referred merely to arrangements considered useful by men in a certain society at a certain time. "Socially useful is that which is actually evaluated as a social interest." [27]

Value-skepticism is carried to an extreme degree by Ross. He declares that the fundamental postulates concerning the nature and existance of man underlying the natural-law philosophy are entirely arbitrary; and the same, he believes, holds true for the moral-legal ideas evolved on this basis.[28] Value-philosophy is to him nothing but ideology put forth to justify certain political or class interests.[29] No rational argument can demonstrate to us whether we shall be brothers, or whether the strong shall oppress the weak.[30] All judgments of right and wrong are founded on emotive-irrational sentiments, and justice can be appealed to for any cause.[31] "To invoke justice is the same as banging on the table: an emotional expression which turns one's demand into an absolute postulate." [32]

The doctrines of the Upsala school have not remained unopposed in Scandinavia. The Danish legal philosopher F. Vinding Kruse has vigorously attacked the value-nihilism implicit in a radically naturalistic form of realism and called for the elaboration of a normative and ethical jurisprudence resting on experimental methods.[33] He takes the

[23] See Olivecrona, *Law as Fact*, p. 152: "It is hardly necessary specifically to refute the contention that the law is based on abstract justice. This view is too openly superstitious."

[24] Lundstedt, pp. 169–170. See also *id.*, p. 203: "The feelings of justice do not direct law. On the contrary, they are directed by law."

[25] Ross, pp. 274, 280.

[26] Lundstedt, pp. 6, 291.

[27] *Id.*, p. 137.

[28] Ross, p. 258.

[29] *Id.*, p. 259.

[30] *Ibid.*

[31] *Id.*, p. 269. See also *id.*, p. 280: "To declare a law unjust contains no real characteristic, no reference to any criterion, no argumentation."

[32] *Id.*, p. 274. For a criticism of value-skepticism see *infra* Sec. 38.

[33] See particularly his *The Foundation of Human Thought* (London, 1949); *The Community of the Future* (New York, 1952); "Zur Ueberwindung des Wert-

position that it was possible to develop fundamental axioms of morality and justice on a scientific basis. In Norway, Frede Castberg has likewise insisted that legal science can never give up the search for an answer to the questions of right and wrong, since "the demand for justice in the community is rooted in our spiritual nature just as strongly as the need for logical connection in our thinking." [34]

---

nihilismus in Rechtsphilosophie und Ethik," 41 *Archiv für Rechts- und Sozialphilosophie* 145 (1954).

[34] *Problems of Legal Philosophy* (Oslo, 1957), pp. 3, 111. See also, *id.*, p. 110: "Philosophical thinking must not turn aside from the problems raised by the seeking after the objectively right law."

IX

THE REVIVAL OF
NATURAL LAW AND
VALUE-ORIENTED
JURISPRUDENCE

Section 33. *Neo-Kantian Natural Law*
From the middle of the nineteenth century to the beginning of the twentieth the theory of natural law was at a low ebb in most of the countries of Western civilization. It was largely displaced by historical-evolutionary interpretations of law and by legal positivism. Historical and evolutionary views of the law sought to explain the law causally in terms of ethnological factors or by reference to certain evolutionary forces which pushed the law forward along a predetermined path. Legal positivists, especially the analytical jurists, sought to discourage philosophical speculation about the nature and purposes of the law and set out to limit the province of jurisprudence to a technical analy-

sis of the positive law laid down and enforced by the state. Inquiries concerning the ends and ideals of legal regulation tended to vanish from jurisprudence and legal philosophy, and at the close of the nineteenth century the philosophical search for the ultimate values of legal ordering had practically come to a halt.[1]

The twentieth century, however, witnessed a revival of natural-law thinking and value-oriented jurisprudence.[2] Certain elements of legal idealism can be noticed already in some versions of sociological jurisprudence. Joseph Kohler saw the end of legal regulation in the promotion of culture but held an entirely relativistic view with respect to the ethical values to be served by a law dedicated to culture.[3] Roscoe Pound defined the aim of the law in terms of the maximum satisfaction of human wants through ordering of human conduct by politically organized society.[4] Although he viewed the rise of a new philosophy of values with sympathy, his own theory of law did not go much beyond a quantitative surveying of the multifarious interests demanding satisfaction or requiring adjustment through the art of legal "engineering." Twentieth-century legal realism was well aware of the role which value judgments and considerations of social policy actually play in the legal process, but it refrained from building up a rational and objective theory of legal ends and social ideals.

A pioneering attempt to create a modernized natural-law philosophy based on a priori reasoning was made in Germany by Rudolf Stammler (1856–1938). As a philosophical disciple of Kant, he was convinced that human beings bring to the cognitive perception of phenomena certain a priori categories and forms of understanding which they have not obtained through the observation of reality.[5] Stammler taught that there exist in the human mind pure forms of thinking enabling men to understand the notion of law apart from, and independently of, the concrete and variable manifestations in which law has made its appearance in history.

Stammler, however, departed from his master Kant by breaking the notion of law down into two components: the *concept* of law and the *idea* of law. Kant had defined law as the aggregate of the conditions

---

[1] Roscoe Pound, "The Revival of Natural Law," 17 *Notre Dame Lawyer* 287 (1942), points out that natural-law thinking survived only in Scotland, Italy, and in the writings of teachers in some Catholic faculties.

[2] See Charles G. Haines, *The Revival of Natural Law Concepts* (Cambridge, Mass., 1930); Joseph Charmont, *La Renaissance du Droit Naturel* (Paris, 1910), partly translated by F. W. Scott in *Modern French Legal Philosophy* (New York, 1921), pp. 65–146; Pound, *op. cit. supra* n. 1.

[3] On Kohler see *supra* Sec. 27.

[4] See *supra* Sec. 29.

[5] On Kant see *supra* Sec. 15.

under which the freedom of one could be harmonized with the freedom of all. Stammler pointed out that this formula was faulty because it confused the concept of law with the idea of "right" or just law. The concept of law, he said, must be defined in such a manner as to cover all possible realizations and forms of law in the history of mankind. Stammler believed that he had found such an all-embracing definition of law in the following formula: "Law is the inviolable and autocratic collective will." [6] A number of different elements are contained in this formula. Law is the collective will, that is, a manifestation of social life. It is an instrument of social cooperation, not a tool for the satisfaction of purely subjective desires of individuals devoid of community value. Furthermore, law is an expression of a collective will which is autocratic and sovereign. The rules of law, once they have been established, claim a compulsory force. They are binding irrespective of the individual citizen's inclination to follow them. This fact, said Stammler, distinguishes law from customs and social conventions, which constitute mere invitations to the citizens to comply with them and do not purport to be absolutely compulsive. Finally, the rules of law contain an element of inviolability. This means that, as long as they are in effect, they are strictly binding not only upon those who are subject to them but also upon those who are entrusted with their creation and enactment. Herein, according to Stammler, lies the difference between law and arbitrary power. We are confronted with the latter when a command is issued which the holder of power does not regard as an objectively binding regulation of human affairs, but merely as a subjective gratification of a present desire or impulse without normative force.[7]

From the concept of law Stammler distinguished the *idea* of law. The idea of law is the realization of justice. Justice postulates that all legal efforts be directed toward the goal of attaining the most perfect harmony of social life that is possible under the conditions of the time and place. Such a harmony can be brought about only by adjusting individual desires to the aims of the community. According to Stammler, the content of a rule of law is just if it is conducive to harmonizing the purposes of the individual with those of society. The social ideal, as Stammler sees it, is a "community of free-willing men." [8] The

---

[6] *Rechtsphilosophie*, 3d ed. (Berlin, 1928), p. 93.

[7] See Stammler, "Recht und Willkür," in *Rechtsphilosophische Abhandlungen und Vorträge* (Charlottenburg, 1925), I, 97. Stammler held, however, that if in a despotic state there exists a written or unwritten rule of law to the effect that the legal relations of the subjects are determined exclusively by the individualized decisions of the ruler, this imparts to the system the character of a legal system. *Id.*, p. 111.

[8] *The Theory of Justice*, transl. by I. Husik (New York, 1925), p. 153.

term "free," as used in this formula, does not denote an act of volition which is directed by the subjective and selfish desire of an individual; in accordance with Kantian terminology, a free act is one that is objectively and rationally justified from the point of view of the common interest.[9]

Stammler pointedly emphasized that his social ideal could serve merely as a formal method for determining whether the content of a specific law was just; it could not be used as a universal substantive standard for passing judgment on the "rightness" of concrete enactments.[10] Stammler's formula has in fact been decried as essentially empty in content.[11] It cannot be denied, however, that Stammler, in contradiction to his own methodological premises, did derive some absolute postulates of "right law" from his social ideal. In any attempt to realize it, he wrote, the legislator must keep four fundamental principles in mind:

1. The content of a person's volition must not be made subject to the arbitrary power of another.

2. Every legal demand must be made in such a manner that the person obligated may remain his own nearest neighbor (retain his self-respecting personality).

3. A member of the legal community cannot be excluded from it arbitrarily.

4. A power of control conferred by law can be justified only to the extent that the person affected thereby may remain his own nearest neighbor (retain his self-respecting personality).[12]

What do these "principles of respect and participation," as Stammler called them, mean in substance? They mean that each member of the community is to be treated as an end in himself and must not become the object of the merely subjective and arbitrary will of another.[13] No one must use another merely as a means for the advancement of his own purposes. "To curb one's own desires through respect of another, and to do so with absolute reciprocity, must be taken as a principle in the realization of the social ideal." [14] This notion of a com-

[9] Stammler, *Wirtschaft und Recht nach der Materialistischen Geschichtsauffassung*, 2d ed. (Leipzig, 1906), pp. 356–357, 563.
[10] *Theory of Justice*, pp. 89–90.
[11] Morris R. Cohen, "Positivism and the Limits of Idealism in Law," 27 *Columbia Law Review* 237, at 241 (1927). Cohen gives a number of examples designed to show the essential vagueness and indeterminateness of Stammler's ideal.
[12] *Theory of Justice*, pp. 161, 163. The translation has been changed and follows in a few places Pound's translation in his *Jurisprudence* (St. Paul, Minn., 1959), I, 150–153.
[13] From the above principles, Stammler inferred, for example, the unjustness of slavery, of polygamy, and of absolute prohibition of divorce.
[14] *Theory of Justice*, p. 162.

munity of free men treating each other as ends in themselves is close to the Kantian idea of law, but differs from it in two respects. First, the *community* of individuals takes the place of the free individual as such; this means that Stammler's formula is somewhat less individualistic than Kant's.[15] Second, Stammler's formula in its abstractness leaves more room for variety and diversity in positive law than Kant's natural-law definition. "There is not a single rule of law," said Stammler, "the positive content of which can be fixed a priori." [16] In his view, two legal systems with widely varying rules and principles of law may both be in conformity with his social ideal. This ideal does not embody a concrete system of natural law but represents merely a broad yardstick by which the justice or injustice of positive rules of law may be tested. It is, at the most, a "natural law with a changing content." [17] With the eternal and immutable law of nature of the classical period it has very little in common.

Like Stammler, the Italian legal philosopher Giorgio Del Vecchio (b. 1878) distinguishes sharply between the concept of law and the ideal of law.[18] The concept of law, he maintains, is logically anterior to juridical experience, that is, constitutes an a priori datum. The essential characteristics of law, according to him, are first, objective coordination of the actions of several individuals pursuant to an ethical principle, and second, bilateralness,[19] imperativeness, and coercibility.[20]

The legal ideal is identified by Del Vecchio with the notion of natural law. "Natural Law is . . . the criterion which permits us to evaluate Positive Law and to measure its intrinsic justice." [21] Accepting the fundamental tenets of Kantian ethics, he derives natural law from the nature of man as a rational being. Respect for the autonomy of the human personality is to him the basis of justice. Every human being may demand from his fellowmen that he should not be treated

[15] See *supra* Sec. 15. In accord: Carl J. Friedrich, *The Philosophy of Law in Historical Perspective* (Chicago, 1958), p. 163.

[16] *Theory of Justice*, p. 90.

[17] *Wirtschaft und Recht*, p. 165. On Stammler see also Morris Ginsberg, "Stammler's Philosophy of Law," in *Modern Theories of Law* (London, 1933), pp. 38–51; George H. Sabine, "Rudolf Stammler's Critical Philosophy of Law," 18 *Cornell Law Quarterly* 321 (1933); Wolfgang Friedmann, *Legal Theory*, 4th ed. (Toronto, 1960), pp. 130–138; Edwin W. Patterson, *Jurisprudence* (Brooklyn, 1953), pp. 389–395.

[18] See Del Vecchio, *Philosophy of Law*, transl. by T. O. Martin (Washington, 1953), p. 248. On Del Vecchio see also Friedmann, pp. 138–142.

[19] This means that the law brings together at least two subjects and gives a norm for both, in the sense that what is allowed to one party may not be impeded by the other. Del Vecchio, p. 277.

[20] See *id.*, pp. 270, 280 ff., 297, 304.

[21] *Id.*, p. 450.

as a mere instrument or object.[22] Del Vecchio is convinced that the evolution of mankind leads to a constantly increasing recognition of human autonomy and thus to a gradual realization and ultimate triumph of natural law.

The absolute value of the person, equal liberty of all men, the right of each of the associates to be an active, not just a passive, participant in legislation, liberty of conscience, and in general the principles in which is summed up, even amid accidental fallacies, the true substance of the classical philosophy of law, *juris naturalis scientia,* have already received important confirmations in the positive juridical orders, and will receive others soon or in the course of time, whatever may be the resistances and the oppositions which they still encounter.[23]

Del Vecchio, though in general he may be classified as a neo-Kantian, differs from Kant in his conception of the purposes of the state. For Kant, the purpose of state power exhausted itself in the promulgation and enforcement of laws designed to protect the equal liberty of all. Del Vecchio holds that the state need not be indifferent to the problems of the economic, cultural, and moral life. It may extend its regulatory power over all aspects of human social life, and it is its highest function to promote the well-being of society generally. But in doing so, the state must always operate in the forms of the law, so that every act of the state has for its basis a law manifesting the general will.[24] With this conviction, Del Vecchio leaves the soil of Kantian individualism and moves into the orbit of the Hegelian philosophy of the state.[25] However, he is willing to recognize a right of resistance against the commands of state power in extreme cases in which these commands come into irreconcilable conflict with the most primordial and elementary requirements of natural law and justice.[26]

The German legal philosopher Gustav Radbruch (1878–1949) started out from a neo-Kantian philosophy of values, which erects a

[22] "Do not extend your will to the point of imposing it upon others, do not try to subject to yourself one who, of his nature, is subject only to himself." *Id.,* p. 443.
[23] *Id.,* pp. 449–450. "Participant in legislation" is my substitution for Martin's translation "participant in social laws."
[24] *Id.,* pp. 382–383.
[25] "The empirical antithesis between the individual and society . . . finds in the State its rational composition. . . . Individuality is tempered in the State and therein 'it reveals its true nature,' as Vico said." *Id.,* p. 383. On Hegel's philosophy of the state see *supra* Sec. 17.
[26] "Legitimate, then, is 'the appeal to Heaven' according to Locke's expression, that is, the struggle against the written laws in the name of the 'unwritten' ones, the vindication of Natural Law against the Positive Law which denies it." *Id.,* p. 456. See also Del Vecchio, *Justice,* ed. A. H. Campbell (New York, 1953), pp. 157, 158.

strong barrier between the "is" and the "ought" and denies that any judgment as to what is "right" can be gained from the observation and apperception of reality. In giving an account of Radbruch's legal philosophy it is necessary, however, to distinguish two phases in the evolution of his thought.

Prior to the Second World War, Radbruch adhered to an essentially relativistic view of law and justice. The chief trend of his thought ran as follows: Law is the sum of the general rules for the common life of man. The ultimate goal of the law is the realization of justice. But justice is a rather vague and indeterminate concept. It demands that those who are equal be treated in an equal manner, while those who are different be treated differently according to their differences. This general maxim leaves open two questions: first, the test by which equality or inequality is to be measured, and second, the particular mode of treatment to which equals as well as unequals are to be subjected.[27] In order to obtain the substantive and specific contents of the law, the idea of justice must be supplemented by a second idea, the idea of *expediency*. The question as to the expediency of a legal regulation cannot be answered unequivocally and generally in one way or another. The answer is colored by political and social convictions and party views. One man or group of men may see the highest goal of the law in the development of the individual human personality (individualism); another may see it in the attainment of national power and glory (supraindividualism); a third one may regard the promotion of civilization and the works of culture as the worthiest aim of the law (transpersonalism).[28] Even though Radbruch expressed preference for the transpersonalist conception, he denied that a choice between the three views could be justified by any scientific argument; the choice was to him a matter of personal preference. But it is obvious, said Radbruch, that the legal order cannot be made the plaything of conflicting political and social opinions. In the interest of security and order, what is right and what is wrong must in some way be authoritatively settled. The ideas of justice and expediency must be supplemented by a third idea, the idea of *legal certainty*, which demands the promulgation and maintenance of a positive and binding legal order by the state.[29]

Thus we have three elements or principles, all of which contribute

[27] Gustav Radbruch, "Legal Philosophy," in *The Legal Philosophies of Lask, Radbruch, and Dabin*, transl. K. Wilk (Cambridge, Mass., 1950), pp. 90–91.
[28] *Id.*, pp. 91–95.
[29] *Id.*, p. 108: "The certainty of the law requires law to be positive: if what is just cannot be settled, then what ought to be right must be laid down; and this must be done by an agency able to carry through what it lays down."

in some degree to the building up of the legal order: the idea of justice, the idea of expediency, and the idea of legal certainty. These three elements, according to Radbruch, "require one another—yet at the same time they contradict one another." [30] Justice, for example, demands generality in the formulation of a legal rule, while expediency may require an individualized treatment adapted to the specific situation of the case. To take another example, the idea of legal certainty postulates fixed and stable laws, while justice and expediency demand a quick adaptation of the legal system to new social and economic conditions. The full realization of one of these ideas will make a certain sacrifice or neglect of the two others indispensable, and there is no absolute standard by which the proportionate relation of these three elements within the legal order can be satisfactorily determined.[31] Different ages will lay decisive stress upon the one or the other of these principles.[32] Radbruch himself, before World War II, was committed to the view that in case of an irreconcilable conflict between them, legal certainty ought to prevail. "It is more important *that* the strife of legal views be ended than that it be determined *justly* and *expediently*." [33]

After the cataclysmic events of the Nazi period and the collapse of Germany in the Second World War, Radbruch undertook a revision of his former theories.[34] He expressed the view that there exist certain *absolute* postulates which the law must fulfill in order to deserve its name. Law, he declared, requires some recognition of individual freedom, and a complete denial of individual rights by the state is "absolutely false law." [35]

Furthermore, Radbruch abandoned his former view that in case of an irreconcilable conflict between justice and legal certainty, the positive law must prevail. He argued that legal positivism had left Ger-

---

[30] *Id.*, p. 109.

[31] *Id.*, p. 109.

[32] Thus, he pointed out, the police state of the Prussian Kings tended to disregard justice and legal security in the interest of political expediency. The epoch of natural law attempted to deduce the whole content of the law from the idea of justice. Nineteenth-century legal positivism looked only to security and neglected the investigation of expediency and justice in law. *Id.*, p. 111.

[33] *Id.*, p. 108.

[34] Not only the extent, but even the occurrence of a revision has been the subject of debate among legal authors. See Erik Wolf, "Revolution or Evolution in Gustav Radbruch's Legal Philosophy," 3 *Natural Law Forum* 1 (1958). Most convincing are the arguments of Alfred Verdross, *Abendländische Rechtsphilosophie* (Vienna, 1958), pp. 200–202, who finds a substantial break. See also Lon L. Fuller, "American Legal Philosophy at Mid-Century," 6 *Journal of Legal Education* 457, at 481–485 (1954).

[35] *Vorschule der Rechtsphilosophie* (Heidelberg, 1947), pp. 27–28.

many defenseless against the abuses of the Nazi regime, and that it was necessary to recognize situations where a totally unjust law must give way to justice. His revised formula regarding the relation between positive law and justice reads as follows: "Preference should be given to the rule of positive law, supported as it is by due enactment and state power, even when the rule is unjust and contrary to the general welfare, unless the violation of justice reaches so intolerable a degree that the rule becomes in effect 'lawless law' and must therefore yield to justice." [36] By this formula Radbruch, in his old age, made himself a convert to natural law in a moderate form.

Section 34. *Neo-Scholastic Natural Law*

Neo-Scholasticism is a modern philosophical movement of Catholic origin which will be considered in this section only with regard to its impact on the philosophy of law. In this field, neo-Scholastic thought has in the last few decades been particularly active in France, Germany, and the United States.

Although neo-Scholastic jurists have developed legal theories with differing emphases and implications, certain basic convictions are held in common by them. The most important of these convictions is the belief in a natural law which exists prior to positive law and is superior to it. This natural law is no longer the law of nature of the classical period of Western legal philosophy. It draws its inspiration from a different source, namely, from medieval Catholic Scholastic thought and particularly from the legal philosophy of St. Thomas Aquinas.[1]

The chief difference between the classical and the Thomist natural law may be sought in the fact that the Thomist consists of very broad and general principles, while many of the classical thinkers developed very specific and detailed systems of natural law. Neo-Scholasticism in this respect definitely follows the Thomist tradition. It rejects the idea that natural law is an unchangeable order of specific and concrete legal norms and contents itself with laying down some broad and abstract principles. Victor Cathrein, for example, a Swiss neo-Thomist, defined the supreme principle obligatory for human action as follows: "You should observe the order which is fitting for you as a rational being in your relations to God, your fellowmen, and yourself." This

---

[36] "Gesetzliches Unrecht und Übergesetzliches Recht," in *Rechtsphilosophie*, ed. E. Wolf, 4th ed. (Stuttgart, 1950), p. 353. The text follows Fuller's translation in *op. cit. supra* n. 34, p. 484. On Radbruch see also Wolfgang Friedmann, "Gustav Radbruch," 14 *Vanderbilt Law Review* 191 (1960). Friedmann's interpretation differs to some extent from the approach taken in the text.

[1] See *supra* Sec. 6.

maxim, as applied to legal ordering, demands above all the recognition of the *suum cuique* principle (to give everybody that which is due him).[2] Natural law, according to Cathrein, embraces only some very fundamental principles and must be made concrete and implemented by the positive law of the state. Heinrich Rommen states that only two self-evident principles belong to the content of natural law in the strict sense. These are: "What is just is to be done, and injustice is to be avoided," and the old axiom, "Give to everyone his own." [3] He assumes that, in the light of these maxims, the legal institutions of private property and inheritance must be deemed to be of natural law, but that the natural law "does not demand the property and inheritance institutions of feudalism, or of liberalist capitalism, or of a system in which private, corporate, and public forms of ownership exist side by side." [4] The supreme maxims of natural law would, of course, prohibit such obviously unjust acts as the killing of innocent persons, and they also require that human beings be granted a certain amount of liberty and the right to found a family.[5] Louis Le Fur, a French author, declares that there exist three principles of natural law: to keep freely concluded agreements, to repair damage unjustly inflicted on another person, and to respect authority.[6] Jacques Maritain states that "there is, by very virtue of human nature, an order or a disposition which human reason can discover and according to which the human will must act in order to attune itself to the necessary ends of the human being. The unwritten law, or natural law, is nothing more than that." [7] Maritain's catalogue of rights to be derived from natural law is more comprehensive than Rommen's. Maritain holds, however, that these rights are not necessarily absolute and unlimited; they are, as a rule, subject to regulation by the positive law for the purpose of promoting the public interest.[8]

---

[2] *Recht, Naturrecht, und Positives Recht*, 2d ed. (Freiburg, 1909), pp. 132–133, 222.

[3] *The Natural Law*, transl. T. R. Hanley (St. Louis, 1948), p. 220.

[4] *Id.*, p. 235.

[5] *Id.*, pp. 222–223, 232, 238 ff.

[6] *Les grands problèmes du droit* (Paris, 1937), p. 181.

[7] *The Rights of Man and Natural Law*, transl. D. C. Anson (New York, 1947), p. 61.

[8] *Id.*, pp. 78–80, 72, 89–90, 113–114. On Maritain's philosophy of law and state see also Clarence Morris, "The Political Philosophy of Jacques Maritain," 88 *Daedalus* 700 (1959); Edgar Bodenheimer, "Some Recent Trends in European Legal Thought—West and East," 2 *Western Political Quarterly* 45, at 46–48 (1949).

A comprehensive legal philosophy on a neo-Thomist basis was developed by Johannes Messner, *Social Ethics*, transl. J. J. Doherty (St. Louis, 1949). Other neo-Scholastic contributions include: Thomas E. Davitt, *The Elements of Law* (Boston, 1959); John C. H. Wu, *Fountain of Justice* (New York, 1955); and the con-

A significant contribution to neo-Thomistic legal thought has been made by Jean Dabin (b. 1889), a Belgian jurist. Dabin conceives of the legal order as "the sum total of the rules of conduct laid down, or at least consecrated, by civil society, under the sanction of public compulsion, with a view to realizing in the relationships between men a certain order—the order postulated by the end of civil society and by the maintenance of the civil society as an instrument devoted to that end." [9] Dabin places a great deal of emphasis on the rule element in law and on compulsion as an essential ingredient of the positive legal order, approaching in this respect the positivistic position.[10] On the other hand, he also undertakes an elaborate analysis of the ends of legal regulation portrayed in terms of justice and the public good. The latter, in Dabin's view, embraces the totality of human values. It requires the protection of the legitimate activities of individuals and groups as well as the institution of public services in aid or supplementation of private initiative. The state, by means of the law, should coordinate and adjust conflicting economic efforts and counteract undue dispersion and waste engendered by unregulated competition.[11]

Nothing which is contrary to morality can, in Dabin's view, be considered as included in the public good.[12] This maxim forms the link between Dabin's conception of the public good and his theory of natural law. He deduces natural law from the nature of man as it reveals itself in man's basic inclinations under the control of reason. More concretely, Dabin appears to identify natural law with certain minimal requirements of ethics postulated by reason.[13]

What happens when the positive law comes at odds with the ethical minimum? Dabin says: "Everybody admits that civil laws contrary to natural law are bad laws and even that they do not answer to the concept of a law." [14] This statement should probably be construed to reflect the general Thomistic and neo-Scholastic position, according to which a flagrantly and outrageously unmoral law, as distinguished from a merely unjust law, must be deemed invalid.

Dabin's theory of justice contemplates three different forms of jus-

---

tributions listed in Harold G. Reuschlein, *Jurisprudence—Its American Prophets* (Indianapolis, 1951), pp. 360–393, and Edgar Bodenheimer, "A Decade of Jurisprudence in the United States," 3 *Nat. L. For.* 44, at 65–66 (1958).

[9] Jean Dabin, "General Theory of Law," in *The Legal Philosophies of Lask, Radbruch, and Dabin,* p. 234. On Dabin see also Patterson, *Jurisprudence,* pp. 355–358.

[10] See, for example, Dabin, pp. 251–252, 259.

[11] *Id.,* pp. 355–358.

[12] *Id.,* p. 456.

[13] *Id.,* pp. 419–431, 455–456.

[14] *Id.,* p. 425. See also *id.,* p. 420: "Natural law . . . dominates positive law in the sense that, while positive law may add to natural law or even restrict it, it is prohibited from contradicting it."

tice: commutative, distributive, and legal justice.[15] The first kind of justice is aimed at the proper adjustment of the relations of private individuals, particularly by means of the legal remedies designed to award adequate damages in contract and tort cases, restore stolen or lost property, grant restitution in cases of unjust enrichment, and the like. Distributive justice determines what is due from the collectivity to its members: it governs the legislative distribution of rights, powers, honors, and rewards. Legal justice, on the other hand, is concerned with what is owed *to* the collectivity by its members. Its object is "ordination for the common good," that is, determination of the duties and obligations which the members of society owe to the social whole, such as revenue, military service, participation in public functions, obedience to laws and legitimate orders. "Legal justice," says Dabin, "is the virtue most necessary to the public good precisely because its object is the public good (of the state or of the public). It is in legal justice that law and morals meet so closely as almost to merge." [16] Although legal justice will come into play only after a demonstration of the insufficiency of the two other forms of justice for the solution of a problem, it will prevail in the case of an irreconcilable conflict with the latter.[17]

Closely linked with the neo-Thomist natural law is the *institutional theory*, which was devised by Maurice Hauriou (1856–1929) and, after his death, developed in detail by Georges Renard (b. 1876).

Hauriou defines the concept of "institution" as follows: "An institution is an idea of an undertaking or enterprise which is realized and which persists in a social environment." [18] For the realization of this idea an authority is constituted which provides itself with organs; in addition, among the members of the social group interested in the realization of the idea, manifestations of communion arise which are directed by the organs of authority and regulated by procedural rules. Expressing the same general thought, Renard defines an institution as "the communion of men in an idea." [19]

---

[15] *Id.*, pp. 443 ff.

[16] *Id.*, p. 463.

[17] Certain aspects of the legal theory of François Gény, another author of an influential neo-Thomist philosophy of law, were described *supra* Sec. 28. On Gény see also Pound, *Jurisprudence*, I, 181–184.

The attention of the reader is also called to Joseph Charmont, "Recent Phases of French Legal Philosophy," in *Modern French Legal Philosophy*, transl. F. W. Scott and J. P. Chamberlain (New York, 1921), pp. 65–147.

[18] "La théorie de l'institution et de la fondation," in *La cité moderne et les transformations du droit* (Paris, 1925), p. 10. On the institutional theory see W. I. Jennings, "The Institutional Theory," in *Modern Theories of Law* (London, 1933), pp. 68–85.

[19] Georges Renard, *La théorie de l'institution* (Paris, 1930), p. 95.

The institution is supposed to symbolize the "idea of duration" in law. An individual is certain to die, and contracts concluded between individuals are of a transitory character. An institution like the state, the Catholic Church, Harvard University, or the British Board of Trade will be likely to endure for a long time to come. The idea to whose realization the institution is consecrated will live and prevail long after the original founders of the institution have died, and this idea is wholly detached from the casual individuals who belong to the institution at some particular time. It may be noted that Renard finds the most perfect definition of the institution in the first article of the former Italian Fascist Charter of Labor, which reads as follows: "The Italian nation is an organization endowed with a purpose, a life, and means of action transcending those of the individuals or groups of individuals composing it." [20]

Institution and contract are sharply contrasted by Renard. The touchstone of a contract is the notion of equality; a contract serves the merely subjective purposes of two or more individuals. The criterion of the institution, on the other hand, is the idea of authority; the organization of an institution implies differentiation, inequality, direction, and hierarchy. It demands subordination of individual purposes to the collective aims of the institution. Subjective rights, typical in the law of contracts, are restricted in institutional law. Status, not contract, is the chief organizational principle of the institution.[21] The relations and qualifications of the members are objectively and authoritatively determined. This does not mean, Renard states, that the members of the institution occupy the position of slaves; it merely means that the common good of the institution must prevail over the private and subjective interests of the individual members. Renard admits that the members of an institution lose their liberty to some degree; but in his opinion they gain in security what they lose in liberty.[22]

The state, according to the theory of institution, is the most eminent manifestation of the institutional phenomenon. But the advocates of the theory do not consider the state as an omnipotent and totalitarian entity. There are other institutions, they say, which enjoy a considerable autonomy and independence from state interference and which should represent an effective counterweight against state power. First, there is the family, which is the oldest of institutions. Second, there is the religious congregation, the Church. Third, there are professional

[20] *Id.*, p. 168.
[21] *Id.*, pp. 329 ff.
[22] *Id.*, p. 365.

associations, corporations, labor unions, employers' associations. Every individual belongs to some institution other than the state, and the autonomy of the various institutions guarantees him a certain amount of liberty, because no institution has an entirely unlimited power over him. The institutional theory is opposed to statism and to that form of socialism which would make the individual a mere cog in the apparatus of an all-powerful state. It believes in corporate or syndicalist pluralism and in the self-government of institutions, subject of course to the state's police power.[23]

Section 35. *Duguit's Legal Philosophy*

A natural-law theory with strongly sociological overtones was propounded by the French jurist Léon Duguit (1859–1928). This doctrine was diametrically opposed to the natural-law doctrines of the age of enlightenment in that Duguit repudiated any natural or inalienable rights of individuals. His objective was to supplant the traditional system of legal rights by a system which would recognize only legal duties. Every individual has a certain task to perform in society, Duguit said, and his obligation to perform this function may be enforced by the law.[1] The only right which any man might be said to possess under this theory is the right always to do his duty. As Corwin has aptly said, this theory is "that of Locke stood on its head." [2]

Notwithstanding his emphasis on social duties, Duguit rejected any absolutist conception of state power. He proposed to strip the state and its organs of all sovereign rights and other attributes of sovereignty with which the traditional doctrine of public law had endowed it. Duguit taught that the governing authorities, like the citizens, have only duties, and no rights. Their activity is to be confined to the performance of certain social functions, and the most important of these functions is the organization and maintenance of public services. It is the duty of governmental officials to guarantee a continuous and uninterrupted operation of the public services. This aim, Duguit believed, would be most efficiently realized by a far-reaching decentralization and technical autonomy of the public utilities under a syndicalist structure of the state.[3]

[23] *Id.*, p. 151. Cf. also Raymond Saleilles, *La personnalité juridique*, 2d ed. (Paris, 1922), p. 626 (Saleilles emphasizes the necessity of state control more strongly than Renard); Georges Gurvitch, *L'idée du droit social* (Paris, 1932), pp. 634 ff.

[1] *Les transformations générales du droit privé*, 2d ed. (Paris, 1920), pp. 24–25.

[2] Edward S. Corwin, "The 'Higher Law' Background of American Constitutional Law," 42 *Harvard Law Review* 365, at 382 (1929).

[3] See Duguit, "The Law and the State," 31 *Harv. L. Rev.* 1 (1917); *Les transformations du droit public* (Paris, 1925), pp. 33 ff.; Harold J. Laski, "M. Duguit's Conception of the State," in *Modern Theories of Law*, pp. 52–67.

The social function of law, according to Duguit, is the realization of *social solidarity*. This is the central concept in Duguit's theory of law. "The fact of social solidarity is not disputed and in truth cannot be disputed; it is a fact of observation which cannot be the object of controversy. . . . Solidarity is a permanent fact, always identical in itself, the irreducible constitutive element of every social group." [4] Thus Duguit regarded social solidarity not as a rule of conduct or imperative, but as a fundamental fact of human coexistence.

The fact of social solidarity becomes, however, converted into a normative principle under Duguit's "rule of law" (*règle de droit*). The rule of law demands of everyone that he contribute to the full realization of social solidarity. It imposes upon the governors as well as the governed the duty to abstain from any act which is motivated by a purpose incompatible with the realization of social solidarity. [5] The rule of law is so conceived by Duguit as to constitute a definite limitation upon the power of all governing authorities. No statute or administrative order is valid which is not in conformity with the principles of social solidarity and social interdependence. Duguit suggests that a tribunal composed of representatives of all social classes should be set up which would be entrusted with the task of interpreting the concept of social solidarity authoritatively, and with determining whether a certain legal enactment is or is not in accord with this supreme requirement. [6]

It was Duguit's professed intention to create an entirely positivistic, realistic, and empirical theory of law, free from any ingredients of metaphysics and natural law. In truth, as Gény has pointed out, Duguit's rule of law based on social solidarity is far removed from legal positivism and empiricism. [7] The theory is essentially metaphysical and must be classified as a peculiar version of natural-law doctrine in a socialized form.

Section 36. *The Policy-Science of Lasswell and McDougal*
Harold Lasswell (b. 1902) and Myres McDougal (b. 1906), two American writers who have joined in an effort to develop a policy-science of the law, have in common with Léon Duguit the objective of build-

---

[4] Duguit, "Objective Law," 20 *Col. L. Rev.* 817, at 830 (1920); see also Duguit, "The Theory of Objective Law Anterior to the State," in *Modern French Legal Philosophy*, pp. 258 ff.

[5] Duguit, *L'État, le droit objective, et la loi positive* (Paris, 1901), p. 87.

[6] *Le droit social, le droit individuel, et les transformations de l'état* (Paris, 1911), p. 58. On Duguit see also Pound, *Jurisprudence*, I, 184–191.

[7] François Gény, *Science et technique en droit privé positif* (Paris, 1919–1925), II, 248 ff.

ing an empirical legal theory free from metaphysical speculation. Unlike Duguit, however, they admit openly that their approach to the law represents a theory of values rather than a mere description of social facts.

The Lasswell-McDougal value system proceeds from the assumption that a value is a "desired event." [1] Thus, inasmuch as men want power (defined as participation in the making of important decisions), power is "unmistakably a value, in the sense that it is desired [or likely to be desired]." [2] Other value categories or "preferred events" gratifying the desires of men are wealth, that is, control over economic goods and services; well-being, or bodily and psychic integrity; enlightenment, or the finding and dissemination of knowledge; skill, or the acquiring of dexterities and development of talents; affection, or the cultivation of friendship and intimate relations; rectitude, or moral responsibility and integrity; and respect, or recognition of merit without discrimination on grounds irrelevant to capacity.[3] This list is regarded as representative, but not necessarily exhaustive. A ranking of the values in question in the order of their importance is held impossible by the authors since "the relative position of values varies from group to group, from person to person, and from time to time in the history of any culture or personality." [4] Nor is it regarded as feasible to assign a universally dominant role to any particular value. What the values controlling a group or individual are in a given situation must in principle be determined separately in each case.[5]

Law is conceived by Lasswell and McDougal as a form of the power value and described as "the sum of the power decisions in a community." [6] It is essential to the legal process, McDougal says, that a formally sanctioned authority to make decisions be conjoined with an effective control ensuring the execution of these decisions.[7] This combination of formal authority and effective control produces a flow of decisions whose purpose it is to promote community values in conformity with the expectations of the community.[8] It is one of the basic

[1] Harold D. Lasswell and Abraham Kaplan, *Power and Society* (New Haven, 1950), p. 16.

[2] Lasswell, *Power and Personality* (New York, 1948), p. 16.

[3] *Id.*, p. 17; Myres S. McDougal, "International Law, Power, and Policy," in 82 *Recueil des Cours* 137, at 168 (Hague Academy of International Law, 1953).

[4] *Op. cit. supra* n. 2, p. 17.

[5] Lasswell and Kaplan, p. 56.

[6] McDougal, "The Law School of the Future: From Legal Realism to Policy Science in the World Community," 56 *Yale Law Journal* 1345, at 1348 (1947).

[7] McDougal, "Law as a Process of Decision: A Policy-Oriented Approach to Legal Study," 1 *Nat. L. For.* 53, at 58 (1956).

[8] Thus, law is viewed as the process of decision-making in a community as a whole, and not as a mere body of rules. McDougal, *op. cit. supra* n. 7, p. 56.

postulates of the authors that the members of the community should participate in the distribution and enjoyment of values, or, differently expressed, that it must be the aim of legal regulation and adjudication to foster the widest possible sharing of values among men. The ultimate goal of legal control as envisaged by Lasswell and McDougal is a world community in which a democratic distribution of values is encouraged and promoted, all available resources are utilized to the maximum degree, and the protection of human dignity is regarded as a paramount objective of social policy.[9]

These authors believe that legal science, in approaching its task of fostering the democratization of values on a global scale and contributing to the creation of a free and abundant society, should minimize and deflate the role of technical legal doctrine, which is referred to as the "authoritative myth." Legal doctrines, McDougal says, have the unfortunate habit of "traveling in pairs of opposites."[10] Conceptual and doctrinal antinomies are endemic to the law, and legal terms take their meaning from the context in which they are used, the person who uses them, and the objective for which they are employed. Thus, reliance on doctrine does not ensure legal certainty and often defeats the attainment of socially desirable ends.

Lasswell and McDougal propose, therefore, that the technical-doctrinal approach to law, although it should not be entirely discarded, ought largely to be supplanted by a "policy" approach. Key legal terms should be interpreted in relation to the goals and vital problems of democratic living.[11] Legal decisions should be viewed as "responses to precipitating events best described as value changes in social processes."[12] Emphasis on definition and orientation upon rules should be replaced by "goal thinking" and functional consideration of the effect of alternative solutions upon over-all community patterns. Legal doctrines should be relegated to the role of "symbols whose function is to serve the total policies of their users."[13] Sharp distinctions between law and policy, between formulations *de lege lata* and propositions *de lege ferenda* should be shunned. "Every application of legal rules," says

[9] See Lasswell and McDougal, "Legal Education and Public Policy," 52 *Yale L. J.* 203, at 212 (1943): "The supreme value of democracy is the dignity and worth of the individual; hence a democratic society is a commonwealth of mutual deference—a commonwealth where there is full opportunity to mature talent into socially creative skill, free from discrimination on grounds of religion, culture, or class." Cf. also McDougal, *op. cit. supra* n. 7, pp. 67, 72.
[10] "The Role of Law in World Politics," 20 *Mississippi Law Journal* 253, at 260 (1949).
[11] Lasswell and McDougal, p. 216.
[12] McDougal, *op. cit. supra* n. 7, p. 65.
[13] McDougal, *op. cit. supra* n. 10, p. 263.

McDougal, "customary or conventional or however derived, to specific cases in fact requires the making of policy choices." [14] While the adjudicating organs may seek guidance from past judicial experience, they should always focus their vision strongly upon the probable impact of the decision upon the future of their community.[15] Such a future-oriented approach to the decision-making process is regarded by McDougal and Lasswell as far superior to the mechanical manipulation of traditional doctrines.[16]

Although both of these authors hold that their legal "policy-science" should not be classified as natural-law doctrine, such a characterization would not appear to be wholly inappropriate. While the eight values recognized by them correspond largely to the actual desires held by people and are therefore empirical in character, the insistence of the authors that these values be democratically shared in a world-wide order, resting on respect for human dignity as a supervalue, would appear to bear the chief earmarks of natural-law thinking.

Section 37. *Other Recent Value-Oriented Philosophies of Law*
In addition to Lasswell and McDougal, a number of other thinkers in the United States have turned their attention in recent decades to the fundamental values which the institution of law should be made to promote. Although the revival of natural law or justice-oriented approaches to the law has not in this country reached the degree and intensity of Western European developments, the trend is at the present time still gaining in momentum and strength.

Edmond Cahn (b. 1906) is in many important aspects of his thought connected with the realist movement in American jurisprudence. Although Cahn realizes the importance of the rational element in the administration of justice, he views legal processes to a far-reaching extent as intuitive ethical responses to concrete and particular fact situations.[1]

Cahn has expressed the conviction that the problem of justice should be approached from its negative rather than its affirmative side. Suggesting that the postulation of affirmative ideals of justice has been "so

---

[14] *Op. cit. supra* n. 3, p. 155. See also p. 144.

[15] McDougal, "Law and Power," 46 *American Journal of International Law* 102, at 110 (1952).

[16] This account of the thinking of Lasswell and McDougal was first published in my article on "A Decade of Jurisprudence in the United States of America: 1946–1956," 3 *Nat. L. For.* 44, at 53–56 (1958) and has been reprinted here with some changes by permission of the editors of that journal. For a critical appraisal of this theory see *id.*, pp. 56–59.

[1] See particularly his book *The Moral Decision* (Bloomington, 1955). See also Cahn, *The Sense of Injustice* (New York, 1949), p. 102.

beclouded by natural law writings that it almost inevitably brings to mind some ideal relation or static condition or set of perceptual standards," Cahn prefers to place the emphasis on the "sense of injustice." [2] The sense of injustice is a blend of "reason and empathy" which forms part of the human biological endowment. Justice is essentially a process of remedying or preventing whatever would arouse the sense of injustice.

How does the sense of injustice manifest itself? First and perhaps most important of all, feelings of injustice are precipitated in a group of human beings by the creation of inequalities which the members of the group regard as arbitrary and devoid of justification. "The sense of injustice revolts against whatever is unequal by caprice." [3] The inequalities resulting from the law must make sense; the law becomes unjust when it discriminates between indistinguishables.

The sense of injustice also makes certain other demands, such as the demand for recognition of merit and human dignity, for impartial and conscientious adjudication, for maintenance of a proper balance between freedom and order, and for fulfillment of common expectations.[4] The last-mentioned demand, Cahn points out, may manifest itself in two different ways. It may assert itself, first, where normal expectations of human beings regarding the consistency and continuity of legal operations have been disappointed by lawmakers or judges. Any retroactive change of substantive law which reaches transactions and acts undertaken in justified reliance on the earlier law presents, therefore, a challenge to the sense of injustice. Second, a similarly unfavorable reaction may be produced by the opposite way of proceeding, namely, by a failure of the law to respond to new moral convictions and new social needs. Thus, the positive law may become unjust not only by breaking its promise of regularity and consistency, but also by violating its commitment to be sensitive to new demands of the social and economic life. Law, in order to be just, must maintain a precarious and hazardous balance between regularity that is uncompromising and change that is inconsiderate. The sense of injustice "warns against either standing still or leaping forward; it calls for movement in an intelligible design." [5]

Lon Fuller (b. 1902) has turned a critical searchlight on both juridical positivism and legal realism. The positivistic attitude, he points out, is as a general rule associated with ethical skepticism. "Its unavowed

---

[2] *Sense of Injustice*, p. 13.
[3] *Id.*, p. 14.
[4] See *id.*, pp. 20–22, 102 ff., 111 ff.
[5] *Id.*, p. 22.

basis will usually be found to rest in a conviction that while one may significantly describe the law *that is*, nothing that transcends personal predilection can be said about the law *that ought to be*." [6] In his opinion, it is impossible to study and analyze the law apart from its ethical context. The legal realists, he charges, have made the same mistake as the positivists, the mistake of assuming that a rigid separation of the *is* and *ought*, of positive law and morality, is possible and desirable.[7]

In the field of purposive human activity, which includes the domain of the law, value and being are not two different things in Fuller's view, but rather, two aspects of an integral reality.[8] A purpose, he declares, is "at once a fact and a standard for judging facts." [9] This conviction has led Fuller to embrace a moderate and strongly qualified philosophy of natural law. Natural law, he maintains, rightly denies the possibility of a rigid separation of the *is* and the *ought* in legal discussion.[10] The central aim of natural law is the search for those principles of social order which will enable men to attain a satisfactory life in common. Men must in a collaborative effort attempt to articulate the purposes and social aims which they share and to discern the means for achieving them.[11]

Fuller maintains that the search for the principles of successful human living must always remain open and unshackled. He rejects the notion of natural law as a body of authoritative "higher-law" axioms against which human enactments must be measured. No natural law theory can be accepted, he insists, that attempts to lay down in advance an eternal, unchanging code of nature.[12]

Because of widespread association of the term "natural law" with doctrinaire and absolutist philosophies of law and ethics, Fuller recommends that a new name be used for an old phenomenon. He suggests the term "eunomics," which he defines as "the theory or study of good order and workable arrangements." [13] He warns that eunomics must

---

[6] Fuller, *The Law in Quest of Itself* (Chicago, 1940), p. 5.

[7] *Id.*, p. 60.

[8] *Id.*, p. 11. See also Fuller, "Human Purpose and Natural Law," 3 *Nat. L. For.* 68, at 69 ff. (1958). For a criticism of Fuller's views see Ernest Nagel, "On the Fusion of Fact and Value," 3 *Nat. L. For.* 77 (1958) and "Fact, Value, and Human Purpose," 4 *Nat. L. For.* 26 (1959).

[9] Fuller, "American Legal Philosophy at Mid-Century," 6 *J. Leg. Ed.* 457, at 470 (1954).

[10] *Op. cit. supra* n. 6, p. 5. For a critical discussion of this view of natural law see Jerome Hall, "Reason and Reality in Jurisprudence," 7 *Buffalo Law Review* 351, at 365–368 (1958)

[11] Fuller, "A Rejoinder to Professor Nagel," 3 *Nat. L. For.* 83, at 84 (1958). Cf. also Fuller, "Positivism and Fidelity to Law," 71 *Harv. L. Rev.* 630, at 660 (1958).

[12] "A Rejoinder to Professor Nagel," p. 84; (1958); *op. cit. supra*, n. 9, p. 473.

[13] *Id.*, p. 477

not attempt to teach any orthodoxy or doctrine of binding ultimate ends, but must see its task primarily in furnishing a doctrine of the *means* which the legal order must employ to attain the aims of a certain form of social organization.[14] However, it may go beyond such concern for the means aspects of social ends and attempt to demonstrate scientifically that there exist unattainable social goals for which no practicable and manageable legal forms can be devised. Fuller believes that there are some constancies and regularities in man's nature which impose limitations upon the desire of legal utopians and social engineers to create radically novel forms of society.[15]

Jerome Hall (b. 1901) is deeply concerned with the question of whether rationality and morality are "of the essence" in law, and his answer to the question is affirmative. He advocates the adoption of a restrictive definition of positive law which would limit the term to "actual ethical power norms" and exclude "sheer power norms." [16] He is convinced that there may be norms enacted by the state which lack the quality of law because they are entirely devoid of ethical content. In an attempt to lay the foundations for a democratic natural law, Hall proposes that the democratic ideal should be included in the essence of our positive law. "Especially, we include therein the 'consent of the governed' and all that that implies in the context of the democratic process. That is the fundamental correction which must be made in the traditional Natural Law theories of positive law." [17]

Law, in Hall's view, is a "distinctive coalescence of form, value, and fact." [18] The value component of law, he points out, is not merely an expression of subjective desires and personal interests, but lends itself to rational analysis. "People sometimes act against their desires and sacrifice their interests because they decide to do the right thing. The

---

[14] *Id.*, p. 478. Fuller realizes, however, that there is a close interaction between means and ends, and that the means chosen may affect the content of the ends. *Id.*, p. 480 and Fuller, *op. cit. supra* n. 8, pp. 72 ff. On this phase of Fuller's thought see the critical discussions by A. P. d'Entrèves, "The Case of Natural Law Re-Examined," 1 *Nat. L. For.* 5, at 31–32 (1956) and Joseph P. Witherspoon, "The Relation of Philosophy to Jurisprudence," 3 *Nat. L. For.* 105, at 109 ff. (1958).

[15] *Op. cit. supra* n. 9, pp. 478, 481. Interesting observations on the notion of freedom are found in the following two articles by Fuller: "Freedom: A Suggested Analysis," 68 *Harv. L. Rev.* 1305 (1955); "Some Reflections on Legal and Economic Freedoms," 54 *Col. L. Rev.* 70 (1954).

[16] *Living Law of Democratic Society* (Indianapolis, 1949), pp. 138–139. For a refutation of legal positivism see also Hall, "Concerning the Nature of Positive Law," 58 *Yale L. J.* 545 (1949).

[17] *Living Law*, p. 85. "Consent of the governed" means to Hall the active participation of the citizens in the processes of government. *Id.*, p. 89.

[18] *Id.*, p. 131. The demand for an "integrative jurisprudence" derived by Hall from this conception of law is discussed *infra* Sec. 38.

naturalistic dogma must condemn Socrates as an idiot." [19] Under the skeptical theory of value judgments, "expressions of delight when witnessing a murder would be just as rational as expressions of intense anger directed at someone who had just risked his life to rescue a drowning child." [20] The fact that it is sometimes very difficult to solve a moral problem does not justify the conclusion that objectivity in valuation is impossible or that justice is, in the words of Kelsen, an "irrational ideal." [21]

Filmer Northrop (b. 1893) agrees with Hall that an evaluative science of the law is possible.[22] According to him, a scientifically meaningful evaluation of legal norms ought to be undertaken on two different levels. First of all, the positive law enacted by the state should be tested with respect to its conformity with the living law of a people or culture. Only a positive law which meets the social and legal needs of the people and is, in general, accepted and acted upon by them can function as an effective legal system.[23] The living laws of nations or groupings of nations in this world, Northrop points out, are not uniform, but pluralistic and widely divergent. This does not mean that the sociological "is" of a culture constitutes the ultimate test for the goodness or badness of its legal system. "The normative ideal for judging today's human behavior and cultural institutions cannot be the de facto 'is' of that human behavior and those social institutions; otherwise the status quo would be perfect and reform and reconstruction would be unnecessary." [24] The criterion of virtue and sin for culture and cultural man, according to him, is the truth or falsity of the philosophy of nature and natural man underlying a culture.[25] This philosophy of nature and natural man is identified by Northrop with natural law, which in his view includes "the introspected or sensed raw data, antecedent to all theory and all cultures, given in anyone's experience in any culture." [26] Ethics, he argues, is nothing but empirically verified natural philosophy applied to human conduct and relations. The ethical principles on the basis of which the Hitler government operated must be

[19] Id., p. 69.
[20] Ibid.
[21] Id., p. 76. Cf. supra Sec. 26.
[22] F. S. C. Northrop, The Complexity of Legal and Ethical Experience (Boston, 1959), p. xi.
[23] Id., pp. 15, 41. Northrop finds himself with respect to this point in agreement with the theories of Eugen Ehrlich, discussed supra Sec. 27.
[24] Id., p. 240.
[25] Id., pp. 155: "Cultural facts are good or bad solely because the propositions concerning natural facts from which they derive are true or false." See also id., p. 11.
[26] These facts are called "first-order facts" by Northrop, while he applies the appellation "second-order facts" to cultural elements or phenomena. Id., p. 254.

adjudged to be bad because Hitler's conduct was the consequence, in part at least, of philosophical beliefs about natural man which scientific method can demonstrate to be false.[27]

Northrop is of the opinion that the natural law of the modern world cannot be based either on the Aristotelian-Thomist conception of this law or on the natural-rights philosophy of Locke and Jefferson. It must be grounded on the conception of nature and natural man supplied by modern physics, biology, and other natural sciences (including psychology). Northrop insists that the building of an effective international law to secure the survival of mankind must of necessity be predicated on the scientific foundations with which this theory of natural law may provide us. Only a truly universal natural law can, in the long run, mitigate and alleviate the hostility and tensions engendered by the living law pluralism of the present world and bring about that modicum of mutual understanding between peoples which is indispensable to world peace.[28] The "dying legal science" of positivism, with its emphasis on legal force and power politics, is inadequate, in his opinion, to furnish us with the tools and the inspiration needed to cope with the momentous problems which the atomic age has thrust upon mankind.[29]

In Western Europe and in Latin America, the modern philosophical movements known as phenomenology and existentialism have to some extent drawn the philosophy of law into their orbit. These developments will not be traced here in detail.[30] Only the views of two legal thinkers who were influenced by these movements will be discussed. The first is Luis Recaséns Siches (b. 1903), an influential Mexican professor of jurisprudence. Recaséns Siches believes, with the German philosophers Max Scheler and Nicolai Hartmann, that values are ideal objects which do not exist in space and time but which can nonetheless claim an objective and a priori validity.[31] Values such as truth, good-

[27] See *id.*, pp. 244–246.

[28] Northrop, "Contemporary Jurisprudence and International Law," 61 *Yale L. J.* 623, at 650 ff. (1952).

[29] *Id.*, p. 654. See also *op. cit. supra* n. 22, pp. 18, 252. On Northrop see also my review in 108 *U. Pa. L. Rev.* 930 (1960).

[30] Reference is made to Alfred Verdross, *Abendländische Rechtsphilosophie* (Vienna, 1958), pp. 190–195, 213–220. On phenomenology and existentialism in general see B. A. G. Fuller and Sterling McMurrin, *A History of Philosophy*, 3d ed. (New York, 1955), II, 549–556, 603–612. Contradictory accounts of the impact of existentialist philosophy on jurisprudence are given by Hans Welzel, *Naturrecht und Materiale Gerechtigkeit* (Göttingen, 1951), pp. 187–195, and Erich Fechner, *Rechtsphilosophie: Soziologie und Metaphysik des Rechts* (Tübingen, 1956), pp. 223–263.

[31] See Max Scheler, *Der Formalismus in der Ethik und die Materiale Wertethik*, 3d ed. (Halle, 1927); Nicolai Hartmann, *Ethics*, transl. S. Coit (London, 1932).

ness, beauty, justice, and security belong to this realm of ideal things; they are not given to us through experience or sense perception, but contact with them is made through intuitive processes. Man is a citizen of two worlds, the world of nature and the world of values, and he endeavors to build a bridge between these two worlds.[32]

The law, according to Recaséns Siches, is not in itself a pure value but is a system of norms designed to realize certain values. Its primary purpose is to achieve security in the collective life; men created law because they wanted to have certainty and protection for their personal and property relationships. But while Recaséns Siches regards security as the primary aim of the law and the chief reason for its existence, it is not to him its supreme end. The highest and ultimate goal of the law is the realization of justice. However, while security and inviolable regularity are part of the very concept of law, this is not true of justice.[33] If the legal order does not represent an order of security, then it is not law of any sort; but an unjust law is nevertheless a law.

It is the task of juridical valuation, according to Recaséns Siches, to find the criteria of value which should be taken into account in molding the content of the positive law. He believes that the supreme value which ought to inspire all lawmaking is the protection of the individual person. He emphatically rejects the philosophies of transpersonalism and collectivism, which see in man an instrument to produce works of culture or to serve the ends of the state.[34] To him, the function of law is to guarantee liberty, personal inviolability, and a minimum of material comfort to the individual, so that he can develop his own personality and fulfill his "authentic" mission.[35]

Like Recaséns Siches, the German jurist Helmut Coing (b. 1912) grounds his philosophy of law on an individualistic attitude toward life. But unlike Recaséns Siches, Coing attempts to develop an elaborate natural-law theory inspired by liberal ideals. The dignity of the human being and his freedom, Coing says, is an absolute value anterior to the law.[36] If an acute conflict should arise between freedom and the principles of social justice, freedom as the highest value of the legal

---

[32] Luis Recaséns Siches, "Human Life, Society, and Law," ed. J. L. Kunz, transl. G. Ireland, in *Latin-American Legal Philosophy* (Cambridge, Mass., 1948), pp. 18–26, 39.   [33] *Id.*, pp. 118–123.

[34] *Id.*, pp. 320 ff. See in this connection the discussion of Radbruch's philosophy of law *supra* Sec. 33.

[35] *Id.*, pp. 328–329, 340. In this emphasis on personalism and individual unique destiny as the supreme values of human life, the influence of existentialist philosophy (Jaspers, Heidegger) is noticeable.

[36] *Grundzüge der Rechtsphilosophie* (Berlin, 1950), p. 136.

order must be given preference.[37] Consistent with this basic assumption, the core of Coing's natural law doctrine is formed by a catalogue of natural rights reflecting and recognizing the dignity of the human personality. These fundamental rights include bodily integrity, private property, privacy, protection of one's reputation, free speech and assembly, education, protection against fraud, chicanery, and overreaching, and others.[38] Coing concedes that these "supreme principles of law" cannot be hypostatized into illimitable absolutes. They are subject to some restrictions necessary to promote the general welfare, but their essential substance may not be touched.

Any theory of law which assumes the existence of a suprapositive body of legal principles must come to grips with the problem of conflicts between the "supreme" and the positive law. Coing takes the position that a statute enacted by the state which violates a "supreme principle of law" is not void, but justifies, in extreme cases, active or passive resistance on the part of the people or the law-enforcing authorities. As far as the position of the judiciary in such a conflict is concerned, Coing believes that the judge, if confronted with an insoluble conflict between a positive law and a supreme principle of just law, must give preference to the latter or, as an alternative, lay down his mandate.[39]

Section 38. *Concluding Observations*

In the preceding chapters, some expanses of the jurisprudential universe have been traversed, while others have remained unexplored. Although only a fraction of the innumerable legal theories advanced by thinkers since the early days of civilization have been discussed, a great number of heterogeneous and conflicting views of the law have crossed our path. No substantial amount of agreement seems to have been reached by the legal philosophers as to the ends to be achieved by legal control and the means by which such control ought to be exercised. Must we, then, despair of discerning the ultimate truth concerning the law and give up the search for the ideas and principles which should

---

[37] *Id.*, pp. 222–223.

[38] Coing, *Die Obersten Grundsätze des Rechts* (Heidelberg, 1947), pp. 64 ff.; *op. cit. supra* n. 36, pp. 170 ff.

[39] *Op. cit. supra* n. 38, pp. 59–61; *op. cit. supra* n. 36, pp. 167–169, 257–258.

The revival of natural-law jurisprudence in post-Hitler Germany, of which Coing's writings are symptomatic, is discussed in Edgar Bodenheimer, "Significant Developments in German Legal Philosophy since 1945," 3 *American Journal of Comparative Law* 379 (1954); Heinrich Rommen, "Natural Law in Decisions of the Federal Supreme Court and the Constitutional Courts of Germany," 4 *Nat. L. For.* 1 (1959); Ernst von Hippel, Note, *id.*, p. 106.

guide the administration of justice? Is it possible for the jurisprudential scholar to do more than express a merely personal preference for some legal ideal that has caught his imagination and appeals to his emotions? Is there any rational thread running through the perplexing multitude of legal theories which were reviewed in the preceding chapters?

It may be observed that the large majority of these legal theories were normative in character in the sense that they were concerned with the paramount objectives to be pursued by social control through law. In other words, they dealt with the "ought" rather than with the "is" of the legal life. This characterization would be applicable to most theories of natural law, to the philosophy of transcendental idealism, to utilitarianism, and to certain versions of sociological jurisprudence. A colorful variety of standpoints were propagated by these diverse schools of jurisprudence with respect to the proper goals and ends of legal regulation. Equality, freedom, conformity to nature or God's will, happiness, social harmony and solidarity, the common good, security, promotion of culture—all of these and some others have at various times and by various thinkers been proclaimed as the supreme values of the law.[1] Is there any possibility of making a rational choice between these seemingly inconsistent views? Or must we conclude that these points of view signify nothing but the subjective and irrational predilections of their authors, with the consequence that no objective validity can be attributed to them?

On more sustained consideration, the picture does not appear to be as black as would seem to be true at first sight. If we accept the thesis that "truth is the summation of man's experience at any given moment," [2] and that the truth of the past may reveal itself to us as a partial and incomplete truth in the light of our new and wider experience, we shall gain a better perspective for appraising the history and present status of legal philosophy than if we pursue this task on the assumption of the nonrational character of valuation. The law is a large mansion with many halls, rooms, nooks, and corners. It is extremely hard to illuminate with a searchlight every room, nook, and corner at the same time, and this is especially true when the system of illumination, because of limitations of technological knowledge and experience, is inadequate, or at least imperfect. Instead of maintaining with the logical positivists that most of the historical philosophies of law must be branded as "nonsense" from a scientific point of view,[3] it would seem to be much more appropriate to argue that the most

---

[1] See the instructive list of "top values" in Arnold Brecht, *Political Theory* (Princeton, 1959), pp. 303–304.

[2] Hyman Levy, *A Philosophy for a Modern Man* (New York, 1938), p. 309.

[3] See *supra* Sec. 24.

significant of these philosophies form valuable building stones in the
total edifice of jurisprudence, even though each of these theories represents only a partial and limited truth. As the range of our knowledge
increases, we must attempt to construct a synthetic jurisprudence
which utilizes all of the numerous contributions of the past, even
though we may find in the end that our picture of the institution of
law in its totality must necessarily remain incomplete.

Proceeding from similar methodological and epistemological premises, Jerome Hall has made a strong plea for present-day scholastic
efforts to create an "integrative jurisprudence." [4] He has castigated
the "particularistic fallacy" in jurisprudence, especially the attempt to
separate from one another value elements, factual elements, and form
elements in legal theory. What is needed today, in the opinion of Hall,
is an integration of analytical jurisprudence, realistic interpretations
of social and cultural facts, and the valuable ingredients of natural-law
doctrine. All of these divisions of jurisprudence are intimately related
to, and dependent on, one another.[5] In Germany, the legal philosopher
Erich Fechner, in pursuance of similar aims, has made a worthwhile
attempt to trace the influence of numerous "ideal" and "real" factors
upon the development of the law and to demonstrate the connections
and interrelations between these multifarious elements of the legal
order.[6]

Such ideas and efforts should be deemed sound and constructive.
Our historical experience has taught us that it is impossible to explain
the institution of law in terms of any one single, absolute factor or
cause. A number of social, economic, psychological, historical, and
cultural components as well as a number of value judgments influence
and condition the making and administration of the law. Although a
certain social force or ideal of justice may exert a particularly strong
impact upon a legal system at a particular period of history, it is impossible to analyze and explain legal control generally, either in terms
of one exclusive sociological factor (such as power, national heritage,
economics, psychology, or race) or in terms of one exclusive legal
ideal (such as liberty, equality, security, or human happiness). The
law is a complicated web, and it is the task of the science of jurisprudence to pull together the various strands which go into the making of
this intricate fabric. Inasmuch as this task is one of immense dimensions
and difficulties, a certain division of labor among jurisprudential schol-

[4] Hall, "Integrative Jurisprudence," in *Studies in Jurisprudence and Criminal
Theory* (New York, 1958), pp. 25–47; see also Hall, "Reason and Reality in Jurisprudence," 7 *Buffalo L. Rev.* 351, at 388–403 (1958). On Hall see also *supra* Sec. 37.
[5] Hall, "Integrative Jurisprudence," p. 44.
[6] Fechner, *Rechtsphilosophie: Soziologie und Metaphysik des Rechts.*

ars becomes an inescapable necessity for a proper performance of the
task.

A few examples will suffice to exemplify the partial usefulness as
well as the over-all inadequacy of single-track, one-dimensional theories of law. As far as the ends of legal control are concerned, it is becoming increasingly clear that equality, freedom, security, and the
common good ought not to be hypostatized into absolutes which,
singly and in isolation, figure as ultimate and exclusive legal ideals. All
of these values, in combination and reciprocal dependence, must find
their proper place in the building of a mature and developed legal
system.[7] It would likewise be one-sided to contend that either reason
as such or experience alone should be the lodestar guiding the administration of justice. As Pound has aptly stated, in the life of the law
"reason has its part as well as experience. Jurists work out the jural
postulates, the presuppositions as to relations and conduct, of civilized
society in the time and place, and arrive in this way at authoritative
starting points for legal reasoning. Experience is developed by reason
on this basis, and reason is tested by experience." [8]

The historical school of law has made a significant contribution to
legal knowledge by teaching that the national genius of a people may
have its share in the creation of a great legal system.[9] It can hardly be
denied, for example, that the Romans possessed a capacity for building
a legal order characterized by rationality and coherence, which the
Greeks, another gifted nation, lacked in considerable measure. English
practical judgment and an intuitive sense for the exigencies of concrete situations contributed to the growth of the only legal system
which was destined to become a true rival of the Roman law. The
historical school erred, on the other hand, when it elevated national
consciousness and peculiar national traits to the rank of the principal
moving force in legal evolution. The historical school cannot adequately explain why Roman law, several centuries after its decline in
the world of antiquity, was revived in a new and different civilization.
Nor can the historical school account for the fact that the legal systems of Germany and Switzerland were transplanted to countries like
Turkey and Japan and were made to work satisfactorily in those countries. These shortcomings of the historical view stem from an insufficient appreciation of the rational element in law, an element which
makes it possible for one nation to utilize the legal system of another if
this system is well constructed and serves the economic and social

[7] This position will be elaborated in Part II.
[8] Roscoe Pound, *Social Control through Law* (New Haven, 1942), p. 112.
[9] See *supra* Sec. 18.

needs of the adopting nation. A truly great legal system will have qualities which raise it above the limitations of national traits and render it, at least in some measure, universal in spirit and practical value.

The Marxian doctrine of law, according to which the productive system of a society forms the substructure and base of its legal system, has demonstrated the close relation which exists between economics and law.[10] But this doctrine has paid insufficient attention to other elements of legal evolution. Power relations, basic biological facts, ethnological data, religious convictions, ideologies and value systems, and, last but not least, the plain dictates of reason must also be assigned their proper place in an adequate sociological analysis of the institution of law.[11] Furthermore, the Marxian doctrine has attributed a wholly disproportionate weight to the class aspects of legal control and has underemphasized the fact that the law very frequently represents an accommodation and adjustment of conflicting group interests.[12]

The positivist view, which identifies law with the commands of the sovereign, has brought to light a characteristic of law in the modern nation-state that can by no means be ignored. In its analytical version, positivism has also made us aware of the fact that a careful elucidation of legal conceptions from a technical-dogmatic point of view may beneficially affect the clarity and consistency of the legal order. On the other hand, the tendency of analytical positivism to divorce law from its psychological, ethical, economic, and social foundations, carried to an extreme by Hans Kelsen,[13] has imparted to us a misleading perspective with respect to the degree of autonomy and self-sufficiency that can be achieved by a legal system. We have to recognize that law cannot thrive in a hermetically sealed container, and that it cannot be blocked off from the nonlegal life around it without harmful consequences for the legal system.[14]

Furthermore, analytical positivism, especially in the form in which it was cast by Kelsen's Pure Theory of Law, has greatly exaggerated the character of law as a system of external compulsion. It has failed to give sufficient recognition to the observation of Hermann Heller, a German teacher of public law, that "in order to secure its power and the foundations of the social order, no government can rely solely on its compulsive apparatus. It must always strive for legitimization, i.e.

[10] See *supra* Sec. 21.
[11] See Fechner, pp. 53–111.
[12] See Pound, *Interpretations of Legal History* (Cambridge, Mass., 1930), pp. 92–115.
[13] On Kelsen see *supra* Sec. 26.
[14] See *infra* Sec. 43.

it must attempt to incorporate the citizens into a community of will and values ready to respect its claim to power; it must also try to justify this claim to power by adherence to ideals, and to secure the inner acceptance of this claim by the subjects in the form of a recognition of normative duties."[15] When the legal sociologist N. S. Timasheff described law as "ethico-imperative coordination," he was referring to the fact that in any workable legal system there is a combination of organized power and group conviction for the purpose of securing effective realization of certain patterns of conduct.[16] It is quite wrong to overaccentuate the power element and to underrate the ethical and societal components in law.

Legal realism in its various versions has had the merit of correcting the one-sided normative and often conceptualist orientation of analytical jurisprudence by calling our attention to the frequent intrusion of subjective-emotional elements and environmental predispositions into the adjudicatory processes.[17] But legal realism has tended to give an insufficient weight to the role of legal rules and legal doctrine in the practical life of the law. It has sometimes (especially in the theories of Jerome Frank) offered to us an overdrawn picture of judicial arbitrariness and cadi justice, and it has failed to provide us with a blueprint for maintaining that degree of rationality and consistency of law which is within the human powers of achievement.

Most unfortunate has been the overskeptical attitude exhibited toward the ultimate values of the legal order by certain representatives of positivism and legal realism, most notably by Hans Kelsen and Alf Ross.[18] Both of these men have regarded the problem of justice as a pseudoproblem, incapable of being intelligently approached by any effort at rational analysis. According to Ross, for example, the words "just" and "unjust" are entirely devoid of meaning for purposes of evaluating a legal rule or legal order. "Justice is no guide for the legislator."[19]

In reality, the problem of achieving justice in human relations is the most challenging and vital problem of social control through law, and it is one that is by no means impervious to the method of rational argument.[20] The use of this method does not demand unanimity or uni-

---

[15] *Staatslehre* (Leiden, 1934), pp. 87–88. On this problem see also *infra* Sec. 54.
[16] See *An Introduction to the Sociology of Law* (Cambridge, Mass., 1939), pp. 15, 245–248.
[17] See *supra* Secs. 31 and 32.
[18] See *supra* Secs. 26 and 32.
[19] Alf Ross, *On Law and Justice* (Berkeley, 1959), p. 274.
[20] The connection between justice and rationality is discussed *infra* Sec. 45. On the problem of rationality in ethical science see also Morris R. Cohen, *Reason and Nature* (Glencoe, Ill., 1931), pp. 438–449.

versality in the reaching of conclusions concerning the justice of a legal measure. It only demands that the problem be approached with detachment and broadmindedness, and that the relevant issues be appraised from all angles, with consideration of the interests and concerns of all people or groups affected by the regulation. An important guide for the rational evaluation of the justice of a law or set of laws is furnished by the status of our scientific knowledge with respect to the psychological, biological, or social assumptions underlying a piece of legal regulation.[21] No law dealing with racial relations, for example, can be just if it rests on a racial theory which the most advanced findings of biological science have demonstrated to be untenable.

The search for justice is unending and beset with many difficulties. It is, on the other hand, aided by certain objectively verifiable factors, such as the existence of cultural uniformities of valuation which draw their roots chiefly from the fact that affirmation of life strongly preponderates over life-negation in the history of the human race.[22] There is no reason for the jurisprudential scholar to shy away from probing into the foundations of a just legal order, even though the task may necessitate side excursions into the field of philosophical anthropology and other nonlegal disciplines. Concern for the "good society" cannot be disavowed by social science, and it should not be relegated by it to the politicians and legislators preoccupied with the pressing practical problems of the day. If the search for justice and reasonableness in law is abandoned by the best minds on the grounds that justice is a meaningless, chimerical, and irrational notion, then there is danger that the human race will fall back into a condition of barbarism and ignorance where unreason will prevail over rationality, and where the dark forces of prejudice may win the battle over humanitarian ideals and the forces of good will and benevolence.

There is one further comment to be made on the one-sidedness of many legal theories of the past. A partial explanation of this shortcoming must be sought in the historical conditions of their origin. Every historical epoch faces certain major problems of social control that require the resourcefulness of the best minds for solution. Many of the absolutist philosophies of law with which we have become acquainted represent attempts on the part of legal thinkers to call the attention of their contemporaries, perhaps in overdramatized fashion, to certain acute and burning problems of their day. Thus, in an era in which inequality in the social order was very marked and led to strong

[21] On the relationship between justice and truth see Brecht, pp. 404–416.
[22] See *infra* Sec. 46 and Edgar Bodenheimer, "The Province of Jurisprudence," 46 *Corn. L. Q.* 1 (1960).

discontent threatening the foundations of society, the stress in the legal philosophy of perceptive thinkers was laid on the need for greater equality, although apologists of the *status quo* were not absent from the scene. In a social order endangered by chaos and anarchy, emphasis on order and legal security must be expected, as evidenced by the legal philosophy of Thomas Hobbes. An age of political absolutism may tend to accentuate, within the limits set by political control or even in disregard of these limits, the antidespotic elements in the law.

It is not possible to overcome the limitations of these precedents altogether. Following this historical introduction, no attempt will be made to delve into all of the numerous subjects and issues which may properly be said to fall into the domain of jurisprudence. In accordance with an almost universal tradition, dictated perhaps by necessity, a selective approach to the problems of jurisprudence will be chosen. Although a strong endeavor will be made to avoid one-sidedness and dogmatism in the presentation, the focus of the inquiry will be centered on those aspects and characteristics of the law which seem to warrant special attention and privileged consideration in our own time.

PART II

THE NATURE

AND FUNCTIONS

OF THE LAW

X

THE NEED FOR ORDER

Section 39. *The Prevalence of Orderly Patterns in Nature*
The institution of law is closely related to man's perennial search for
order, regularity, and fixity in human social relations. Although, as we
shall see later,[1] law by no means exhausts its significance in the quest
for the realization of order, its functions and aims in society cannot be
understood in isolation from this fundamental striving of human beings. Wherever men have created units of social organization, they
have attempted to avoid unregulated chaos and to establish some form
of a livable order.

This striving for orderly patterns in human coexistence is not an
arbitrary or dispensable trait of human beings. It is deeply rooted in
the whole fabric of nature, of which human life is a part. Nature exhibits approximate uniformities, repeated sequences, recurrent associations of events. At least in those manifestations of external nature
which affect human life on this planet most significantly and decisively,
order appears to prevail over disorder, regularity over deviation, rule
over exception. Our earth follows its course around the sun in a fixed
orbit and under conditions which have permitted the existence of life

[1] See *infra* Sec. 44.

for millions of years. There is a dependable alternation of seasons, enabling men, during the food-producing seasons, to provide and store for the times of the year in which the soil is barren. The elements of the physical universe, such as water, fire, and chemical substances, have certain more or less unvarying characteristics which permit us to rely on their permanent properties and to predict their effects in utilizing them for human purposes. Our entire control of nature is predicated on the existence of a number of determinate, often mathematically calculable, physical laws on whose uniform operation we rely in building tunnels, navigating ships and airplanes, controlling floods, and harnessing electricity for industrial and other purposes. The physical processes of living beings are likewise subject to a number of laws. The normal metabolism of the human body, for instance, takes place according to an orderly system whereby only as many cells are produced as are required for the replacement of worn-out or damaged ones. Most illnesses show typical symptoms and follow characteristic courses; if this were not true, all medical therapy would rest on guesswork or on purely fortuitous success in treatment.

It is conceivable, on the other hand, that the normal "lawfulness" of natural events is subject to exceptions, or breakdowns in the orderly movements of nature. While such breakdowns may themselves come about through the operation of certain hitherto undiscovered laws, they appear to our incomplete understanding as cataclysmic events upsetting the normal order of things. Whole species of living creatures, like the Saurians of prehistoric times, have become extinct without a clearly ascertainable cause. The metabolic mechanisms of the living body may be disrupted by the disorderly, wasteful growth of cancerous tissue, which ignores all normal bounds. Illnesses that defy classification may befall the human body, or known forms of sickness may take an unusual and unforeseeable course which sets at naught long-established therapies and well-tested cures. We cannot even reject as wholly unimaginable the notion that, over a span of many millennia, the laws of nature themselves may be subject to change.

As long as the irregular and totally unpredictable occurrences in nature do not predominate over the recurrent regularity of physical phenomena, human beings are able to plan their lives in reliance on the foreseeable course of events. In order to visualize what the effect of the opposite state of affairs would be, one need only contemplate a general suspension of the laws of gravitation (with the result that matter would freely move around in space in all imaginable directions), or an interruption of the regular orbit of our planet (with the result that it would aimlessly roam around in space, perhaps colliding with other celestial bodies, or becoming removed from its life-sustaining source, the sun).[2] These examples show that the predominant regularity of the processes of nature is deeply beneficial to human life. In its absence, we would be living in a mad and deranged world, in which we would be tossed around like puppets by a whimsical and wholly uncontrollable fate. All human attempts to lead a rational, meaningful, and purposive life would be thwarted and frustrated in a chaotic universe.

It would seem that the foregoing account of lawfulness in nature does not depend for its correctness on the ultimate outcome and solution of a controversy which is waged among the natural scientists of our day. There is a group of physicists who believe that, in the light of the findings embodied in quantum mechanics and Heisenberg's principle of uncertainty, physical laws lack the element of inexorable certainty and uniformity which was ascribed to them by classical physics, and that they must be viewed merely as statistical or probability laws. According to this view, undetermined chance governs the behavior of the finer particles of nature, and law arises only statistically in mass phenomena owing to the cooperation of a myriad of chances at play in these phenomena.[3] Another group of scientists, on the other hand, maintains that the notion of strictly determined causality ought to be upheld in modern physics, and that apparent instances of lawless or acausal behavior in nature seem so only because of our imperfect understanding of its ways. It is assumed that the behavior of each elementary particle of nature is in every instance strictly determined, and that what we apprehend as "chance" is the cooperation of innumerable partial causes which cannot be completely perceived by our inadequate mental equipment and research instruments; thus chance, according to this view, is something wholly subjective—a name for our inability to understand the interplay of numerous small component causes and to predict the outcome of their intricate interactions with certainty.[4]

[2] Amusing illustrations of what a discontinuous and lawless universe might look like are found in Henry Drummond, *Natural Law in the Spiritual World* (New York, 1889), pp. 38–39.

[3] Erwin Schrödinger, *Science and the Human Temperament*, transl. J. Murphy and W. H. Johnston (New York, 1935), pp. 41 ff., 143 ff.; Niels Bohr, *Atomic Theory and the Description of Nature* (New York, 1934), p. 4; Bertrand Russell, *Philosophy* (New York, 1927), p. 294; Hermann Weyl, *The Open World* (New Haven, 1932), pp. 46–48, 51.

[4] Max Planck, *Where Is Science Going* (New York, 1932), pp. 99 ff. Planck says, on page 100: "I have not been able to find the slightest reason up to now, which would force us to give up the assumption of a strictly law-governed universe, whether it is a matter of trying to discover the nature of the physical or the spiritual forces around us." See also prologue by Albert Einstein, *id.*, p. 11; F. S. C.

Even if we accept the former view, the "statistical" theory of physical laws, according to which absolute determinism must give way to the assumption of noncausal occurrences in nature, the predominantly law-governed character of at least all large-scale operations of nature must still be admitted. While chance and unpredictability may govern the behavior of individual electrons and atoms, the action of large aggregates of elementary particles will generally be subject to a predictable course; departures from law will mostly be small and infrequent.[5] The foes of a deterministic theory of nature are quite willing to concede that gravitational and electrodynamic phenomena, as well as energy and momentum principles, lend themselves to extraordinary accuracy in forecasting future occurrences.[6] Thus even if absolute determinism is denied, even if "nature exhibits loopholes in its uniformity and inflexibility," [7] causal laws indicating regularity and uniformity in the operation of nature still remain in effect on a wide scale.

Section 40. *Order in Human Individual and Social Life*
As in nature, order plays a significant role in the life of human beings. Most people follow certain habits in the conduct of their lives and organize their work and leisure time in a certain way. There exists, of course, also the "bohemian" type of man who disdains the pedantic orderliness of the "bourgeois" and prides himself on the spontaneity and unregulated impulsiveness of his mode of life. Some great creative artists have preferred this "romantic" way of existence to the planned and often routine activities of the average citizen. But there is little doubt that the wholly "bohemian" conduct of life is and always has been the exception rather than the rule.[1]

In family life, too, certain patterns or customary ways are usually observed by the members of the family group. Meals are taken at certain hours; some chores are assigned to certain members of the family; some time is set aside for common family activities. Such family order

---

Northrop, *The Logic of the Sciences and the Humanities* (New York, 1947), ch. xi; Henry Margenau, *The Nature of Physical Reality* (New York, 1950), p. 420.

[5] Schrödinger, p. 45; Friedrich Weismann, "Verifiability," in *Essays on Logic and Language,* ed. A. Flew (New York, 1951), p. 131. See also A. C. Benjamin, *An Introduction to the Philosophy of Science* (New York, 1937), p. 376.

[6] Schrödinger, pp. 145–146.

[7] Jerome Frank, *Fate and Freedom* (New York, 1945), p. 145, who is inclined to magnify the element of chance and "free will" in nature. See in this connection also Frank, " 'Short of Sickness and Death': A Study of Moral Responsibility in Legal Criticism," 26 *New York University Law Review* 545, at 618 (1951).

[1] It might also be mentioned in this connection that the enjoyment of music is usually enhanced by its rhythmical character—another manifestation of the human proclivity for regularity.

not only prepares the children for the highly organized and regulated activities of professional, commercial, and industrial life in modern society, but also represents an important demand of economy, since a constant reshuffling and rearrangement of family schedules would be a time-consuming and wasteful affair. A certain amount of ordering and scheduling is probably found in the majority of all family groups.

Even in aggregations of men haphazardly thrown together, there is a strong tendency to resort to orderly forms of organization. It has been observed, for example, that prisoners of war will rapidly establish some rules of conduct to govern life in the camp, sometimes without any intervention on the part of the camp administration.[2] Shipwrecked people cast ashore on an uninhabited island will almost immediately proceed to set up some improvised system of "government" and "law."

Society as a whole, depending upon the coexistence and cooperation of many different individuals and groups, is in even greater need of organization and "pattern." Societies have undertaken to regulate sexual relations and to determine the basic structure of family entities. They have allocated property rights to individuals, groups, or collective units. They have punished certain palpable manifestations of antisocial conduct, such as murder, rape, and other severe crimes of violence. They have often lent uniformity and direction to political and legal action by the adoption of a "basic law" defining the fundamental elements of the political and social system. As societies progress and become more populous, diversified, and complex, the measure of regulatory social control tends to increase and intensify. In a modern civilized state, the number of official and unofficial prescriptions designed to insure a smooth and ordered running of the major social processes is exceedingly large.

Without some degree of regulation by means of legal institutions, life in society would hardly be tolerable.[3] If human actions were subject entirely to the vicissitudes of chance, if no attempt were made to mitigate the impact of the numerous irrationalities and incalculabilities incident to human life, progress toward the higher forms of civilization would be impossible. An unregulated social life would be as unendurable as a chaotic physical universe. The totality of our psychological and historical experiences fully warrants the conclusion that some form of legal order holding human societies together is an inescapable requirement of human coexistence.

[2] See Helmut Coing, *Die Obersten Grundsätze des Rechts* (Heidelberg, 1947), p. 19.
[3] On the meaning of rationality as related to the problems of law and justice see *infra* Sec. 45.

Section 41. *Anarchy and Despotism*

There are two types of social structure characterized by the absence of institutional devices for the creation and maintenance of orderly and regular social processes. These two types are anarchy and despotism, in their pure and undiluted forms. While we hardly know of any societies which have (at least for any considerable length of time) operated on either a purely anarchic or a totally despotic basis, a consideration of these extreme or "marginal" forms of political and social existence is helpful for an understanding of the nature and functions of law as an agency of social control.

Anarchy means a social condition in which unlimited power is given to all members of the community. Where anarchy reigns, there are no obligatory rules which each individual is bound to recognize and obey. Everybody is free to follow his own impulses and to do whatever comes to his mind. No state or governnment sets limits to the arbitrary exercise of private power.[1]

Opinions differ as to how men would actually behave if states and governments were abolished and anarchy were enthroned as the legitimate form of political and social life. Men like Bakunin and Kropotkin, who adhered to a creed of collectivist anarchism, were convinced that men were essentially good by nature, and that only the state and its institutions had corrupted them. They believed that men were imbued with a deep instinct of solidarity, and that after the forcible destruction of organized governments they would be able to live together under a perfect system of freedom, peace, harmony, and cooperation. In place of the coercive state, there would exist a free association of free groups; everyone would be permitted to join the group of his choosing and to withdraw from it whenever he wished. Leo Tolstoy also believed in the possibility of a noncoercive society in which all members would be tied together by the bonds of mutual love. Cooperation and reciprocal aid, instead of ruthless competition, would become the supreme law in such a society.[2]

It is extremely unlikely, however, that the complete elimination of the state or other form of governmental constraint would bring about an undisturbed, harmonious association between men. Even if we assume that the majority of men are by nature social-minded and good,

---

[1] See the description of anarchy in Shakespeare's *Troilus and Cressida* I. iii. 116–124.

[2] A good survey of the various anarchist doctrines is given by Oscar Jásci in his article, "Anarchism," *Encyclopedia of the Social Sciences*, II, 46; see also C. E. Merriam and H. E. Barnes, *History of Political Theories (Recent Times)* (New York, 1924), pp. 197–216.

there will always be a noncooperative minority against whom coercion has to be used. A few unbalanced or criminal elements can easily disrupt a community. Recent statistics have also shown that high economic prosperity—such as envisaged by the anarchists as a foundation of their ideal society—does not in and of itself solve the problem of criminality. Irrespective of economic conditions, "men are of necessity liable to passions," [3] and even the normally rational man may, under the spell of an uncontrolled impulse, commit an act that society will not tolerate. For these reasons, a completely free, unregulated society without community sanctions appears to be impossible. Order in human affairs, unfortunately, is not self-executing.

The extreme opposite of anarchy in social life would be a political system in which one man holds an unlimited, tyrannical sway over his fellow men. If the power of this man is exercised in a totally arbitrary and capricious way, we are confronted with the phenomenon of despotism in its pure form.

The pure despot issues his commands and prohibitions in accordance with his free and unrestricted will and in response to his casual whims or passing moods. One day he will sentence a man to death because he has stolen a horse; the following day he will perhaps acquit another horse thief because the man, when brought before him, tells an amusing story. The favorite courtier may suddenly find himself in jail because he has beaten the pasha at a chess game, and an influential writer may suffer the unforeseen fate of being burned at the stake because he has written a few sentences displeasing to the ruler. The actions of the pure despot are unpredictable because they follow no rational pattern and are not governed by ascertainable rules or policies.

Most of the historically known forms of despotism have not exhibited these extreme features of a purely arbitrary rule because firmly ingrained community or class customs ordinarily have been respected by the despot, and the property and family relations of private persons have usually not been disturbed. Moreover, in modern totalitarian states an "impersonal" ideological element is introduced into the social structure which slightly mitigates its arbitrary character and makes possible a limited amount of prediction of official action in the light of general policies announced beforehand. In Soviet Russia after the Revolution of 1917 a despotic power was exercised for the purpose of liquidating the bourgeoisie and promoting the revolution of the proletariat. In Fascist Italy, undiluted power was exercised for the glory and aggrandizement of the nation; in National Socialist Germany racial policies

[3] Benedict Spinoza, *Tractatus Politicus*, transl. R. H. M. Elwes (London, 1895), ch. i.5.

determined the actions of the government in many areas. It should be realized, however, that power may be arbitrary even though its holder is actuated by ideological objectives. We know as a matter of experience that in a modern totalitarian state many acts of a purely arbitrary and capricious nature are justified and sanctioned in the name of the sacred purpose. A revolutionary statute which decrees that the power given to the Soviets is to be exercised in the interests of the toiling masses and the proletarian revolution grants a practically unlimited amount of discretion to the ruling authorities. If there are no guaranties against an abuse of this discretion (such as recourse to an independent law court), the discretion is often hardly distinguishable from arbitrary power. An act done by an official for purely personal motives might easily be rationalized as having been done "in the interest of the proletarian revolution," and there would be no court that would be able to inquire into the real motives of the act. A German National Socialist statute authorizing the judge to punish "according to the healthy sentiment of the people" [4] vests in him, in the name of a general and abstract principle, a latitude which can easily be abused in an irresponsible fashion.

Instances of arbitrary rule, which to a greater or lesser degree will be found in all totalitarian states, promote a feeling of danger and insecurity among the people.

It is decisive for the behavior of the subjects within a despotic power structure that they cannot count on the behavior of the dominators as being in conformity with the general commands; for these commands do not bind their authors, and strict obedience to a general order issued yesterday may, today or tomorrow, call forth anger and revenge on the part of the dominators. Every individual must be aware of the passing whims of the dominators and try to adjust his conduct to them. Troubled and insecure must be the ordinary state of mind of the subjects in a power structure of this type.[5]

But there is a way to avoid such a condition. It is the way of the law.

Section 42. *The Normative Element in Law*

Law, being essentially a restraint upon the exercise of arbitrary power, is hostile to anarchy as well as to despotism. To avoid the anarchy of numerous conflicting wills, law limits the power of private individuals. To avoid the tyranny of an arbitrary government, law curbs the power of the ruling authorities. It seeks to maintain a mean or balance between the two extreme forms of social life which we have described

---

[4] Statute of June 28, 1935, *German Official Legal Gazette*, 1935, pt. I, p. 839.
[5] N. S. Timasheff, *Introduction to the Sociology of Law* (Cambridge, Mass., 1939), p. 216.

by introducing order and regularity into the dealings of private individuals as well as the operations of governmental organs. A complete and fully developed system of law would be equidistant from the two opposite poles of anarchy and despotism. By an effective system of private law, it would attempt to delimit the spheres of action of private individuals or groups so as to avoid or combat mutual encroachments, aggressive interferences with the liberties or possessions of others, and social strife. By an effective system of public law, it would endeavor to define and circumscribe the power of public officials in order to prevent or remedy improper tampering with guaranteed private spheres of interest and to forestall a tyrannical rule of whim. Thus, law in its purest and most perfect form would be realized in a social order in which the possibility of an arbitrary or oppressive use of power by private individuals as well as the government has been reduced to naught.[1]

The attempt of the law to introduce ordered relations into the dealings of private individuals and groups as well as into the operations of government cannot be accomplished without *norms*, generalized pronouncements relating to human actions and conduct.[2] A certain degree of generality is the hallmark of legal regulation.[3] This does not mean, however, that legal norms must apply with equal force to the whole population or to a substantial portion of it; they may apply to a narrowly limited circle of persons as long as they purport to establish patterns of conduct or frameworks of organization rather than merely to regulate single or particular situations and acts.

Although it has been asserted that "if the leader of a small community decided each case not by rules but by his subjective sense of justice, few would go so far as to say that there was no law in the community," [4] this statement cannot be accepted without qualification. If the leader's "subjective sense of justice" manifested itself in such a way as to produce uniform decisions in essentially similar cases, a nor-

---

[1] For an elaboration of the relation between power and law see *infra* Sec. 55.

[2] "Norm" is derived from the Latin word *norma*, meaning rule or yardstick.

[3] Kelsen describes the concrete command contained in a judicial decision (as distinguished from the statutory or judge-made rule applied in the case) as an "individual legal norm." See Hans Kelsen, *General Theory of Law and State*, transl. by A. Wedberg (Cambridge, Mass., 1949), p. 38; Kelsen, "The Pure Theory of Law," 51 *Law Quarterly Review* 517, at 521 (1935). This use of the term would appear to be a *contradictio in adiecto*. A norm must always contain a generalized statement. It will be shown later, however, that the legal system in a broader sense will usually contain mechanisms for the dispensation of "individual equity" in situations where the generality of the law causes unjust results. See *infra* Sec. 50. Thus, while "a law" or "norm of law" must have an element of generality, the legal order as a whole may possess agencies of individualization.

[4] George W. Paton, *A Textbook of Jurisprudence*, 2d ed. (Oxford, 1951), p. 56.

mative content would in fact have been imparted to his adjudications, and the standards of decision followed by him would soon become known to the community. If, on the other hand, the leader's subjective approach to the administration of justice resulted in irrational, whimsical, and totally unpredictable decisions, it is likely that the community would view this condition of affairs as the antithesis of an order of law. Law and arbitrariness, as we have seen, are opposites. As Sir Frederick Pollock correctly pointed out, "An exercise of merely capricious power, however great in relation to that which it acts upon, does not satisfy the general conception of law, whether it does or does not fit the words of any artificial definition. A despotic chief who paid no attention to anything but his own whim of the moment could hardly be said to administer justice even if he professed to decide the disputes of his subjects." [5]

The close connection between law and the notion of generality has often been noticed by philosophers and legal authors. "Law is always a general statement," said Aristotle.[6] Cicero emphasized that law was a *standard* by which justice and injustice are measured.[7] Several famous Roman jurists quoted in Justinian's *Corpus Juris* expressed similar opinions. Papinian described law as "a general precept." [8] Ulpian pointed out that legal prescriptions are not made for individual persons but have a general application.[9] Paul, cognizant of the normative nature of law, observed that "to that which happens only once or twice, the legislators pay no attention." [10] Jean Jacques Rousseau remarked that "the object of laws is always general." [11] Friedrich Carl von Savigny likewise emphasized the generality inherent in the concept of law.[12]

Several English and American legal thinkers have taken the same position. Thomas Hobbes understood by "civil law" those *rules* which the Commonwealth had imposed on its subjects.[13] John Austin held that only a command which "obliges *generally* to acts or forbearances of a *class*" is a law.[14] He pointed out that, if Parliament prohibited the

---

[5] Pollock, *A First Book of Jurisprudence*, 6th ed. (London, 1929), p. 34.
[6] *The Nicomachean Ethics*, transl. H. Rackham (Loeb Classical Library ed., 1947), Bk. V. x. 4. Cf. also *Politics*, transl. E. Barker (Oxford, 1946), Bk. III. 1286a.
[7] *De Legibus*, transl. C. W. Keyes (Loeb Classical Library ed., 1928), Bk. I. vi. 19.
[8] *Dig.* I. 3. 1.
[9] *Dig.* I. 3. 8.
[10] *Dig.* I. 3. 6.
[11] *The Social Contract* (Everyman's Library ed., 1913), Bk. II, ch. 6.
[12] *System des Heutigen Römischen Rechts* (Berlin, 1840), vol. I, sec. 52.
[13] *Leviathan* (Everyman's Library ed., 1914), ch. xxvi.
[14] Austin, *Lectures on Jurisprudence*, 5th ed. by R. Campbell (London, 1885), I, 96. Austin's view was followed by W. E. Hearn, *The Theory of Legal Duties and Rights* (Melbourne, 1883), p. 9.

exportation of corn, either for a given period or indefinitely, a law would be established. But an order issued by Parliament to meet an impending scarcity, stopping the exportation of corn *then shipped and in port*, would not be a law, though issued by the sovereign legislature.[15] Sir Frederick Pollock said: "The sum of such rules as existing in a given commonwealth, under whatever particular forms, is what in common speech we understand by law."[16] In the United States, a similar position was taken by James Wilson,[17] John Chipman Gray,[18] and Edwin Patterson,[19] among others.

To the extent that these definitions seek to restrict the notion of law to those general precepts and norms that have received express recognition in a formal source of the law, they may be open to challenge and criticism. It should be conceded that in all legal systems the numerous gaps in the positive law are filled by the application of general policies or social norms, which supply at least subsidiary standards for the decision of legal controversies. But such general policies or social norms possess the same distinctive trait which in the opinions of the aforementioned authors characterizes the institution of law as such. They are designed to furnish general yardsticks for shaping or judging human conduct rather than transient or particular directions for the solution of specific problems. In this sense, the nonformalized sources of law, which are indispensable to a proper administration of justice, are endowed with normative character in the same manner and to the same extent as the formal and technical rules of the law.[20]

For two chief reasons, it seems desirable to hold that the element of generality is an important ingredient of the concept of law (in the sense of a system of norms). First, this approach produces a semantic uniformity in the use of the term law.[21] In the physical sciences, the word law is reserved for the description of uniform patterns or at least

[15] Austin, I, 93. This use of terminology leads to the result that special acts of a legislature, such as granting a pension to a particular person, allowing individual exemptions from income tax laws, or deporting a designated person cannot be regarded as law in the true sense. See Edgar Bodenheimer, "Separation of Powers and the Steel Seizure," 6 *Virginia Law Weekly Dicta* 103 (1955). Some of these special acts constitute dispensations from general laws for reasons of individual equity.

[16] Pollock, p. 8.

[17] *Works*, ed. J. D. Andrews (Chicago, 1896), I, 49, 55.

[18] *The Nature and Sources of the Law*, 2d ed. (New York, 1921), pp. 84, 161.

[19] Edwin W. Patterson, *Jurisprudence* (Brooklyn, 1953), pp. 97–116.

[20] On the nonformal sources of law see *infra* Secs. 68–73.

[21] It is of interest to observe here that, as a matter of history, there was a close connection between the origins of Ionian philosophy, inaugurating the scientific description of physical laws in Western civilization, and the birth of the constitutional city-state showing the faint beginnings of the rule of law. See Werner Jaeger, *Paideia: The Ideals of Greek Culture*, 2d ed. (New York, 1945), I, 110.

statistical regularities in the operations of nature, and it is not applied to unusual events inexplicable in terms of repetitive experience. There is a great deal of merit in preserving the basic connotation of a linguistic symbol for all or most of the uses of the term. Tolstoy pointed out, "The only means for the mental intercourse of men is the word, and, to make this intercourse possible, words have to be used in such a way as to evoke in all men corresponding and exact concepts. But if it is possible to use words at random, and to understand by them anything we may think of, it is better not to speak at all but to indicate everything by signs." [22] Although this goal of semantic uniformity can seldom be reached in full measure, there appears to exist no convincing reason why the term law should be employed in the social sciences in a sense which differs very materially from its meaning in the natural sciences. We should fully concur in Justice Cardozo's statement that "as in the processes of nature, we give the name of law to *uniformity of succession*." [23]

Second, in imparting to human-made laws a meaning coterminous with that of physical laws, we not only retain consistency in the use of a linguistic term but also impress upon the mind one of the most important functional characteristics of societal law. By applying a uniform standard of adjudication to an indefinite number of equal or closely similar situations, we introduce an element of stability and coherence into the social order which guarantees internal peace and lays the groundwork for a fair and impartial administration of justice. Without this necessarily imperfect striving for stability, law cannot exist. As Morris Cohen has well said, "The law cannot abandon the effort at consistency. We must remember that the law always defeats the expectation of at least one party in every lawsuit. To maintain its prestige, in spite of that, requires such persistent and conspicuous efforts at impartiality that even the defeated party will be impressed." [24] Furthermore, because of the generality of law, "men can be enabled to predict the legal consequences of situations that have not yet been litigated, and hence can plan their conduct for a future which is thereby rendered less uncertain." [25] In a large community, where the task of adjudication is usually entrusted to a great number of

[22] "On Life," in *Complete Works of Count Tolstoy*, transl. L. Wiener (Boston, 1904), XVI, 233.
[23] Benjamin N. Cardozo, *The Growth of the Law* (New Haven, 1924), p. 40 (italics mine). See also Vernon J. Bourke, "Two Approaches to Natural Law," 1 *Natural Law Forum* 92, at 94 (1956): "(A) law always has some generality to it."
[24] Morris R. Cohen, "Law and Scientific Method," in *Law and the Social Order* (New York, 1933), p. 194.
[25] Patterson, p. 97. See also *id.*, pp. 101–106 for an account of the advantages of generality in law.

officials—whose views as to what constitutes the just and proper solution of a legal controversy may be at considerable variance—there would be great danger of capricious and subjective administration of justice in the absence of a normative system.[26]

Section 43. *The Striving of the Law*
for Independence and Autonomy

In order to endow the law with logical consistency, predictability, and stability, highly developed legal systems strive to create an autonomous apparatus of legal concepts, legal techniques, and legal norms. There prevails, at least during certain important epochs in the life of a legal system, a tendency to set up the law as a self-sufficient science, resting completely on its own foundations and insulating itself from the external influences of politics, ethics, and economics. The law during this period of its development attempts to fashion the course of its growth primarily from within and to deduce answers to legal questions as much as possible from the logic of its own notions and concepts. By building up a technical apparatus and an internal organization, creating a special caste of legal experts characterized by specialized training and knowledge, and elaborating an indigenous legal technique and method, the law seeks to guarantee and preserve its own autonomy. This does not mean that the law stands still or fails to develop and improve, but an attempt is made to make it lead a life of its own. Thus, the facts of a legal controversy are often rendered amenable to judicial cognition and analysis only after having been molded to fit the requirements of the technical system. The idea underlying this process is apparently that the law shall be freed from exposure to political or other outside pressures, immunized against dependence on fluctuating economic currents, removed from the impact of transient social trends, and armored by a protective covering against the danger of improper bias and personal administration of justice.[1] The insulation may also come in part from the inertia of those of the judiciary and the legal profession who are content to work with the tools at hand and refuse to look beyond at the world at large.

[26] The proposals by Jerome Frank for an "unblindfolding" and a greater "individualization" of justice must be assessed in the light of this danger. See Jerome Frank, *Courts on Trial* (Princeton, 1949), pp. 378 ff., 423. While Frank recognizes the desirability of general rules as pointers or guideposts, he wishes to inject a large dose of judicial discretion into all or most legal rules, making them as pliant as possible. It would seem that his approach overestimates the scope of "uniqueness" in legal controversies, although one may go along with him in recognizing the necessity for certain areas of discretion in the adjudicative process.

[1] See Rudolph von Jhering, *Der Geist des Römischen Rechts*, 2d ed. (Leipzig, 1866), vol. II, pt. 1, pp. 19 ff.

This endeavor to enthrone the law as an untouchable goddess residing in a sealed-off enclosure can be observed in certain periods of Roman as well as English legal history. As Fritz Schulz pointed out, "Private Roman law as portrayed by classical writers attains an extraordinary, almost logical, definiteness. The number of juristic conceptions which play a part in it is comparatively small, as all which pertain to special or non-Roman variations are set aside. The legal rules take on the character of apodictic truths, as any limitations imposed by public law or extra-legal duties are ignored." [2] A highly technical system of pleading was evolved during the period of the formulary procedure in Rome, with the result that the stereotyped and thoroughly formalized rules of pleading often did not comport with the demands of life and common sense.

In English law, too, some attempts to establish a "pure" system of law, characterized chiefly by the virtue of internal self-consistency, may be observed in the course of its history. As F. W. Maitland pointed out, "Our old lawyers were fond of declaring that 'the law will suffer a mischief rather than an inconvenience,' by which they meant that it will suffer a practical hardship rather than inconsistency or logical flaw." [3] In the period when the common-law system of actions and pleading reached its culmination, the needs of justice and utility were often sacrificed to the postulates of strict logic and legalistic-technical orthodoxy.

The attempt to emancipate the law from the social and economic forces that are instrumental in shaping its institutions can at best have a partial success. In the long run, logic is apt to yield to life, and technicality to justice and social need. A juristic dialectic which "clothes the Positive in the shining garments of logic," [4] and which in a dogmatic fashion tries to prove the inevitability of a legal result without any regard to its practical or ethical consequences is often self-defeating and deceptive. While a system of concepts and rules is necessary in order to guarantee the reign of law in society, it must always be kept in mind that such rules and concepts were created in order to meet the needs of life, and that care must be taken lest life be unnecessarily and senselessly forced into the strait jacket of an overrigid legal order. [5] Law cannot be reduced to a system of mathematics or scholastic logic. While its normative standards and generalizations will pre-

[2] *Principles of Roman Law,* transl. M. Wolff (Oxford, 1936), pp. 34-35; see also pp. 38-39.
[3] Introduction to *Publications of the Selden Society,* XVII (London, 1903), xviii-xix (vol. I of the Yearbooks of Edw. II).
[4] Jhering, III, 318.
[5] See *infra* Secs. 74 and 75.

vent the law from becoming excessively fluid or ephemeral, its arrangements are subject to periodic appraisals in the light of the necessities of human social life and the requirements of fairness and justice. Thus, the autonomy of the law can be a partial one only. An attempt to keep the law completely insulated from the external social forces beating against the armor by which the law seeks to protect its internal structure will necessarily be doomed to failure.

XI

THE QUEST FOR JUSTICE

Section 44. *The Problem of Justice*

The order element in law is concerned solely with the adoption by a group or political society of certain rules of organization, standards of behavior, and patterns of conduct designed to delimit spheres of activity and avoid unregulated chaos. It tells us nothing about the character and content of these rules, standards, and patterns. A family might adopt an order according to which all family decisions are entrusted to the youngest child and are to be faithfully obeyed by all members of the family. A state may adopt a legal system in which judges are selected on the basis of the amount of property they possess or in which bribery and fraud are rewarded, while integrity is proscribed. Whether or not such an order is fair and reasonable is not directly and immediately relevant in an analysis of the order function of the law. Consequently those writers who see the concept of law exhausted in its function of laying down formally valid and authoritatively binding legal precepts leave aside in their investigations the substantive content of the law and the reasonableness of its precepts. In the words of a spokesman for this point of view, Hans Kelsen, "Any content whatsoever can be legal; there is no human behavior which could not function as the content of a legal norm." [1]

If, on the other hand, we look upon the institution of law as being closely linked not only with the need for order, but also with the quest for justice, we turn our attention from a consideration of the formal structure of the legal system to a study and evaluation of the substantive rules, principles, and standards which are the component parts of the normative structure. From the point of view of justice, we are deeply interested in the fairness and reasonableness of these rules, principles, and standards, their effect upon human beings, and their worth as measured in terms of their contribution to human happiness and productive human effort. Speaking of justice in the broadest and most general terms, we might say that justice is concerned with the fitness of a group order or social system for the task of accomplishing its essential objectives. The aim of justice is to coordinate the diversified efforts and activities of the members of the community and to allocate rights, powers, and duties among them in a manner which will satisfy the reasonable needs and aspirations of individuals and at the same time promote maximum productive effort and social cohesion. This broad description of the general goals of justice will be analyzed in greater detail later.

It is by no means widely conceded that a scientific theory of law should concern itself with the problem of justice. Most questions of justice belong to the domain of ethics, and according to a view which has wide currency today, normative ethical theory cannot be considered a legitimate branch of scientific knowledge.[2] Thus Ayer, a proponent of logical positivism, says: "The fundamental ethical concepts are unanalysable, inasmuch as there is no criterion by which one can test the validity of the judgements in which they occur. . . . The reason why they are unanalysable is that they are mere pseudo-concepts." [3] Kelsen, in a similar vein, remarks with special reference to the ethical concept of justice: "To determine . . . whether this or that order has an absolute value, that is, is 'just,' is not possible by the methods of ethical knowledge. Justice is an irrational ideal. However indispensable it may be for the willing and acting of human beings, it

---

[1] "The Pure Theory of Law," 51 Law Quarterly Review 517, at 517–518 (1935). On Kelsen see supra Sec. 26.

[2] According to this view, ethics may be treated by the scholar as a department of psychology or sociology, ethical investigations being confined to a study of the moral feelings and habits of persons or groups of persons, and the reasons causing them to have these feelings and habits.

[3] Alfred J. Ayer, Language, Truth, and Logic (London, 1950), p. 107. See also supra Sec. 24.

is not viable by reason. Only positive law is known, or more correctly is revealed, to reason." [4] In the opinion of the Swedish legal realist A. V. Lundstedt, the often-heard assertion that lawmakers and courts should be guided by ideals of justice is "completely senseless." [5] Such skeptical viewpoints have their origin in an unconscious or conscious belief that expressions of ethical judgments are mere "ejaculations," [6] that is, irrational articulations of emotions, feelings, and subjective preferences.

The philosophy which excludes ethical valuations completely from the domain of scholarship and social science has already been rejected. [7] The conviction has been expressed that scholarly effort may, within certain limitations, legitimately be applied to a study of the foundations and postulates of the "good society." With special reference to the problem under discussion, the notion of justice, as a specialized category belonging to the realm of ethics, is amenable to rational cognition. The affirmation of this belief is aided by the undeniable fact that positive legal systems fulfilling the "order" requirements of law have sometimes proved unworkable and for this reason have been abandoned or overthrown. History teaches the lesson that men will not put up with all systems of law, however "orderly" and formally consistent the integrated normative structure of such systems may be. There are conditions under which men, groups, and nations will, for entirely rational reasons, either rebel against a positive legal system, evade some of its major commands, or make a strong effort to change it. These conditions are usually anchored in fundamental traits of human nature itself or in historically caused disparities between human potentialities and a social and economic system ignoring or thwarting these potentialities. [8] Without a thorough consideration of the factors which render legal systems workable or unworkable, acceptable or unacceptable, a scientific theory of law becomes stale and lifeless. No philosophical or sociological treatment of the law which refuses to face the question of the "goodness" of the law in addition to that of its formal validity and technical organization can provide us with an adequate insight into legal reality.

However, when we delve into the problem of justice and endeavor

---

[4] "The Pure Theory of Law," 50 *L. Q. Rev.* 474, at 482 (1934). See also Kelsen, *General Theory of Law and State*, transl. by A. Wedberg (Cambridge, Mass., 1945), p. 13.

[5] "Law and Justice," in *Interpretations of Modern Legal Philosophies*, ed. P. Sayre (New York, 1947), p. 450. On Lundstedt see *supra* Sec. 32.

[6] Ayer, p. 103.

[7] See *supra* Preface and Sec. 38. Cf. also Edgar Bodenheimer, "The Province of Jurisprudence," 46 *Cornell Law Quarterly* 1 (1960).

[8] These thoughts will receive further elaboration in Sec. 46.

to unravel its perplexing secrets, discouragement and despair are likely to befall us. We shall find that many diverse and discrepant theories of "true" justice, each claiming absolute validity, have been set forth by thinkers and jurists in the course of the centuries. Which one of these, if any, shall we accept as the correct one? Furthermore, a historical inquiry into the practical realization of philosophical conceptions of justice in the life of social groups and nations is also apt to yield baffling and confusing results. It will be found that innumerable solutions for the problem of establishing a just political and social order have been attempted by organized associations of men since the beginnings of recorded history, and that many of them were in irreconcilable conflict with other attempted solutions. Can we discover any reliable yardstick which will help us to measure and appraise social orders, to honor some of them with the commendatory term "just," and castigate and condemn others with the derogatory epithet "unjust"?

Let us first briefly review some of the most influential theories of justice advanced by the philosophers. Plato, in his *Republic*, fashioned a doctrine of the just commonwealth strongly ir   ed with collectivistic ideals. In his view, justice consists in a harmonious relation between the various parts of the social organism. Every citizen must do his duty in his appointed place and do the thing for which his nature is best adapted. Since Plato's state is a class state, divided into rulers, auxiliaries, and the producing class, Platonic justice signifies that the members of each class must attend to their own business and not meddle with the business of the members of another class. Some people are born to rule, some to assist the rulers in the discharge of their functions, and others are destined to be farmers or artisans or traders. A man who attempts to govern his fellow men when he is only fit to be a farmer or craftsman must be deemed not only foolish but also unjust. The rulers of the state, assisted by their aides, must see to it that each person is assigned his proper station in life, and that he adequately performs the duties of this station.[9] The idea underlying this concept of justice rests on the assumption that an individual is not an isolated self, free to do whatever he likes, but a dependent member of a universal order who must subordinate his personal wishes and preferences to the organic unity of the collective whole.

A different approach to the problem of justice was taken by Aristotle. Justice, in his opinion, consists in "some sort of equality."[10] It demands that the things of this world shall be equitably allotted to

[9] See Plato, *The Republic*, transl. A. D. Lindsay (Everyman's Library ed., 1950), Bk. IV, 433-434. See also *supra* Sec. 2.
[10] *The Politics*, transl. E. Barker (Oxford, 1946), Bk. III. 1282b.

the members of the community or state; it also requires that this just distribution of things shall be maintained by the law as against any violations. According to this twofold function of justice, Aristotle distinguishes between two forms of justice. The first he calls *distributive* justice. This form of justice is meted out primarily by the legislator and consists in the distribution of offices, rights, honors, and goods to the members of the community according to the principle of proportionate equality. Equal things should be given to equal persons, unequal things to unequal persons. "There will be the same equality between the shares as between the persons, since the ratio between the shares will be equal to the ratio between the persons; for if the persons are not equal, they will not have equal shares; it is when equals possess or are allotted unequal shares, or persons not equal equal shares, that quarrels and complaints arise." [11] The standard which Aristotle proposes for the measurement of equality is that of worthiness and merit. If X is twice as deserving as Y, his share should be twice as large. But what are the criteria by which worthiness and merit are to be judged? According to Aristotle, it is the person of highest civic excellence, making the greatest contribution to the good life in society, who should be entitled to the greatest recognition in matters of monetary reward, honor, political office, and the like.[12]

The second kind of justice in the Aristotelian scheme is called *corrective* justice. Assuming that an allocation of rights, duties, and offices has been accomplished by legislative or other means, it is the function of justice to guarantee, protect, and maintain this distribution against illegal attacks and to restore the distributive equilibrium after it has been disturbed. This corrective function of justice is chiefly administered by the judge. If one member of the community has encroached upon the rights, privileges, or property of another member, corrective justice will re-establish the *status quo* by returning to the victim that which belonged to him or by compensating him for his loss. By the same token, if one man has become unjustifiably enriched at the expense of another man, the improper gain must be taken away from him.[13] According to Aristotle, the principle of equality operative in

[11] Aristotle, *The Nicomachean Ethics*, transl. H. Rackham (Loeb Classical Library ed., 1934), Bk. V. iii. 6.

[12] See *The Politics*, Bk. III. 1281a.

Wolfgang Friedmann, *Legal Theory*, 4th ed. (Toronto, 1960), p. 10, asserts that Aristotle's distributive justice orders "the equal treatment of those equal before the law." This is an erroneous interpretation of Aristotle's view. The Aristotelian theory is concerned with the *just content of laws*, and not merely with their non-discriminatory application.

[13] See *Nicomachean Ethics*, Bk. V. iv.

corrective justice differs from that which should obtain in distributive justice. Distributive justice demands a relative, proportionate, "geometrical" equality which takes account of the natural differences in the physical and mental endowments of men. The equality postulated by corrective justice, on the other hand, is an "arithmetical" one, being concerned with the computation of losses suffered and the restoration of gains illegally made.

Related to the Aristotelian notion of justice, but differing from it in formulation and emphasis, is the concept of justice set forth in Justinian's Corpus Iuris Civilis. The definition of this concept is attributed to the Roman jurist Ulpian and reads as follows: "Justice is the constant and perpetual will to render to everyone that to which he is entitled." [14] This description of the aim of justice can be traced back to Cicero,[15] and it was adopted and reiterated at later periods of history by a number of influential thinkers and jurists.[16] For purposes of brief identification, it might be called the *suum cuique* ("to each his due") formula of justice. It differs from the Aristotelian approach in that no reference to the concept of equality is made in the formula. There is implicit in the *suum cuique* notion, however, an assumption that two persons to whom the same things are "due" are entitled to equality of treatment.

A fundamentally divergent attitude toward justice was taken by the English philosopher and sociologist Herbert Spencer. The supreme value he linked to the idea of justice was not equality, but *freedom*. Every individual, Spencer argued, has the right to reap whatever benefits he can derive from his nature and capabilities. Each man should be allowed to assert his selfhood, acquire property, carry on a business or vocation of his choosing, move freely from place to place, and express his thoughts and religious feelings without hindrance. The only limitation upon the exercise of these rights and freedoms which Spencer wished to recognize is the individual's consciousness of and respect for the unimpeded activities of other men, who have like claims to freedom. The liberty of each is to be limited only by the equal liberties of all. This conception of justice was cast by Spencer into the mold

[14] *Dig.* I. 1. 10: *Iustitia est constans et perpetua voluntas ius suum cuique tribuendi.*

[15] *De Finibus Bonorum et Malorum,* transl. H. Rackham (Loeb Classical Library ed., 1951), Bk. V. xxiii. On Cicero see *supra* Sec. 4.

[16] St. Thomas Aquinas, *Summa Theologica,* transl. Fathers of the English Dominican Province (London, 1913–1925), pt. II, 2d pt., qu. 58, arts. 1 and 12; Thomas Hobbes, *Leviathan* (Everyman's Library ed., 1914), ch. xv; Giorgio Del Vecchio, *Justice,* ed. A. H. Campbell (New York, 1953), p. 85; Emil Brunner, *Justice and the Social Order,* transl. M. Hottinger (New York, 1945), p. 17.

of a celebrated formula: "Every man is free to do that which he wills, provided he infringes not the equal freedom of any other man." [17]

A position very similar to Spencer's was taken by the German philosopher Immanuel Kant. He also used the concept of liberty for the purpose of defining the meaning of law and justice. Proceeding from the premise that liberty was the only original, natural right belonging to each man in his capacity as a human being, he described law (in the sense of just, adequate law) as "the totality of the conditions under which the arbitrary will of one can coexist with the arbitrary will of another under a general law of freedom." [18]

A decisive return from freedom to the concept of equality as the chief constitutive element in a theory of justice will be found in the social philosophy of the American sociologist Lester Ward. In the opinion of Ward, justice consists in the "enforcement by society of an artificial equality in social conditions which are naturally unequal." [19] While Ward concurs with Aristotle in making equality the central idea in describing the goals of justice, his notion of equality is different from Aristotle's. Aristotle was ready to accept many natural inequalities, such as those created by sex and superior intelligence, and to make these natural inequalities the basis and justification for the unequal treatment of persons by the law. Ward, on the other hand, was convinced that natural inequality had nothing to do with justice. The "artificial equality" by which he sought to cut down the incidence and consequences of natural inequality was to be the deliberate objective of a social policy designed to achieve an unlimited equalization of opportunity for all members of a community or state. Every individual, regardless of sex, race, nationality, class, and social origin, was to be given a full chance to make good in life and lead a worthwhile existence.

The first and foremost condition for creating the widest possible equality of opportunity, in Ward's view, is the necessity for equalizing intelligence among the members of the upper and lower classes of society. "I have never cherished much hope for any permanent social reform," he said, "so long as society consists of two classes . . . , an intelligent or well-informed class and an ignorant or uninformed class." [20] Ward was convinced that intelligence was unrelated to class origin and depended chiefly on environmental factors, especially on

---

[17] *Justice* (New York, 1891), p. 46. On Spencer see also *supra* Sec. 20.
[18] *Metaphysik der Sitten*, ed. K. Vorländer (Leipzig, 1922), pp. 34-35 (translation mine). On Kant see also *supra* Sec. 15.
[19] *Applied Sociology* (Boston, 1906), p. 22.
[20] *Id.*, p. 93.

access to all sources of information and an opening up to all persons of the entire heritage of knowledge and wisdom of the past. He admitted that not all men are equals intellectually, but insisted that intellectual inequality was common to all classes. The general level of intelligence prevailing in the various strata of society could be equalized, in his view, and under a condition of universal enlightenment it would appear that the lower class was not inferior in intellectual ability to the upper class. Any more far-reaching schemes for the equalization of the material resources of society would depend for their success on the prior attainment of equalization of intelligence.[21]

Most of the theories discussed thus far made either equality or freedom the focal point for approaching the problem of justice. A Scottish philosopher, W. R. Sorley, claimed that no satisfactory doctrine of justice could be developed without finding a place for both equality and freedom in the scheme of societal organization and without attempting to reconcile the potentially antithetical character of these two human values. He pointed out that liberty and equality may easily come into opposition in the social order, since the extension of liberty does not necessarily promote human equality. A social system fixing upon freedom as the sole or almost exclusive principle of governmental policy may produce wide differences of condition between rich and poor, employers and employed, educated and uneducated. Each step taken for the purpose of preventing gross inequalities from arising in the social and economic sphere involves some interference with the abstract right to freedom.

The social ideal which Sorley proposed as an alternative to either abstract liberty or abstract equality was the ideal of *positive freedom*. Its realization requires the following conditions: (1) The development and direction of human mental and physical powers by education; (2) such access to the materials and instruments of production as would give suitable employment to people; and (3) the establishment of physical and social surroundings which will aid, not hamper, individual development. An order fashioned upon such principles, Sorley maintained, would foster the growth of genuine freedom while it would at the same time bring the ideal of freedom into closer harmony with equality.[22]

When we turn from the blueprints and speculations of the philosophers to the historical scenes of political and social action, we experience an equally strong sense of bewilderment. Presuming that most of the architects of social and legal systems have acted in accordance with

[21] *Id.,* p. 281.
[22] Sorley, *The Moral Life* (Cambridge, Eng., 1911), pp. 95–113.

what they understood to be the best interest of the community, we find that the conceptions of political, social, and economic justice actuating them in their community-building activities were most diverse and heterogeneous. Political regimes such as democracies, benevolent autocracies, patriarchal monarchies, and responsible aristocracies have all been able at times to discharge the tasks of government successfully and to command the loyalties of their subjects. Feudalistic, capitalistic, and socialistic systems of economics have been able to claim substantial economic achievements, sometimes in the face of limiting historical conditions that had to be overcome. Social systems built on egalitarian ideals have exhibited considerable stamina and staying power along with systems inspired by nonegalitarian principles. Recorded history has furnished no proof so far that one particular conception of justice in human social affairs must be looked upon as so superior to all rival conceptions that the latter are a priori condemned to failure and bankruptcy.

In the light of such widely discrepant views on justice, in theory as well as in the practice of states, is it not necessary to resign oneself to the position of the skeptic who believes that justice is entirely a matter of irrational, subjective valuation or transient community consensus? In the remaining sections of this chapter, an endeavor will be made to demonstrate that an attitude of despair or a posture of cynical contempt vis-à-vis the problem of justice is not demanded or warranted by the teachings of history.

Section 45. *Justice as an Attitude of the Mind*
It was noted in the preceding section that the Roman jurist Ulpian defined justice as "the constant and perpetual will to render to everyone that to which he is entitled." [1] Similarly, Cicero described justice as the disposition of the mind to render to everyone his due.[2] St. Thomas Aquinas observed that justice was "a habit whereby a man renders to each one his due by a constant and perpetual will." [3]

The subjective element in these definitions, which is of far-reaching importance, has not always received the attention it deserves. In each of the three definitions set forth above, justice is identified with a certain *attitude* or *disposition of the mind*. Justice, according to this point of view, demands an objective, unbiased, and considerate attitude toward others, a willingness to be fair, and a readiness to give or leave

[1] *Dig.* I. 1. 10.
[2] *De Finibus,* transl. H. Rackham, Bk. V. xxiii. 65–67.
[3] *Summa Theologica,* transl. Fathers of the English Dominican Province, pt. II, 2d pt., qu. 58, art. 1.

to others that which they are entitled to have or retain. The just man, either in private or in public life, is a person who is able to see the legitimate interests of others and to respect them. The just father does not arbitrarily discriminate between his children. The just employer is willing to consider the reasonable claims of his employees. The just judge administers the law with even-handed detachment. The just lawgiver takes into account the interests of all persons and groups whom he is under a duty to represent. Thus understood, justice is a principle of rectitude which requires integrity of character as a basic precondition.

This subjective element in the idea of justice is of a generally valid and truly universal character. In its absence, justice cannot flourish in society. As was clearly seen by Aristotle, justice is a social virtue which is concerned with relationships between persons. "Justice alone of the virtues is the 'good of others,' because it does what is for the advantage of another." [4] In order to function effectively, it requires liberation from one's exclusively self-regarding impulses. The pure egotist levies claims upon the goods of the world without regard to the justified claims of others. Justice opposes this tendency by the demand that the rights and claims of all be respected. Without integrity, an "other-regarding" attitude, and the will to be fair, the goals of justice cannot usually be attained.

These considerations make evident the close connection that exists between justice and rationality. A rational individual may insist on scrupulous respect for his own feelings and due recognition of his personal rights, but at the same time he accords an equal respect to the personality of other human beings. Rationality, in the sense in which the term is relevant to this discussion, is the capacity of individuals to abstract themselves from their own egos, to put themselves in the position of others, to generalize their own sentiments and reactions and project them into the persons of others. This capacity enables human beings to view their mutual relationships, within certain limits set by the self-centered constituent of human nature, in an objective light.[5]

A rational being tends to act in a moral and socially responsible manner, while antisocial and immoral action is normally irrational in character. The rational man realizes that certain moral and legal restraints are indispensable for the purpose of adapting our own needs to the needs of others and for making life in a community tolerable. It is this capacity to reflect with detachment upon the inevitable or most desira-

---

[4] *Nicomachean Ethics*, transl. H. Rackham, Bk. V. i. 17; see also Plato, *Republic*, transl. A. D. Lindsay, Bk. I. 341–342.
[5] See also the observations on "reason" *infra* Sec. 70.

ble conditions of social coexistence which makes it possible for human beings to frame generalized ethical systems and codes of law.

What, then, is the difference between the rational man and the just man? The difference lies simply in the fact that rationality is a term of broader import than justice because it encompasses the entire area of moral, legal, and social conduct. The approach of justice is confined to respect for rights and recognition of duties deemed to involve a degree of obligation superior to that of purely moral commitments, but the notion is broad enough to include not only solicitude for rights and duties sanctioned by the positive law, but also for those which "ought" to be recognized by the legal order.[6] Thus, justice may be described as a form of rationality pertaining to that sphere of societal life which is concerned with demands and obligations considered to be endowed with an obligatory character of particular strength and definiteness. The view propounded by Hans Kelsen[7] and Alf Ross[8] that justice is a purely "irrational" ideal cannot claim to have even a shadow of justification.

While the mental attitude which is a concomitant of just conduct is indispensable for the successful accomplishment of the objectives of a "good society," it is only one of the components of the concept of justice. A good will alone, unsupported by determined action to carry its promptings into effect, is powerless to produce a just order of things. There are objective conditions of social life and social organization which must be realized in order to attain the final goals of justice. These conditions will be discussed in the following sections of this chapter.

Section 46. Justice and Natural Law

In the history of jurisprudential thought, the idea of justice has frequently been closely linked or even identified with the concept of natural law. So deeply is the evolution of human thought on justice enmeshed with speculation concerning the existence and significance of an assumed "law of nature" that no adequate theory of justice can afford to ignore this enduring problem.

Any general discussion of the problem of natural law has to face the initial difficulty that, in the development of jurisprudential theory, natural law has meant different things to different thinkers. St. Thomas

---

[6] See Sorley, The Moral Life, p. 98: "The just man may observe the rights sanctioned by society, but he will respect others also of which the society is careless, and he may attempt to modify the social standard by an appeal to what may be called Ideal Justice." See also infra Sec. 47.

[7] See supra Sec. 26.

[8] See supra Sec. 32.

Aquinas considered natural law as a set of barriers or restrictions which human instincts and the rational impulse of sociability impose upon the powers of human lawmakers. Under this view, natural law is conceived of as an aggregate of minimum requirements of the social order stemming from universal and ineradicable traits of human beings.[1] The classical law-of-nature school took a less restrictive view of the contents of the natural law.[2] Men like Grotius, Pufendorf, and Wolff were convinced that many specific rules of national and international law could be devised by the exercise of the powers of the human intellect, and that these rules could claim general validity by virtue of their consonance with "natural reason." Locke and Jefferson converted the natural-law philosophy into a doctrine of "natural rights," insisting that men were endowed with inherent and inalienable rights, such as life, liberty, and property. In the twentieth century, Rudolf Stammler introduced into natural-law thinking the idea of a "natural law with a changing content," denoting by this phrase a set of axioms and principles which, although in basic accord with the postulates of justice, were responsive to the contingent needs of a particular place and time.[3] More recently, Justice Cardozo—again in a relativistic manner—identified natural law with standards of justice and fair dealing prevalent among reasonable men, who are mindful of the habits of life in a community.[4] A return to a more absolute approach is advocated by F. S. C. Northrop, who insists that natural-law jurisprudence provides us with a criterion for measuring the goodness or badness of the living law of a particular civilization by means of a scientifically verified theory of the "first order facts" of nature and natural man, representing the raw data of human experience in any cultural setting.[5]

Notwithstanding the divergencies and disagreements existing among

---

[1] See *supra* Sec. 6. On the problem of natural law in general see A. P. d'Entrèves, *Natural Law* (London, 1951) and "The Case for Natural Law Re-examined," 1 *Natural Law Forum* 5 (1956); Heinrich A. Rommen, *The Natural Law*, transl. T. R. Hanley (St. Louis, 1948).

[2] See *supra* Chapter III.

[3] See *supra* Sec. 33.

[4] Benjamin N. Cardozo, *The Nature of the Judicial Process* (New Haven, 1921), p. 142; see also Morris R. Cohen, *Reason and Nature*, rev. ed. (Glencoe, Ill., 1953), p. 405: "The domains of life . . . not provided for in the positive law are regulated by the customary rules of what people think fair, which thus constitute a natural or non-positive law."

[5] "Naturalistic and Cultural Foundations for a More Effective International Law," 59 *Yale Law Journal* 1430, at 1435, 1448 (1950); Northrop, "Contemporary Jurisprudence and International Law," 61 *Yale L. J.* 623, at 650 (1952); and *The Complexity of Legal and Ethical Experience* (Boston, 1959), pp. 252–260. On Northrop see *supra* Sec. 37.

the philosophers of natural law, it would appear possible to reduce the aforementioned points of view to a common denominator. There is consensus among all or at least the large majority of these writers that natural law consists of principles and norms which are entitled to recognition regardless of whether or not they have found formal expression in the positive law of the state or community. However indefinite, elusive, or contradictory the various historical versions of natural-law thinking may be, the above description would serve to lend a certain bond of unity to them.

There would, indeed, appear to exist some postulates of a normative character which, independently of the will of the positive lawgiver, require recognition by the legal order of the community. Some of these requirements are grounded in the physical or psychic constitution of man. Nature demands of man a certain amount of food and of sleep; it has endowed him with sexuality; and it has instilled in him a love for his offspring. It may be said, therefore, that laws providing a working day of twenty-two hours, prescribing a starvation diet (in the absence of conditions of serious famine), prohibiting all sexual intercourse between men and women, or depriving people of the right to bring up their offspring [6] are repugnant to the "law of nature." Nature has also given to man a desire for self-preservation. Laws requiring the maiming or killing of oneself, or forbidding the use of self-defense against unlawful attacks must therefore, under ordinary circumstances, be looked upon as incompatible with primordial instincts of human nature.[7]

Other norms imposing limitations upon completely free volition in lawmaking are those which are imposed by the dictates of human reason and which are inevitable or indispensable to enable man to live as a social being. It must be kept in mind that human nature includes the faculty of reason, and so these dictates may therefore be regarded as "natural" in a different sense. These types of norms have the tendency to regulate and restrict some of the physical and psychic inclinations in man (especially his aggressive impulses) in order to make life in society possible and to avoid chaos. Inasmuch as these postulates embody the minimum requirements of legal control, they are apt to

[6] Plato advocated that the guardians of his ideal state should not be permitted to rear or even to know their own children. It is important to note that he wished to compensate the ruling authorities for this severe deprivation by granting them an immense amount of powers and privileges. See Plato, *Republic*, transl. A. D. Lindsay, Bk. V. 457 ff. Endeavors during the early period of the Bolshevik revolution to make children the wards of the state miscarried.

[7] This does not mean that exceptions to the legal recognition of the instinct of self-preservation may not be decreed for purposes of war or punishment for crimes.

be found, in one form or another, in the legal systems of all peoples.

For example, because of the strong passions engendered by sexual relations and the possible social disturbances resulting from their unregulated indulgence, all societies (except possibly the earliest and most primitive ones) have evolved definite rules governing sexual behavior. All societies that have emerged from the crudest forms of barbarism punish incest (subject, perhaps, to some limited exceptions) and—although the definition of the offense varies a great deal—rape. The vast majority of societies frown upon complete sexual promiscuity and recognize marriage as a social necessity, although the form which marriage takes may be monogamy, polygamy, or polyandry. Practically all societies recognize adultery as undesirable, and offenders are often punished.[8]

Modern anthropologists are also in agreement that no human society has ever permitted killing within an organized group in the absence of some form of justification. It is true that private killing was often allowed in early society as a form of retaliation for a wrong, but the exercise of the right was subject to supervision and control by the group. Homicide was usually sanctioned in the case of self-defense. Some societies have commanded a killing of the aged to save food, as some Eskimo tribes have done. Others have approved of the ritual sacrifice of members of the community to please the gods, or the burning of the widows of deceased husbands to symbolize the complete unity of the spouses. Many societies have authorized the killing of slaves on the ground that they lack the attribute of human personality. These historical exceptions, impressive as they appear to be as evidence for the theory of ethical relativity, do not affect the validity of the fact that the intentional killing of an innocent person without justifiable cause has been considered reprehensible and blameworthy by all societies.[9] This is in itself an important exemplification of the existence of a "natural" social law. Furthermore, the advance of civilization has generally brought in its train an increased respect for human life and a corresponding decrease in permissible homicide. Killing in war is, of course, a universal fact in civilized as well as less civilized

[8] On these and other uniformities in cultural patterns, see Ralph Linton, "Universal Ethical Principles," in *Moral Principles in Action*, ed. R. N. Anshen (New York, 1952), pp. 645 ff., Clyde N. Kluckhohn, "Ethical Relativity: Sic et Non," 52 *Journal of Philosophy* 663 ff. (1955); G. P. Murdock, *Social Structure* (New York, 1949), pp. 265, 284, 297; E. Adamson Hoebel, *Man in the Primitive World* (New York, 1949), pp. 191, 219; Franz Boas, "Methods of Research," in *General Anthropology*, ed. F. Boas (Boston, 1938), p. 677.

[9] See Edward Westermarck, *The Origin and Development of Moral Ideas* (London, 1906), I, 331; Max Scheler, *Der Formalismus in der Ethik und die Materiale Wertethik* (Halle, 1927), pp. 321-329, esp. 326.

cultures. We have to keep in mind, however, that the natural-law doctrine is concerned with certain essential contents of *legal* systems, while war—in spite of certain recent attempts to regulate some of its rigors—is basically an extralegal phenomenon.

In the area of property relations, it has been shown that all societies have recognized personal property in tools, utensils, ornaments, and the like; the only exceptions have been the few completely collectivistic societies which communized all goods under the inspiration of a strong religious or ethical idea but which were incapable of preserving this extreme system indefinitely.[10] It has also been found true that all societies have imposed some requirements of good faith in living up to the terms of contractual agreements and have proscribed serious forms of fraud. All societies recognize that there are instances in which the interests of individuals must be subordinated to those of the state or organized community. Such widely observed cross-cultural correspondences and congruences led a leading modern anthropologist, Clyde Kluckhohn, to ask the question: "Is there not a presumptive likelihood that these moral principles somehow correspond to inevitabilities, given the nature of the human organism and of the human situation?" [11]

Human nature, however, is not static and immutable. While there exist universal traits of human beings which are shared by cavemen and highly civilized human beings, the growth and refinement of civilization and culture brings in its train adjustments and changes in human reactions and sensibilities that cannot remain without influence on the law. Thus, civilized man may regard certain general principles of fair dealing and justice as imperatively demanded by reason which a member of a tribe of aborigines may not as yet recognize as essential. Among these basic principles of civilized justice may perhaps be counted the requirements that there must be impartial tribunals for the redress of wrongs and the protection of elementary rights; [12] that no one should be the judge in his own case; that agreements should be kept subject to certain qualifications established by law; and that a person should not be punished for an act which, at the time of its commission, he had no reason whatever to consider blameworthy.[13] Imposing capital punishment for a slight offense may also be looked

---

[10] Linton, p. 655.

[11] Kluckhohn, p. 673.

[12] See the decision of the Supreme Court of the Federal Republic of Germany of July 12, 1951, 3 *Entscheidungen des Bundesgerichtshofes in Zivilsachen*, 94 (1951), where the Court stated that "among the inalienable rights of human beings is the right not to be deprived of one's life without judicial proceedings" (p. 107).

[13] See *Calder v. Bull*, 3 Dall. (U.S.) 386 (1798).

upon as violation of civilized decency.[14] Furthermore, an outrageous and totally unjustifiable disregard for minimum human claims to freedom and equality may be said to offend against the "natural reason" of civilized man.[15] In the case of a serious violation of any of these basic postulates, the problem of the "legality" of the departure may under certain conditions present itself to a court.[16]

The term "natural law" has been extended by some writers to embrace certain legal axioms and institutions which, while not common to men generally, or to civilized nations, are natural and indigenous to a particular form of civilization. Thus in a genuinely feudal society, in which the chief political and economic institutions are anchored in a personal bond of fidelity between the lord and his vassal, it would be contrary to the basic premises of the social system to permit the free alienation of land by a vassal to a third person, with the consequence that the lord might become saddled with a tenant who is unreliable or a personal enemy of the lord. Irrespective of statutory recognition of the principle, the courts would be inclined to recognize at least a strong presumption against free alienability. In a capitalist society, freedom of transaction would appear to be demanded as a cardinal postulate of a free enterprise economy, and although the law inevitably imposes restrictions on the conclusion of certain contracts, freedom is considered the rule rather than the exception. A socialist society considers it natural to look with disfavor upon any antisocial exercise of private rights and to give preference to the concerns of the collective whole over those of individuals. When Justice Cardozo made the statement that "the system of law-making by judicial decisions which supply the rule for transactions closed before the decision was announced, would indeed be intolerable in its hardship and oppression if natural law . . . did not supply the main rule of judgment to the judge when precedent and custom fail or are displaced," [17] he

---

[14] See Oliver Goldsmith, *The Vicar of Wakefield*, ch. xxvii. A decision of the West German Supreme Court held that a judgment of a Nazi Court imposing the death penalty for a criticism of Hitler made by a husband to a wife in the privacy of their home must be considered null and void because of an excessive disproportion between deed and punishment. 3 *Entscheidungen des Bundesgerichtshofes in Strafsachen*, 110 (1952). On this case see H. L. A. Hart, "Positivism and the Separation of Law and Morals," 71 *Harvard Law Review* 593, at 618–621 (1958), and Lon L. Fuller, "Positivism and Fidelity to Law," 71 *Harv. L. Rev.* 630, at 652–655 (1958).

[15] The relationship of justice to equality and freedom is discussed *infra* Secs. 47 and 48. Also relevant to a discussion of natural law is the human urge for self-perfection, discussed *infra* Sec. 59.

[16] See *infra* Sec. 53; cf. also Edgar Bodenheimer, "The Natural Law Doctrine before the Tribunal of Science," 3 *Western Political Quarterly* 335, at 344 ff. (1950).

[17] Cardozo, *op. cit. supra* n. 4, p. 142.

used the term "natural law" more or less as a synonym for the prevailing convictions, widely accepted ideals, and jural postulates of a particular type of civilization. When Holmes referred to the "felt necessities of the time" and "prevalent moral and political theories" as formative influences in the development of law, he was obviously speaking about the same thing.[18]

For the sake of semantic uniformity, and in deference to an impressive tradition of natural-law thinking, it would seem desirable to stop short of the broad view just outlined and to restrict the use of the term natural law to those minimum requirements of reasonableness and justice in the absence of which there can be no genuine order of law in society. Natural law in this sense constitutes the rock-bottom layer of justice which is indispensable to the legal life of an organized society. Because of an element of necessity in natural law which is derived from the ineradicable traits of human nature, this form of law exhibits a certain measure of uniformity and universality. As pointed out above, however, it is not incapable of development and growth, since not only man's knowledge of human nature may improve with the advance of civilization, but man's moral sense itself may undergo a certain strengthening and refinement. Thus, any conclusions with respect to basic necessities of lawmaking which rest on a contemplation of man's essential nature are subject to revision in the light of an advance in the psychological and biological sciences, resulting in deeper and more penetrating insights into the mysteries and complexities of the human personality.

It has sometimes been objected that the identification of "natural law" with certain fundamental postulates of human rationality is misleading and artificial. It has been pointed out that the irrational, aggressive, and destructive instincts of man, which the so-called "natural law" is designed to curb and domesticate, also form a permanent part of human nature.[19] The argument has some merit, but may be obviated by pointing out that the primary object of our investigation is not "nature" but "natural law." The rational component in natural-law thinking is anchored in the fact that, although some men have natural impulses to kill or do harm to other men, it is "natural" for the law

---

[18] Oliver W. Holmes, *The Common Law* (Boston, 1881), p. 1; cf. Harold J. Laski, "The Judicial Function," 2 *Politica* 115 (1936).

[19] See Jeremy Bentham, *The Theory of Legislation*, ed. C. K. Ogden (London, 1931), p. 83. Cf. also Morris R. Cohen, "Moral Aspects of the Criminal Law," 49 *Yale L. J.* 987, at 994 (1940): "Unless we believe in supernatural ordinances or a devil who interferes with our nature, we must apply the term natural to everything that actually takes place, in the field of legislation as well as in the field of 'unnatural' or 'abnormal' animal behavior."

to erect barriers against the aggressive and socially destructive inclinations of men, and that all societies have in fact enacted such restrictions
in order to preserve themselves. Thus, the natural law is to a large
extent rooted in the cognitive faculty of human beings, which recognizes the social dangers resulting from man's irrational impulses as well
as the necessity for a rational control of these impulses through the
agency of the law.[20]

The theory here advanced holds that the words "justice" and "natural law" should not be used as synonyms. The natural law forms
merely the bottom layer of a just order of law, comprising those minimum standards of fairness and reasonableness without which there can
be no genuine order of law. The concept of justice, on the other hand,
also includes certain jural principles of a general character which a
particular political and social system regards as just and which play
an important part in the decision of cases, even though these principles
may not have found express recognition in a formalized source of law.[21]
Finally, there is a third and top layer, consisting of blueprints for a
better and more ideal order which the positive law of the state has
fallen short of achieving. The concept of justice, in this view, is concerned with the pressing and immediate as well as with the more remote and ultimate ends of legal ordering.

Section 47. *Justice and Equality*

It has been pointed out before that the idea of justice is closely connected with the problem of equality in human social life.[1] Justice requires the equal treatment of equal persons in equal or essentially
similar circumstances. The realization of justice demands that two
situations in which the relevant circumstances are the same should be
dealt with in an identical way.

This aspect of justice may be illustrated by an example. The father
of two boys who are twins forbids them to climb the roof of the

---

[20] Ranyard West, *Conscience and Society* (New York, 1945), p. 165: "We ourselves are as much the victims of the aggressiveness which conflicts with our
major character and our 'social solidarity' as those upon whom we vent our aggressiveness. . . . The prime operative duty of the law is the control of human
aggressiveness."

[21] On these principles see *infra* Sec. 69.

[1] See *supra* Sec. 44 and Aristotle, *Nicomachean Ethics*, transl. H. Rackham,
Bk. V. iii. 3–6; Ward, *Applied Sociology*, pp. 22 ff.; Gerhart Husserl, "Justice,"
47 *International Journal of Ethics* 271 (1937); Edmond N. Cahn, *The Sense of
Injustice* (New York, 1949), p. 14; Gustav Radbruch, "Legal Philosophy," in
The Legal Philosophies of Lask, Radbruch, and Dabin, transl. K. Wilk (Cam-
bridge, Mass., 1950), p. 109; Carl J. Friedrich, *The Philosophy of Law in Historical
Perspective* (Chicago, 1958), pp. 192–199.

house because it is unsafe. One day he notices one of the boys sitting on the roof and punishes him by confining him to his room. A few days later the other boy climbs the roof and is seen by his father, but goes unpunished. Both boys, under these circumstances, will have the feeling that their father acted unjustly. By the same token, a judge who imposes unequal and grossly discrepant sentences on two persons who have committed identical offenses would, in the absence of special circumstances justifying different treatment, violate an essential command of justice.[2]

It would likewise be unjust if a judge should decree the same penalty for two men who have committed crimes of very different magnitude and gravity, unless in the case of the person guilty of the more severe offense a strong showing of mitigating circumstances could be made. The command to treat equal men in equal circumstances in an equal way contains as a corollary the proposition that fundamentally unequal situations may have to be treated in an unequal way to meet the requirements of justice. For instance, it would be unjust for a teacher to give the same grade to two students if one had done excellent work in an examination, and the other had performed very poorly. Justice, by its very nature, abhors caprice and arbitrariness. As Edmond Cahn has well said: "The sense of injustice revolts against whatever is unequal by caprice." [3]

Two major shortcomings, however, are inherent in the equality-definition of justice. First, it fails to clarify the obvious truth that an equality of *mistreatment* does not live up to the expectations of mankind for a just order of things. If all or most members of a collective entity are subjected to an equal status of slavery or oppression, there is no reason to assume that justice has been achieved through equal treatment of equals. If a number of criminals who have committed identical derelictions of a light character all receive the death sentence or terms of life imprisonment, the mere fact that equality of punishment was accorded to them does not constitute compliance with the notion of justice.[4] Second, the equality view of justice fails to articulate the fact that justice is concerned not only with a comparison of individuals, social groups, and legally relevant situations for the purpose of determining their essential likeness or dissimilarity, but also aims at the proper judicial treatment of unique situations and unusual com-

---

[2] See the example given by Cahn, p. 14.
[3] *Ibid.* See also Arnold Brecht, "Relative and Absolute Justice," 6 *Social Research* 58, at 76 (1939): "It is unjust to discriminate arbitrarily among equal cases."
[4] On the injustice of meting out severe penalties for light offenses see Goldsmith, *The Vicar of Wakefield*, ch. xxvii.

binations of events not lending themselves to such a comparison.[5] For instance, justice seeks to administer a fitting punishment for a particular crime committed under a highly exceptional constellation of facts, defying analysis according to stereotyped and generalized criteria of judgment. Also, in cases where justified and reasonable interests of two private parties come into conflict, or where a legitimate private interest is found to have clashed with an important public need, justice may have to undertake a "balancing of the equities" and a painstaking appraisal of the relative weight of the opposing claims with a view to adjust them, if possible, in a way which is fair to both sides under the particular circumstances of the case.

Because of the deficiencies attendant upon a description of justice as equality or "equal treatment of equals," this approach has from early times encountered a complement in a second conception of justice which we have referred to as the *suum cuique* formula.[6] Under this formula, justice is identified with the endeavor to render to everyone that to which he is entitled. It differs from the equality view in that it leaves room for differentiation and individualized consideration of justified claims, where the equality view stresses the need for generality and universality in the treatment of persons or things falling into the same category or class. There is, however, implicit in the *suum cuique* notion an assumption that two persons to whom the same things are "due" are entitled to distributive equality. But the *suum cuique* formula directs our attention to another factor which is neglected in the equality definition: namely, that if A does not get as much as he deserves, it does not help the situation appreciably if B receives an equally unsatisfactory share.

Notwithstanding the shortcomings of the view which equates justice with "some sort of equality," [7] this view brings out an extremely important element in the concept of justice. It gives expression to the universal experience that human beings are strongly inclined to rebel against a discriminatory treatment which they feel to be unreasonable, unjustified, and capricious.

It is not true, as has sometimes been asserted, that what is "capricious" depends wholly on the personal and irrational reactions of individuals, and that the concept of justice is therefore unamenable to rational, scientific analysis. Professor Jean Piaget, in his studies on the moral judgment of children, found that, while the children's ideas

---

[5] See Jerome Frank, *Courts on Trial* (Princeton, 1949), p. 391, who is inclined to focus his attention almost exclusively on this particular element in justice.

[6] See *supra* Sec. 44.

[7] Aristotle, *The Politics*, transl. E. Barker, Bk. III. 1282b.

of right and wrong and fair and unfair differ to some extent according to the age and experience of the child, the majority of the children in a given age group evince the same general attitude toward moral questions, and that the development from one attitude to another follows a fairly definite pattern.[8] As Bienenfeld has shown in an able study,[9] the feeling for justice is innate in the child and deeply rooted in his sense of personality. It manifests itself in an essentially similar way in all children. The child demands equality with his brothers and sisters, although in a more advanced stage of his development he will understand inequalities of treatment if they are rationally explained to him. A child will rebel in his innermost soul against discriminations felt by him to be entirely arbitrary and capricious.[10] His reactions in this respect are not basically different from those of a social group in which differentiations are created that the members of the group regard as wholly unjustified and oppressive. In the words of Bienenfeld, "it is the degree of impartiality in respect of quarreling children and their contradictory basic desires that makes for peace or disharmony in the family. Similarly in society, co-operation will be promoted by impartiality and impeded by discrimination."[11]

It cannot, of course, be assumed that there has existed in history a universal agreement on what does and what does not constitute unreasonable discrimination. While it is unlikely that in any nation or epoch of history the people would make eligibility for public office dependent on whether the candidate was left- or right-handed, differentiations in terms of birth, wealth, and sex have been regarded as highly material in some social units and as immaterial in others. The Middle Ages, emphasizing inequality over equality, built a hierarchical structure of society predicated upon a complex gradation of ranks and privileges. Many democracies in the nineteenth century considered the differences between the sexes so fundamental as to justify an unequal treatment of men and women with respect to suffrage and other legal rights. A number of countries look upon racial differences as highly significant and accord a different status to groups within the social order on the basis of race. Even in countries recognizing as axiomatic the idea of a general equality before the law, men of property and wealth sometimes enjoy actual privileges and a preferred so-

[8] Piaget, *The Moral Judgment of the Child,* transl. M. Gabain (London, 1932), pp. 197 ff.

[9] F. R. Bienenfeld, *Rediscovery of Justice* (London, 1947), pp. 19–27.

[10] Thus any boy would be shocked if his twin brother, without explanation or obvious reason, received a large piece of birthday cake while he himself was given a small one or none.

[11] Bienenfeld, p. 26.

cial position. Against such differentiations are directed the attacks of modern socialists who claim that political equality must be supplemented by a greater amount of economic equality.

In all these instances there exists a controversy as to the degree of equality or inequality that should exist in the social order. This controversy has its roots in the undeniable fact that a strict and absolute equality hardly ever exists in nature or human social life. No two persons look, behave, or act in an exactly identical way. No two situations are completely alike. The term equality denotes an *approximate* equality only. "Equality is but an abstraction from actual inequality, taken from a certain point of view." [12] When two persons or things are considered equal, some existing difference is deemed to be insignificant and inessential.

Undoubtedly the question of whether certain factual differences between men and things warrant a differentiating treatment by the law has received diverse and inconsistent answers in the course of history. Such divergences of opinion lend apparent strength to the argument that the notion of justice is not amenable to rational cognition and, even if not totally subjective, represents at best a social convention resting on majority conviction or at worst a forcible imposition of standards of equality and inequality by a ruling class.

It is believed that such a skepticism concerning the possibility of an objective theory of justice mistakes surface appearances for a deeper truth. It is undoubtedly correct to say that the concept of justice includes a large *relative* component which makes it necessary for us to interpret and appraise systems of justice in the context of their historical, social, and economic settings. But this does not mean that the ideal of justice at a particular time is nothing but a product of fortuitous and arbitrary social conventions, accepted perhaps by the people on the basis of ruling-class propaganda attempting to demonstrate the eternal reasonableness of the existing social system. While this may have been true in certain historical epochs, it must also be realized that the degree of equality and inequality accorded to people and groups is often contingent upon objective conditions of production, on more or less uncontrollable social realities, and on the existing level of knowledge and understanding. At a time when technology was not sufficiently developed to provide educational facilities for all, it was not necessarily capricious to restrict all forms of higher education to male persons on the ground that the women were needed at home. Villeinage, a condition in which the agricultural laborer is bound to the

[12] Radbruch, *op. cit. supra* n. 1, p. 109.

soil, seems unjust to us; yet there is a serious question as to whether the Middle Ages could have achieved maximum productivity in agriculture under a system of free mobility of agricultural labor. It should also not be forgotten that when compared with its predecessor, chattel slavery, villeinage represented an advance in the promotion of justice.

A system of food rationing, such as was in effect in several European countries after World War II, under which workers performing the heavy tasks of physical reconstruction were given larger rations than people engaged in lighter and less exhausting work, with intellectuals receiving the smallest allotments, would be considered totally intolerable in an economy of abundance. It can be defended as reasonable and just under conditions of famine or food shortage when the rebuilding of houses and other essential facilities had to be made the first order of business. When a race just emerging from the state of savagery lives under the same sovereignty with a culturally highly developed group, inequalities in treatment will almost inevitably become a feature of the coexistence of these groups, with or without legal sanctions. Such inequality of treatment—as long as it is temporary and its effect will not be to hold down the more primitive race and the stultification of its growth under some "master-race" theory—may not in every respect be unjust.

The sense of justice will ineluctably assert itself, however, when an existing inequality, due to a change in conditions or an advance in scientific knowledge or human understanding, is felt to be no longer justifiable, necessary, or acceptable. Thus, when it became clear that women were capable of intellectual achievements as great as those of men, the struggle for equal participation of women in the political, professional, and educational life of the community received a strong impetus and resulted in the breaking down of many legal and extralegal barriers that had previously stood in the way of female equality. In the fifth century B.C., the plebeians in Rome revolted against the exclusive rule of the patricians on the ground that the existing political inequalities had no basis in social reality and that the plebeians were just as fit to participate in government as the aristocratic elements of the population. The French Revolution was waged against discrimination by the feudal class against the middle classes; the American Revolution directed its force against what was felt to be an unjust treatment of the colonies; and the European Chartist movement of the 1830's fought for granting the franchise to the laboring classes because it was regarded as untenable to deny voting rights to people solely on the ground that they had little property. The elevation of the living standards, levels of intelligence, and cultural needs of a disfavored race will bring about a struggle on its part for emancipation and equality of rights. In such struggles the victims of discrimination have often won the sympathy and support of outsiders, including members of the ruling group, whose sense of justice was aroused by the unequal treatment devoid of rational justification. Nothing aids the cause of a group subjected to an inferior status more effectively than showing that there exists no factual basis for unequal treatment.

It may therefore be said that the battle for justice is in many instances waged for the purpose of removing a legal or custom-approved inequality for which there is no foundation in fact and reason. From the beginnings of recorded history all great social struggles and reform movements have raised the banner of justice against certain iniquities of the positive law that were felt to be in need of correction. Frequently the success of a new idea of justice is ensured by an advance in psychological or sociological knowledge which demonstrates that the lines governing the classification of persons, groups, and things for the purpose of equal or unequal treatment by the law must be redrawn in order to redress a political or social wrong.

These considerations help us to understand the chief cause for the historical relativity of the notion of justice in many of its concrete manifestations: Deficiencies of knowledge as well as the harsh, limiting facts of reality, often prevent the establishment of an equality of status and rights which a perfect society would be likely to guarantee. Trial and error, experimentation and failure, progress and retrogression will affect and modify our ideas as to what should be treated equally and unequally. Thus justice has its dynamic and fluid components. It does not permit us to adopt stereotyped solutions for our social problems regardless of time, state of social evolution, development of productive forces, and other contingent factors. But this does not mean that justice is a purely subjective or irrational ideal.[13] The possibilities for its approximate realization are grounded in the objective conditions of life, and reason is the chief instrument for appraising and, if necessary, revising the political, economic, and social system if it does not satisfy the legitimate demands and constructive aspirations of individuals and groups. We must hope that the social science of the future will provide us with more reliable guides than have hitherto been offered to us in solving the momentous problems of justice.

[13] See Friedrich, *op. cit. supra* n. 1, p. 198. Friedrich points out that justice, although it must be understood as a changing reality, is nevertheless an *objective* reality, "transpersonal and not subjective."

Section 48. *Justice and Freedom*

The desire for freedom is deeply ingrained in all human beings. It is innate in the child, who has a strong urge to do whatever the mood of the moment suggests to him and often chafes at restrictions imposed by parents and educators.[1] The adult human being, as Spencer has pointed out, is "irritated by invisible restraints as well as by visible ones";[2] he feels joy in being able to use his bodily and mental powers to the fullest and to reap the resulting benefits. The value attributed by human beings to freedom is attested by the fact that imprisonment, or threat of imprisonment, is considered an effective way of punishment for and deterrence from unlawful or criminal acts.

Entire philosophies of law and justice have been erected around the concept of freedom. "The end of law is not to abolish or restrain, but to preserve and enlarge freedom," asserted John Locke.[3] Jefferson was convinced that liberty was an inherent and inalienable right of human beings. "Man is born free; and everywhere he is in chains," said Rousseau.[4] Herbert Spencer believed that the idea of justice exhausted its meaning for human society in the demand that a maximum amount of liberty be granted to each individual, limited only by the like liberties of others.[5]

When we study the history of civilizations, we find, however, that freedom has by no means been viewed by all political and social systems as a natural and inalienable right of every human being. Large masses of men and women were reduced to slavery in the ancient world, and the institution has not entirely vanished even in modern times. The Middle Ages practiced a mitigated and more humanized type of bondage known as serfdom. Certain modern dictatorships have subjected their peoples to a form of unfreedom which, although not amounting to slavery in the legal sense, exhibits some of the characteristic features of this institution. Must we, then, conclude that freedom, although we may cherish it as a desirable and praiseworthy goal which all systems of law and justice should endeavor to attain, can in no sense be regarded as a "natural right" and indispensable ingredient of every legal system?

The question of whether freedom is or is not a necessary attribute

---

[1] See Bienenfeld, *Rediscovery of Justice*, p. 21.

[2] Spencer, *Justice*, p. 28. On justice and liberty see also Carleton K. Allen, *Aspects of Justice* (London, 1958), pp. 106–153.

[3] *Of Civil Government* (Everyman's Library ed., 1924), Bk. II, ch. vi, sec. 57.

[4] *The Social Contract*, transl. G. D. H. Cole (Everyman's Library ed., 1913), Bk. I, ch. i.

[5] Spencer, p. 45. See *supra* Sec. 44.

of the human personality occupied the minds of Greek and Roman philosophers. Aristotle, assuming that some men were by nature destined to be masters while others were born to be servants, came to the conclusion that for servants the condition of slavery was both beneficial and just.[6] Being aware, however, that the actual practice of slavery in his time was not controlled by this criterion, he added the reservation that "it is easy to see that those who hold the opposite view are also in a way correct," [7] and his entire position with respect to slavery is in fact ambivalent. Quite obviously, even if his cardinal premise as to the division of mankind into masters and servants, leaders and led, is sound, it does not carry with it as a logical corollary the proposition that the servants must be divested altogether of human personality and be degraded to the status of mere "chattels." For some of the Stoic philosophers and legal thinkers of a later period of antiquity, Aristotle's doubts regarding the justification of slavery became a certainty, and they held with Sabinus, the Roman jurist, that "so far as the civil law is concerned, slaves are not considered persons; but this is not the case according to natural law, because natural law regards all men as equal." [8] This position prepared the ideological ground for the gradual amelioration of the status of the slaves in the Roman Empire and the eventual demise of the institution in the Europe of the Middle Ages.

Bishop Isidore of Seville, in the seventh century A.D., also proclaimed "the universal freedom of all" as a command of natural justice.[9] St. Thomas Aquinas, quoting this passage, argued that Isidore's postulate had undergone a change in the course of time, and that some form of serfdom had been found to be useful for society.[10] St. Thomas insisted, however, that unfree men and women should at least be accorded the right to life, sustenance and family relations.[11] The philosophers of the Enlightenment went further and demanded freedom for all men without reservation.

As was pointed out in the beginning of this section, the desire for freedom is undoubtedly a characteristic trait of human beings generally. Toynbee remarks that "man cannot live without a minimum of free-

[6] *The Politics,* transl. E. Barker. Bk. I. 1255a.

[7] *Id.,* Bk. I. 1255a. See also Aristotle, *Nicomachean Ethics,* transl. H. Rackham, Bk. VIII. xi. 7.

[8] *Dig.* L. 17. 32. See also *Inst.* I. 2. 2: "Wars have arisen, and captivity and slavery, which are contrary to natural law, as according to natural law all men were originally born free."

[9] *Etymologia* (in Migne, *Patrologia Latina,* vol. 82), Bk. V, ch. 4. See *supra* Sec. 5.

[10] *Summa Theologica,* transl. Fathers of the English Dominican Province, pt. II, 1st pt., qu. 94, art. 5.

[11] *Id.,* pt. II, 2d pt., qu. 105, art. 4; pt. III, suppl., qu. 52, art. 2.

dom, any more than he can live without a minimum of security, justice, and food. There seems to be in human nature an intractable vein . . . which insists on being allowed a modicum of freedom and which knows how to impose its will when it is goaded beyond endurance." [12] People have a strong desire to realize the potentialities of their personalities and to make productive use of the powers with which nature has endowed them. In the words of Hocking: "It is objectively 'right' that an individual should develop his powers, whatever they are." [13] Provided that we limit this axiom to the *constructive* powers of men, a statement to the effect that some measure of liberty should be held to constitute a "natural right" is not at all devoid of positive meaning. A high civilization benefiting the largest possible number of human beings can only be built if the energies of men are not bound by oppressive shackles. From the point of view of perfect justice, therefore, slavery and serfdom cannot be justified. These institutions can only be explained in terms of possible or probable economic necessity and as historical stepping stones in the endeavor to create greater and richer civilizations.[14] Aristotle saw quite clearly that slavery was a concomitant of a technologically undeveloped society which had not as yet solved the problem of production satisfactorily. He said: "There is only one condition on which we can imagine managers not needing subordinates, and masters not needing slaves. This condition would be that each instrument could do its own work . . . as if a shuttle should weave of itself, and a plectrum should do its own harp-playing." [15] And the distinguished modern anthropologist Bronislaw Malinowski has told us that "perhaps the most positive function of slavery was the creation of a leisure group. The aimless, unwilling, and unpurposeful labor of some gave others more scope for the development of culture. However amoral this may sound, it is a fair description of facts." [16]

If, from the point of view of justice, we decide to recognize a right of universal freedom rooted in the natural inclinations of human beings, we cannot, however, construe this right as being absolute and bound-

[12] Arnold Toynbee, *An Historian's Approach to Religion* (London, 1956), p. 245.
[13] William E. Hocking, *Present Status of the Philosophy of Law and of Rights* (New Haven, 1926), pp. 71–72.
[14] See Rudolph von Jhering, *Geist des Römischen Rechts* (Leipzig, 1866), part II (1), p. 66: "For all peoples which know or have known personal unfreedom either in the form of slavery or serfdom there comes a time when they become cognizant of the unlawfulness thereof and feel obliged in their conscience to terminate this condition."
[15] *The Politics*, Bk. I. 1253b.
[16] Malinowski, *Freedom and Civilization* (Bloomington, Ind., 1960), p. 302. He also points out that "under conditions where large numbers of human beings were necessary for the performance of engineering tasks on a large scale, slave labor was an asset." *Id.*, pp. 299–300.

less. It has been the experience of free societies that all liberties are liable to abuse by unscrupulous individuals and groups, and that they must therefore be subjected to certain restraints in the interest of the public weal. A large part of the constitutional history of the United States can be understood only if it is interpreted as an attempt on the part of the United States Supreme Court to create a workable equilibrium and synthesis between the two polar ideas of liberty and authority. In the words of Chief Justice Stone:

> Man does not live by himself and for himself alone. There comes a point in the organization of a complex society where individualism must yield to traffic regulations, where the right to do as one will with his own must bow to zoning ordinances, or even on occasion to price-fixing regulations. Just where the line is to be drawn which marks the boundary between the appropriate field of individual liberty and right and that of government action for the larger good, so as to insure the least sacrifice of both types of social advantage is the perpetual question of constitutional law.[17]

The character of the synthesis between liberty and restraint has varied throughout the history of this nation. It must necessarily differ according to whether a commonwealth goes through a period of peace or war, prosperity or crisis, disciplined morality or moral disintegration. But while no generally valid precepts or panaceas for reconciling freedom and restraint can be offered, it might be possible (since the results of considerable experimentation with free forms of social organization are available today) to summarize certain conclusions regarding this problem which are likely to be concurred in not only by the large majority of Americans but by informed observers in other civilized communities in the modern world as well. These conclusions (which are not in any sense meant to be exhaustive) are the following: Speech cannot be tolerated which untruthfully defames others. Organized activities aiming at immediate violent revolution need not be countenanced.[18] The use of private property in a manner which seriously and unjustifiably harms or discomforts other members of the community must be curbed. Freedom of transaction should not be extended to include agreements repugnant to morality or prevailing public policy. The conduct of business by means of practices which are regarded as thoroughly unfair by other businessmen or the com-

[17] Harlan F. Stone, "The Common Law in the United States," 50 *Harv. L. Rev.* 4, at 22 (1936).

[18] Here we can perhaps speak of a "natural right" of self-defense of political units, corresponding to the right of self-defense of individuals. See art. 51 of the United Nations Charter, providing that "nothing in the present Charter shall impair the inherent right of individual or collective self-defense." However, it might be argued that a highly oppressive government forfeits its right of self-defense.

munity at large should be subjected to legal restrictions. Freedom of manufacturing is to be limited by the government's power to protect the health of the community, by food and drug laws, for example. Freedom to engage in certain vocations which require special skill ought to be confined to persons who have undergone the requisite professional education and training. Freedom to build should be made subordinate to certain restraints imposed in the interests of public safety and public convenience. The right of free motion should be regulated by traffic laws. Public education should be promoted even though it restricts the liberties of both parents and children. While the details and the manner of operation of these limitations on freedom will vary considerably in different civilized countries, there would seem to exist nearly universal agreement today as to their necessity or desirability.[19]

No discussion of freedom can be complete which fails to recognize that the ideal of freedom has a negative as well as a positive component. Freedom does not only consist in the removal of external restraints and exemption from arbitrary control. It also embraces the opportunity to develop one's natural gifts and acquired skills in the service of the great enterprise called human civilization. Freedom in this sense can be described as "the conditions necessary and sufficient for the formation of a purpose, its translation into effective action through organized cultural instrumentalities, and the full enjoyment of the results of such activity." [20] A man may be completely free from coercive or other harmful restraints, from physical or legal fetters placed on his freedom of movement or expression, but if society affords him no opportunity for useful work and constructive activity, he will not have the sense of being a truly free man. Hence freedom to pursue and attain purposes is as much a significant and vital aspect of the concept in its essential meaning as freedom from external impediment.[21]

Negative freedom from interference may sometimes come into irreconcilable conflict with the positive freedom of realizing one's personal and social capacities. A law forcing parents to send their children to school and keep them in school until they have reached a certain age does not promote freedom from restraint on the part of parents as well

[19] On the relation between freedom and organization see Lon L. Fuller, "Freedom—A Suggested Analysis," 68 *Harv. L. Rev.* 1305 (1955). A different position is taken by Allen, *Aspects of Justice*, pp. 117–118. On the problem of freedom generally see Mortimer J. Adler, *The Idea of Freedom* (Garden City, 1958).

[20] Malinowski, p. 25. See also *id.*, pp. 82, 91, 95.

[21] See Sorley, *The Moral Life*, pp. 103–113. In the view of Fuller, "Freedom—A Suggested Analysis," p. 1305, "the deterioration of the meaning of freedom has been caused in part by a shift of interest away from the notion of 'freedom to' in favor of 'freedom from.'"

as children; but there is little doubt that such a law is beneficial to freedom of self-realization and enlarges the opportunities of children in later life, especially their freedom of vocational choice. Inasmuch as individual development needs to be aided by cultural institutions and proper social surroundings, it is clearly within the competence of the law as a tool of the general welfare to advance the cause of positive freedom, even at the expense of some sacrifice of the negative freedom from restraint.

It is also necessary to emphasize that activities or conditions which increase or guarantee the freedom of one man or group of men may result in the infringement or curtailment of the freedom of another man or group of men. Thus the rights of private property owners may in some cases become pitted against the legitimate interests of agricultural or industrial groups.[22] The freedom of labor unions to enter into closed shop agreements with employers may operate as a reduction of the freedom of workingmen or employees to stay free of union affiliation. In such cases, justice may require "the balancing and the portioning out of freedom." [23] The postulates of freedom may also come into opposition with a social policy designed to maintain a reasonable degree of economic or social equality in the societal order. Therefore, the freedom given to business enterprise to combine and organize the market may result in the growth of monopolies which may endanger the maintenance of equal opportunity in the economic world. What is the measuring rod to be used by the law in attempting to reconcile conflicting freedoms or to harmonize a measure of freedom with the realization of some degree of equality?

Section 49. *Justice and the Common Good*
Justice, as we have seen, requires that human beings be accorded a certain measure of freedom and equality. A social order striving to be just must also grant to men certain other basic rights which may be regarded as aspects of freedom in a larger sense. Among these may be counted the right to life, the right to the security of the person, and the right to own property, together with the necessary legal implementation of these rights.[1] If the state of productivity and the height of the development of the social order permits it, further rights con-

---

[22] See, for example, *Miller v. Schoene,* 276 U.S. 272 (1928); *Head v. Amoskeag Mfg. Co.,* 113 U.S. 9 (1885).
[23] Malinowski, p. 22.
[1] Thus the legal order must provide redress for invasions of the integrity of the person, must restore wrongfully taken property to its owners, and compensate men for other losses which they have suffered through unlawful acts. Without corrective justice, i.e., the defense of the system of rights and duties established by distributive justice, the latter would be ineffective.

tributing to the fullest unfolding of men's constructive powers should be granted. A rich and mature civilization is scarcely attainable unless people are given the right to education. The right to productive work may be viewed as part of freedom in its more inclusive sense. A certain amount of rest and leisure is necessary in order that men and women may effectively perform their chosen tasks. Protection against the hazards of old age, sickness, and unemployment would seem to be called for in a civilization intent upon assuring everybody a full and satisfactory life free from burdensome fear.[2]

None of these rights, however, should be viewed as an absolute to be extended by the legal order to the limits of its bounds. It has already been pointed out that the right to freedom, in its various manifestations and ramifications, is amenable to being abused and perverted by individuals and groups for socially deleterious ends, and, furthermore, that the freedom of one man or group may come into conflict with that of another man or group.[3] All social systems have therefore imposed limitations on freedom in the interest of public welfare. Similar limitations must be recognized with respect to the right of equality. An uncompromising theory of absolute equality will lead logically to the doctrine of communism, according to which each person must receive "according to his needs." Although from the point of view of the individual the materialization of this postulate could hardly be objected to as "unjust," it is unlikely that the principle would function satisfactorily as a proper rationale of social organization. Its realization would tend to stifle incentive and initiative, two values which, according to past human experience, are stimulated by the promise of special rewards for special merit. Men should have enough equality to enable each person to reach the station for which he is best fitted, but this equality should not be held to stand in irreconcilable opposition to the idea of unequal recompense for unequal achievements.

We must come to the conclusion, therefore, that a perspective of appraisal which takes into account not only the desires of individuals, but also the effects of the system of distribution viewed in terms of the total social good accomplished by it, must recognize the reasonableness and justice of certain limitations placed upon human equality. As W. D. Lamont has pointed out correctly, certain inequalities appear to be necessary for the promotion of progress and creative effort and cannot, for this reason, be condemned as "unjust." [4]

It follows that the notions of liberty, equality, and fundamental

[2] See in this connection the *Declaration of Human Rights* adopted by the UN Assembly Dec. 10, 1948.
[3] See *supra* Sec. 48.
[4] *The Principles of Moral Judgement* (Oxford, 1946), pp. 154–161.

rights are not entirely sufficient to explain and determine the idea of justice. A realistic conception of justice—reckoning with the imperfections of human nature, the shortcomings of human knowledge, and the limiting conditions of technology, economic development, and natural resources—must make the basic rights of the individual to some extent subject to the needs engendered by social interdependence and the requirements of cooperative human effort.[5] Justice, in other words, requires some accommodation and synthesis between individual and community values. The relation between individual rights and the public welfare in the realization of justice may be expressed in the following formula: *Justice demands that freedom, equality, and other basic rights be accorded and secured to human beings to the greatest extent consistent with the common good.*[6]

This formula leads us to the analysis of the concept of the common good, an analysis which is attended with great difficulties because a very large number of variables must necessarily enter into the definition of the concept.[7] Nevertheless a few general principles for determining the content and scope of the concept can perhaps be stated.

First of all, the common good or public welfare clearly cannot be identified with the sum total of the demands and desires of individuals, since we know from experience that some demands of individuals are unreasonable from the point of view of the welfare of society, and that individuals are capable of actions harmful to the common weal. Second, it is similarly impermissible to identify the common good with the demands or desires of rulers or ruling groups. Government officials may misconceive the community interest, make serious and unquestionable mistakes in framing and executing public policies, and may lead the state to ruin and disaster. The large majority of rational human beings would certainly reject a view according to which the wishes, conveniences, or actions of the rulers were deemed to be auto-

---

[5] Cf. art. 20 (2) of the *Declaration of Human Rights:* "In the exercise of his rights and freedoms, everyone shall be subject only to such limitations as are determined by law solely for the purpose of securing due recognition and respect for the rights and freedoms of others and of meeting the just requirements of morality, public order, and the general welfare in a democratic society." See also Hermann Heller, *Staatslehre* (Leiden, 1934), p. 218.

[6] John Salmond points out correctly that "the rule of justice determines the sphere of individual liberty in the pursuit of individual welfare, so as to confine that liberty within the limits which are consistent with the general welfare of mankind," but fails to discuss the role of equality and other basic rights in the realization of justice. See Salmond, *Jurisprudence*, 11th ed. by G. Williams (London, 1957), p. 63.

[7] The following definition is given by Vera Bolgár, "The Concept of Public Welfare," 8 *American Journal of Comparative Law* 44, at 47 (1959): "The legal definition of public welfare is . . . the extent to which a given society accepts regulation by law in the sphere of individual rights and, conversely, the extent to which these rights, if violated, are given protection by law."

matic expressions of the common good regardless of their consequences for society. Neither individual desire nor governmental expediency as such can provide the basis for a meaningful conception of the common good.

In order to arrive at a conception of the common good which, presumably and presumptively, would comport with the true interests and aspirations of mankind, it would appear necessary to introduce the idea of *civilization*. A general determination of the content and scope of the common good must start from the insight that an individual can have a full and satisfying life only if he makes a contribution in some measure to that great enterprise called "the building of civilizations." The erection of stately and livable cities, the cultivation of the soil in order to secure the means for sustaining life, the production of goods designed to reduce the hardships or increase the amenities of life, the invention of devices for transportation and communication in order to promote traffic and intercourse between men and to give men access to the beauties of nature, the search for knowledge and the fostering of the spiritual powers of men, the creation of great works of literature, art, and music—these endeavors have through the centuries aroused the admiration of men and harnessed their energies at the highest level.[8] As Gustav Radbruch has wisely observed, history has always judged nations and peoples by the contributions they have made to culture and civilization.[9]

Our concept of civilization would be too narrowly delimited, however, if it were held to comprise only the material, technological, intellectual, and artistic elements of human culture. It must also be held to include the ethical aspects of human social life, whether they manifest themselves in religious or secular form. In the words of the educator Friedrich Wilhelm Foerster:

> The whole gigantic enterprise of technology, with all the as yet unimaginable consequences of atomic discoveries, requires for its success much more than a mere scientific and material apparatus; this enterprise makes such tremendous demands upon the social and ethical culture of the living person, who is supposed to harmonize the various functions of the giant machinery and to prevent their misuse, that in reality all technology represents a lost cause unless a spiritual and moral rebirth comes to its succor. Technology without ethics would be like a living being without soul and without a conscience.[10]

[8] See the further comments on this subject *infra* Sec. 59.
[9] "Legal Philosophy," in *Legal Philosophies of Lask, Radbruch, and Dabin*, p. 97.
[10] *Die Hauptaufgaben der Erziehung* (Freiburg, 1959), p. 163 (translation mine).
The ethical element in culture is insufficiently emphasized by Joseph Kohler, *Philosophy of Law*, transl. A. Albrecht (New York, 1921), pp. 4-5, 22. On Kohler see *supra* Sec. 27.

A materially and intellectually advanced civilization will be unable to guarantee the "good life" unless it has also taught men to temper self-interest by self-restriction in the interest of others, to respect the dignity of fellow men, and to devise proper rules for coexistence and co-operation on the various levels of group life, including the international community.

If it is true that the principal goal of mankind should be the development of all constructive forces latent in man, the crucial question as to the proper relation between individual and social effort in this process of building civilizations arises at the outset. Quite obviously the individual cannot attain the self-realization to which his nature impels him as an isolated being in a social vacuum. Without the framework of a social system affording him opportunities for productive effort he cannot develop his powers to the fullest. On the other hand, the human personality is much more than a functional element in an organized group endeavor. Those tasks which make a social order worthy of being called a civilization can never be executed by a group or collective entity as such; their fulfillment requires the cooperation of creative individuals. Thus, there must be an active interplay between individual and social effort in the building of civilizations. Under favorable conditions, for example, where there is a new and rich continent to develop, the degree of individual effort may far outweigh the volume of group control of the societal processes. Under unfavorable conditions, as, for instance, when natural resources or human manpower are scarce in a country or when a community or nation is threatened by external enemies, a strong collective effort may be necessary to ensure survival or growth. A general formula for the right proportion between individual initiative and collective direction can, therefore, never be given. It can be asserted as an invariable axiom, however, that no workable form of society can be imagined in which individual action is not subject to some degree of social control.

While there must be interplay between individual and social effort, there need not be full congruence or coordination between these two. Historical and sociological experience would seem to demonstrate conclusively that advancement in culture, science, economics, and political forms has often been due to the ideas, teachings, or actions of individuals dissenting from and at odds with the generally accepted beliefs of the community. A social authority which is intent solely upon preserving its own power and prestige and which suppresses all individual attempts at social criticism and all challenges to group purpose, will stagnate and be unable to carry out the aims which, according to the thesis here advanced, alone will justify the existence of a coercive social power. There must be room for cooperation as well as for healthy tension between the individual and the group within the social order.

These broad outlines of a general frame of reference within whose confining limits the notion of the common good would have its operating radius leave innumerable questions unanswered. Many of these questions cannot be answered generally and abstractly. The needs of society cannot be the same under different historical and sociological conditions. In times of crisis, stress, and war, for instance, the public welfare usually makes more stringent and burdensome demands upon individuals and groups than in times of peace and prosperity. It is believed, however, that a general determination of the concept according to which the measures designed to realize the public good should be directed toward the task of securing the productive use of all human faculties and capabilities comports with the aspirations of the large majority of men in our age.[11]

[11] Verdross defines the concept of the common good as follows: "*Bonum commune* is neither the sum of the goods desired by individual persons nor the advantage of a human collective whole but the aggregate of the things of value produced in a community through the collaboration of individuals which must exist in order to enable human beings, by effort and labor, to shape their own life so that it comports with the dignity of the human personality." Alfred Verdross, *Abendländische Rechtsphilosophie* (Vienna, 1958), p. 245. See also the discussion of the "Principle of the Common Need," by Lon L. Fuller, *The Problems of Jurisprudence*, temporary ed. (Brooklyn, 1949), pp. 694–701.

XII

LAW AS A SYNTHESIS
OF ORDER AND JUSTICE

Section 50. *The Relation Between Order and Justice*
The attempt has been made in the two preceding chapters to demonstrate that a legal system, in order to fulfill its function properly, must aim at the creation of order as well as the realization of justice. This assertion will perhaps be questioned on the ground that no human institution can serve two masters at the same time. This may be true where the two masters pursue entirely different objectives, give inconsistent and irreconcilable orders, and find themselves at cross-purposes almost every time they embark on a certain course of action. Where, on the other hand, the two masters strive for the same major goals, cooperate in the pursuit of these goals, and do not part ways except on relatively infrequent occasions, service for one of them does not exclude service for the other. In a healthy legal system the values of order and justice are not normally at cross-purposes; on the contrary, they are locked together in a higher union. A legal system that cannot meet the basic demands of justice will be unable, in the long run, to

provide order and peace for the body politic.[1] On the other hand, justice cannot be accomplished without an orderly system of judicial administration which will insure the equal treatment of equal situations.[2] Thus the maintenance of order is to some extent conditioned by the existence of a reasonably healthy system of law, while justice needs the helping hand of order to perform some of its essential functions.

Nevertheless there will be occasions when order and justice will part company. As a general rule, in the interest of legal security and calculability of the law, the existing positive structure of the law must be deemed the basis of legal administration and adjudication.[3] But there may occur some very rare and unusual situations, under special political conditions, where certain deficiencies and inadequacies of the enacted positive law have become so glaring, irremediable, and intolerable that a breakthrough of elementary justice must be permitted as an *ultima ratio*.[4]

The view here taken ascribes to order and justice positions of equivalence in accomplishing the objectives of the law. This standpoint is by no means generally accepted. St. Augustine and St. Thomas Aquinas considered justice to be the overriding objective of the law and consequently came to the conclusion that an unjust law lacked the attribute of a law.[5] Conversely, legal positivists like Austin and Kelsen regarded law predominantly as a system of order designed to impart certainty and regularity to human relations, and these writers relegated the problem of justice entirely to the nonlegal and wholly subjective domain of personal evaluation.[6] The modern Latin American legal philosopher Luis Recaséns Siches takes the position that certainty and security constitute the primary and immediate aims of the law, its "basic motiva-

---

[1] This will be shown later in this section and also *infra* Sec. 54.

[2] See *supra* Sec. 47. In accord: H. L. A. Hart, "Positivism and the Separation of Law and Morals," 71 *Harvard Law Review* 593, at 624 (1958): "It is . . . true that *one* essential element of the concept of justice is the principle of treating like cases alike."

[3] It will also be shown, however, that the existing positive structure of the law is necessarily incomplete and gapridden, and that numerous opportunities for introducing considerations of justice, reason, and equity will present themselves to those concerned with the application and interpretation of the law. See particularly *infra* Secs. 69–71. See also Sec. 80 on the right to overrule obsolete or unreasonable judicial precedents.

[4] See *infra* Secs. 53 and 69.

[5] See *supra* Secs. 5 and 6. St. Thomas Aquinas made a concession to the idea of order, however, by pointing out that sometimes a person subjected to an unjust law should yield his right of opposing its application "in order to avoid scandal and disturbance." *Summa Theologica*, transl. Fathers of the English Dominican Province (London, 1913–1925), pt. II, 1st pt., qu. 96, art. 4.

[6] See *supra* Sec. 44.

tion"; justice, on the other hand, should be sought after by the law-makers as a more remote and ultimate end. He says: "Law was not born into human life by reason of the desire to render tribute or homage to the idea of justice, but to fulfill an inescapable urgency for security and certainty in social life. The question of why and wherefore men make Law is not answered in the structure of the idea of justice . . . but in a subordinate value—security—corresponding to a human need." [7]

There is serious doubt, however, whether a social system fulfilling the requirements of order and legal certainty can be effective without the presence of a substantial ingredient of justice. If the feelings of fairness of a large part of the population are outraged by a system of law purporting to establish "orderly" conditions of life, it will be extremely difficult for the public authorities to maintain such a legal system against attempts at evasion or subversion. Men will not stand long for an order they feel to be totally unreasonable and unbearable, and a government bent on perpetuating such an order will run into serious difficulties of enforcement. Thus an order which does not have a substantial anchorage in justice will rest on an unsafe and precarious basis. As John Dickinson points out: "We come upon the need for not merely a system of fixed general rules, but of rules based on justice, or in other words, on a regard for certain demands and capacities of human nature. Otherwise the system would not be workable; offending ingrained proclivities and standards of judgment, it would be continually violated and so fail to yield the certainty which is the excuse for its existence." [8]

It might be objected that for many centuries large aggregates of human beings have endured the oppressive condition of slavery, and that in other historical instances the lower classes have frequently borne poverty, disease, and substandard conditions of life without murmur or complaint. The answer, insofar as slavery is concerned, must be that the law of slavery delegated unlimited authority over the slaves to the master, and that the treatment to which the slaves were

---

[7] "Human Life, Society, and Law," transl. G. Ireland, in *Latin-American Legal Philosophy* (Cambridge, Mass., 1948), p. 119. See also *id.*, p. 123: "Security is the fundamental value of juristics, without which there can be no Law. . . . It is true, moreover, that the Law ought to be just, to serve the common good, etc. . . . But, on the other hand, if it does not represent an order of security, then, it is not Law of any sort." Cf. also pp. 309–319. On Recaséns Siches see also *supra* Sec. 37.

[8] *Administrative Justice and the Supremacy of Law* (Cambridge, Mass., 1922), p. 113.

Various problems involving the relation between order and justice are discussed by Carl J. Friedrich, *The Philosophy of Law in Historical Perspective* (Chicago, 1958), chs. xx and xxii.

subjected depended entirely on the "law" laid down by the master for the slave estate. The history of Roman slavery teaches us that during those periods in which the treatment of slaves by their masters was frequently cruel and inhuman, public order was sometimes seriously disturbed by slave uprisings and even protracted slave wars.[9] Even slaves will not tolerate conditions they feel to be totally unbearable. With respect to the second objection, it is undoubtedly true that large masses of people have sometimes humbly accepted misery, sufferings, and deprivations by virtue of religious or other beliefs in the inevitability and God-given necessity of the existing order of things. Assuming that this belief was unjustified and that these disfavored classes could actually have been accorded a greater share of rights and benefits than they were permitted to enjoy, the example proves merely that the sense of injustice contains a subjective ingredient which requires consciousness of unreasonable discrimination as a condition of its emergence. This is one of those factors which render justice subject to certain historical and psychological contingencies. Where, on the other hand, the feelings of justice of substantial numbers of people have been thoroughly aroused, some form of vigorous social action has usually been the consequence. Oppressed minorities have sometimes caused serious difficulties to their oppressors.

We turn next to the question of whether a system of law would be feasible which dispenses entirely with ordered regularity and certainty and concentrates its efforts solely on administering an individualized justice to the members of the community. The answer to this question must be that such a system would not be workable and has in fact never been operative in the practice of communities or states. The human desire for normative guidance is so strong that a system which abandons any and all standards of judgment and relies solely on the free and unfettered intelligence of its judges will, by its very nature, fall. This statement is not meant to imply, however, that such normative guidance must necessarily be provided by legal rules, statutes, ordinances, or precedents. The canons of conduct lending a modicum of consistency to the administration of the law may be of a social, ethical, or religious character, they may rest on usage and custom, or they may be shaped by the intrinsic logic of the social institutions which prevail in a particular society. Even Plato, who in his earlier writings went far in decrying the use of fixed and circumscribed rules and principles in the administration of justice,[10] desired his judges to

[9] See Wilhelm Kroll, *Die Kultur der Ciceronischen Zeit*, II, 83 (Leipzig, 1933); M. I. Rostovtzeff, *History of the Ancient World* (New York, 1930), II, 118.
[10] See *supra* Sec. 2.

be bound by the social and moral philosophy of his ideal common-wealth, whose contents he laid down in considerable detail in his *Republic*.

Order and regularity are in another and equally significant sense essential to the accomplishment of justice. As we have seen, justice requires the equal treatment of equal or substantially similar situations. Since there may be serious differences of opinion among the various judges in an organized community as to what situations require like or similar decisions, the recognition of a body of binding standards of adjudication is well-nigh indispensable for the proper discharge of the judicial function. Here again justice and the need for certainty join hands in calling for some measure of normativeness in law.

It was pointed out earlier, however, that the notion of justice does not exhaust its vitality in the postulate of equal treatment.[11] It also requires an individualized treatment of situations which exhibit unique or extraordinary features and cannot be adequately handled by the application of strict rules or by comparing the case before the court with previously decided cases. In such instances, a departure from or relaxation of fixed norms may be necessary and desirable in the interest of justice, whereas order tends to favor regularity and invariant ad-herence to rules.

This problem was recognized by Aristotle, who pointed out that "there are some cases for which it is impossible to lay down a law, so that a special ordinance becomes necessary." [12] The solution which he proposed for the disposition of such cases was as follows: "When therefore the law lays down a general rule, and thereafter a case arises which is an exception to the rule, it is then right, where the lawgiver's pronouncement because of its absoluteness is defective and erroneous, to rectify the defect by deciding as the lawgiver would himself decide if he were present on the occasion, and would have enacted if he had been cognizant of the case in question." [13] We must be conscious, how-ever, that such a judicial engrafting of an exception or qualification upon a previously existing rule of law may in many cases be no more than the initiation of a new normative standard to be applied to all similarly situated cases in the future. The judge finds that the classifica-tions and differentiations made by the *lex lata* are too crude or too sweeping, and that they should be replaced by more refined and highly restricted generalizations.

[11] See *supra* Sec. 47
[12] *The Nicomachean Ethics*, transl. H. Rackham (Loeb Classical Library ed., 1944), Bk. V. x. 6–7.
[13] *Ibid.*

Examples of this process can be found in English as well as Roman law. Thus, when the English Chancery for the first time granted specific performance of a contract, it did so on grounds of equity or conscience, because the chancellor felt that the common-law remedy of damages could not adequately compensate the plaintiff for the harm inflicted on him by the defendant's breach of contract. However, as soon as specific performance was granted as a matter of course in other and similar cases in which the remedy at law was found inadequate, the original equitable departure from the letter of the common law became transformed into a "rule of equity jurisprudence." By the same token, when the Roman praetor permitted new actions and defenses in instances where the ancient *jus civile* was found defective because of its rigidity and narrowness, such innovations became incorporated into a separate body of law known as *jus honorarium*. Such developments throw a great deal of light on the nature of law as a vehicle of what might be called *progressive differentiation*, that is, an increasing adaptation of the classifications and distinctions of the law to the boundless complexities and variations of life. Sir Henry Maine was fully justified when he characterized the two great historical systems of equity jurisprudence as instrumentalities of legal growth and law reform.[14] But it must be kept in mind that this evolution of equity jurisprudence furnishes evidence in favor of, and not against, the essentially normative character of law.

The term "equity" may, however, also be used in a different and more restricted sense. An equitable decision may be one that is neither based on an existing rule of law nor designed to inaugurate a new sequence of precedents. Its sole aim may be to do justice to the parties in a case characterized by a configuration of facts unlikely ever to be repeated in reality in the same or a similar way. As H. G. Hanbury has well said: "Every legal system must at times find the peculiarly hard case that cries aloud for relief, the case which no judge could decide according to rule without putting an intolerable strain on his own conscience." [15] In view of the historical connotations associated with the Anglo-American system of equity jurisprudence, it might perhaps be desirable to use a term other than equity to describe this aspect of the judicial process. The Germans speak of *Billigkeit;* we might possibly adopt the Greek word *epieikeia* or the phrase "individual equity" to identify the phenomenon. Whatever terminology is chosen, this judicial vehicle for accomplishing justice, since it lacks the normative element typical for legal regulation, should clearly be distinguished

---

[14] *Ancient Law*, Pollock's ed. (London, 1930), pp. 31, 34–35.
[15] *Modern Equity*, 7th ed. (London, 1957), p. 4.

from "law" in the proper sense, a distinction which Aristotle lucidly drew in his *Nicomachean Ethics*.

While the number of occasions calling for the application of *epiei-keia* may not be as large as is sometimes believed, most legal systems have developed some mechanisms to cope with the problem. The Romans granted their emperors broad prerogatives in dispensing from the law. Whenever the emperor (or the jurists advising him) felt that the application of a statutory or other rule would lead to an inadequate or iniquitous result, he had the power to set aside the rule for this particular case. The same kind of dispensing power is exercised by the Pope under canon law. Under the American legal system, the judge is given discretion to "balance the equities" in certain types of situations; the judge in most states is given power to consider individual circumstances in the award of custody of minors and the distribution of property in divorce cases; the power of pardoning possessed by the chief executive is essentially the power to minister equity or grace where extenuating factors were not, or could not be, sufficiently taken into account by the court; and juries have sometimes corrected rigidities and inadequacies in the law by exercising what Judge Frank has called "fact discretion." [16] As long as the power to mete out *epieikeia* is kept within narrowly confined and reasonable bounds and is not used to an extent destructive of the normative system, it might be safe and desirable to invest the judge with such a power even in those legal systems which do not entrust the judges with the prerogative to effect substantial innovations in the body of the law.[17]

Apart from the cases in which an individualization of justice becomes necessary, disparities between the claims of order and justice may arise in another context. An existing legal system may be felt to be just, or at least tolerably reasonable, by the community as long as it satisfies the basic needs and demands of the people. By virtue of a change in economic or social conditions, technological advances, governmental mismanagement, or deterioration of a ruling elite, this state of general satisfaction may give way to discontent and a widespread conviction that the existing legal order should be displaced by one better adapted to the people's sense of justice. If a piecemeal adaptation of the law to newly arising conditions and problems cannot be made because of inertia or resistance to needed change, a social crisis or revolution will sometimes bring about a substantial reform or overhauling of the legal system which will close or at least lessen the distance between the two paramount goals of the law.

[16] Jerome Frank, *Courts on Trial* (Princeton, 1949), p. 328.
[17] A further discussion of this problem is found *infra* Sec. 71.

Section 51. *Stability and Change in Law*

"Law must be stable, and yet it cannot stand still." [1] These words of Roscoe Pound are the expression of a lasting and irrefutable truth. A legal order completely devoid of stability would be nothing but a cluster of *ad hoc* measures designed to cope merely with the ephemeral exigencies of the moment. It would lack cohesion and continuity. In entering into agreements or consummating other transactions, people could never be sure whether the law of yesterday would still be the law of tomorrow. "Law as a guide to conduct is reduced to the level of mere futility if it is unknown and unknowable." [2] Conditions of excessive fluidity and chronic instability, resulting in day-to-day changes in the law, are therefore incompatible with the very idea of the law.

Stability and certainty alone, however, are not sufficient to provide us with an effective, vital system of law. Progress also has a justified claim upon the law. A legal system which is out of gear with the necessities and demands of the day and which perpetuates the transient ideas of a past epoch has little to recommend itself. In a fluid world, law cannot function effectively if it is conceived solely as an instrument of permanence. Some reconciliation must be brought about between the contradictory forces of mobility and rest, conservation and innovation, constancy and change.[3] Law, being the cement which holds the social structure together, must intelligently link the past with the present without ignoring the pressing claims of the future.

This whole problem is closely related to the subject discussed in the preceding section. Insofar as the law strives to promote the social value of order, it is bound to pay homage to the ideas of continuity and stability. Order in social life, as we have seen,[4] is concerned with the establishment of patterns for human action and conduct, and such patterns cannot be accomplished without relating and assimilating the behavior of today to that of yesterday. If the law did not act as a brake on incessant and indiscriminate change, chaos rather than order would be the result. The command of *stare decisis* and the observance of enacted statutory norms are therefore apt instruments for the promotion of order.[5]

The pursuit of justice in the administration of the law, on the other hand, may sometimes call for considerations of a different character.

---

[1] *Interpretations of Legal History* (Cambridge, Mass., 1923), p. 1.
[2] Benjamin N. Cardozo, *The Growth of the Law* (New Haven, 1924), p. 3.
[3] Excellent reflections on this problem are found in Cardozo, pp. 1–3, 143–145; see also Cardozo, *The Paradoxes of Legal Science* (New York, 1928), pp. 1–30.
[4] See *supra* Sec. 42.
[5] See *infra* Secs. 79 and 80.

While the doctrine of precedent, born of the desire for order and regularity, demands that a fact situation which in the past has been decided in a certain way should be decided in the same fashion today, the equality contemplated by justice is not necessarily an equalization of past and present decisions. Justice, under certain conditions, will postulate an equality in space rather than an equality in time. It is just to treat two persons, groups, or situations equally which under the current standards of society deserve equality of treatment. Thus, conflicts between *stare decisis* and justice will arise whenever the value judgments of the past no longer comport with those of the present. In such cases, the difficult task of maintaining a salutary equilibrium between respect for precedent and deference to justice is presented to the organs of judicial administration.[6] A good example of the existence of such a conflict and its solution by judicial action is offered in the case of *Oppenheim v. Kridel*,[7] where the New York Court of Appeals held that a woman may maintain an action for criminal conversation against her husband's paramour. The common-law precedents, resting on the doctrine of the married woman's disability to bring suits, had limited such actions to husbands. The court rejected these precedents on the ground that social, political, and legal reforms had changed the relations between the sexes, so as to put men and women on a plane of equality.[8] In the School Segregation Case, the United States Supreme Court repudiated an earlier decision upholding segregation of races on the ground that contemporary notions of racial equality rendered its continued validity nugatory.[9]

To reconcile equality in point of time, that is, the application of prior decisions to equal or essentially similar situations, with spatial equality, the equal treatment of persons and things which under the social philosophy of the present should be dealt with alike, is a task of considerable difficulty. It involves the proper gauging of the speed with which the law should be adapted to the fluctuating currents of the day and also an appraisal of the permanence and finality of newly emerging social ideals or trends. Some other things must also be taken into account when a court is confronted with the task of discarding an earlier judicial doctrine; among them are, for example, the degree of faith that has been placed by a party to the suit on the continued force of the rule embodied in the precedent, as well as the effect of the court's reversal of position on legal relations and transactions not in-

[6] See Cardozo, *Paradoxes*, p. 30.
[7] 236 N.Y. 156, 140 N.E. 227 (1923).
[8] The case is discussed in Cardozo, *Growth of the Law*, p. 105.
[9] *Brown v. Board of Education*, 347 U.S. 483 (1954).

volved in the litigation at hand but contracted in reliance on the earlier rule. In England, where the most important courts are not free to set aside their own precedents, this problem does not possess the same importance as in the United States.[10]

The order function of law reflected in the twin doctrines of precedent and compliance with statutes has a tendency to freeze and stiffen the law, and to preserve the social and economic *status quo*. It promotes the retrospective and inertial forces inherent in the law and makes the institution of law to some extent resistant to change. It is not easy to remedy this shortcoming entirely from within the legal system, through judicial action. Relief often comes from the outside, either through the exercise of political power to improve the law through legislation, or by setting up a system of equity as a complement and corrective to the system of law in the strict sense. It is instructive and revealing to note that the Romans as well as the English developed special procedures and institutions of equity as an antidote to the formalism and inflexibility of their strict law, and for the purpose of rectifying the deficiencies resulting from the conservatism of the orthodox body of law.[11] Such procedures demonstrate the force of *justice* in the law, that is, of a largely teleologically directed force which acts to keep the law in balance with the conscience of the community.

In conclusion, it might be observed that both the backward pull and the forward push are essential to the proper working of any legal system. The relative strength of the past-oriented and future-oriented forces in legal development varies in different epochs of the history of a nation. An ideal system of law would presumably be one in which the necessary revisions of the law were brought about at the appropriate time by orderly procedures and with a minimum of hardship upon those who might become innocent victims of the change.

Section 52. *The Imperative and the Societal Elements in Law*
Those jurisprudential writers who regard the maintenance of order and internal peace as the exclusive or foremost task of the law will be inclined to look upon the law as a mandate or command from the government, designed to realize and guarantee the effectuation of these goals. Without some range and coordination of governmental action, it is difficult to maintain public order, especially in a complex and differentiated society. Government, however, always involves the employment of directive and, if necessary, coercive power by a mi-

[10] For a further discussion of this question see *infra* Sec. 80.
[11] See *supra* Sec. 50.

nority of the population. It is usually impossible to obtain the consent of every member of the community to those measures of social control which affect their interests and well-being, and the enactment of such measures must therefore be committed to a smaller body endowed with special authority and prerogatives. John Austin and his followers designated the organ vested with the right to exact obedience to its enactments "the sovereign," and the commands issued by the sovereign power constituted for them the substance and heart of the law.[1]

There exists, however, another school of legal philosophy, founded by Eugen Ehrlich, whose representatives regard the law as an aggregate of the arrangements, daily usages, and principles of justice observed by the members of a society rather than as a body of commands issued by the organs of sovereignty.[2] To them, the law as lived by the people, finding reflection in their marriage arrangements, property dealings, inheritance dispositions, and in the internal laws of their groupings and associations, is of greater significance for an understanding of the legal order than a study of the ways by which the government enforces its commands through court judgments (which are regarded by Ehrlich as exceptional occurrences). This sociological school tends to emphasize those elements in the institution of law which render it apt to serve as an instrument for the spontaneous, noncoercive adjustment of the mutual claims and demands of ordinary men living together in society and entering into various kinds of relations with each other.

In passing judgment upon these two opposing theories, one is not forced to accept the conclusion that they are necessarily incompatible or exclusive of each other. Government, in issuing its laws and decrees, may heed and observe the basic dictates of justice; its formal codes may essentially be a reflection of the prevailing convictions of the people. On the other hand, many of the arrangements, customs and practices of the community may be in perfect harmony with the promptings of public order. Hence, an absolutistic theory which links law either exclusively with government and order or identifies it one-sidedly with the folkways of the people and their ideals of justice cannot be said to portray reality correctly.

There is, however, a strong possibility that a gap may occur between the decreed law of the government and the living law of the people. The populace may refuse to accept portions of the imposed law and attempt to evade it wherever possible. Conversely, the government may refuse to accept the prevailing folkways and attempt to

[1] On Austin and the analytical school of law see *supra* Sec. 25.
[2] On Ehrlich and the sociological school of law see *supra* Sec. 27.

change them by force if necessary. In that case, a dispute may arise as to whether governmental command or popular conviction represents the "true" law.

In a democratic system, the potential gap between governmental fiat and societal interest is assumed to be reduced to a narrow margin by a mode of popular election of legislative bodies under which the primary obligation of the elected representatives is seen in the faithful representation of the interests of the governed. It is postulated that the law as enacted by the legislators should do no more than to record and register the wishes and needs of the people. In the reality known to us, this postulate is not always lived up to in democratic states. The legislators may misconceive the desires of the people or sacrifice them to the special interests of economically powerful groups. They may enact laws which they regard as necessary in order to strengthen internal security or to meet an emergency, but which severely curb and restrict the rights and freedoms of the population and do not for this reason meet with popular approval. In nondemocratic forms of society, the possibilities for a discrepancy between governmental policy and the wishes and feelings of the people are greatly multiplied; it may happen that the machinery of the state is employed chiefly for the purpose of maintaining and solidifying the existing political regime, with only scant attention paid to the reactions of the masses to the enacted measures or to the intrinsic justice of the legal order.

A discriminating philosophy of law will recognize that under no political or social system is law either wholly governmental or wholly societal. Such a philosophy will hold that law arises from the tensions and adjustments between society and its rulers, and that the institution of law represents a subtle interplay between imperative and sociological factors, with one of the two elements frequently prevailing over the other in different nations and in different phases of their history. Some modus vivendi between the government and the people must be found in order to preserve the integrity and effectiveness of the legal system. If the government is too far ahead of what the people are ready to accept, or if, conversely, a forward-moving nation is held back by a retrogressive-minded government, the legal system, in whole or in part, is headed for trouble.

The ideal situation is attained when the norms of the lawgiver conform completely to the value judgments and genuine interests of the entire community, but political reality often falls far short of this ideal. It may be that the lawmakers are the representatives of a group of conquerors who impose their system of value judgments upon the masses of the conquered. It may be that they are the agents of an economically or politically dominant group whose views on desirable social policy are colored by class bias or class interest. There exists also the possibility that the governmental leaders are high-minded reformers resolved to elevate the ethical standards of the community or to remedy a retardation of development caused by stubborn adherence to obsolete custom.[3] It might be observed in connection with this last possibility that it would be shortsighted to hold that the positive law enacted by the government can under no circumstances do more than faithfully reflect and record popular opinion and custom. The instrumentality of positive law may legitimately be used to overcome social inertia and pave the way for basic readjustments in the mode of living of a people.[4]

When we reach the extreme borderline situations in this area of "ethico-imperative coordination," [5] we may come to a point where we may be stepping outside of the proper institutional limits of the law. If there is a complete lack of normative direction by the appointed organs of government, we may be confronted with a condition in which law has dissolved into anarchy; [6] this may be true, for instance, in a situation where different classes or factions in society espouse and practice totally irreconcilable forms of "living law." If this occurs, law may entirely or largely disappear, and a battle or civil war of antagonistic groups may temporarily displace it.

The other extreme would be presented in the case of a totally despotic order of society. In such an order, the law might—at least in part—be filled with a content which completely lacks reasonableness and which large groups of the population regard as unacceptable. If the degeneration of law into oppressive tyranny reaches a degree of repugnance to the people's sense of justice which can be described as unbearable, the problem of the validity of such totally unjust legal measures comes to the fore and calls for a solution.

Section 53. *The Validity of Unjust Law*

A legal philosophy which regards law as an aggregate of governmental commands designed to keep order in society will be inclined to uphold the validity and binding force of such commands regardless of their

[3] These various possibilities are mentioned by Max Rheinstein in "Sociology of Law," 48 *Ethics* 232, at 235 (1938).

[4] In India, for example, the government by positive enactments set about to accelerate the demise of an outworn caste system.

[5] This, according to Timasheff, is the chief issue confronting the law as a political and social institution. See N. S. Timasheff, *Introduction to the Sociology of Law* (Cambridge, Mass., 1939), pp. 15, 245–248.

[6] See *supra* Sec. 41. Such situations, as was pointed out there, are rare.

intrinsic and substantive content. This has been the position of such positivistic philosophers as John Austin and Hans Kelsen. In their opinion, law constitutes a social mechanism engendered by a certain formalized procedure; as long as the constitutional or institutional directives for the production of valid law are observed, law has authoritative force and must be applied and obeyed regardless of the reasonableness of the enacted measures.[1] According to this view, justice is not an independent criterion to be used in determining the "rightness" of law. On the contrary, the concept of justice tends to become completely merged in the notions of positiveness and formal legality;[2] and if the term injustice is used in a sense which suggests disagreement with the content of a legal norm, it is held that its only meaning can be the expression of a subjective and irrational preference by the utterer of the criticism.[3]

Those legal philosophers who see the overriding goal of the law in the realization of justice in society, on the other hand, are likely to view the problem of the validity of unjust law in a different light. They will consider the enactment of a totally unjust law as a frustration of the paramount goal of legal regulation and will hold such a law to be tainted with serious vice. St. Augustine, a representative of this philosophy, came to the conclusion that a law that was not just was no law at all.[4] St. Thomas Aquinas held that an unjust law was not a law, but "a perversion of law."[5] John Locke pointed out that legislators passing oppressive and arbitrary laws "put themselves into a state of war with the people, who are thereupon absolved from any farther obedience."[6] Jefferson, under the influence of Locke, enunciated in the American Declaration of Independence the principle that in the case of a "long train of abuses" the people should have a right to rebel against the execution of tyrannous laws.

[1] See John Austin, *Lectures on Jurisprudence,* 5th ed. by R. Campbell (London, 1885), I, 218; Hans Kelsen, "The Pure Theory of Law," 50 *Law Quarterly Review* 474, at 488 (1934), 51 *L. Q. Rev.* 517, at 518, 534 (1935).

[2] See Austin, I, 218: "The law itself is the standard of justice"; Kelsen, "The Pure Theory of Law," 50 *L. Q. Rev.* 474, at 482 (1934): " 'Just' is only another word for 'legal' or 'legitimate.' "

[3] According to John Austin, "the terms just and unjust imply conformity to the standard set by the law and a deviation from it; or else they signify mere dislike which it would be far better to signify by a grunt or a groan than by a mischievous and detestable abuse of articulate language." See Austin, I, 218; see also Kelsen, *op. cit. supra* n. 2, p. 482.

[4] "The City of God," Bk. XIX, ch. 21, in *Basic Writings of Saint Augustine,* ed. W. J. Oates (New York, 1948), II, 497.

[5] *Summa Theologica,* transl. Fathers of the English Dominican Province, pt. II, 1st pt., qu. 95, art. 2; qu. 96, art. 4. He was not, however, willing to grant a right of resistance against every law that was unjust. See *supra* Sec. 6.

[6] *Of Civil Government* (Everyman's Library ed., 1924), Bk. II, ch. xix, sec. 222.

A theory of law which considers the values of order and justice to be entitled to equal recognition as supreme goals of the law will be disinclined to assert the invalidity of every legal enactment that does not live up to the fundamental tenets of justice. Since a determination of whether a law is just or unjust cannot always be made with firm assurance, and since there is often considerable disagreement as to the fairness and reasonableness of a particular piece of legislation, a broad recognition of the right to ignore or disobey an unjust law would subject the certainty and authority of the legal system to an unbearable strain and burden. It would therefore appear necessary to establish a very strong presumption in favor of the validity of positive law produced by the proper legislative procedures. In those countries where the right to review the constitutionality of legislation is entrusted to the judiciary, this presumption can sometimes—as in the United States—be rebutted by showing that the normative content of a statute or ordinance does not meet the criteria of reasonableness, equality or "due process," as laid down by the constitution; if this showing is properly made, the judges can be expected to ignore the deficient enactment in whole or in part. Where such institutional channels for the obliteration of objectionable law exist, there is every reason—in the absence of highly unusual conditions indicating a complete or almost complete lack of independence on the part of the judiciary—to regard these channels as exclusive means of redress against injustices committed by the legislator.

A different problem may arise under a despotic regime. If rules of law are enacted under such a system which utterly defy all civilized standards of decency and fairness, and if (as will usually be the case) no bona fide legal procedures for challenging the authority of such rules are available, there may be ground for questioning the presumptive validity of such positive law in some cases. "The period of National Socialism in Germany has taught us," said the Constitutional Court of the West German Republic, "that it is possible for the legislator to enact wrongful statutes. In order to have a protective armor against such a historically thinkable development, legal practice must have the opportunity in extreme cases to give the principle of justice preference over the principle of public order." When the outer bounds of justice have been transgressed by the lawmaker, the court continued, the law must be held invalid.[7]

In such unusual cases, the right to resist the application and execution of such commands on the part of legal officials as well as private

[7] 3 *Entscheidungen des Bundesverfassungsgerichts* 225, at 232 (1953).

citizens might have to be recognized.[8] The exigencies of legal security demand, however, that this right be limited to extreme and inextricable situations in which an outrageous wrong is being committed by the government. Furthermore, the person making use of the right of resistance must be held to the risk of having misjudged the stringent prerequisites for the legitimate exercise of this right.

The West German Supreme Court in the post-Hitler period went even one step further and adjudged that in the case of totally obnoxious and unbearably unreasonable commands by the state the right to resist their execution may under certain circumstances become transmuted into a legal duty not to obey such mandates.[9] The Court held in one case that a decree stating that any bearer of arms was placed under a duty to execute any person deserting the army without necessity for a hearing violated basic canons of "natural law" and could not with impunity be observed. A statute or other official act, the court declared, "reaches the ends of its bounds at a point where it comes into conflict with generally recognized principles of international law, or where the contrast between positive law and justice becomes so unbearable that the positive law, being 'false law,' must yield to justice." [10] Such a position imposes high standards of moral responsibility on persons who, by the very nature of the conditions under which the duty of resistance becomes operative, will find themselves under an exceedingly strong pressure to comply with the unconscionable command.[11] It would seem that great wisdom and understanding of human nature must in such circumstances be displayed by the judges, and that

[8] As a matter of general principle (subject to certain modifications and qualifications) the following modern authors would appear to be in accord with this position: François Gény, *Science et technique en droit privé positif* (Paris, 1924), IV, 125–134; Jean Dabin, *La Philosophie de l'ordre juridique positif* (Paris, 1929), pp. 712 ff.; Giorgio Del Vecchio, *Justice*, ed. A. H. Campbell (New York, 1953), pp. 157–158; Gustav Radbruch, "Gesetzliches Unrecht und Übergesetzliches Recht," in *Rechtsphilosophie*, 4th ed. by E. Wolf (Stuttgart, 1950), pp. 352–355; Helmut Coing, *Die Obersten Grundsätze des Rechts* (Heidelberg, 1947), pp. 58–61.

[9] The decisions of the West German Federal Supreme Court dealing with the validity of Nazi legislative and judicial acts are discussed in Edgar Bodenheimer, "Significant Developments in German Legal Philosophy since 1945," 3 *American Journal of Comparative Law* 379, at 387–391 (1954); Heinrich Rommen, "Natural Law in Decisions of the Federal Supreme Court and of the Constitutional Courts in Germany," 4 *Natural Law Forum* 1 (1959).

[10] Decision of the Bundesgerichtshof of July 12, 1951, 3 *Entscheidungen des Bundesgerichtshofs in Zivilsachen* 107 (1951); see also Decision of the Bundesgerichtshof of May 8, 1951, 2 *Entscheidungen des Bundesgerichtshofs in Strafsachen* 235 (1951). See the further discussion of the problem *infra* Sec. 69. See also H. L. A. Hart, "Positivism and the Separation of Law and Morals," 71 *Harv. L. Rev.* 593, at 615–621 (1958); Lon L. Fuller, "Positivism and Fidelity to Law," 71 *Harv. L. Rev.* 630, at 644–661 (1958).

[11] A Biblical example of such a command is the order of King Herod to slay all boys under two years of age. Matt. ii:16.

the character and severity of the compulsion exercised to ensure compliance should be taken into account by them in adjudging liability for failure to resist the unlawful decree. It must be realized, on the other hand, that unless we are ready to produce a generation of robots who will render slavish and unquestioning obedience to even the most tyrannical and inhuman regime of gangsterism, the exercise of critical judgment in carrying out monstrous commands ought to be required of a responsible human being, even though he may thereby incur the risk of severe deprivations. Legal science can do little more in this area than propose some broad standards for dealing with such problems and leave the details to the judicious consideration of such situations in the light of their particular facts.

Section 54. *The Significance of Sanctions*

It is contended by a number of jurisprudential writers that the criterion for whether a certain rule of conduct qualifies as a rule of law must be sought in the character of the sanction employed in enforcing the rule. If compliance is secured by a threat of compulsion imposed by the state or an organized community, then, these writers say, the rule partakes of the nature of a legal rule. If, on the other hand, the pressure used to bring about conformity with a societal arrangement is merely that of public opinion or community disapproval, manifested in loss of reputation, social ostracism, or perhaps private reprisals, then the norm must be held to be of a nonlegal character. In the opinion of Patterson, it is typical for a legal sanction to consist in "a harmful consequence imposed by state officials"; the attachment of a legal sanction to a norm of conduct is "a necessary characteristic of a body of law and of every legal provision." [1] In a similar vein, the anthropologist Hoebel wishes to classify a societal norm as legal if "its neglect or infraction is regularly met, in threat or in fact, by the application of physical force by an individual or group possessing the socially recognized privilege of so acting." [2]

Under this theory, coercibility of a specified type is the touchstone and distinguishing element of legal regulation. In the words of Del Vecchio, "Where coercibility is lacking Law, too, is lacking"; to him the concepts of law and coercibility are in logic and fact inseparable.[3]

This point of view cannot be fully accepted. It is true that a legal

[1] Edwin W. Patterson, *Jurisprudence* (Brooklyn, 1953), p. 169.
[2] E. Adamson Hoebel, *The Law of Primitive Man* (Cambridge, Mass., 1954), p. 28; for a criticism of this definition see the review of this book by F. S. C. Northrop in 16 *Louisiana Law Review* 455 (1956).
[3] Giorgio Del Vecchio, *Philosophy of Law*, transl. T. O. Martin (Washington, D.C., 1953), p. 304; see also Rudolf Stammler, *Die Lehre vom Richtigen Rechte* (Berlin, 1902), p. 235.

system unequipped with the teeth of enforceability may prove ineffective to restrain noncooperative, antisocial, and criminal elements and may therefore fail to carry out its basic functions to maintain order as well as justice in society. It is also true that all mature and highly developed legal orders attempt to achieve a maximum degree of legal compliance by putting the coercive machinery of the state at the disposal of the law-administering agencies and officials. In this sense, it may be asserted that the forward march of the law is accompanied by a *tendency* to guarantee the efficacy of legal norms by the establishment and maintenance of official procedures for their execution and enforcement.

This view, however, must be differentiated from the one which sees in politically organized coercion the *conditio sine qua non* and the chief criterion for the existence of a body of legal rules. This latter view ignores the fact that the primary guaranty for the efficacy of a legal order must be its acceptance by the community, and that compulsive sanctions can merely form a secondary and auxiliary guaranty. A reasonable and satisfactory system of law will be obeyed by most members of the community because it serves their interests, is respected by them, or at least does not arouse in their hearts any feelings of hostility or hatred.[4] Compulsion is used only against a noncooperative minority; in any normal and effectively working commonwealth the number of lawbreakers against whom sanctions must be employed is much smaller than the number of law-abiding citizens.

The objection might be raised against this thesis that there are legal systems or portions of legal systems which are not accepted as reasonable and just, and which are complied with by the citizens only out of fear that forcible sanctions might be employed against them in case of disobedience. It is likely, however, that in such a situation acts of sabotage and resistance against the legal order will be widespread and will gradually undermine the foundation and strength of this order. Even if this should not be the case, the duration of such an order cannot be expected to be long, since it is extremely difficult for a minority of governmental officials to force an unacceptable system of law upon the bulk of the population. As Freehof has said: "Police power is, of course, essential, yet never quite sufficient. If a large percentage of the citizens decided to be violent, as has happened repeatedly, the police power is helpless. The true source of order comes from within. It is

---

[4] In accord: George W. Paton, *A Textbook of Jurisprudence*, 2d ed. (Oxford, 1951), p. 59; on the motives for submission to law in primitive society see Bronislaw Malinowski, *Crime and Custom in Savage Society* (New York, 1926). See on this problem also Gerhart Niemeyer, *Law without Force* (Princeton, 1941).

conscience which makes citizens of us all." [5] Coercion is meaningless, and threat of coercion impotent, if a majority of the citizens are unwilling to obey the law.

We are justified, therefore, in taking the position that the necessity for primary reliance on governmental force as a means for carrying out the mandates of the law evinces a weak and morbid rather than a strong and healthy condition of the legal order. Since we should not define or describe a social institution in terms of its pathological manifestations, the imperative theory of law, which sees the essence of law in the governmental compulsion necessary to vindicate its authority against lawbreakers, provides us with an erroneous perspective. As Paton has aptly said: "Academic preoccupation with the sanction leads to a false view of law. The idea of health does not at once suggest to our minds hospitals and diseases, operations and anaesthetics, however necessary these things may be to maintain the welfare of a community. The best service of medicine is the prevention of disease, just as the real benefit of law is that it secures an ordered balance which goes far to prevent disputes." [6]

A further reason for the inadequacy of the sanction theory of law lies in the fact that every legal order contains a greater or lesser number of norms which are not supported by compulsive sanctions. Under the American constitutional system, for example, provisions of the Constitution and federal statutes which direct the state legislatures to reapportion their congressional districts after each decennial census cannot, in the opinion of the United States Supreme Court, be judicially enforced.[7] Furthermore, in those areas of Anglo-American law where the doctrine of sovereign immunity is operative, torts or other violations of law by the sovereign cannot be vindicated in the absence of special legislation authorizing suits against the government. Outside the United States, especially in those countries where the power of the judiciary to guarantee the execution of constitutional directives is absent or highly limited, there exist many norms in the domain of constitutional and public law which are incapable of enforcement at the behest of private parties injured by their nonobservance. Compliance with these rules and principles depends on the good will and conscientiousness of executive or administrative officials or, in democratic orders, on the deterrent effect of the fear of being defeated at the next election (which is not an enforcement sanction in the technical sense).

[5] Solomon Freehof, "The Natural Law in the Jewish Tradition," 5 *University of Notre Dame Natural Law Institute Proceedings* 15, at 22 (1953).
[6] Paton, p. 60.
[7] *Colegrove v. Green*, 328 U. S. 549 (1946).

Yet the provisions in question are clearly considered to be of a legal character.

One of the most challenging testing grounds for the sanction theory of law is the field of international law. John Austin denied the legal character of international law on the ground that its rules and principles are not laid down by a sovereign political superior and because no legal sanctions are prescribed which guarantee compliance with its precepts.[8] To him, international law represented merely an aggregate of rules of "positive morality." Hans Kelsen disputed the validity of this position by pointing out that, under international law, coercive acts in the form of war, reprisals, reparations, economic boycotts, and the like are authorized as a reaction against international derelictions. He considered it immaterial for the purpose of establishing the legal nature of international law that these sanctions, in most instances, are administered by the state which has suffered the wrong rather than by a superior and impartial international agency or international government.[9] Common to both these points of view is the disposition to regard sanctions as an essential ingredient of all law; they differ merely in their conception of the type of enforcement procedure which is held to fulfill the requirement of a legally relevant sanction.

A sounder conception of the law of nations as a body of genuine law will have to proceed from the recognition of the fact that no system of international law can be effective which does not rest on the acceptance of its prescriptions by the international legal community, or at least the majority of its members. It must be emphasized that the bulk of the customs and treaty provisions controlling international relations are for the most part observed because it is in the interest of the nations concerned to preserve their peaceful existence and to court international good will by adhering to them. This does not mean that international law has not frequently been violated by nations on grounds of egotistical interest, desire for self-aggrandizement, or perhaps occasionally for reasons of national survival. But the fact of such violations would compel us to deny the legal character of international law only if the frequency of the breaches were such as to render the entire system ineffective and utopian. Such a far-reaching conclusion cannot be drawn on the basis of the available evidence. As Jessup and Moore have shown, the rules of international law are more frequently observed than flouted.[10] Even if there are hectic periods in history

---

[8] *Lectures on Jurisprudence*, I, 226.
[9] Kelsen, *Principles of International Law* (New York, 1952), pp. 18 ff.
[10] See Philip Jessup, "The Reality of International Law," 18 *Foreign Affairs* 244 (1940).

where turbulence and national aggressiveness drown out the strong human desire for peace, such periods always alternate with other epochs in which international order is relatively stable and violations of international law form the exception rather than the rule.

It must, of course, be admitted that the deficiencies in the enforcement procedures of international law detract greatly from its forcefulness and usefulness as a pacifier of nations. In this respect, international law has sometimes been compared with primitive law, which is also lacking in efficacious sanctions administered by a government. But these considerations merely help us to understand that international law is still an inchoate and weakly developed system of law; they do not force us to the conclusion that it is no law at all.

XIII

LAW AS DISTINGUISHED FROM OTHER AGENCIES OF SOCIAL CONTROL

Section 55. *Law and Power*

Power in a sociological sense is the ability of an individual or group to carry out its will, even against the resistance of others.[1] Its acquisition or exercise may be due to physical, psychological, or intellectual characteristics of a person. A man may obtain power merely because he is physically stronger than some of his fellow men, or he may become powerful because he is capable of exercising an irresistible psychological or even hypnotic influence upon other men or crowds. Great intellectual capacities may also, under favorable circumstances, secure to their possessor a position of power within a community or nation. The power of a single individual may be considerably enhanced if he succeeds in gaining the devoted cooperation of a sympathetic group for

[1] Bertrand Russell defines power as "the production of intended effects" in *Power* (New York, 1938), p. 35

the execution of his aims, such as a political party, a secret society, or a religious order. If the relations between the leader and the members of such a group are based on the principle of strict submission and obedience to the leader's command, the organization may be described as a "power structure." [2] Such a structure may also arise where a collective leadership group, consisting of men fanatically imbued with determination to achieve certain political or social objectives, is able to impose its domination upon a people.

Many philosophers and sociologists have realized the great importance of the power concept in an analysis of human individual and social life. Hobbes and Spinoza based their philosophical systems on the assumption that every living creature, by natural instinct, is driven to expand his power as far as he can.[3] "Life is a search after power," exclaimed Emerson.[4] Friedrich Nietzsche looked upon the "will to power" as the basic motivating force in nature and human life.[5] All things, he argued, are dynamic quanta standing in a relation of tension to other dynamic quanta. The American sociologist Lester F. Ward described the law of nature as the "right of might." Under the normal operation of the psychological and social forces, he said, the weaker yield to the stronger as though they were under the compulsion of a law of physics. To Ward, human civilization consists in the successful teleological control of these forces of nature.[6] Later, Bertrand Russell argued that power constitutes the fundamental concept in social science in the same way that energy is the fundamental concept in physics. He maintained that love of power is the chief motive producing the changes that social science has to study, and that the laws of social dynamics are capable of being stated only in terms of the various forms of power.[7] Modern political scientists and sociologists of law have similarly emphasized the significance of the power concept in describing the phenomena of politics and law.[8]

[2] N. S. Timasheff, *Introduction to the Sociology of Law* (Cambridge, Mass., 1939), p. 172.
[3] Thomas Hobbes, *Leviathan* (Everyman's Library ed., 1914), pt. I, chs. 10, 14; Benedict Spinoza, *Tractatus Theologico-Politicus,* transl. R. H. M. Elwes (London, 1895), ch. 16.
[4] Ralph Waldo Emerson, "Power," *Complete Works* (New York, 1884), VI, 55.
[5] *The Will to Power,* transl. A. M. Ludovici, in *Complete Works,* ed. O. Levy (London, 1924), vol. XV, Bks. III and IV.
[6] *Dynamic Sociology,* 2d ed. (Boston, 1897), I, 34 ff., 503 ff.
[7] Russell, pp. 12–15. A good refutation of Russell's basic thesis is found in Martin Buber, *Zwischen Gesellschaft und Staat* (Heidelberg, 1952).
[8] Karl Loewenstein, *Political Power and the Governmental Process* (Chicago, 1957), says on p. 3: "Politics is nothing else but the struggle for power." See also Charles E. Merriam, *Political Power* (New York, 1934); Timasheff, pp. 171–244; Barna Horvath, *Rechtssoziologie* (Berlin, 1934), pp. 198 ff.

Indeed it can hardly be denied that the will to power is often a strong impelling force in individual as well as social life. In individual life, the power impulse may manifest itself in many forms, depending upon the particular qualities of the individual; it may direct its force to the attainment of political or social influence, the acquisition of money and property, the conquest of women, or mental and intellectual achievements. In social life, the struggle of groups, classes, and nations for power and dominance accounts for many decisive events in the pageant of history. In our own day, the role of power in the life of nations is amply demonstrated. Unchecked political power is one of the most dynamic and aggressive forces in the world, as the history of modern dictatorships clearly proves. "It is an ever-recurring experience," said Montesquieu, "that every man who has power is apt to abuse it; he will go further and further, until he meets a barrier." [9] In a similar vein, the German historian Friedrich Meinecke pointed out that a person invested with power is exposed to a constant temptation to expand this power beyond the limits set by law and morality. "One may call it a curse reposing on power—it is an inevitable one." [10]

Granting the tremendous significance of the power concept for any description of political and other societal processes, it must nevertheless be noted that there has been a tendency in recent times to overrate the role which the power impulse plays in the conduct of human affairs. A considerable number of men, among them some of the most valuable servants of mankind, have acted from motives other than the will to acquire or increase power. They may have acted for the unselfish motive of serving the public good or under an impulse of sympathy with the burdens and sufferings of their fellow men. This has been true not only of the great religious and ethical leaders of mankind, but also of some of the most outstanding political leaders. If such men, in order to be able to accomplish their purposes, have sought to gain power over other men, the acquisition of such power was to them only a secondary aim, subservient to the attainment of worthier objectives. Only a cynical and unrealistic psychology will assert that men like Moses, Buddha, Jesus, Confucius, Socrates, Pericles, Marcus Aurelius, George Washington, and Abraham Lincoln were motivated in their actions exclusively or primarily by a desire to increase their power.

Furthermore, Friedrich Nietzsche and his followers committed a serious error when they hypostatized the "will to power" into the su-

---

[9] Charles Louis de Montesquieu, *De l'esprit des lois* (Paris, 1748), Bk. XI, ch. 4 (translation mine).

[10] *Die Idee der Staatsräson*, 2d ed. (Munich, 1925), p. 16.

preme and dominant principle governing human life. In the lives of many human beings, the will to obtain or increase power plays no conspicuous part. They seek to conform to the prevailing patterns of existence and are content to occupy a modest position in the social order as long as that position enables them to satisfy their basic wants. They are unwilling to accept changes in their way of life which would require a greater expenditure of effort and energy. The tendency to save energy is as much a part of the physical and psychological reality of human existence as the opposite tendency to expend it.[11]

More important perhaps, where the will to power manifests itself on the social scene, it is met, countered, and checked by an organizing principle of equal weight and strength—the will to law. While the will to power has its roots in the desire to dominate other men and subject them to one's influence and control, the will to law stems from a human inclination opposing this impulse, namely, the desire to be free from the arbitrary domination of other men. The institution of law, in one of its most significant aspects, may be viewed as an instrument to check and curb man's appetite for power.[12]

It would, however, be quite unrealistic and inappropriate to assert that power and law, conceived as forces by which the actions and conduct of men may be controlled, must always and in every respect be understood as antithetical notions occupying positions at opposite poles. To correct such a possible misapprehension, it need only be pointed out that a state or government without power could not fulfill its basic function of maintaining the legal order and protecting it against those who set about to flout and infringe its mandates. It is likewise true that the law itself sometimes establishes and guarantees spheres of power for individuals, collective units, or governmental organs, and by so doing acts as an agency for the allocation and distribution of power in the social system. Conversely, it can be observed that holders of power endowed with unlimited authority may be quite willing to submit to certain restraints established by law and to forego the prerogative of overturning such restraints whenever it appears convenient to them. On the other hand, it must be insisted that power in its pure and naked form, a power which "results merely from the power-loving impulse of individuals or groups, and wins from its subjects only submission through fear, not active co-operation," [13] constitutes the polar opposite of law in its mature and developed form. The

[11] See in this connection Franz Alexander, *The Age of Unreason* (Philadelphia, 1942), pp. 199, 210.
[12] See *supra* Sec. 42.
[13] Russell, *Power*, p. 41.

institution of law can flourish only in a political and social setting where effective restraints exist against the arbitrary and unprincipled exercise of power.

Pure power tends to symbolize the element of struggle, war, and violent change in the world of social reality. In its uncontrolled form it may be compared to free-flowing, highly charged energy, which is often destructive in its effect. The exercise of power is frequently marked by ruthlessness and impatience of restraints; [14] where it reigns unchecked, it is apt to produce tensions, frictions, and conflicts. In a social system where power has unlimited sway, the tendency will be toward oppression or exploitation of the weaker members of society by the stronger ones. In an international system dominated by power politics in its unscrupulous form, the big nations will be inclined to impose their will upon the smaller members of the international community and to pursue their aims by expansion and conquest, if necessary. Since unconfined power is a consuming force which is apt to burn itself out by the violent thrust of its action, it is usually shortlived as an exclusive vehicle of social control. But where it functions temporarily as a dynamic, expansive, or revolutionary force in the national or international area, it is sometimes able to accomplish fundamental and necessary changes and to prepare the ground for new forms of human society.

Law in its pure form, on the other hand, by setting barriers to the unlimited exercise of power and attempting to maintain a certain social equilibrium, must in many ways be viewed as a restrictive force in social life. In contrast to the aggressive and expansionist tendencies of naked power, law seeks compromise, peace, and agreement in the political and social sphere.[15] In a political system where social control is primarily exercised through law, every effort will be made to adjust

---

[14] Because of this fact, Jakob Burckhardt observed that "power in itself is evil regardless of who exercises it." Burckhardt, *Weltgeschichtliche Betrachtungen* (Leipzig, n.d.), p. 97.

[15] Those who glorify power, struggle, and war will necessarily have a critical attitude toward law. Friedrich Nietzsche, an outstanding exponent of a power philosophy, made the following remarks about the law: "Viewed from the most advanced biological standpoint one must realize that conditions of law should be *exceptional conditions* only, in that they are partial restrictions of the real life-will, which strives after power; they should be subordinated to the life-will's general end, as a particular means, namely, as a means to create larger power units. A legal order, conceived of as sovereign and universal, not as a weapon in the fight of power complexes, but as a weapon against strife in general, somewhat after the style of Dühring's communistic method of treating every will as equal to every other will, would be a principle *hostile to life*, a destroyer and dissolver of man, an outrage on the future of mankind, a symptom of fatigue, a hidden avenue to nothingness." Nietzsche, *Gesammelte Werke* (Musarion ed., Munich), XV (1925), 342.

human relations by specific means and to avoid constant and needless struggle. While the rule of power tends to increase tensions in the political and social world, the rule of law is apt to neutralize such tensions. An important device by which a developed legal system will often attempt to forestall the rise of oppressive power structures is the dispersion and consequent balancing of power by a wide distribution of rights and privileges among individuals and groups.

When a state of balanced power and social equilibrium has been achieved, the law will strive to protect it from serious disturbances and disruptions. This is one of the essential functions of the law. The elimination of tensions which the law attempts to bring about would be largely illusory and of little value if the adjustments and arrangements made through legal control were of an entirely temporary and fleeting character. Law, wherever its reign is securely established, will seek to avoid and thwart indiscriminate, chaotic, and perpetual change and to surround the existing social structure with certain guarantees of continuity and durability. A totally ephemeral system of law which does not aim at least at temporary consolidation and self-perpetuation of its normative arrangements is hardly consistent with the stabilizing objectives of the institution.

The endeavor of the law to impart a certain amount of continuity and stability to the social order gives it, to some extent, the antidynamic property of inertia; this observation provides us with a valid explanation of the fact that the law often lags behind the times, as many of its critics have noted.[16] The truly far-reaching changes in the legal order usually come from the outside, through the exercise of political power by means of legislative action, and the more incisive these changes are, the greater the role of power in effectuating them is likely to be. There is a constant interaction between power and law in the social process, and the actual relations between these two phenomena are complex and unstable. Power may become transformed into law, and law may disintegrate into power (as in the case of revolution and war). In times of crisis and social change, new groupings or alignments of interests will press for recognition of their claims, and the law in such periods can save itself from breakdown only by exhibiting a large degree of flexibility and adaptability. The dynamic forces operating in human social and political life will always strive to tear into the protective armor with which the law surrounds existing institutions and spheres of interest; differently expressed, power is constantly tugging at the substance of the law. While the law, as we have seen, seeks to establish barriers against the undiluted rule of power, we must also recognize

---

[16] On the time lag in the law see also *infra* Sec. 62.

that power is sometimes apt to set limits on the attempt of the law to make social life reasonably stable and to protect it against disruptive change.

Section 56. *Law and Administration*

Administration is an exercise of power for the accomplishment of a private or public purpose. A landowner administers his estate by giving orders for the proper cultivation or conservation of his land. A corporate officer who administers the affairs of a corporation is concerned with expedient and useful measures for promoting its business; he gives orders to the employees, draws up plans for production, hires and fires workers. These are examples of private administration. Where administrative measures are taken in the public interest by government officials, we enter the sphere of public administration. The conduct of foreign affairs, the building of roads and dams, the preservation of national parks, and the establishment of public health services are typical acts of public administration.

What is the relation between public administration and law? This problem was discussed by two German teachers of public law, Georg Jellinek and Paul Laband. According to the theory of Jellinek, the purely administrative activity of the state does not fit within the concept of law. He argued that the creation of executive organs by the state, the administration of governmental property, and the issuance of instructions and orders to the state officials are outside the field of the law. In his view, not everything which is put in the form of a statute should be considered as an act of law. For instance, a statute ordering the building of a canal or railway by the state, providing for the establishment of a university, granting relief to the inhabitants of a flooded community, or organizing a governmental expedition to the Antarctic is regarded as an administrative rather than a legal measure by Jellinek. No rule can be law which operates only within the administration itself and which does not create any obligations or rights for anyone who is outside the administration.[1] Such rules have as little to do with law as an instruction by a private individual regarding the management of his household or estate. All law, said Jellinek, is conditioned by relations between two or more persons.[2] Only a rule that delimits the sphere of the free activities of persons in their relation to each other is a legal rule.[3]

[1] Jellinek, *Gesetz und Verordnung* (Tübingen, 1887), pp. 240 ff. See also Paul Laband, *Staatsrecht des Deutschen Reichs* (Berlin, 1901), I, 168.
[2] Jellinek, *System der subjektiven öffentlichen Rechte*, 2d ed. (Tübingen, 1905), p. 193.
[3] Jellinek, *op. cit. supra* n. 1, p. 240.

In this view Jellinek was supported by Laband. Law, according to Laband, consists in the "delimitation of rights and duties of particular subjects against each other: by its very nature law presupposes a plurality of persons who may come into collision." [4] There is no room for law, according to Laband and Jellinek, so long as the sphere of volition of the administering state, or of any other natural or legal person, does not come in touch with some other sphere of volition, thereby making possible a mutual encounter, a collision, or a compromise between various wills. The state, to the extent that it is concerned with the exercise of free discretion in administering its affairs, may be judged as a political and ethical phenomenon, but not as a legal configuration. The state enters the domain of law only when it grants rights to private individuals or when it delimits its own free sphere of activity by imposing obligations toward private individuals upon itself.[5]

Starting from wholly different philosophical premises, the Soviet jurist E. B. Pashukanis reached conclusions very similar to those of Jellinek and Laband.[6] Pashukanis distinguished between legal rules on the one hand and social-technical rules on the other. All law, he asserted, is conditioned by the existence of separate and conflicting private interests. It is the typical instrument of social control in a society of private, isolated commodity producers who exchange their products by way of contract. Law, according to Pashukanis, is out of place in a society where there are no conflicting individual interests requiring adjustment. In a socialist society undefiled by the clash of contradictory interests, he argued, legal rules will be replaced by social-technical rules. These constitute the typical form of regulation in a social organization in which a "unity of purpose" prevails. Pashukanis illustrated his theory by the following examples:

The juridic norms of the responsibility of railways presuppose private claims and private isolated interests; whereas the technical rules of railway movement presuppose a single purpose—the attainment of maximum hauling capacity, let us say. The treatment of a sick person—to take another example —presupposes a series of rules, both for the patient himself and for the medical personnel; but inasmuch as these rules are established from the point of view of a single purpose—the restoration of the patient's health—they are of a technical character.[7]

---

[4] Laband, p. 168.

[5] Jellinek, *op. cit. supra* n. 2, p. 195.

[6] See the instructive article by S. Dobrin, "Soviet Jurisprudence and Socialism," 52 *Law Quarterly Review* 402 (1936).

[7] Pashukanis, "Theory of Law and Marxism," in *Soviet Legal Philosophy*, ed. J. N. Hazard, transl. H. W. Babb (Cambridge, Mass., 1951), p. 137.

Other examples of merely technical regulations, according to Pashukanis, are plans of production in a collectivized economy, mobilization directives in wartime, and instructions given to members of the Jesuit order by their leaders. Arrangements of this character do not involve the adjustment or adjudication of conflicting private claims but aim at the accomplishment of a collective purpose. In the words of Pashukanis, "The more systematic the development of the principle of authoritarian regulation (which excludes any inkling of a separate and autonomous will), the less ground there is for the application of the category of law." [8]

An entirely different approach to the problem is taken by Hans Kelsen. He recognizes no essential distinction between administration and law. According to his theory, practically every act of public administration is at the same time an act of law.[9] He arrives at this conclusion by stretching the term law to cover any variety of compulsive norms established by the state. A considerable portion of what we call administration, he argues, cannot be distinguished functionally from judicial activity. Public policy is pursued in both instances in an identical fashion, namely, by achieving a desired condition of affairs by attaching to its opposite an act of compulsion.[10] The state, being the agency which administers compulsion, is a "King Midas in whose hands everything he touches is converted into law." [11]

To those who see in law a limitation rather than an exercise of power, Kelsen's refusal to distinguish clearly between law and administration is unacceptable. Public administration unrestrained in its power to pursue its objectives by any and all means considered expedient by the officials of the government is the antithesis of law. It is pure power rule. In the words of Mr. Justice Frankfurter, "Discretion without a criterion for its exercise is authorization of arbitrariness." [12] Administrators who do as they please and who are not bound by "considerations capable of rational formulation" [13] cannot be said to operate within a framework of law. In the law state, the administrative activity of the government takes place within a framework of rules or standards, and the administrator, before making a policy determination or

---

[8] Pashukanis, p. 154. On Pashukanis see also Lon L. Fuller, "Pashukanis and Vyshinsky," 47 *Michigan Law Review* 1157 (1949); Edgar Bodenheimer, "The Impasse of Soviet Legal Philosophy," 38 *Cornell Law Quarterly* 51 (1952).

[9] Kelsen, *Allgemeine Staatslehre* (Berlin, 1925), p. 242.

[10] Kelsen, "The Pure Theory of Law," 51 *L. Q. Rev.* 517, at 521 (1935); cf. also Kelsen, *General Theory of Law and State*, transl. A. Wedberg (Cambridge, Mass., 1949), p. 114.

[11] Kelsen, *op. cit. supra* n. 9, p. 44.

[12] *Brown v. Allen*, 344 U.S. 443, at 496 (1952).

[13] *Id.*, p. 497.

individual decision, must check to see if his action moves within the orbit of discretion allowed to him by the law.

This leads us to a discussion of the problem of administrative law. What is the nature and function of this branch of law? On this question the opinions of legal authors seem to be widely divergent. Berle characterizes administrative law as "the law applicable to the transmission of the will of the state, from its source to the point of its application." [14] Other writers describe administrative law as the "law of statutory discretions." [15] These definitions fail to distinguish between public administration and administrative law. Administrative law is not primarily concerned with the transmission of the will of the state in any of its forms. It is concerned, in its most essential manifestations, with the *limits* which are set to the exercise of this will. It is not correct to say that it is the task of administrative law to enumerate and describe the discretionary powers vested in government officials and administrative agencies. Administrative law is principally interested in the *restraints* which the legal order has placed on the exercise of such discretion. This does not mean, however, that a statutory provision which contains a grant of administrative power without at the same time limiting or circumscribing the exercise of this power thereby forfeits the quality of an act of law. In order to determine whether the public administration of a country is controlled by legal restraints, the system of public law *as a whole* must be consulted. If the executive and administrative organs of the country follow regular procedures in discharging their functions, if their activities are governed by rules which impose certain checks upon the exercise of unrestricted discretion, and if certain safeguards exist against an abuse of power by these agencies, then there is a system of administrative law in effect in this country. It should be emphasized that the rules controlling discretion do not necessarily have to emanate from the legislature or the judiciary; they may be the product of the rule-making activity of the executive or administrative agency itself. However, it is hard to conceive of an effective system of administrative law capable of preventing an arbitrary abuse of power by government officials which does not provide for at least a limited review of their actions by the courts or some other impartial board or tribunal.[16]

[14] Adolf A. Berle, "The Expansion of American Administrative Law," 30 *Harvard Law Review* 430, at 431 (1917).

[15] John Willis, "Three Approaches to Administrative Law," 4 *Selected Essays on Constitutional Law* 35, at 36 (1935); J. A. Corry, "Administrative Law in Canada," 5 *Proceedings of the Canadian Political Science Association* 190 (1933).

[16] Goodnow defines administrative law as "that part of the public law which fixes the organization and determines the competence of the administrative authorities,

Jellinek and Laband took the position that rules and regulations operating within the administration itself and merely affecting the internal distribution of governmental powers should be excluded from the province of the law. This view lacks persuasive force. A system of organization which sets the functions and competence of one agency apart from those of other agencies and defines their respective operational spheres, thereby preventing intragovernmental friction and conflicts of jurisdiction, would seem to be well within the proper frame of reference of the law.

In the nineteenth century, the emphasis in American government was almost exclusively on the legal restraints designed to keep administration within confined bounds. The discretionary domain in administration was held down to an unavoidable minimum. As Roscoe Pound pointed out,

Law paralyzing administration was an every-day spectacle. Almost every important measure of police or administration encountered an injunction. . . . What in other lands was committed to administration and inspection and supervision in advance of action we left to the courts, preferring to show the individual his duty by a general law, to leave him free to act according to his judgment, and to prosecute him and impose the predetermined penalty in case his free action infringed the law. It was deemed fundamental in our polity to confine administration to the inevitable minimum. In other words, where some people went to one extreme and were bureau-ridden, we went to the opposite extreme and were law-ridden.[17]

In the twentieth century, especially in the thirties, the pendulum has swung to the other side. A great number of administrative agencies charged with supervision of various areas of the economic and social life grew up in quick succession. A certain tendency developed to take away or curtail judicial review of the actions of these agencies. The low estimate of administrative power in the nineteenth century gave way to a high praise of its blessings in many quarters. Pound, in an interesting comparison, likened this "recrudescence of executive justice" to the rise of equity jurisprudence in sixteenth-century England. He pointed out that equity started its career as a form of execu-

---

and indicates to the individual remedies for the violation of his rights." F. J. Goodnow, *Comparative Administrative Law* (New York, 1903), p. 8. Frankfurter gives the following definition: "Administrative law deals with the field of legal control exercised by law-administering agencies other than courts and the field of control exercised by courts over such agencies." Felix Frankfurter, "The Task of Administrative Law," 75 *University of Pennsylvania Law Review* 614, at 615 (1927). These definitions bring to light important elements in administrative law.

[17] "Justice According to Law," 14 *Columbia Law Review* 1, at 12–13 (1914).

tive justice, as a movement away from the law courts; later, however, it became a well-established part of the law. "The common law survived and the sole permanent result of the reversion to justice without law was a liberalizing and modernizing of the law." [18] He expressed his conviction that a similar development would take place in regard to the new administrative justice in the United States, and the events of the last few decades would seem to bear out his prediction. An integration and absorption of administrative law into the total body of the public law appears to be slowly in the making.

An increase in administrative control has been inevitable and necessary in the United States in order to achieve efficiency in the management of public business in the face of a complicated industrial world. In a complex society where numerous conflicting interests are in need of adjustment and where the public welfare must be preserved against antisocial and disruptive trends, there is an impelling need for regulation by direct government action.[19] Certain dangers inherent in administrative control must, however, be clearly recognized and met. A system of public administration interested solely in results and unconcerned with human rights may lead to autocracy and oppression. The example of the totalitarian states proves clearly that a purely administrative state may have little regard for the dignity of the human personality. Administrative discretion must therefore be subjected to reasonable restraints in order that the rule of law may be maintained in society.

Where to draw the line between administrative discretion and legal restraint cannot be determined by a simple formula. The exercise of a substantial margin of discretion may be absolutely essential to the effective accomplishment of some important social purpose. On the other hand, it will be possible in many instances, by way of statute or administrative regulation, to define the ways and means through which the administrative purpose is to be executed beforehand and to inform the public of the typical operations of the agency. Furthermore, however large the undefinable area of discretion granted to the agency may be, the individual affected by its actions should always have some form of recourse to an impartial tribunal in the case of arbitrary abuse of such discretion. As long as efficiency in government is not considered an ultimate end in itself, the realization of adequate safeguards for the protection of human rights must be looked upon as an essential postulate of an enlightened administrative justice.

[18] *Id.*, p. 21.
[19] See on this point John Dickinson, *Administrative Justice and the Supremacy of Law* (Cambridge, Mass., 1927), pp. 10–15.

Section 57. *Law and Morals*

According to an influential theory, the distinction between law and morals is found in the fact that the law regulates the external relations of men, while morality governs their inner life and motivations. This theory was first announced by Thomasius [1] and subsequently elaborated by Kant; [2] it has since found acceptance with numerous students of jurisprudence. [3] Since it is common to identify this view primarily with the name of Kant, we shall hereafter refer to it as the "Kantian theory."

According to this view, law requires merely external compliance with existing rules and regulations, while morality appeals to the inner conscience of man. Moral law demands that men act from praiseworthy motives, above all from a sense of ethical duty, and that they strive after good for its own sake. A modern advocate of this doctrine, the Hungarian jurist Julius Moór, summarizes thus:

> The norms of morality do not threaten the application of external means of compulsion; no external guaranties for the enforcement of their postulates are of avail to them. The guaranty of their enforcement rests exclusively within the soul of the individual concerned. Their only authority is grounded on the insight that they indicate the *right* way of acting. Not outward physical compulsion and threats, but the inner conviction of their inherent rightness will bring about the realization of moral norms. Thus the moral command appeals to our character, to our conscience. [4]

The law, on the other hand, says Moór, demands an absolute subjection to its rules and commands, whether a particular individual approves of them or not, and it is characterized by the fact that it always applies the threat of physical compulsion. Morality, according to this view, is autonomous (coming from within man's soul), while the law is heteronomous (being imposed upon man from without).

This theory, although it contains an element of truth, is not acceptable as a generally valid explanation of the relationship between law and morals, First of all, the formula does not accurately describe the relation between these two agencies of social control from a historical

[1] Christian Thomasius, *Fundamenta Iuris Naturae et Gentium* (Halle, 1705), Bk. I. ch. 1. 4–6.

[2] *The Philosophy of Law*, transl. W. Hastie (Edinburgh, 1887), pp. 14, 20–23.

[3] See for instance Hermann Kantorowicz, *The Definition of Law*, ed. A. H. Campbell (Cambridge, Eng., 1958), pp. 43–51; Otto Gierke, "Recht und Sittlichkeit," 6 *Logos* 211, at 228–233 (1917); Gierke, *Deutsches Privatrecht* (Leipzig, 1895), I, 115; Julius Moór, *Macht, Recht, Moral* (Szeged, 1922), p. 15; Max E. Mayer, *Rechtsphilosophie*, 2d ed. (Berlin, 1926), p. 46; W. R. Sorley, *The Moral Life* (Cambridge, Eng., 1911), p. 8.

[4] *Macht, Recht, Moral*, pp. 15–16.

point of view. This relation is, in itself, a product of evolution and change.[5] Second, the Kantian theory needs to be modified in various important respects even when we undertake to analyze the difference between law and morality in a highly developed social system.

In the early stages of legal development, no clear-cut distinction between the two spheres of social regulation is apparent. The customary law of primitive society was closely linked with religious and moral convictions. With the growing complexity of social life, a certain "division of labor" in matters of social control took place, and organized political society took upon itself the function of regulating authoritatively the most essential relations between the members of society, especially those which might most easily become the source of friction and strife. But even the sophisticated civilization of the Greeks does not seem to have provided a workable segregation of legal rules from moral postulates. There is every reason to believe that the unguided lay juries which administered justice in the Greek popular courts did not in their minds perceive a clear distinction between what was legally prohibited and what was morally opprobrious. In Rome, for the first time in history, law emerged in its peculiar and independent character, emancipated from custom and morality. The philosophical and sociological significance of this emancipation was not, however, fully recognized by the Roman jurists themselves. In Justinian's *Institutes*, the command to "live honestly" (*honeste vivere*) [6] is mentioned as a fundamental precept of the law, although it must also be regarded partly as a moral postulate. The definition of Celsus, *Ius est ars boni et aequi* (Law is the art of the good and the just),[7] also draws no clear distinction between law and morality. In actual practice, however, the Roman jurists probably were fully conscious of the border which separates law from morals.

After the Roman Empire had perished, the European world relapsed again into relatively primitive conditions. During most of the Middle Ages, law was not differentiated sharply from morals and theology. The medieval chancellors administered equity according to the dictates of their conscience, which had been shaped by the prevailing moral ideals and the religious doctrines of the Roman Catholic Church. The judges of the common law often imposed punishment for crimes in cases where they felt the perpetrator had outraged the moral feelings of the community and in the absence of a statute clearly defining the

---

[5] A sketch of this historical process is found in Giorgio Del Vecchio, *Philosophy of Law*, transl. T. O. Martin (Washington, D.C., 1953), pp. 273-276.
[6] *Inst.* I. 1. 3.
[7] *Dig.* I. 1. 1.

elements of the crime and the measure of punishment to be visited upon the offender.

It was not until the beginning of modern times that a new emancipation of law from morals took place. The classical law-of-nature school investigated the peculiar character of the law and prepared the ground for the establishment of jurisprudence as an independent science. Law tended more and more to become the only strictly compulsory agency of social regulation. Thomasius and Kant merely expressed the trend of their time when they relegated to the realm of mere conscience those principles of morality which had not been incorporated into the law.

Yet the Kantian theory, with its sharp separation of the respective spheres of law and morality, exhibits serious shortcomings, even as applied to the conditions of modern society. To Kant, morality pertains solely to the relationship between a man's actions and the motives underlying these actions; in other words, he saw its regulatory force as operative only within the psyche of the individual. But morality may also with good reason be looked upon as the recognition of an objective hierarchy of basic values which are to guide the conduct of human beings toward one another in a given society. Ethical or moral doctrine understood in this sense furnishes us with some essential criteria for the evaluation of human acts and human behavior. In relating these moral criteria to the normative standards of the law, it is necessary to realize that in every form of social organization there exist certain tenets of moral rightness which are considered so basic and imperative for social intercourse that society will use all the means at its disposal to uphold their obligatory character and binding force. Murder, rape, robbery, and physical assaults upon others are usually looked upon as immoral acts, but the law will also render these acts illegal and often punishable by informal prohibitions or specific formal commands. In Christian civilization, monogamy in sexual relations is viewed as a fundamental postulate of morality, and the law protects this value by the recognition and regulation of monogamous marriage. Legal rules against fraud and fraudulent transactions, breaches of solemnly entered agreements, and cruel treatment of prisoners in war are also indicative of the incorporation of moral principles into the law. When Georg Jellinek defined law as the "ethical minimum," [8] he was guided by the thought that every society regards certain axioms of moral behavior as so essential to its preservation and well-being that

[8] Die Sozialethische Bedeutung von Recht, Unrecht und Strafe (Vienna, 1878), p. 42; cf. also Roscoe Pound, Law and Morals, 2d ed. (Chapel Hill, N.C., 1926), pp. 103–104.

it surrounds these axioms with effective guarantees for observance. There is a strong tendency to ensure compliance with these basic requirements of proper conduct by the establishment of organized community sanctions, including the possible use of force, but the existence of such coercive sanctions is not, as we have seen, an indispensable condition of social control by law.[9]

The line of demarcation between those moral principles which are part of the legal system and those which have not been absorbed into the law is not permanent and fixed; it tends to waver and shift in the course of legal growth and evolution. Up to this day, for example, the common law has not recognized a legal obligation to assist another human being who is in grave danger of life or limb. Thus a physician is under no duty to answer the call of one who is dying and might be saved; no one is required to play the part of a good Samaritan and bind up the wounds of a stranger who is bleeding to death, or to cry a warning to one who is walking into the jaws of a dangerous machine.[10] At some time in the future, the duty to give aid to someone in serious peril may perhaps, with certain reasonable limitations, pass from the domain of common morality and decency into the realm of obligatory law.

In the law of unfair competition, many changes accomplished in recent times by courts and legislatures must be attributed to a sharpening and refinement of the moral sense, accompanied by a conviction that the business community must be protected against certain reprehensible and unscrupulous trading practices by means more effective than moral disapproval. Thus in a reversal of earlier trends in the law, the pirating of news from a competitor by a well-known news-gathering agency was condemned by the United States Supreme Court,[11] and the decision gave an impetus to new developments in that branch of business torts which is concerned with the unjustifiable appropriation by one person of commercial values created by another. The slowly increasing protection which the right of privacy is receiving at the hands of courts and legislatures is another illustration of the same phenomenon.[12] Such examples prove, in the apt words of Hocking, that

[9] See *supra* Sec. 54.
[10] See William L. Prosser, *Handbook of the Law of Torts,* 2d ed. (St. Paul, Minn., 1955), p. 184.
[11] *International News Service v. Associated Press,* 248 U.S. 215 (1918).
[12] See *Peay v. Curtis Pub. Co.,* 78 F. Supp. 305 (1948); *Pavesich v. New England Life Ins. Co.,* 50 S.E. 68 (Ga., 1905); *Melvin v. Reid,* 297 Pac. 91 (Cal., 1931); *Restat. of Torts,* Sec. 867; several states have in recent decades passed statutes giving a limited protection to the right of privacy.

law falls in behind the advance of ethical reflection, attempting to make unanimous in behavior what ethical sense has made almost unanimous in motive, and in so doing (a) to make the motivation itself more nearly unanimous, and (b) to transfer the released ethical energy to a new level of issues, which in turn will eventually become material for new law. Law is the great civilizing agency it is, not because it throws conduct into artificial uniformity and order, but because it is a working partner with the advancing ethical sense of the community.[13]

Even where no decisive change in the pre-existing law is involved, the ethical convictions of the judges as to the "rightness" or "wrongness" of a certain solution or result will often have a bearing upon the interpretation of a statute or the application of an established rule to a novel situation. As Justice Cardozo has stated, judges will stretch a point here and there "in response to a moral urge." [14] Law and morals do not represent entirely separate or mutually exclusive vehicles of social control; they converge and overlap on various occasions in the actual operation of a legal system.[15]

Another shortcoming of the Kantian approach lies in the fact that it limits the juridical orbit to the adjudication of the legality of external acts, while morality is relegated to the evaluation of mental attitudes. In reality, the law is often deeply interested in the disposition of the mind of a person whose actions are to be judged by its norms and standards. In the criminal law, for example, the proof of a guilty mind (*mens rea*) is an essential prerequisite for the punishment of the majority of crimes. It is also to be kept in mind that the kind and severity of the penalty will often depend on the inner motives and intentions which induced the accused to commit the crime. The law of torts, too, is often concerned with the subjective psychological springs of human actions. Thus in several states of the Union, the truth of a libelous statement will exculpate the maker of the statement only if it was published with good motives and for justifiable ends. Persons may be

[13] William E. Hocking, "Ways of Thinking About Rights: A New Theory of the Relation Between Law and Morals," in *Law: A Century of Progress* (New York, 1937), II, 258.

[14] Benjamin N. Cardozo, *The Paradoxes of Legal Science* (New York, 1928), p. 43. See also Samuel E. Stumpf, "The Moral Element in Supreme Court Decisions," 6 *Vanderbilt Law Review* 41 (1952), with examples, and *infra* Sec. 72.

[15] As Hocking observes, there is "a natural and minimal organic connection of the living law with the living ethical convictions of a people." *Op. cit. supra* n. 13, II, 245.

On the relationship between law and morals see also Patrick Devlin, *The Enforcement of Morals* (London, 1959); Eugene V. Rostow, "The Enforcement of Morals," *Cambridge Law Journal*, Nov. 1960, p. 174; H. L. A. Hart, "Positivism and the Separation of Law and Morals," 71 *Harv. L. Rev.* 593 (1958); Lon L. Fuller, "Positivism and Fidelity to Law," 71 *Harv. L. Rev.* 630 (1958).

deprived of rights ordinarily belonging to them if they exercise these rights out of pure malice or spite.[16] Thus, where a man opens a business not for the sake of financial gain but with the sole and exclusive intent to drive another person out of business for reasons of personal animosity, the malevolence of the motive may give rise to an action in tort.[17]

While intentions are frequently important from the point of view of the law, it is also conversely true that morality is not entirely disinterested in actions. Good intentions unaccompanied by moral acts, or praiseworthy motives resulting in unintended consequences of an immoral or harmful character, can hardly be looked upon as meaningful manifestations of social morality.[18] Society will usually exercise some kind of pressure to induce people to convert their moral intentions into socially approved deeds. Immoral behavior is often met by the sanction of popular condemnation, even though the act in question may stay within the authorized precincts of the law. While it is true that the law does not put a man in prison for not exercising the moral virtues of charity and forbearance, a man whose actions persistently violate the moral sense of the community may find it difficult to remain a self-respecting member of his group.

The chief difference between law and morality in the developed legal systems of the world today must be sought in the fact that morality, insofar as it may be regarded as a separate and distinct agency of social control, stands outside the more or less definitely circumscribed network of rights, duties, and obligations which make up the fabric of the law. As Petrazycki has shown, it is typical of a solely moral obligation that it is not accompanied by a corresponding right on the part of another person to insist on compliance with the obligation.[19] Although I may release the debt of a person who owes money to me in order to help him out of his financial difficulties, the debtor has no right to demand such generosity on my part.[20] The moral duty which I am dis-

---

[16] See A. H. C. Chroust, "Law and Morals," 25 *Boston University Law Review* 348, at 354 (1945).

[17] See *Tuttle v. Buck*, 119 N.W. 946 (Minn., 1909); *Dunshee v. Standard Oil Co.*, 132 N.W. 371 (Iowa, 1911); *Boggs v. Duncan-Schell Furniture Co.*, 143 N.W. 482 (Iowa, 1913).

[18] " 'Dictates of the heart' are meaningless unless they affect first the arm-and-leg action of the individual, and then institutions." Hocking, II, 257.

[19] Leon Petrazycki, *Law and Morality*, transl. H. W. Babb (Cambridge, Mass., 1955), pp. 45–49.

[20] See F. S. C. Northrop, "Petrazycki's Psychological Jurisprudence: Its Originality and Importance," 104 *U. Pa. L. Rev.* 651 (1956). In the words of Northrop, "The obligation is unilateral in the case of a moral relation and bilateral in the case of a legal relation." *Id.*, p. 654.

charging by the release of the debt is one which is imposed upon me solely by the dictates of my conscience. It is characteristic of the situation in this particular example that, in response to the promptings of the moral impulse, I renounce a right which the legal order has accorded to me. In other cases, where no abandonment of a legal right is involved, the elements of a moral act may nevertheless be present. Thus, when I give alms to an indigent person, he cannot be said to have a right to my ethical action.

Moral conduct, in what may perhaps be considered its most significant aspect, is "conduct which is actuated by a wise sympathy." [21] Morality, insofar as it operates beyond the confines of the legal order, seeks to limit the play of self-centered instincts more than the law regards as necessary for the preservation of the essential conditions of the social order. Morality thus leaves room for the exercise of man's altruistic impulses and the demonstration of benevolence and love in an area left untouched by the law. Lamont, using the term "ideal morality" to describe the domain of moral conduct as transcending the scope of legal obligation, follows Bosanquet's theory that "the positive nature of this attitude [is] that it is concerned not with a world of rights and duties, claims and counter-claims, but with an ideal of service and counter-service." [22] Moral man is intent upon promoting the good of others even if this necessitates a sacrifice of his own legal rights. This does not, of course, imply any inherent contradiction or opposition between the requirements of law and morality. Renunciation or neglect of one's rights for the sake of sympathy or benevolence toward one's fellow men is in no sense looked upon with disapproval by the law.

A bridge obviously exists between the view here expounded and the position taken by Kant. Whether the tenets of that higher morality which exceeds the average moral behavior demanded by the law are or are not carried out by actual deeds of benevolence or love depends to a far-reaching extent upon personal commitment and motivation. However, the postulates and norms of this higher morality are not fashioned entirely by the dictates of the individual conscience; they are frequently also grounded on general and objective social values or on religious ideals. Inasmuch as the law, as we have seen, is also strongly influenced by the prevailing values of society, law and morality may

---

[21] Alexander Sutherland, *The Origin and Growth of the Moral Instinct* (London, 1898), p. 19.
[22] W. D. Lamont, *The Principles of Moral Judgement* (Oxford, 1946), p. 166. Lamont defines ideal morality as a "righteousness which fulfils and exceeds that minimum of respect for other persons which justice requires." *Id.*, p. 171.

be said to have a common axiological foundation. In the words of Del Vecchio, "Between law and morals there will be a distinction, but not a separation, and much less opposition." [23] Despite the essential correctness of this statement, it must be conceded that clashes and encounters between legal norms and moral ideals are also within the range of possibility.

Section 58. *Law and Custom*

Customs are habits of action or conduct which are generally observed by classes or groups of people. They may relate to dress or to etiquette or to rites surrounding important events of life, such as birth, marriage, or death. They may also pertain to the conclusion of transactions or the fulfillment of obligations.

There exist customs in every society which are concerned with the less important aspects of social life.[1] Most societies have certain usages with respect to the kind of dress one is expected to wear on various occasions. It is the custom in many countries to give wedding presents to friends and relatives. Well-established customs are observed at burials and other solemn ceremonies. When a custom of this type is violated, society usually reacts by showing social displeasure or disapproval; and if the norms of social intercourse are repeatedly or constantly violated by some person, he may soon find himself outside the pale of society. But it is characteristic of social customs of this type that sanctions directly affecting the liberty, property, or status of the offender (such as imprisonment, fines, or loss of civil rights) are not employed.

There may be other kinds of customs which in a more definite and stringent sense are regarded as the specific duties and obligations of men. Such customs may regulate the obligations of marriage and the upbringing of children, the transmission of property at death, or the modes of consummating and fulfilling agreements. Such customs do not pertain to the sphere of social formalities, outward decorum, or esthetics; rather, they are concerned with the serious business of society, the work that must be accomplished in order to secure and guarantee satisfactory conditions for collective life. There is every likelihood that such customs will become absorbed and incorporated into the body of the law, and that their violation will eventually be met by the typical sanctions employed by the legal order, including perhaps the use of direct constraint by governmental authorities. The

---

[23] *Philosophy of Law*, p. 276.
[1] See James C. Carter, *Law: Its Origin, Growth, and Function* (New York, 1907), pp. 120, 138.

term customary law will hereafter be used to designate customs which, although they have not been authoritatively promulgated by a legislative or judicial body, have become transformed into rules or arrangements to which a legal character is attributed.

It has often been asserted that law and custom were entirely undifferentiated in early society, and that the drawing of a line between social custom and customary law was the product of a long and gradual legal evolution. The anthropologist Bronislaw Malinowski disputed this view. He attempted to show that even in early society some rules of custom stood out from other social rules in that they were felt to represent the definite obligations of one person and the rightful claims of another. "On close inquiry," he said, "we discover a definite system of division of functions and a rigid system of mutual obligations, into which a sense of duty and the recognition of the need of cooperation enter side by side with a realization of self-interest, privileges, and benefits." [2] He pointed out that it is not the sheriff who stands ready to enforce such rights and obligations in primitive society; they are usually self-enforcing because men need the good will and the services of others. A man requires a boat in order to fish, but he can obtain it only if he delivers part of the catch to the owner of the boat. The native who shirks his obligations knows that he will suffer for it in the future.[3]

Thus it is Malinowski's thesis that primitive society recognized the distinctive character of legal rules, that is, rules invested with a definite binding obligation, He maintained further that these rules were not necessarily enforced by modes of constraint resembling modern legal sanctions; the psychologically dictated necessity of reciprocal observance was the chief guaranty of compliance. There is much in Malinowski's argument which is highly suggestive and persuasive. Whether the rules of law in primitive society formed as well-defined a category within the general body of custom as he seems to assume may to some extent remain subject to doubt and debate.

There is substantial agreement among legal historians that primitive law was to a large extent based on customary rules which were not promulgated by a legislator or formulated in written form by professionally trained judges.[4] With regard to the origin of this primitive

[2] Malinowski, *Crime and Custom in Savage Society* (New York, 1926), p. 20.
[3] Malinowski, pp. 23, 28–30, 41, 59.
[4] See Paul Vinogradoff, *Common Sense in Law* (New York, 1926), p. 149; Vinogradoff, "The Problem of Customary Law," in *Collected Papers* (Oxford, 1928), II, 422; T. F. T. Plucknett, *A Concise History of the Common Law,* 5th ed. (Boston, 1956), p. 307; Carter, p. 18; Charles S. Lobingier, "Customary Law," *Encyclopedia of the Social Sciences,* IV, 662 (1931).

customary law, however, a number of different points of view have been set forth.

According to an influential opinion, customary law arises as soon as certain usages and customs felt to be legally obligatory are generally and continuously observed among the members of a family, group, tribe, or people. No formal recognition or compulsory enforcement of these usages and arrangements by a superior authority is regarded as necessary for the formation of customary law. In this view, law in early society arose out of the nonlitigious customs of everyday life which were approved by public opinion. "It is not conflicts that initiate rules of legal observance, but the practices of every-day directed by the give and take considerations of reasonable intercourse and social cooperation." [5] This view rests upon a theory of law which draws its chief support from the jurists of the historical school, especially from Savigny and Puchta.[6] The historical school of law assumed that in early society rules of law were not imposed from above, but grew from below as a result of the physical and mental collaboration and the mutual relationships of the members of a community. According to Savigny, customary law arose from the social arrangements of the people, consolidated by tradition and habit and conforming to the legal consciousness of the people; it did not, in his opinion, originate through the decrees of a governmental authority.

The general correctness of this view may in some respects be open to doubt. It presupposes a democratic structure of primitive society, in the sense that only those rules of conduct which arose out of the legal consciousness of the entire group attained the force of law. Modern research into primitive society has revealed that, at least in numerous instances, its structure was patriarchal rather than democratic. It is very likely that many sibs or *gentes*, especially in the Indo-European world, were ruled in an authoritative and patriarchal manner by one man, who sometimes had the power of life and death over the members of his group. If we believe in the existence of such ancient patriarchal authority, we have to assume that the rules of conduct in primitive society were often determined by its autocratic chief, or at least that only those customs and usages which met with his approval could become part of the legal fabric.

In many instances, the early monarchic system gradually gave way to the rule of a caste or aristocracy.[7] It may have been a council of

[5] Vinogradoff, *Historical Jurisprudence* (Oxford, 1920), I, 368.

[6] On Savigny and Puchta see *supra* Sec. 18. The view that law comes out of the mores of the people was also propounded by William G. Sumner, *Folkways* (Boston, 1907), pp. 55–56.

[7] See Henry Maine, *Ancient Law*, ed. F. Pollock (London, 1930), p. 8.

chiefs or elders or a college of priests. It is likely that this aristocracy became to some extent the agent for the administration of customary law. Some customs might have been unsettled or in conflict, and the uncertainty or conflict would have had to be resolved by some authoritative decision. Even Vinogradoff, who was, by and large, an adherent of the Savigny-Puchta theory, admitted that "we are . . . driven to assume . . . that there was a conscious activity of elders, priests, judges, witans, or experts of some kind directed towards the discovery and declaration of what is right and just."[8] This aristocratic caste tended to monopolize the knowledge of the law. Since writing was not known, some other effective means for the preservation of the customs of the community had to be employed. By confiding the recognized modes of conduct to the memory of a small group of men who transmitted their experience from generation to generation, a certain stability and continuity in the development of customary law was insured.

In one important respect, however, the historical school was right. Only such customs as suited the general way of life of early society and the economic requirements of the epoch could be administered by the chief or ruling aristocracy. No authority can, for a long time, enforce rules or arrangements which are contrary to the social necessity of the time and place. If we look at the problem from this point of view, Savigny's opinion that law arises from the legal consciousness of the people contains an important element of truth. In order to function successfully, the administration of rules of conduct requires some degree of cooperation and support from the community in which the rules are operative. "Laws repugnant to the notions of right of a community or to its practical requirements are likely to be defeated by passive resistance and by the difficulty of constant supervision and repression."[9] Thus, it may be assumed with good reason that there was a continuous interaction between popular sentiment, usage, and practice on the one hand and the activity of authoritative interpreters on the other in the operation of early customary law.[10]

Some writers have taken the view that only those customs and usages which were enforced by some governmental authority can be considered as legal rules.[11] Others have gone further, regarding as law

---

[8] *Common Sense in Law*, p. 165.

[9] Vinogradoff, "Customary Law," in *The Legacy of the Middle Ages*, ed. C. G. Crump and E. F. Jacobs (Oxford, 1926), p. 287.

[10] This is the view of Carleton K. Allen, *Law in the Making*, 6th ed. (Oxford, 1958), pp. 123–126.

[11] John Austin, *Lectures on Jurisprudence*, 5th ed. by R. Campbell (London, 1885), I, 36, 199; G. T. Sadler, *The Relation of Custom to Law* (London, 1919), p. 85; Thomas E. Holland, *The Elements of Jurisprudence*, 13th ed. (London, 1924), p. 58.

only those rules of conduct whose observance was guaranteed by the infliction of penalties affecting the person or his property.[12] These views will be critically examined in a later section dealing with the problem of customary law and the significance which this form of law retains in our modern age.[13]

[12] Munroe Smith, *A General View of European Legal History* (New York, 1927), p. 285.
[13] See *infra* Sec. 73.

XIV

THE BENEFITS
AND DRAWBACKS OF
THE RULE OF LAW

Section 59. *The Channeling of Creative Human Energies*
Man is so constituted by nature that his creative faculties and energies
are not fully absorbed or used up in his efforts to preserve his own life
and reproduce new life. There is a reserve of excess energy in him,
without which the great collective enterprise which we call human
civilization would be impossible. If man's resources of energy were exhausted and consumed in his struggle to find food and shelter, protect
himself against the dangers of nature, and reproduce his kind, there
would be no energy left for the higher-minded, cultural activities,
which go beyond satisfying the bare, immediate necessities of life. It is
this surplus strength flowing into cultural activity which, perhaps more
than anything else, distinguishes man from the lower species of life.[1]

[1] Max Scheler, *Die Stellung des Menschen im Kosmos* (Darmstadt, 1930), pp.
46–47, 71–73; Arnold Gehlen, *Der Mensch* (Bonn, 1958), pp. 60–65, 385–400. On the
idea of civilization see also *supra* Sec. 49.

It is true, as Franz Alexander has demonstrated, that the urge of the human being to actualize his potentialities to the fullest degree in the service of the manifold tasks of civilization is opposed and impeded by the contradictory "principle of economy," which causes men to save energy and to relax ambition as soon as the necessary conditions for their existence are safeguarded.[2] Initiative is often stultified by inertia, active creativity by regressive indolence, productivity by sloth. Since the tendencies toward growth and effort on the one hand and inertia on the other are both inherent in individual and social life, the former must be stimulated by every available reasonable means in order to bring to fruition the constructive and creative potentialities of the human race. It is more and more recognized by modern psychologists that true happiness for human beings can be achieved only if the capacities of the total human organism (including its mental and emotional branches) are realized to the fullest possible extent.[3] The lack of an integrated social system able to satisfy all the various aspirations of the human body and mind may cause serious psychological frustrations among the masses of the people, which may lead to disintegration of the social order, with all its concomitant effects.[4] Man's cravings are not satisfied by procuring food and shelter and by reproducing his kind. He desires to participate in something greater and more inspiring than a mere technical organization for the gratification of consumers' wants.[5] He must therefore be given an opportunity to fulfill the higher purposes of life, that is, to develop his capabilities and talents to be of service to humanity. No adequate philosophical anthropology can ignore this human urge for self-perfection.

In the great endeavor to build a rich and satisfying civilization, the institution of law plays an important and indispensable part. The law cannot, of course, directly initiate or promote the erection of the edifice of civilization; it cannot order people to be inventors or dis-

---

[2] Alexander, *Our Age of Unreason* (Philadelphia, 1942), pp. 199–200, 210; Kurt Goldstein, *Human Nature in the Light of Psychopathology* (Cambridge, Mass., 1951), p. 111.

[3] Erich Fromm, *The Sane Society* (New York, 1955), pp. 67–69, 202–203; Fromm, *Man for Himself* (New York, 1947), pp. 20, 27; Goldstein, pp. 112, 140 ff., 171, 221–223.

[4] If the goal of channeling man's surplus energies is not successfully accomplished by the social order, there is danger that these energies will be deflected into socially undesirable and destructive pursuits. Participation in an adventurous gang engaged in criminal activities may serve as a substitute for desired but frustrated cooperation in a worthwhile and challenging enterprise. Membership in a secret organization operating under rituals inspiring awe or fear may attract individuals whose lack of moral directives makes them amenable to misuse for antisocial ends.

[5] "All men are 'idealists' and are striving for something beyond the attainment of physical satisfaction." Fromm, *Man for Himself*, p. 49.

coverers, to contrive new ways of city-building, or to compose good music. But it can make an indirect contribution toward achieving the "good life" in society by establishing the conditions in whose absence the higher tasks of human social organization could not be discharged.

The success of a social system depends largely upon its ability to direct the surplus energies which are not absorbed by economic or sexual pursuits into socially desirable channels. This can be achieved only if the base of the entire structure is so solidly constructed that the top layers may be superimposed without causing the collapse of the foundation. Only a society which has set up a working system for the primary satisfaction of basic wants can afford to direct or encourage activities which are designed to enrich and embellish the material and spiritual world in which we live and to satisfy the urges of all human beings to participate in a great and worthwhile undertaking.

In order to insure that the creative powers of men are directed toward the worthiest goals of civilization, important groundwork has to be done. Care must be taken that the energies of men are not consumed or dissipated in constant friction with their neighbors, in private warfare between individuals and groups, or in perpetual vigilance and preparation against aggressive and predatory acts of antisocial individuals. Unless society guarantees a certain amount of security to individuals and groups, they will be unable to devote themselves to the more comprehensive aims that are within the reach of human cooperative effort.

The beneficial effect of the law upon society stems largely from the fact that it creates and maintains a sphere of security for individuals in certain basic conditions of life.[6] The law protects the life, bodily integrity, property transactions, family relations, and perhaps even the subsistence and health of the members of the body politic. It makes it unnecessary for people to set up private systems of protection against invasions of their privacy. It promotes the growth and maturing of human personalities by creating ordered conditions beneficial to the development of their mental and spiritual powers. It curbs physical or social adventure by those whose nature drives them to seek mastery and arbitrary power over others. Furthermore, it sets up institutional frameworks to provide means and proper environments for carrying out the manifold political, economic, and cultural tasks which a progressive society must successfully accomplish in order to achieve

---

[6] Rudolf von Jhering, *Law as a Means to an End*, transl. I. Husik (Boston, 1913), p. 380, advocated the thesis that the security of conditions of social life is the paramount objective of legal regulation. Jhering did not, however, sufficiently emphasize that only an order fulfilling the cardinal requirements of justice can accomplish this goal. On Jhering see *supra* Sec. 23.

satisfaction of the demands of its members. By performing these functions, the law helps the creative, life-affirming powers latent in the social body to flow into constructive channels, and it thereby proves to be an indispensable instrument of civilization.[7]

Section 60. *The Promotion of Peace*

The desire for peace is deeply rooted in the structure of the human personality. A chaotic state of society in which individuals or groups would be engaged in constant strife, attempting to harm or annihilate each other, would not be conducive to developing in men those constructive faculties whose affirmative exercise is a condition of human happiness.[1] The entire energies of men, in such a state of affairs, would be applied to self-protection and the devising of destructive means for warding off aggressors or committing aggressive acts. Fortunately the psychology of human beings is not so constituted as to make likely the existence of an endless and perpetual condition of struggle, conflict, and war. All societies have succeeded in establishing various ways of coexistence and cooperation among their members, as well as legal institutions designed to promote harmony and peace within the social unit and to regulate the relations with other and potentially hostile social groups.

In this human endeavor to form orderly and peaceful "polities," the law has played a vital and leading part. Law is an instrument for the rational distribution and limitation of power in society, and by undertaking this difficult task the law makes a significant contribution to peace and to the security of life. Without excluding or stifling healthy competition between individuals and groups, it purports to allocate rights, duties, powers, and liabilities according to a plan which takes account of the capabilities and needs of individual persons as well as of the concerns of society as a whole. The legal system of a social body also sets up machinery for the adjustment of conflicts arising between various members of the unit and also perhaps between these members and their government.

While domestic law strives to safeguard intragroup harmony and cooperation, international law pursues the same aim on a transnational or world basis. It seeks to reduce the causes for international strife by producing norms and procedures to facilitate political and economic intercourse between nations, adjust disputes and grievances among

---

[7] The role of the law in the building of civilizations was emphasized by Joseph Kohler, *Philosophy of Law*, transl. A. Albrecht (New York, 1921), pp. 4, 22, 58–62. On Kohler see *supra* Sec. 27.

[1] See *supra* Sec. 59.

them, and protect the nationals of one country residing under the temporary sovereignty of another country. It will be generally conceded, however, that because of the incomplete character of its normative system, and certain serious weaknesses inherent in its processes of enforcement, international law has been only partially successful thus far in eliminating the sources of international friction and in composing severe differences between nations.

In a world threatened by nuclear war and the specter of total destruction, an enlargement of the jurisdiction of international law with the aim of guaranteeing a peaceful solution of all international controversies appears to be imperative. In case a strengthening of international law should prove to be impossible, the only alternative would be the establishment of a world government vested with power to settle all disputes between the political units subordinate to it through compulsory legal means and instrumentalities. There appears to be grave doubt, however, whether the formation of a supranational government endowed with a sovereignty sufficient to preserve universal peace could be achieved, under present world conditions, without the occurrence of another major war or series of wars that might destroy large parts of the world. The present insistence of at least the major nations of the world on full preservation of their political sovereignty being as strong as it is today, the only hope for the immediate future of the world seems to lie in the strengthening of international-law procedures which will deal effectively with all serious threats to peace.

The desire for peace is an innate longing of man which, on an overall scale and in the long run, is normally superior in strength to the traits of pugnacity and ruthless self-assertiveness which are also found in human beings and groups. Although the struggles between these two conflicting impulses may be intense and prolonged, and although there may be serious setbacks for the cause of collective sanity, it need not be held that mankind is condemned to an eternal stalemate between social cooperation and antisocial aggression on the community level as well as on the international plane.[2] This view, to be sure, is not accepted by all students of human nature. Sigmund Freud, for example,

---

[2] In accord: Ranyard West, *Conscience and Society* (New York, 1945). The following passage from this book is relevant to our discussion: "The most significant social fact about the operation of these two main instinct groups—the social instinct of self-realization through others and the self-assertive instinct of self against others —is that, whether in a happy normal personality, or in the self-restrained individualist, or in the repressed and unhappy neurotic, *the social instinct nearly always wins.* Except in the case of the conscious-free bully (with whom a stable society can readily cope), the trouble of modern society springs less from the individual self-assertiveness of its individual members than from its failure to master collective aggressiveness." *Id.*, p. 153.

was convinced—at least in the later periods of his life—that the sociable and creative impulses of human beings are fully matched and counteracted by a negative force, the "death instinct," which finds one of its outlets in the human desire for aggression and destruction.[3] Man's psyche, he believed, is a battlefield on which two equally powerful biological forces are struggling with each other: the drive to live and the drive to die; the latter may under certain circumstances seek its aim either in self-destruction or in the destruction of others.

This deeply pessimistic view has been convincingly refuted by Malinowski and Fromm. Both demonstrate that aggression and destructiveness are merely secondary potentialities of the human psychological constitution, which arise from the thwarting of basic desires and the frustrations or deflections of the creative and cooperative impulses.[4] In the words of Malinowski, "Human beings fight, not because they are biologically impelled, but because they are culturally induced . . . War is not the original or natural state of mankind." [5] He points out that if war came from an innate biological urge, it would most certainly occur at the earliest stages of anthropological development, where these inclinations manifest themselves in their most direct and uninhibited way. Evidence shows, however, that in these stages pugnacity is directed only against the individual or individuals guilty of violence or malice (real or supposed), and that it does not engender any collective organized fighting. Fighting and war may break out when one organized group feels threatened in its interests and security as a collective unit by the actual or anticipated interference by other units. Hunger may also drive an aggregation of human beings to the warpath. Fighting in these cases does not occur for its own sake, but under the impulses of anger, fear, or desperation. While wars of conquest occur at later stages of history, they are, as Malinowski shows, mostly occasional affairs and do not necessarily absorb the total energies of the peoples involved. They are not, in his opinion, perpetual conditions of social existence impelled by a supposed "animal of prey" constitution of human nature.[6]

Fromm presents a reasoned argument, from the point of view of the psychologist, in which he attempts to demonstrate that the good and

---

[3] Freud, *The Ego and the Id*, transl. J. Riviere (London, 1949), pp. 54–57; Freud, *Civilization and Its Discontents*, transl. J. Riviere (New York, 1930), pp. 102–103; see also pp. 85–87, 97–102; Freud, "Warum Krieg?" in *Gesammelte Schriften*, XII (Vienna, 1934), 356.

[4] See Bronislaw Malinowski, *Freedom and Civilization* (Bloomington, Ind., 1960), pp. 276 ff.; Fromm, *Sane Society*, pp. 37–38; Fromm, *Man for Himself*, pp. 210–226.

[5] Malinowski, pp. 279, 280.

[6] *Id.*, pp. 280–282, 301.

evil forces in human nature are not of equal strength. He points out that the destructive impulses of human beings come to the fore only under abnormal conditions and that "the degree of destructiveness is proportionate to the degree to which the unfolding of a person's capacities is blocked. . . . If life's tendency to grow, to be lived, is thwarted, the energy thus blocked undergoes a process of change and is transformed into life-destructive energy. *Destructiveness is the outcome of unlived life.*" [7] Its evil potential, in most instances, will materialize only when the proper conditions for growth and development are lacking. In other words, the life instinct in human beings is primary, the instinct of destruction secondary.

Such interpretations of the psychology of man give us hope that man may be able increasingly to master the problem of aggression in the various areas where it occurs, or at least to reduce its incidence considerably. It is essential today for the accomplishment of this goal that the law must attempt to implement and strengthen the social instinct not only on an intracommunity but on a worldwide level. Unless the inborn desire for peace is strong enough to overcome the counteracting destructive tendencies, mankind, through a momentary lapse of its collective reasoning powers, might easily plunge itself into darkness and utter ruin.

Section 61. *The Adjustment of Conflicting Interests*
In a society which leaves any leeway for the exercise of individual initiative and self-assertion (and it may be doubted whether there has ever been a society which for any sustained period of time has been able to eradicate completely these natural impulses of human beings), there will necessarily be conflicts and clashes between contradictory individual interests. Two persons may covet the same property and may have taken steps to obtain it which have entangled them in a serious dispute. Several persons may have entered into a partnership and encountered disagreements in the management of the enterprise or in the computation of individual shares of gain or loss. One person may have injured another person and may have been exposed to a claim for damages on the part of that person, but may have denied his obligation or responsibility to make good the other's loss.

Societies are not, however, troubled only by contradictions and conflicts between the interests of individuals (or groups of individuals). There may also arise incompatibilities between the interest of a single individual or group of individuals on the one hand and the interests of society viewed as an organized collective unit on the other. The gov-

[7] Fromm, *Man for Himself,* p. 216.

ernment may wish to build roads or erect structures in places occupied by a private owner. It may wish to impose curbs and restrictions in the interest of internal security or national self-preservation that infringe upon the freedom of individuals to act or speak. In wartime, organized society may have to go as far as to require individuals to sacrifice their lives for the sake of the collective whole.

It is one of the chief functions of the law to adjust and conciliate these various conflicting interests, individual as well as social. This must be done, in part at least, by the promulgation of general rules assessing the weight of various interests and providing standards for their adjustment. Without certain general yardsticks of a normative nature, organized society would flounder around in uncertainty in determining what interests should be regarded as worthy of protection, what the scope and limits of their guaranty should be, and what relative rank and priority should be assigned to various claims and demands. Without measuring rods of this type, the adjustment of such interests would be left either to chance or happenstance, with fatal consequences for social cohesion and harmony, or to the arbitrary fiat of a group having the power to enforce its decisions.

Interests, as we have seen, may be either individual or social. Among the *individual* interests may be counted the interest in one's own life, in private property, freedom to make contracts, and freedom of expression. The *social* interests requiring recognition and protection by the legal order and which in part overlap with the individual interests mentioned were classified and described by Roscoe Pound.[1] Among the interests to be encouraged and promoted, according to him, are the following: interest in general security, which includes safety from internal and external aggression and public health; security of social institutions, such as government, marriage, the family, the religious institutions; social interest in general morality; conservation of physical and human resources; interest in general progress, especially economic and cultural advance; and, last but not least, social interest in individual life, requiring that each individual be able to live a human life according to the standards of the society.

The most difficult question arising in relation to these individual and social interests is their relative ranking and importance if all of them cannot be satisfied at the same time. What determines or should determine the value judgments that may have to be made in assigning preferences and priorities to one or another of the interests mentioned?

[1] See his "A Survey of Social Interests," 57 *Harvard Law Review* 1 (1943). An account of Pound's theory of interests is given in Edwin W. Patterson, *Jurisprudence* (Brooklyn, 1953), pp. 518–527. See also *supra* Sec. 29.

This raises the problem of a "valuation of interests." Is the interest in general security superior to the individual interest in property protection and maximum self development? Does the social interest in conservation of natural resources prevail over the individual interest in full exploitation of private property, such as oil property?

Pound himself declines to commit himself to a rigid canon of evaluation. His approach to the problem is pragmatic and experimental. The jurist should be aware of the nature of his responsibility and should do the best he can on the basis of the best information he can get. The final goal, as Pound sees it, is the satisfaction of as many interests as is possible with a minimum of sacrifice and friction.

It is not possible to undertake, by the methods of philosophy, a generally valid and authoritative ranking of the interests entitled to recognition and protection by the law. This does not mean, however, that all interests must be regarded by jurisprudence as necessarily being on the same plane and that no qualitative evaluation is ever feasible. The interest in life, for instance, being the normal precondition for the safeguarding of other interests (especially all individual interests), will be entitled to claim precedence over the interest in property. The interest in health would appear to rank above the interest in pleasure or entertainment. In the case of a legitimate war, the interest in the preservation of the commonwealth would have precedence over human life and property. The protection of the natural resources of a country for the sake of future generations would appear to be superior to the desire of an individual or group to gain wealth through the exploitation of such resources, especially if an element of waste were present in unregulated private control. In dealing with such problems it must always be kept in mind, however, that the special historical and sociological conditions of an age may prescribe or necessitate particular priority rankings among such interests, and that there is little merit in an attempt to establish a permanently valid or rigid value hierarchy for the legal order.

Section 62. The Drawbacks of the Law

Although the law is an indispensable and highly beneficial institution of human life, it possesses—like most institutions—its drawbacks and defects. These negative aspects of the law stem in part from its normative nature and in part from its conservative tendencies.

The deficiencies resulting from the normative character of the law were clearly seen and described by Plato and Aristotle. Plato was convinced that the law, because of the differences of men and actions, and the infinite variety of things and circumstances, was incapable of ordaining by a general and universal rule what is best for all. Simple principles, he argued, cannot be applied to human relations, which are nearly always complex.[1] Aristotle pointed out that the law, though a necessary social institution, may by its rigidity and abstract form cause hardships and injustices in individual cases; he proposed, therefore, that the law must be corrected by *epieikeia* (equity) where it was found to be defective because of its generality. We have shown above that most legal systems have created certain methods for the equitable individualization of the law, and that these methods should not be included in the definition or description of law in its strict sense, but should be distinguished from it by a special linguistic term.[2]

The second shortcoming of the law is related to the first. By setting forth the social policy of a particular time and place in constitutional or statutory precepts, or by making the precedents of the past binding or nearly binding on the judges of the present, the law often tends to perpetuate the *status quo*. Quick changes responding to new social needs and exigencies are not always possible after a legal rule has become formalized and settled; furthermore, such changes are not always desired by those who have a vested interest in the maintenance of things as they are. Legislative procedure is often slow and cumbersome, and legislatures are prone to attend to issues of immediate political advantage more expeditiously than to the revision of outmoded codes or the modernization of a tradition-clogged judicial law. Judges may follow outdated precedents even though they have the power to overrule them. A constitution, especially if it is very detailed and specific in its provisions, may under some circumstances operate as a fetter to progress and change.

All of these factors are responsible for the "time lag" in the law.[3] The established law of society often comes into conflict with the fluid forces of social growth, and this conflict may assume grave and acute proportions. Dynamic and critical minds have castigated the law for its inertial tendencies and sluggish path; few disciplines have received as many curses from disciples as well as from outsiders as the science of law. In times of crisis and social change, the law has frequently broken down, making room for new and revolutionary adjustments. In such times, the law has a chance of preserving itself only by ex-

---

[1] Plato, *The Statesman*, transl. J. B. Skemp (New York, 1957), 294c. See also *supra* Sec. 2.

[2] See *supra* Sec. 50.

[3] See *supra* Sec. 55.

hibiting great flexibility and adaptability, capacities which it often does not possess in the degree required to surmount or survive a social cataclysm.

The truly great systems of law are those which are characterized by a peculiar and paradoxical blending of rigidity and elasticity. In their principles, institutions, and techniques they combine the virtue of stable continuity with the advantages of evolutionary change, thereby attaining the capacity for longevity and survival under adverse conditions. This creative combination is very difficult to achieve. It requires statesmanlike acumen on the part of the lawmakers, a sense of tradition as well as sagacious discernment of the trends and needs of the future, and a training of prospective judges and lawyers which accentuates the peculiar and enduring features of the technical juridical method without losing sight at the same time of the claims of social policy and justice. These qualities can be acquired and developed only in a slow and painful process through centuries of legal culture.

PART III

THE SOURCES

AND TECHNIQUES

OF THE LAW

XV

THE FORMAL SOURCES
OF THE LAW

Section 63. *Introduction*

After attempting in Part II to determine the nature of law and to ascertain and describe its functions in human social life, we shall turn now to questions of a somewhat more technical character. We must investigate the apparatus of tools, methods, and techniques of which the institution of law avails itself in order to carry out its social goals most adequately and effectively. An investigation of this type is well within the province of jurisprudence, which is devoted to the general theory and philosophy of the law, since it is concerned with issues of methodology, modes of reasoning, and processes of interpretation common to the various fields of the law, rather than with the treatment of problems, principles, and rules pertaining to specialized areas.

We shall inquire here into the formal sources of the law, and take up next what we propose to call its nonformal sources. This use of terminology, inasmuch as it does not follow a commonly accepted pattern, requires some explanation and justification. First of all, since the term "source of law" has thus far not acquired a uniform signification in Anglo-American jurisprudence,[1] a few words must be said about this concept itself.

John Chipman Gray, an influential American jurist, drew a sharp distinction between what he called "the law" on the one hand and "the sources of the law" on the other. To him the law consisted of the rules authoritatively laid down by the courts in their decisions, while he looked for its sources to certain legal and nonlegal materials upon which judges customarily fall back in fashioning the rules which make up the law. Five such sources are listed by Gray: (1) acts of legislative organs; (2) judicial precedents; (3) opinions of experts; (4) customs; (5) principles of morality (including axioms of public policy).[2] Other writers have taken a different approach and have equated the sources of the law with the official, authoritative texts from which formulated legal rules usually derive their force: constitutions, statutes, treaties, executive orders and ordinances, judicial opinions, and rules of court.[3] In Civil Law countries, legislation, customary law, and (under certain circumstances) treaties are often declared to be the only sources of law.[4] The phrase has also been used in another sense to identify certain bodies of law which have served as traditional reservoirs of legal rules and principles, such as the common law, equity, the law merchant, and the canon law.[5] Others again have designated as sources of law literary materials and bibliographical repositories of the law, as, for instance, statute books, judicial reports, digests of case law, treatises, encyclopedias, and legal periodicals.[6]

Here, the term sources of law will be given a meaning which bears some similarity to Gray's definition, but differs from it in several important respects. First, for reasons to be set forth later,[7] the line of demarcation which Gray drew between the law and its sources has

---

[1] For an enumeration of the various senses in which the term has been employed in legal literature see Thomas E. Holland, *The Elements of Jurisprudence*, 13th ed. (Oxford, 1924), p. 55, and Roscoe Pound, "The Sources and Forms of the Law," 21 *Notre Dame Lawyer* 247-248 (1946).

[2] Gray, *The Nature and Sources of the Law*, 2d ed. (New York, 1921), pp. 123-125. Gray's view is followed, with some modifications, by Edwin W. Patterson, *Jurisprudence* (Brooklyn, 1953), pp. 195 ff. On Gray see also *supra* Sec. 25.

[3] These are called "legal sources" by John Salmond, *Jurisprudence*, 11th ed. by G. Williams (London, 1957), pp. 135-136, who, however, adds custom to the list.

[4] See, e.g., L. Enneccerus, T. Kipp, and M. Wolff, *Lehrbuch des Bürgerlichen Rechts*, 14th ed. by H. C. Nipperdey (Tübingen, 1952), I, 144 ff.; this view is criticized by Hans Kelsen, *General Theory of Law and State*, transl. A. Wedberg (Cambridge, Mass., 1949), p. 131.

[5] See, e.g., Edmund M. Morgan, *Introduction to the Study of Law*, 2d ed. (Chicago, 1948), pp. 40-47; Charles H. Kinnane, *A First Book on Anglo-American Law*, 2d ed. (Indianapolis, 1952), pp. 258 ff.

[6] See W. S. Holdsworth, *Sources and Literature of English Law* (Oxford, 1925).

[7] See *infra* Sec. 67.

not been adopted. For purposes of the ensuing discussion, we mean by the term "law" the aggregate and totality of the sources of law used in the legal process, in their connectedness and interrelatedness. Second, while we agree with Gray in identifying the sources of law with the materials and considerations upon which legal decisions may legitimately be based, we consider these sources relevant for the making of legal decisions of *any* type, and not only those rendered by the courts. Third, the number of legal source materials which we believe should be recognized in the legal order has been materially increased beyond those in Gray's list.

It appears proper and desirable to divide legal sources into two major categories, to be designated as *formal* and *nonformal* sources. By formal sources, we mean sources which are available in an articulated textual formulation embodied in an authoritative legal document. The chief examples of such formal sources are constitutions and statutes (discussed below under the general heading of legislation), executive orders, administrative regulations, ordinances, charters and by-laws of autonomous or semiautonomous bodies and organizations (discussed below under the general heading of delegated and autonomic legislation), treaties and certain other agreements, and judicial precedents. By *nonformal* sources we mean legally significant materials and considerations which have not received an authoritative or at least articulated formulation and embodiment in a formalized legal document. Without necessarily claiming exhaustive completeness for this enumeration, we have subdivided the nonformal sources into standards of justice, principles of reason and considerations of the nature of things (*natura rerum*), individual equity, public policies, moral convictions, social trends, and customary law.

The avowed positivist will be inclined either to dismiss the nonformal sources as irrelevant for the legal process or to relegate them to a decidedly secondary position in the framework of judicial administration. We agree with the second position to the extent that where a formalized, authoritative source of law provides a clear-cut answer to a legal problem, the nonformal sources need not and should not, in the large majority of instances, be consulted. An exception may become necessary in certain rare and extreme situations where the application of a formal source of law would clash with fundamental, compelling, and overriding postulates of justice and equity.[8] Where a formalized legal document reveals ambiguities and uncertainties making alternative courses of interpretation possible—as is so often the case—the nonformal sources should be resorted to for the purpose of

[8] See, e.g., *infra* Sec. 69.

arriving at a solution most conducive to reason and justice. And where the formal sources entirely fail to provide a rule of decision for the case, reliance on the nonformal sources becomes, of course, mandatory.[9]

Section 64. *Legislation*

In its most significant present-day sense, the term "legislation" is applied to the deliberate creation of legal precepts by an organ of government which is set up for this purpose and which gives articulate expression to such legal precepts in a formalized legal document. These characteristics of legislative law distinguish it from customary law, which manifests its existence through actual observance by the members of a group or community unaccompanied by authoritative approval by a governmental organ (at least until it receives formal recognition in a judicial decision or legislative enactment).

Legislation as described above must also be differentiated from normative pronouncements emanating from judicial tribunals. The verbal expression of a legal rule or principle by a judge does not, as we shall see,[1] have the same degree of finality as the authoritative formulation of a legal proposition by a legislative body. Furthermore, although it has often been asserted that adjudication, as well as legislation in the strict sense, involves the deliberate creation of law by an organ of government, it must be kept in mind that the judiciary is not an organ set up primarily for the purpose of making law. Its main function is to decide disputes under a pre-existing law; and although, because of the necessary incompleteness and frequent ambiguity of this pre-existing law, the judiciary has never been able to restrict itself exclusively to its primary function and has always found it necessary to augment and supplement the existing law by something which may not inappropriately be called judge-made law, such law-creating functions of the judges must be held to be incidental to their primary functions.[2] While the very reason for the existence of a legislature is the making of new law, this is by no means true for the courts; the creation of new law is for the judge an *ultima ratio* only, to which he must resort when the existing positive or nonpositive sources of the law give him no guid-

[9] More detailed observations with respect to the hierarchy of sources and their interrelation will be found in the text below.

[1] See *infra*, Sec. 67; cf. Salmond, *Jurisprudence*, p. 149.

[2] As Justice Holmes pointed out in *Southern Pacific Ry. Co. v. Jensen*, 244 U.S. 205, at 221 (1917), judges find themselves under a necessity to legislate, but "they can do so only *interstitially*" (italics mine). For a more elaborate discussion of the problem see *infra* Sec. 82.

ance, or when the abrogation of an obsolete precedent becomes imperative. Because of this essential difference between legislative and judicial lawmaking, the term "judicial legislation"—although it conveys a meaningful thought if properly understood—should be used with care, or perhaps be avoided altogether.

Another typical feature of a legislative act, as distinguished from a judicial pronouncement, was brought out in Mr. Justice Holmes's opinion in *Prentis v. Atlantic Coast-Line Co.*[3] As he pointed out in this opinion, while a "judicial inquiry investigates, declares, and enforces liabilities as they stand on present or past facts and under laws supposed already to exist," it is an important characteristic of legislation that it "looks to the future and changes existing conditions by making a new rule to be applied thereafter to all or some part of those subject to its power." These passages must be understood as elucidating certain *normal and typical* aspects of legislation rather than stating a *conditio sine qua non*, an essential condition, of all legislative activity. The large majority of enactments passed by legislatures take effect *ex nunc*, that is, they are applied to situations and controversies that arise subsequent to the promulgation of the enactment. It is a fundamental requirement of fairness and justice that the relevant facts underlying a legal dispute should be judged by the law which was in existence when these facts arose and not by a law which was made *post factum* (after the fact) and was therefore necessarily unknown to the parties when the transactions or events giving rise to the dispute occurred. The Greeks frowned upon *ex post facto* laws, laws which are applied retrospectively to past-fact situations.[4] The Corpus Juris Civilis of Justinian proclaimed a strong presumption against the retrospective application of laws.[5] Bracton introduced the principle into English law;[6] Coke and Blackstone gave currency to it;[7] and the principle is recognized today

---

[3] 211 U.S. 210, at 226 (1908); see also *Sinking Fund Cases*, 99 U.S. 700, at 761 (1878).

[4] See Paul Vinogradoff, *Outlines of Historical Jurisprudence*, II (London, 1922), 139–140; cf. Elmer E. Smead, "The Rule Against Retrospective Legislation: A Basic Principle of Jurisprudence," 20 *Minnesota Law Review* 775 (1936).

[5] *Code* 1, 14, 7: "It is certain that the laws and constitutions regulate future matters, and have no reference to such as are past, unless express provision is made for past time, and for matters which are pending." S. P. Scott, *The Civil Law* (Cincinnati, 1932), XII, 87.

[6] Henry de Bracton, *De Legibus et Consuetudinibus Angliae*, ed. G. E. Woodbine (New Haven, 1940), III, 181; *Item tempus spectandum erit cum omnis constitutio futuris formam imponere debeat et non praeteritis.*

[7] Edward Coke, *The Institutes*, 4th ed. (London, 1671), p. 292; William Blackstone, *Commentaries on the Laws of England*, ed. W. C. Jones (San Francisco, 1916), vol. I, sec. 46.

in England as a basic rule of statutory construction.[8] In the United States, *ex post facto* laws in criminal cases and retrospective state laws impairing the obligation of contracts are expressly forbidden by the terms of the federal Constitution;[9] in other types of situations, a retroactive legislative infringement of vested rights may present a problem of constitutional validity under the due-process clause of the Constitution.[10]

The principle of nonretroactivity of laws is not always carried to its ultimate conclusion, and certain types of retroactive laws are countenanced or at least tolerated by legal systems. In the United States, for instance, curative statutes designed to validate technically deficient legal proceedings, acts of public officials, or private deeds and contracts have frequently been upheld by the courts, although such statutes operate on past facts or transactions.[11] Likewise, the principle of nonretroactivity is usually not applied to laws of a procedural character. This means that in civil and even in criminal cases a defendant is ordinarily not entitled to be tried in the exact mode that was prescribed at the time when suit was brought or when the offense was committed.[12] The conclusion must be reached, therefore, that although a legislative act presumptively and in the large majority of cases operates *in futuro* only, it would be improper to assert dogmatically that nonretroactivity is a necessary prerequisite of all legislation.[13]

A more controversial problem concerning the essential nature of a legislative act arises in connection with the question of whether such an act must necessarily be of a *normative* character, that is, whether it must in a generalized fashion oblige persons to a certain course of conduct. It has been widely asserted that a law in the true sense of the word must contain a general regulation, and that a disposition which merely deals with an individual, concrete situation cannot qualify as a law or legislative act. The imposing array of jurists and political philosophers who can be cited in support of this view has already been presented.[14] In the practice of legislatures, the important difference between a generalized regulation and an individual command or dis-

---

[8] Carleton K. Allen, *Law in the Making*, 6th ed. (Oxford, 1958), pp. 447, 454.
[9] Art. I, secs. 9 and 10; see *Calder v. Bull*, 3 Dall. 386 (1798).
[10] Fifth and Fourteenth amendments.
[11] For a listing of American cases see 50 *American Jurisprudence*, sec. 479.
[12] See *Constitution of the United States*, ed. E. S. Corwin (Washington, D.C., 1953), p. 329. See, on the other hand, the case of *Thompson v. Utah*, 170 U.S. 343 (1898), where retroactive application of a law reducing the number of jurors in a criminal trial from twelve to eight was denied on the ground that it would deprive the defendant of the valuable right to have his guilt determined by a certain number of persons.
[13] The problem of retroactive lawmaking by judges will be dealt with elsewhere. See *infra* Sec. 80.   [14] See *supra* Sec. 42.

position found recognition in Rome in the distinction between a *lex* and a *privilegium*,[15] in Germany in the distinction between legislative enactments in a material and a formal sense,[16] and in the United States in the distinction between a general and special (private) act of Congress. An example of a special act of Congress would be a legislative enactment granting relief to A (but not to other similarly situated persons) for property damage, permitting B to immigrate to, and become a resident of, the United States, declaring Y to be the natural-born child of X, or granting Z a personal exemption from a tax law.[17]

It would seem highly desirable to reserve the term "law" or "legislative act" in the strict sense for enactments of a general or normative character, and to exclude from the scope of the concept enactments which exhaust their significance in the disposition of a concrete case or single-fact situation. The mere fact that both types of enactments proceed from a duly constituted legislative assembly does not furnish sufficient reason for using an identical nomenclature for them. Inasmuch as the predecessor of the English Parliament, the *Curia Regis*, and the antecedents of legislatures of other countries often indiscriminately combined legislative with various nonlegislative functions, remnants of these nonlegislative functions have been retained by such legislatures up to our own day. Thus the House of Lords in England has the power to decide judicial cases in the last instance, and the American Senate has the power to try impeachments of the President, Vice President, and all civil officers of the United States. Although such appellate decisions and impeachments are entrusted to a legislative body, they have always—and properly—been viewed as an exercise of the judicial function rather than as legislative acts.

The proper classification of governmental acts may become one of great practical importance under a system in which a general division of powers into legislative, executive, and judicial is regarded as one of the cornerstones of the political structure. But one must be aware that the line between a general law containing a normative regulation and a special act dealing with a particular, concrete situation cannot always be drawn with accuracy and ease. The line is clear when we compare an act of Congress conferring the Congressional Medal of Honor on a distinguished war hero with a law defining the responsibilities of persons guilty of negligent driving; it becomes indistinct in situations

[15] See Rudolf von Jhering, *Law as a Means to an End*, transl. I. Husik (New York, 1924), p. 256, n. 44. The *privilegium* was a disposition restricted to a particular individual.

[16] Thus the granting of an appropriation to a governmental agency for a certain year or for a particular purpose is regarded as law in a merely "formal" sense.

[17] State constitutions in the United States commonly prohibit such special laws.

where an individual act of a legislature—for instance, the grant of a franchise to a public utility—does not exhaust its significance in the grant itself, but creates rights and obligations on the part of the grantee which may persist far into the future. A general discussion of jurisprudence cannot undertake a thorough investigation of this borderline area; to the extent that the problem may become a practical one, it would furnish an interesting topic for detailed consideration.[18]

In conclusion it should be noted that those countries which operate under a written constitution deemed to have the force of law recognize a particular high-level form of legislation which is superior to other, ordinary forms of legislation. Constitutions are frequently created by constitutional conventions specially set up for this purpose, and their provisions may usually be amended only under procedures which make a revision or change more difficult than in the case of regular legislative acts. A constitution is viewed as the fundamental law of the state or country, and in many instances it contains norms designed not only to determine the organization, procedures, and competences of legislative and other governmental organs, but also mandates which control the permissible contents of ordinary legislation. Thus, for example, the United States Constitution provides that Congress shall make no law abridging freedom of speech or of the press.[19] The highest court of the United States has held that guarantees of this character must not be construed as mere moral exhortations addressed to the Congress, but that they form binding and obligatory norms of the law. The Constitution is thereby elevated to a source of law superior to ordinary legislation.

Section 65. *Delegated and Autonomic Legislation*
In a modern, highly developed state, the tasks confronting a legislative body are so manifold and complex that they cannot be performed in all of their details and technical minutiae without putting an exorbitant burden and strain on the shoulders of such a body. Furthermore, some types of legislative activity in the area of specialized governmental regulation demand such thoroughgoing acquaintance with the organizational and technical problems existing in the particular field that they can be more adequately discharged by a group of experts than by a legislative assembly lacking the requisite specialized knowledge. For these and other reasons,[1] modern legislatures frequently delegate some

[18] Georg Jellinek's *Gesetz und Verordnung* (Tübingen, 1919), contains a valuable discussion of the problem.
[19] First Amendment.
[1] The various reasons speaking in favor of delegation of certain legislative functions to special agencies are summarized in *Report of the Lord Chancellor's Com-*

legislative functions to an administrative agency of the government, to a bureau or commission, or to the chief executive of the state. It may also happen that a legislature will entrust certain legislative undertakings to the judiciary. In the United States, for example, the Congress has charged the United States Supreme Court with the task of prescribing rules of procedure for use in the federal district courts,[2] and the legislatures of a number of states have passed similar enabling acts.

Far-reaching delegations of legislative power by Congress to the President of the United States and to various executive and administrative agencies have taken place in recent decades, notwithstanding certain pronouncements by the Supreme Court to the effect that Congress cannot surrender its legislative powers.[3] The meaning of such judicial pronouncements is in its practical significance reduced to the proposition that Congress cannot abdicate its legislative functions in a particular field of regulation unreservedly and *in toto;* Congress must at least fix a general policy guiding the concrete exercise of the legislative function by the administrative body. This means that as long as Congress, by law, sets forth a broad and general standard of regulation and devolves upon executive officers or administrative agencies the power to carry out the general directives and purposes of the statute, such a delegation of powers is likely to withstand the test of judicial scrutiny.[4] Since some of the congressional pointers which have accompanied the vesting of rulemaking powers in executive or administrative organs have been extremely broad and elastic,[5] it can be asserted with confi-

---

mittee on Ministerial Powers (London, 1932), pp. 51-52, and *Report of the U.S. Attorney General's Committee on Administrative Procedure* (Washington, D.C., 1941), p. 14.

[2] Act of June 19, 1934 (28 U.S.C.A. § 2072). It might be argued that this authorization represents merely the recognition of a power deemed inherent in the courts under the common-law tradition.

[3] See, for example, *U.S. v. Shreveport Grain and Elevator Company,* 287 U.S. 77, at 85 (1932): "That the legislative power of Congress cannot be delegated, is, of course, clear"; *Field v. Clark,* 143 U.S. 649, at 692 (1892): "That Congress cannot delegate legislative power to the President is a principle universally recognized as vital to the integrity and maintenance of the system of government ordained by the Constitution."

[4] See *U.S. v. Shreveport Grain and Elevator Company, supra* n. 3; Kenneth C. Davis, *Administrative Law Text* (St. Paul, Minn., 1959), p. 33.

[5] Thus the following delegations of power were upheld by the court: (1) A statute conferring upon the Secretary of Agriculture the power to determine what are the "just and reasonable" charges for the services of stockyard brokers, *Tagg Bros. and Moorhead v. U.S.,* 280 U.S. 420 (1930); (2) A statute empowering the administrator of the Office of Price Administration to fix prices which "in his judgment would be generally fair and equitable and will effectuate the purposes of this Act," *Yakus v. U.S.,* 321 U.S. 414; (3) A statute empowering the Wage and Hour Administrator to issue regulations providing for a minimum wage up to 40

dence that the constitutionality of substantial delegations of legislative functions to such organs is well established today in the United States. Other countries likewise permit far-reaching transfers of lawmaking powers to specialized agencies.[6]

As mentioned above, the United States Congress has frequently conferred powers upon the chief executive to promulgate measures of a legislative character. Thus the President of the United States has been authorized to proclaim embargoes in the event of foreign wars, or to issue detailed regulations concerning trading with the enemy in war time. The President usually exercises his delegated lawmaking functions either in the form of proclamations or executive orders.[7] He does not, in the opinion of the Supreme Court, possess any inherent or implied legislative powers in addition to the specific powers conferred upon him by Congress.[8]

Delegated legislation must be distinguished from *autonomic* legislation, even though the lines of demarcation between these two types of legislation sometimes become clouded. By autonomy we mean the power of persons or organizations other than the government to make laws or adopt rules essentially similar in character to laws.[9] Thus the ancient Roman *pater familias* was endowed with comprehensive powers to lay down the law for the members of his household and his slaves, including the power to provide severe punishment for acts of household members he considered reprehensible. Since his autonomous powers preceded those of the state, it would be improper to say that the state merely "delegated" a certain sphere of legislative activity to the head of the family. It is a more correct interpretation of the phenomenon to point out that in early times, when state power was still weak, the autonomy of family units was a primary and unquestioned fact. Only gradually and in the course of time did the public power of the state supplant or restrict the private power of individual family

---

cents per hour "if conveniently feasible without substantially curtailing employment," *Opp Cotton Mills v. Administrator*, 312 U.S. 126 (1941). A delegation of power exceedingly broad in scope was invalidated in *Schechter v. U.S.*, 295 U.S. 495 (1935).

[6] On the situation in England, see Allen, *Law in the Making*, pp. 521 ff. The German Constitution of 1949 permits delegation of legislative powers if standards for the guidance of the executive agencies are provided (Art. 80). The French Constitution of 1946, on the other hand, prohibited such delegation (Art. 13).

[7] Ervin H. Pollack, *Fundamentals of Legal Research* (Brooklyn, 1956), p. 139.

[8] *Youngstown Sheet and Tube Co. v. Sawyer*, 343 U.S. 579, at 587 (1952): "In the framework of our Constitution, the President's power to see that the laws are faithfully executed refutes the idea that he is to be a lawmaker." The case leaves open the question, discussed *infra* Sec. 70, whether the President has inherent *executive* powers to act in an emergency without congressional authorization.

[9] Allen, p. 529; Salmond, *Jurisprudence*, pp. 143-144.

groups governed by their head. State power in later times often inter-
vened for the purpose of protecting the wife, children, and slaves of
the chief of the household from an arbitrary and high-handed exercise
of his prerogatives.[10]

The Roman Catholic Church, during the Middle Ages, enjoyed a
high degree of lawmaking authority, and there were periods of history
when its independence and sovereignty competed with, or even surpassed that of, the secular state. Even today, churches in many parts of
the world possess autonomic powers to regulate their own affairs and,
since the state often claims no right or intention to enter the field
of ecclesiastical activity, the scope of self-government enjoyed by
churches cannot, as a general proposition, be said to owe its existence
to a mere delegation of powers by the state.[11]

Furthermore, private corporations and other associations are today
invested with the power of enacting articles of association and bylaws
for the regulation of intracorporate relations, and the courts will often
recognize such articles and bylaws as determining the claims and obligations of members of such associations. Labor unions regulate the
rights and duties of union members, often in a minute fashion; industrial producers have in some countries organized themselves nationally
or internationally into associations which regulate output, supply, and
prices, often without legislative authorization or recognition by the
government. Professional associations of lawyers and doctors have also
developed a considerable body of autonomic law, in the form of rules
of discipline and professional ethics. It may even be reasonable to
argue that, if a modern family father promulgates a family code assigning definite chores to the various members of the family or determining
the amount of allowances due to the children, this would amount to
an exercise of a right to legislate autonomically within a certain sphere.
The purpose of such a family code is essentially the same as that of a
code for a larger group of human beings, namely, to provide for a
measure of order and to attempt to guarantee justice by the adoption
of rules of uniform and equal application to those to whom they are
addressed.

The existence or potential existence of such enclaves of autonomic
legislation in contemporary society stems from the fact that even a
modern state which has appropriated a tremendously large share of
legislative powers is not in a position to make laws with respect to
everything and everybody. There are still numerous areas left vacant
by governmental law which must or can be filled by the exercise of

[10] See *supra* Sec. 4.
[11] In accord, with respect to the Church of England: Allen, p. 529.

private or semiprivate lawmaking powers. The mere fact that these unoccupied areas exist today by leave and permission of the state and could within the limits of the constitutional system be filled in by public regulation, does not deprive those areas of their autonomic character as long as a substantial amount of private power to regulate within their bounds is left intact by the general law of the state.

Section 66. *Treaties and Other Consensual Agreements*

A treaty is an agreement entered into by countries, nations, or other legal persons recognized in international law. If only two nations or other international persons are the contracting parties, the treaty is called bilateral; if more than two are involved, it is usually called multilateral. A multilateral treaty adopted by a large number of countries and designed to codify important phases of their mutual relations is sometimes referred to in modern legal literature as an act of international legislation. This terminology need not be objected to if the essential difference between treaty-making and ordinary legislative processes is kept in mind. The typical legislature of a modern nation-state may pass laws which a minority of the legislators are unwilling to approve, and these laws will bind everybody subject to the jurisdiction of the legislating body.[1] Norms imposed by multilateral treaties, on the other hand, ordinarily bind only those countries which have manifested their approval by signing the treaty or otherwise adhering to it.[2]

The question arises—and may become intensely practical under certain circumstances—whether a treaty entered into between two or more nations according to proper legal procedures constitutes a genuine source of law. In England, a treaty affecting private rights or requiring for its enforcement a modification of common law or statute must have been converted into an act of municipal legislation by Parliament in order to be binding upon the national courts.[3] With respect to such treaties, the only question that arises is whether the treaty is a source of law within the domain of international law. In other coun-

---

[1] See Arnold D. McNair, "International Legislation," 19 *Iowa Law Review* 177, at 178 (1934).

[2] An important exception is contained in Article 108 of the United Nations Charter, which provides that "amendments to the present Charter shall come into force for all Members of the United Nations when they have been adopted by a vote of two thirds of the members of the General Assembly and ratified . . . by two thirds of the Members of the United Nations, including all the permanent members of the Security Council." This introduces a qualified-majority principle into the amending process.

[3] See L. Oppenheim, *International Law*, 7th ed. by H. Lauterpacht (London, 1948), I, 38; J. L. Brierly, *The Law of Nations*, 5th ed. (New York, 1955), p. 85.

tries, such as the United States, where a validly executed treaty normally becomes operative without a domestic enabling act (United States Constitution, Art. VI), the question presents itself in its broader aspects.

Two answers have been given to this question. According to the first, a distinction must be made between lawmaking treaties and other treaties. The distinction is based on the fact that some treaties establish new general rules for the future international conduct of the signatories or modify or abolish existing customary or conventional rules, while other treaties do not have this purpose. It is held that only lawmaking treaties may be referred to as representing a source of law.[4] The distinction is rejected by Hans Kelsen, who believes that it is the essential function of *any* treaty to make law, "that is to say, to create a legal norm, whether a general or an individual norm." [5] According to this view, there exists no valid distinction between a treaty which establishes a network of reciprocal rights and duties between nations for an indefinite period of time and one which transfers title to a ship in consideration of an antecedent debt.

According to the general position taken here with respect to the nature of law,[6] Kelsen's view is not considered tenable. The term "law," in deference to an impressive tradition and prevailing common usage, and in view of the functional characteristics of law, should essentially be limited to norms of action or conduct which contain an element of generality. The phrase "individual norm," as was shown earlier, is a contradiction in terms.[7] It should be concluded, therefore, that an agreement by which the United States turns over some battleships to the Commonwealth of Australia in exchange for an air base on Australian territory is devoid of normative elements. It is a fully executed transaction, leaving in force no continuing rights or obligations on the part of the contracting nations; the obligation to do nothing inconsistent with the grant [8] follows automatically from the general principles of the law of property and does not have to be read into the agreement as an independent obligation created by its terms. However, a treaty which mutually binds its signatories to allow freedom of religion, freedom of movement, and freedom to engage in commerce and trade to the nationals of the other participating countries, lays down certain general rules of conduct which clearly have the quality of law. A treaty of this type may, therefore, be properly classified as a law-

[4] See Oppenheim, I, 26–27; Brierly, pp. 58–59.
[5] *Principles of International Law* (New York, 1952), p. 319.
[6] See *supra* Sec. 42.
[7] *Ibid.*
[8] Cf. *Fletcher v. Peck*, 6 Cranch 87 (1810).

making treaty. This interpretation is supported by Article 38 of the Statute of the International Court of Justice, which designates as sources of law only those international conventions, either general or particular, which establish *rules* expressly recognized by the contesting states.

It must be realized, however, that the borderline between general regulation and individual action often becomes indistinct and blurred when concrete situations have to be faced. Obviously no difficulty would be presented by an agreement whereby the governments of two countries obligate themselves to exchange for a period of ten years all inventions pertaining to the peaceful use of atomic energy. A treaty of this kind would clearly be a lawmaking treaty. But should the same label be attached to an agreement by which the government of country A agrees to turn over to country B within a period of six months an invention concerning a certain missile in return for the payment of a stipulated price? And what would be the character of a treaty by which State A, as reparation for a denial of justice inflicted on a national of State B, agrees to pay an indemnity of $100,000 in two annual installments? In the last two cases, while rights and obligations of an executory character are created, these rights and obligations are single and particular, as compared with the general and more lasting obligations established in the treaty providing for an exchange of atomic energy inventions. Do the two last-mentioned agreements, then, create law? It may not be possible to give a sweeping theoretical answer to this question. Whether the term "lawmaking treaty" should be extended to the twilight area where the difference between a norm and an individual act becomes indistinct may well depend on the concrete nature of the legal problem in the context of which the distinction becomes relevant and material.

These considerations ought to help us in understanding the implications of certain distinctions made in the laws of some countries between treaties and agreements of a non-treaty character. The United States Constitution, for instance, provides that the President "shall have Power, by and with the Advice and Consent of the Senate, to make Treaties, provided two thirds of the Senators present concur." [9] It is, however, widely conceded in the constitutional theory and practice of the United States that, notwithstanding this provision, the President of the United States may enter into a variety of other agreements with foreign powers, either on his own responsibility or with the prior or subsequent consent of a simple majority in both houses of Congress.

[9] Art. II, sec. 2.

The latter types of agreements are referred to as executive agreements, or, in the case of a participation by Congress, as executive-congressional agreements.

Where should we draw the line of demarcation between treaties and other international agreements? There is no unanimity of opinion on this question. There are writers who would allow a very broad scope to the powers of the Senate in the treaty-making area and would confine presidential authority in this sphere to relatively minor matters.[10] Others would go a little further and permit the President to handle international matters of rather substantial importance "if there can be shown an undisputed practice of long standing on the part of the President to make certain types of executive agreements." [11] The radical view has also been advanced that presidential and executive-congressional agreements have become interchangeable with treaties in diplomatic practice and law; according to this position it is in most instances within the discretion of the President either to submit an international agreement to the Senate for ratification as a treaty or to conclude it either in reliance on his own extensive powers in the field of foreign relations or with the consent of a majority in both houses of Congress.[12]

This view must be rejected as unsound. First of all, when the Constitution gave power to the President to make treaties with the advice and consent of two thirds of the Senate, it certainly did not wish to leave compliance with this mandate to the pleasure of the chief executive. Second, the Constitution in another provision clearly recognizes a legal distinction between treaties and other types of international agreements.[13] Third, the framers of the Constitution, who were strongly convinced of the desirability of establishing a general (though not ironclad) system of separation of powers, wanted to place the exercise of legislative powers to the widest possible extent in a repre-

[10] See Edwin Borchard, "Shall the Executive Agreement Replace the Treaty?" 53 *Yale Law Journal* 664 (1944); Borchard, "Treaties and Executive Agreements: A Reply," 54 *Yale L. J.* 616 (1945).
[11] Henry S. Fraser, "Treaties and Executive Agreements," Sen. Doc. 244, 78 Cong., 2 sess. (1944), p. 26; cf. also Charles C. Hyde, *International Law*, 2d ed. (Boston, 1945), pp. 1416–1418.
[12] Wallace McClure, *International Executive Agreements* (New York, 1941), pp. 5, 32, 343, 363; M. S. McDougal and A. Lans, "Treaties and Congressional Executive or Presidential Agreements: Interchangeable Instruments of National Policy," 54 *Yale L. J.* 181, 534 (1945).
[13] See Art. I, sec. 10, which provides that "no State shall enter into any Treaty, Alliance, or Confederation," while permitting the states, with the consent of Congress, to enter into any *agreement or compact* with another state, or with a foreign power. See also *Holmes v. Jennison*, 14 Pet. 540, at 571–572 (1840).

sentative assembly, and for this reason they repudiated the English constitutional rule which vested the lawmaking power in the international field in the British crown.

It is above all this last consideration which points the way toward a solution of our problem. It can safely be assumed as being in concordance with the general ideas guiding the framers in allocating powers under the constitutional scheme that participation of a qualified majority of the Senate in matters of international concern was to be limited to those important and momentous acts which involve the exercise of *lawmaking* powers.[14] It may be asked, however, why the fathers of the Constitution, if this was their objective, did not express their intention unmistakably in the constitutional text by drawing a distinction between lawmaking treaties on the one hand and treaties dealing with matters of an executive and administrative nature on the other, confining the necessity of Senate consent to the former. The answer may well be that in their minds treaties and lawmaking treaties actually were synonymous terms. The leading men in the constitutional convention were quite familiar with the work of the Swiss diplomat and international jurist Emmerich de Vattel, whose treatise on the law of nations had become a pervasive influence in the international theory and practice of the United States and was frequently cited in the writings of the founding fathers.[15] Vattel had distinguished between treaties and other international agreements as follows:

Sec. 152. A treaty, in Latin, *foedus,* is a compact entered into by sovereigns for the welfare of the State, either in perpetuity or for a considerable length of time.

Sec. 153. Compacts which have for their object matters of temporary interest are called agreements, conventions, arrangements. They are fulfilled by a single act and not by a continuous performance of acts. When the act in question is performed these compacts are executed once and for all; whereas treaties are executory in character and the acts called for must continue as long as the treaty lasts.[16]

These passages identify treaties with executory undertakings which are of some magnitude and call for continuous or at least repeated acts

[14] No view is expressed here on the question of whether Congress, within the framework of its delegated powers, may exercise a lawmaking authority in the foreign field concurrent with that of the Senate under Art. II, sec. 2.

[15] See A. C. Weinfeld, "What Did the Framers of the Federal Constitution Mean by 'Agreements or Compacts'?" 3 *University of Chicago Law Review* 453 (1936); David M. Levitan, "Executive Agreements," 35 *Illinois Law Review* 365, at 368 (1940), with citations of pertinent sources; Fraser, p. 7.

[16] *The Law of Nations or the Principles of Natural Law,* transl. C. G. Fenwick (Washington, D.C., 1916), p. 160.

of performance; whereas agreements of a transitory, temporary nature which can be executed by a single act are excluded from the purview of the concept. It is highly likely that the framers, when they regulated the treaty power in Article II, section 2 of the Constitution, contemplated Vattel's interpretation of this power and sought to limit Senate participation to international compacts establishing reciprocal rights and obligations on more than a short-term basis. This approach to the problem would as a general rule leave executed agreements, such as an exchange of goods, and executory agreements of a minor nature, transient interest, or short duration, and not involving the imposition of substantial legal obligations on the United States, in the hands of the President, to be dealt with by means of an executive agreement.[17]

Critics of this view of the treaty power might argue that according to it the President of the United States could probably consummate any executed transaction, including a cession of federal territory to another country, without the constitutional necessity of securing the approval of a representative body. Whatever the answer to this question in the light of the treaty power might be in a concrete case, the objection would be devoid of merit. In exercising his executive powers, the President is subject to numerous constitutional restrictions other than those established in the treaty-power clause. The most important of these is the Fifth Amendment, which prohibits the President from depriving any person of his liberties or property without due process of law. Furthermore, the Constitution of the United States was ordained for the purpose, among others, of forming "a more perfect union"; [18] this declaration of principles imposes an obligation on the President to preserve and strengthen the American union, rather than to weaken it or reduce its size. It should also be considered that the threat of impeachment for misfeasance in office will normally operate as an effective deterrent to presidential acts detrimental to the fundamental interests of the nation.

No extended discussion will be undertaken with respect to the question of whether agreements other than treaties, such as collective bargaining agreements, industrial agreements for the exchange of patents and technical information, and other types of contracts between private persons or between private persons and the government, may

---

[17] Also into this category would fall the executive agreement entered into in 1940 between the United States and Great Britain, by which the United States transferred certain overage ships and obsolescent military materials to Britain in exchange for naval and air bases. See opinion of Attorney General Jackson of Aug. 27, 1940, 39 *Op. Atty. Gen.* 484 (1937–1940). The opinion is largely in accord with the position taken in the text.

[18] See Preamble to Constitution.

under certain circumstances be regarded as sources of law. It follows logically from the general position taken here on the nature of law that such agreements, insofar as they contain provisions of a normative character, may properly be so viewed.[19] There would seem to be no reason, for example, why a collective bargaining agreement, constituting an accord which governs the hiring, discharge, wage rates, working hours, and disciplining of employee groups, should not be deemed a source of law just as much as a labor code enacted by a legislature which deals with exactly the same subjects. It must be kept in mind that a valid collective bargaining agreement may serve in court suits as well as arbitration proceedings as the sole legal foundation for the recognition and adjudication of substantial rights and obligations on the part of employers and employees.[20] Other types of agreements regulating the mutual conduct of the parties and forming a continuing basis for reciprocal rights and duties may likewise be included in the class of formal sources of the law.

Section 67. *Precedent*

It is today the prevailing opinion in the Anglo-American legal world that a decision of a court of law—especially of a court of last resort—which explicitly or implicitly lays down a legal proposition constitutes a general and formal source of law. It must be kept in mind, however, that this view, while it is rarely disputed in our own day, has by no means always been accepted in Anglo-American legal theory. A doctrine ascribing authoritative force to a precedent is to some extent grounded on the assumption that court decisions are a source of law because judges are entitled to make law in much the same sense in which the legislator is empowered to create law; but this idea was rejected by some of the greatest Common Law judges and legal authors. Sir Matthew Hale, for instance, a famous English seventeenth-century judge, said: "The decisions of courts of justice . . . do not make a law properly so-called (for that only the King and Parliament can do); yet they have a great weight and authority in expounding, declaring, and publishing what the law of this kingdom is, especially

---

[19] See for instance *supra* Secs. 42 and 65; cf. also *Kirkpatrick v. Pease*, 202 Mo. 471, at 493, 101 S.W. 651, at 657 (1906): "[A] contract is but a law unto the parties thereto"; Jerome Frank, *Courts on Trial* (Princeton, 1949), p. 308.

[20] Apparently in recognition of this fact, the United States Supreme Court held in *Steele v. Louisville & Nashville R. R. Co.*, 323 U.S. 192 (1944) that a collective bargaining agreement entered into between railroad companies and a union of railway firemen could not discriminate against a minority of the employees covered by the agreement. The court felt that collective bargaining representatives are clothed with powers similar to those of legislators and must therefore observe certain restraints imposed upon those empowered to make laws for others.

when such decisions hold a consonancy and congruity with resolutions and decisions of former times, and though such decisions are less than a law, yet they are a greater evidence thereof than an opinion of a many private persons, as such, whatsoever." [1] Lord Mansfield remarked in the eighteenth century: "The law of England would be a strange science if indeed it were decided upon precedents only. Precedents serve to illustrate principles and to give them a fixed certainty. But the law of England, which is exclusive of positive law, enacted by statute, depends upon principles, and these principles run through all the cases according as the particular circumstances of each have been found to fall within the one or the other of them." [2] He also said: "The reason and spirit of cases make law, not the letter of particular precedents." [3]

Sir William Blackstone, the well-known legal author and judge of eighteenth-century England, made the following observations on precedents:

The only method of proving, that this or that maxim is a rule of the common law, is by showing that it hath been always the custom to observe it. But here a very natural, and a very material, question arises: how are these customs or maxims to be known, and by whom is their validity to be determined? The answer is, by the judges in the several courts of justice. They are the depositaries of the law; the living oracles who must decide in all cases of doubt, and who are bound by an oath to decide according to the law of the land . . . And indeed these judicial decisions are the principal and most authoritative evidence, that can be given, of the existence of such a custom as shall form part of the common law.[4]

In the United States, Chancellor James Kent maintained: "The great body of the common law consists of a collection of principles, to be found in the opinions of sages or deduced from universal and immemorial usage, and receiving progressively the sanction of the courts . . . The best evidence of the common law is to be found in the decisions of the courts of justice, contained in numerous volumes of reports, and in the treatises and digests of learned men." [5] James Coo-

---

[1] Matthew Hale, *History of the Common Law*, 4th ed. (London, 1739), p. 67. Cf. the view of Thomas Hobbes, a nonlegal writer: "No man's error becomes his own Law; nor obliges him to persist in it. Neither (for the same reason) becomes it a Law to other Judges, though sworn to follow it. . . . Therefore, all the Sentences of precedent Judges that have ever been, cannot altogether make a Law contrary to naturall Equity." *Leviathan* (Everyman's Library ed., 1914), ch. xxvi.

[2] *Jones v. Randall* (1774), Cowp. 37.

[3] *Fisher v. Prince* (1762), 3 Burr. 1363.

[4] *Commentaries*, vol. I, secs. 82–83.

[5] Kent, *Commentaries on American Law*, 14th ed. by J. M. Gould (Boston, 1896), I, 643, 645–646.

lidge Carter declared emphatically that a "precedent is but authenticated custom." [6]

All these statements suggest that, in the opinion of their proponents,
it is not the precedent itself, but something behind it or beyond it
which gives it its authority and force. The agency which validates a
judicial decision, according to this view, is not the will or fiat of the
judges, but the intrinsic merit of the principle, or the reality of the
custom which has become embodied in the decision. It is clear, as Sir
William Holdsworth has pointed out, that "the adoption of this point
of view gives the Courts power to mould as they please the conditions
in which they will accept a decided case or a series of decided cases as
authoritative. If the cases are only evidence of what the law is, the
Courts must decide what weight is to be attached to this evidence in
different sets of circumstances." [7] In accordance with this position,
Chancellor Kent argued that a former decision need not be followed
later, "if it can be shown that the law was misunderstood or misapplied
in that particular case." [8] This position is basically incompatible with
the view that a precedent forms a source of law, unless the latter term
is used in a loose and untechnical sense.

This approach to the problem of precedent was made the target of
a scathing attack by a number of authors. John Austin, following the
lead of Jeremy Bentham,[9] castigated what he called "the childish fiction employed by our judges, that judiciary or common law is not
made by them, but is a miraculous something made by nobody, existing, I suppose, from eternity, and merely *declared* from time to time
by the judges." [10] Sir John Salmond also contended that judges unquestionably make law and that one should recognize "a distinct law-
creating power vested in them and openly and lawfully exercised." [11]
John Chipman Gray maintained that judges customarily make law *ex
post facto,* and that the rules laid down in their decisions are not only
sources of law but the law itself.[12]

The relative merits of these two theories, which may be termed the
declaratory and creative theories of the judicial process, respectively,
will be discussed elsewhere.[13] At this point they are of relevance only

[6] *Law: Its Origin, Growth, and Function* (New York, 1907), p. 65.
[7] "Case Law," 50 *Law Quarterly Review* 180, at 185 (1934).
[8] Kent, p. 648.
[9] Bentham, *A Comment on the Commentaries,* ed. C. W. Everett (London, 1928),
p. 190.
[10] Austin, *Lectures on Jurisprudence,* 5th ed. by R. Campbell (London, 1885),
II, 634.
[11] "The Theory of Judicial Precedent," 16 *L. Q. Rev.* 376, at 379 (1900); see also
Salmond, *Jurisprudence,* p. 164.
[12] *Nature and Sources of the Law,* pp. 100, 84, 94–95, 104.
[13] See *infra* Sec. 82.

insofar as they may throw some light on the problem of the sources of law. Attention should be called to the statement by Holdsworth that "when we talk of the binding force of judicial decisions, we do not mean that all of the words used by the judge, still less all of his reasons, are law." [14] The letter of a particular precedent, that is, the verbal formulation into which the rule or principle of a case is cast does not, under the Anglo-American system, enjoy the same degree of authority as the words employed in a statute. As will be shown later,[15] judicial formulations of rules are frequently revised and restated by the courts in subsequent cases presenting the same or a similar problem. A judge may hold that the statement of a rule of law in an earlier case was too broad, too narrow, incorrect, or inartistically phrased. If the judge is bound by the precedent under the doctrine of *stare decisis,* he will attempt to reconstruct the principle of policy underlying the earlier case and to apply it in the case before him, regardless of the exact words used in the first case. In consideration of this fact, it has been said that a precedent is not a dogmatic formula, but only an "illustration of a principle." [16] In other words, it is the reason or principle of public policy supporting the decision which counts in applying the doctrine of *stare decisis,* and not the formulation of a *regula iuris.*

And yet when we compare an unarticulated principle of public policy, hovering, so to speak, over the social scene, or an unconfirmed axiom of reason allegedly dictating the solution of a legal problem, with a legal principle of policy or maxim of justice which has been judicially recognized, confirmed, and cast in the form of a normative pronouncement, the difference would seem to be so conspicuous as to merit recognition in a doctrine of legal sources. Where the principle was previously in doubt and led an uncertain existence, it now becomes solidified in a judicial decision. Furthermore, it also bears emphasis that many judges, especially lower-court judges, will not be inclined to go behind the verbal expression of a principle found in an earlier case. They will often accept the precise language used in the precedent and apply it in a subsequent case without any critical analysis or re-examination. Regardless of how broad or vague or undiscriminating the statement of the law in the earlier case may have been, it will frequently be carried over into subsequent decisions as representing the true "rule of the case." [17] In this way some rules of law which initially should perhaps have been formulated in a less apodictic

---

[14] W. S. Holdsworth, *Some Lessons from Our Legal History* (New York, 1928), p. 17.

[15] See *infra* Sec. 81.

[16] Allen, *Law in the Making,* p. 213.

[17] See on this question Karl N. Llewellyn, *The Bramble Bush,* rev. ed. (New York, 1951), pp. 67–68; see also *infra* Sec. 81.

and categorical form ultimately have become part of our legal heritage through repetition and unquestioning reception into the body of the law.

In the light of these considerations, issue might be taken with the declaratory theory insofar as it suggests that a precedent is not a source of law while a legal principle correctly stated therein may be regarded as such. It would seem preferable to consider the recognition of a vaguely conceived principle in a judicial opinion, coupled with the fact that a concretely formulated rule or principle will often be accepted as authoritative in later cases, as sufficient warrant for the inclusion of precedents among the formal sources of the law. On the other hand, the substantial freedom with which judges have frequently and properly handled earlier decisions throughout most of the history of the Common Law makes it necessary to use the term source of law, as applied to precedents, with greater caution and in a weaker and more restrictive sense than is appropriate in the case of statutes or constitutional provisions.[18]

According to the theory prevailing in the Civil Law countries a judicial precedent is not to be regarded as a formal source of law. In these countries, the instrument of codification has been used to larger extent than is true for the countries of the Anglo-American legal tradition, and the statute is regarded as the chief source of law to which the judge must pay homage. Thus Justinian's mandate that "cases should be decided on the basis of laws, not precedents" [19] is, as a general proposition, still recognized as controlling. Even a judge of a lower court may depart from a judgment of a higher court—unless special provision is made in the law of a particular country for giving an authentic effect to certain classes of higher-court judgments—if he believes that the higher court misinterpreted a statutory provision in an earlier case. It should be noted, however, that this freedom of the judge toward previously decided cases obtains more in theory than in practice. The *de facto* authority of a court decision, especially of a court of last resort, is a very high one, and the weight of such precedents increases in proportion to the number of decisions reiterating and reaffirming the principles enunciated in them. A series of decisions containing identical statements of legal propositions carries an authority almost equal to that of an Anglo-American court decision or series of

---

[18] The operation of the rule of *stare decisis* in the Anglo-American system and the judicial methods used in handling precedents will be discussed *infra* Sec. 80; cf. also *Mason v. American Wheel Works*, 241 F. 2d 906, at 909 (1957) and *Barnette v. West Virginia Board of Education*, 47 F. Supp. 251, at 252–253 (1942).

[19] *Codex* VII. 45. 13. See on this problem in general Charles Szladits, *A Guide to Foreign Legal Systems: French, German, Swiss* (New York, 1959).

court decisions. It is of interest to observe that in Germany, for instance, the supreme court has held that an attorney disregarding a decision published in the official reports of the court makes himself liable to his clients for the consequences.[20]

In the light of such developments, some civil-law writers have argued that judicial precedents should be formally recognized as authoritative sources of law,[21] but this view has not as yet been widely accepted. An intermediate position that has gained a considerable amount of currency on the European continent maintains that a course of judicial action that has persisted for some time and has found more or less unqualified approval within and outside of the legal profession may become crystallized into a norm of customary law and thereby acquire the full force and effect of law.[22]

[20] See Ernst Rabel, "Civil Law and Common Law," 10 *Louisiana Law Review* 431, at 441 (1950).

[21] Josef Esser, *Grundsatz und Norm* (Tübingen, 1956), p. 23, with further citations.

[22] See Enneccerus, Kipp, and Wolff, *Lehrbuch des Bürgerlichen Rechts*, I, 168; François Gény, *Méthode d'interprétation et sources en droit privé positif*, 2d rev. ed. (Paris, 1954), II, 51-52.

XVI

THE NONFORMAL
SOURCES OF THE LAW

Section 68. *Introduction*

It was one of the cardinal errors of legal positivism that it limited its theory of the sources of law exclusively or almost exclusively to those which we have termed formal sources of law. This shortcoming must be attributed to the fact that legal positivism considered law as a command of the state and for this reason looked for its sources primarily to those formalized precepts and mandates which had been promulgated or issued by a legislature, a constitutional convention, a court, or an administrative agency. Some positivist writers, however, especially on the continent of Europe, were willing to allow a modest place for nonlitigious customary law in their theory of sources; this was a concession to the historical school of law, which for a long time enjoyed a tremendous authority and prestige on the Continent, especially in Germany.[1]

---

[1] Hans Kelsen, a consistent positivist, maintains that customary law is a form of law if and only if the written or unwritten constitution of the state sanctions its law-creating force. Thus he upholds the necessity of an explicit or implicit state com-

As long as positivists and analytical jurists were convinced that the positive legal order was a complete, exhaustive, and logically consistent body of norms providing an answer to any and all legal problems with which a court might become confronted, the cardinal issues of legal methodology seemed to have found an easy and satisfactory solution. When this belief in the self-sufficiency of the legal order broke down in the nineteenth and the early part of the twentieth century, a serious dilemma presented itself to positivist thinking. If the formal sources of the law sometimes failed the judge, if there were cases for which the legal system would have no answers, what means were available to legal decision-makers to supply the deficiency? We shall discuss the solutions for this problem proposed by two representative advocates of legal positivism, John Austin and Hans Kelsen, and weigh the merits of their arguments.

John Austin said that all the judge can do in situations where the positive law offers him no guidance and advice is to act as a legislator and create a new rule fit to dispose of the problem satisfactorily. In making such a new rule, Austin said, the judge may derive it from "any of various sources: e.g., a custom not having force of law, but obtaining throughout the community, or in some class of it; a maxim of international law; his own views of what the law ought to be (be the standard which he assumes, general utility or any other)." [2] Such judiciary law, in his opinion, must necessarily be *ex post facto*. The judge applies the newly fashioned rule to transactions and events that have occurred in the past, which may easily lead to situations where men, to their surprise and dismay, "find themselves saddled with duties which they never contemplated." [3] John Austin deplored this condition and recommended extensive codification of the law as the most desirable expedient for coping with the difficulty. [4]

A similar though not identical position toward the problem of gaps in the law was taken by Hans Kelsen. He realized, like Austin, that the positive law, as embodied in its formal sources, does not contain an express answer to all of the manifold questions which may have to be faced by a court of law. There may be instances where one party makes a claim or demand upon another party in a lawsuit and the judge finds that the positive law is silent about whether the claim or demand

---

mand. See his *General Theory of Law and State,* transl. A. Wedberg (Cambridge, Mass., 1949), p. 126. On the historical school of law, see *supra* Sec. 18.

[2] *Lectures on Jurisprudence,* 5th ed. by R. Campbell (London, 1885), II, 638–639. On Austin's position toward judicial legislation see W. L. Morison, "Some Myth about Positivism," 68 *Yale Law Journal* 212 (1958).

[3] Austin, II, 653; see also *id.,* pp. 633–634, and I, 218, 487.

[4] *Id.,* pp. 653 ff., 663–681.

should be allowed. There may be other instances where the point in litigation might possibly be covered by a statute or rule of law, but the statute or rule of law is so vaguely or ambiguously worded that its applicability to the case at hand is not clear and free from doubt. Kelsen deals with these two situations separately.

Where the legislator is silent about whether a certain cause of action is maintainable, this silence must be construed, in Kelsen's view, as a denial of the claim. This solution is dictated to him by his conviction that no person can demand of another person an act or course of conduct to which that other person is not obliged under the rules of the positive law. "In obliging persons to a specific behaviour, the law permits, outside of these obligations, freedom." [5] Kelsen adds that the positive law may, of course, authorize the judge to allow the claim in such a case if equitable considerations make it appear desirable to him.[6] Such an authorization is construed by Kelsen as a leave granted to the judge to decide the case *contrary* to the law. "The actually valid law could be applied to the case—by dismissing the suit. The judge, however, is authorized to change the law for a concrete case, he has the power to bind an individual who was legally free before." [7]

In the second situation where two or three interpretations of a norm are possible, leading to different results, what guides are available to the judge in determining which of these two or three solutions is the correct one? Kelsen answers that the law provides the judge with no guides whatsoever. "From a positive law standpoint, there is no criterion on the basis of which one out of several possibilities can be selected. There is no method, which could be characterized as positively legal, by which out of several meanings of a norm only one can be shown to be 'correct.' " [8] Thus, within the framework permitted by the language of the norm, *any* construction of the norm is legally proper, regardless of whether it leads to an unreasonable, unjust, or even absurd result.

It is submitted that the theories of Austin and Kelsen do not reflect the realities of legal life accurately, and that they should be rejected on the ground that they are dangerous and misleading. It is not correct, as John Austin says, that a judge may seek the answer to a case unprovided for by formal law simply in his own convictions, based perhaps on

---

[5] Kelsen, "The Pure Theory of Law," 51 *Law Quarterly Review* 517, at 528 (1935).

[6] An example of such an authorization is Article 1 of the Swiss Civil Code, which permits the judge to decide cases unprovided for by statute or customary law according to the rule "which he himself would lay down as a legislator."

[7] *General Theory*, p. 147.

[8] "Pure Theory of Law," p. 526.

considerations of social utility or "any other" considerations. There are guides other than formal law available to the judge, as will be shown in following sections, and although these guides are less concrete and direct than many rules of the positive law, they are greatly preferable to reliance by the judge on his own uncontrolled discretion. It is also not true, as Hans Kelsen asserts, that the silence of the lawgiver with respect to the existence or nonexistence of a cause of action in a case pending before a court must be construed as a negative norm disallowing the plaintiff's claim. Without any specific authorization by the lawmaker, courts have often fashioned new remedies in analogy to existing ones and have granted relief where the denial of a remedy would have appeared unconscionable to them. Examples of cases allowing a form of redress not authorized by a positive norm are Lord Mansfield's decision in *Moses v. Macferlan*,[9] extending the boundaries of quasi-contract, and the United States Supreme Court's decision in *International News Service v. Associated Press*,[10] making an epochal innovation in the law of unfair competition. As to Kelsen's further assertion that, from the point of view of the law as such, *any* interpretation of a statute or other legal source warranted by the words of the norm must be considered correct, it should be stated that conscientious judges for the most part have not heeded this advice, but have considered it their duty as organs of the law to adopt an interpretation consonant with reason, equity, and the spirit of the legal system.

The interpretative nihilism to which a radically conceived legal positivism may easily lead makes a theory of the nonformal sources of the law not only desirable but imperative. We know today that the positive system established by the state is inescapably incomplete, fragmentary, and full of ambiguities. These defects must be overcome by resorting to ideas, principles, and standards which are presumably not as well articulated as the formalized source materials of the law, but which nevertheless give some degree of normative direction to the findings of the courts. In the absence of a theory of the nonformal sources, nothing remains outside the boundaries of fixed, positive precepts but the arbitrariness of the individual judge. If the judge, where the formal law fails him, could make law according to *any* considerations he regards as desirable, as Austin suggests, court decisions would frequently depend on whether the judge was politically conservative, liberal, or radical, whether he believed in tradition or reform in lawmaking, whether he was a friend of capital or labor, whether he favored strong or weak government, or on whatever else his idiosyncratic

[9] 2 Burr 1005 (1760).
[10] 248 U.S. 215 (1918).

convictions might be. This would be an intolerable condition which would undermine the beneficial authority of the law and in the course of time lead to a judicial crisis.

Some groundwork for a doctrine of nonformal sources was laid by Roscoe Pound in his trail-blazing article "The Theory of Judicial Decision." [11] His constructive suggestions may serve as the basis for a more elaborate attempt, undertaken here, to classify the nonformal sources, analyze their character and the scope of their legitimate use, and explain their relationship to the formalized sources of the law.

Section 69. *Standards of Justice*

In discussing the question whether and to what extent considerations and principles of justice have a direct and practical bearing on the administration and application of the law, two separate and not necessarily related problems must be distinguished. The first is the problem of whether justice may be regarded as a source of law *praeter legem* (besides the written law). Is it proper or even mandatory for the judge to resort to notions of justice in cases where the positive sources do not provide an answer to the point of law to be adjudicated, or where its provisions are vague or susceptible of different interpretations? Second, Do situations ever arise where the judge is justified in employing principles of justice *contra legem* (against the written law)? In other words, does the judge, in certain cases, have the power to refuse to apply a positive norm of law on the ground that a fundamental injustice would be perpetrated by the application of the norm? The first problem is a common and ubiquitous one in judicial administration, and a substantial amount of case law is available to illustrate its significance and ramifications. The second problem will arise rarely and only in cases bearing unusual features, and jurists of the positivist creed will deny that even in such instances the problem is one that deserves serious consideration.

The first problem comes up, for example, when a plaintiff in a law suit makes a claim which he is unable to substantiate by the citation of a statute or precedent directly in point. Is the court, under certain circumstances, justified in allowing him redress on the ground that the attainment of justice between the parties demands the granting of the remedy to the plaintiff? Or is it preferable to hold, with Kelsen, that the absence of express recognition of the claim by the positive law must be construed as a determination by the legislator that the claim

---

[11] 36 *Harvard Law Review* 641, at 643, 652, 655, 657, 807, 948 (1923). Pound says on p. 655: "Courts and jurists have always proceeded on the basis of something more than the formal body of legal precepts for the time being." See also his "The Ideal Element in American Judicial Decision," 45 *Harv. L. Rev.* 136 (1931).

will not lie (unless express authority is given to decide according to equity)? [1]

There are a number of judicial decisions, especially under the Anglo-American system of law, where the courts, without any special authorization by the positive law to decide the "unprovided case" according to considerations of equity, have granted relief in novel situations on grounds of "natural justice and reason." There is, for example, the case of *Moses v. Macferlan,* which has already been mentioned,[2] in which the English Court of King's Bench under the leadership of Lord Mansfield enlarged the scope of quasi contractual remedies. Lord Mansfield stated in this case that a recipient of money "which ought not in justice be kept" was obliged "by the ties of natural justice and equity" to refund it. In another instance, the case of *Pavesich v. New England Life Ins. Co.,*[3] the Supreme Court of Georgia permitted the plaintiff to recover damages for violation of a hitherto unrecognized right of privacy, on the ground that the right was founded in the "instinct of nature" and entitled to be regarded as a legal right under the conceptions of natural justice. And in *Woods v. Lancet,*[4] the New York Court of Appeals permitted an infant to recover damages for injuries sustained while in his mother's womb during her ninth month of pregnancy. The court overruled earlier precedents for the declared purpose of bringing the common law into accordance with the needs of justice.

In ancient Roman law, the praetors sometimes granted *actiones in factum* for the purpose of meting out justice in an individual case where neither the Roman civil law nor prior praetorial edicts provided a remedy.[5] In a modern Roman law jurisdiction, Germany, the highest court has inaugurated certain causes of action for which no direct authorization in the provisions of the Civil Code can be found. Thus, the court has sanctioned the principle of liability on the part of a person who, after making an offer or entering into contractual negotiations with another person, has committed a negligent or otherwise culpable act in connection with such offer or negotiations, regardless of whether an agreement was finally reached (*culpa in contrahendo*). The same court has devised a nonstatutory remedy for certain cases of malfeasance in the performance of contractual agreements.[6]

In cases not involving the granting of remedies in novel situations,

---

[1] See *supra* Sec. 68.
[2] 2 Burr 1005 (1760); see *supra* Sec. 68.
[3] 50 S.E. 68 (Ga., 1905).
[4] 102 N.E. 2d 691 (N.Y., 1951).
[5] See H. F. Jolowicz, *Historical Introduction to the Study of Roman Law* (Cambridge, Eng., 1932), p. 416; Rudolph Sohm, *The Institutes,* transl. J. C. Ledlie, 3d ed. (Oxford, 1907), p. 258; *Dig.* 19. 5. 1
[6] See Philipp Heck, *Grundriss des Schuldrechts* (Tübingen, 1929), pp. 123, 118.

reliance by the judges on conceptions of justice is perhaps even more common. Such adjudications can be found in the Anglo-American and other legal systems. In *Valentini v. Canali*,[7] for example, an infant sued to recover money he had paid on a contract to rent a house and to buy furniture. The claim for a refund was predicated on the assumption that contracts entered into by infants for the supply of goods are totally void under statutory law. The plaintiff had occupied the premises and had used the furniture for some months. The British Court of Queen's Bench refused to permit the action, pointing out that "when an infant has paid for something and has consumed or used it, it is contrary to natural justice that he should recover back money which he has paid." In *Maclean v. The Workers' Union*,[8] the Chancery Division of the English Supreme Court of Judicature maintained that under "the principles of natural justice" a person against whom proceedings for expulsion from a private organization had been commenced must be given a reasonable opportunity to be heard, so that he can defend himself against the charges leveled against him and explain his conduct.[9] In 1792, the Supreme Court of South Carolina voided a legislative act transferring a freehold from the heir-at-law of a certain man and vesting it in a second son, on the ground that such a statute was against "common right and reason."[10] The Supreme Court of Utah held in 1944 that it could issue a letter of prohibition barring a lower court from proceeding in a matter in which the lower court had jurisdiction, for the purpose of preventing some "palpable and irremedial injustice."[11]

In the area of conflict of laws, general considerations of fairness and justice have played a particularly important part in developing this branch of the law.[12] Thus, in *Banco Minero v. Ross*,[13] a judgment of a Mexican court was denied recognition because in the opinion of the court, although material questions of fact were raised by the record, the defendant was arbitrarily and unjustly denied the right to present

[7] 24 Q.B.D. 166 (1889).

[8] 1 Ch. D. 602, at 625 (1929).

[9] See also *Young v. Ladies' Imperial Club* (1920), 2 K.B. 523; *Local Government Board v. Arlidge* (1915), A.C. 120. Cf. Percy H. Winfield, "Ethics in English Case Law," 45 *Harv. L. Rev.* 112 (1931).

[10] *Bowman v. Middleton*, 1 Bay (S.C.) 252 (1792); for other examples see Lowell J. Howe, "The Meaning of 'Due Process of Law' Prior to the Adoption of the Fourteenth Amendment," 18 *California Law Review* 583, at 590–594 (1930).

[11] *Olsen v. District Court*, 106 Utah 220 (1944). Some German decisions resting on considerations of justice are discussed by Charles Szladits, *Guide to Foreign Legal Materials: French, German, Swiss* (New York, 1959), p. 171.

[12] This was particularly true during the formative period of conflicts law, when precedents upon which the courts could rely were scarce.

[13] 172 S.W. 711 (Tex., 1915).

his defense. Sometimes the courts of one country have applied a rule of law of another country in a case justiciable under domestic law when they found that the domestic law was silent on the question and the foreign rule was in accordance with reason and justice.[14] As Mr. Justice Cardozo has pointed out, many gaps have been filled in the development of the Common Law by borrowing from Roman law or other legal systems.[15]

Considerations of justice may also be thrown decisively into the scale where two principles of positive law or two judicial precedents pointing in different directions and suggesting different conclusions both appear to be, from the point of view of logic, applicable in a case. Mr. Justice Cardozo, in dealing with this question,[16] cited the case of *Riggs v. Palmer* [17] as an illustration of such conflict. The case decided that a legatee under a will who had murdered his testator would not be permitted to take the property bequeathed to him. The terms of the will as well as the statutes regulating the effects of wills and the devolution of property clearly supported the title of the murderer. On the other end of the scale stood the maxim that a person should not be allowed to profit from his own intentional wrong and to acquire property by the commission of a crime. Two judges of the New York Court of Appeals found the language of the applicable statutes so unmistakable and clear that they were unwilling to depart from their wording. The majority held, however, that the letter of the written law ought in this case to yield to the superior force of the equitable maxim. This choice between two competing principles of law was undoubtedly dictated by strong sentiments of justice, which provided the ultimate source for the solution of the problem. "The claims of dominant opinion rooted in sentiments of justice and public morality are among the most powerful shaping-forces in lawmaking by courts." [18]

Courts have also resorted to considerations of justice in interpreting vague and ambiguous clauses in constitutional and statutory documents. Thus in interpreting the due-process clause of the Fourteenth Amendment to the American Constitution—a clause whose language

[14] An example is *Snedeker v. Warring*, 12 N.Y. 170 (1854), where in the absence of English and American precedents on the question as to whether a statue of Washington placed on a pedestal in front of a dwelling house was personalty or realty, the French rule of law was applied.

[15] Benjamin N. Cardozo, *The Nature of the Judicial Process* (New Haven, 1921), p. 123.

[16] *Id.*, p. 40.

[17] 22 N.E. 188 (N.Y., 1889).

[18] Justice Felix Frankfurter in *National City Bank v. Republic of China*, 348 U.S. 356, at 360 (1955).

conveys little meaning to the uninitiated—the Supreme Court of the United States has held that those guarantees of the Federal Bill of Rights which impose "fundamental principles of liberty and justice" must be observed by the laws and judicial procedures of the individual states as a prerequisite of due process. By virtue of these decisions, the rights of free speech and assembly, the right of free exercise of religion, the right to counsel in capital cases, and the right to a fair trial have been held to be indispensable guarantees of justice under our form of society and government.[19]

The conclusion to be drawn from these examples must be that the notion of justice has been used rather extensively by the judiciary and has played a prominent part in the decision of controversies. This should be characterized as a wholesome and desirable attitude by anyone who regards the law as an institution designed to accomplish peace, stability, and order in society, without neglecting or sacrificing basic postulates and demands of justice.[20] In the cases discussed and other similar ones, judges have not been governed by an irrational, meaningless, and entirely subjective notion of justice, which according to certain positivist writers is the only conceivable content of justice.[21] On the contrary, it is possible to explain the results in these cases rationally and justify them by objective considerations; it can also be assumed that these decisions were accompanied by widespread approval. It is particularly in situations where the scales are heavily weighted on one side and where a strong need for relief is apparent that the courts are willing to allow new claims or defenses on grounds of essential justice and equity.[22]

Of course the task of the judge in arriving at an objective standard of justice and achieving a reconciliation and synthesis of the needs of

[19] See among other cases, *Hurtado v. California*, 110 U.S. 516, at 531–532 (1884); *DeJonge v. Oregon*, 299 U.S. 353 (1937); *Powell v. Alabama*, 287 U.S. 45 (1932); *Palko v. Connecticut*, 302 U.S. 319 (1937); *Brown v. Mississippi*, 297 U.S. 278 (1936); *Moore v. Dempsey*, 261 U.S. 86 (1923).

[20] In accord: François Gény, *Méthode d'interprétation et sources en droit privé positif*, 2d rev. ed. (Paris, 1954), II, 91–92, 105–167.

[21] See Kelsen, "The Pure Theory of Law," 50 *L. Q. Rev.* 474, at 482 (1934); Austin, *Lectures on Jurisprudence*, I, 218; A. V. Lundstedt, "Law and Justice," in *Interpretations of Modern Legal Philosophies*, ed. P. Sayre (New York, 1947), p. 450.

[22] In the case of *International News Service v. Associated Press*, 248 U.S. 215 (1918), often regarded as a revolutionary innovation in the law of torts, the United States Supreme Court enjoined the unauthorized copying of news by the International News Service from early bulletins and news releases of the Associated Press and selling them to its customers. It is likely that the uneven distribution of the equities in this case had a strong bearing on the decision of the court to recognize the appropriation of values created by another through effort and expense as an actionable tort.

stability and justice is by no means an easy one. In the course of the administration of the law, situations will always arise where the claims of legal certainty will come into conflict with the exigencies of justice and where a clearcut choice must be made between two values found to be in opposition to each other. As a general rule, subject to certain rarely occurring exceptions to be discussed later here and elsewhere,[23] the judge must apply the positive and unambiguous mandates of the constitutional and statutory law, even though he is firmly convinced that these mandates are not or are no longer consonant with basic contemporary notions of justice. This is true not only where a single, isolated provision of the positive law categorically requires a certain solution, but also where a comparison of various positive norms and a consideration of their relation within the framework of the whole system inescapably point the way toward a particular disposition of a legal problem. In other words, where a frame of order has been provided by the positive law, the judge is normally bound by it and cannot depart from it in the interest of justice.

It bears emphasis, however, that the situations in which a legal result can be clearly derived from the logical pattern of the positive system or the general spirit suffusing its mandates are not as frequent as some writers have assumed. A judge will often be in great doubt as to whether he should extend a certain positive prescription to a case not directly covered by it, or whether he should limit it to the situation for which it was originally devised. In such a situation, he should not heed Kelsen's advice that from the point of view of the law it makes no difference whatever whether he resorts to an analogy (an extension of a principle to a related case) or to an *argumentum e contrario* (a conclusion that the facts of a case fall outside the scope of a formulated principle and are therefore not covered by it), but should let considerations of justice weigh heavily in the balance. For instance, a court may become confronted with a question as to whether the principle of sovereign immunity, which may have firm anchorage in the legal system and may clearly be applicable to all official acts of the organs of the state, should be extended to the acts of officials of government corporations. In deciding this question, the realization of the serious injustice caused by the principle in obviating relief against wrongful acts of public officers may legimately induce the court to confine the principle narrowly to situations in which its applicability has been authoritatively established.

Where the positive law has left a problem before the court entirely unsettled, standards of justice must play a prominent part in bringing

[23] See *infra* Secs. 71 and 79.

about a satisfactory solution of the dispute. Unfortunately, the mental processes which lead to the adoption of a rule of justice fit to dispose of the problem in an adequate fashion lend themselves to a very limited general description only. What is due to a party can often be determined only in the light of the circumstances of a particular case. Although an objective rationalization of the result is possible, such a rationalization cannot always be developed in advance in a theoretical and dogmatic way, but must be elaborated in the context of a concrete problem. The desire to allow the fullest scope to the assertion of individual rights may have to be balanced against arguments appealing to the common good and public advantage.[24] Furthermore, considerations of justice are often blended with supporting arguments resting on other informal sources of the law, such as public policies, social trends, customs, and accepted moral standards.[25]

The desire to achieve justice between the parties will sometimes be outweighed in the minds of the judges by the determination to avoid a sharp break with the past. Although good reasons may be available to support the award of a new remedy or the allowance of a new defense, the court may legitimately feel that in the absence of any available analogy to existing remedies or defenses the action asked for would constitute such a revolutionary and unprecedented innovation upon the law that it cannot be undertaken without legislative authorization. Such an argument would carry special weight in cases where the scales of justice are not heavily weighted on one side, or where a number of alternatives for a solution of the problem would appear to be open. Sometimes it may become necessary to prescribe detailed rules or limitations for the enjoyment of a new right or to set up an administrative machinery for its enforcement.[26] In such instances, courts will often take the position that the regulation of the matter must be left to the legislature.

We must now turn to the second question raised at the beginning of our discussion. In an earlier section, the problem of the validity of unjust law was subjected to analysis,[27] and the position was taken that there may be rare, extreme, and unusual situations in which the legality of a positive law may be questioned by a court even in the absence of a written constitution prescribing standards to which legislative acts must conform. Problems of this type will hardly ever come up in a democracy governed by humanitarian ideals, but they may become

[24] See *supra* Sec. 49.
[25] See in this connection Cardozo, *op. cit. supra* n. 15, p. 112.
[26] See here the dissenting opinion of Mr. Justice Brandeis in *International News Service v. Associated Press*, 248 U.S. 215, at 262–267 (1918).
[27] See *supra* Sec. 53.

acute under either a tyranny or a political and social order replacing a tyrannical regime. In the latter case, the order succeeding the system of dictatorship may be compelled to pass judgment on outrageous acts of violence and brutality committed during the era of despotic rule under cover of the positive laws of the state. As a matter of general principle, it should be held that resort to elementary considerations of justice *contra legem* should not necessarily, in a proper historical setting, be regarded as a transgression of judicial authority. There may be types of laws so utterly repugnant to the postulates of civilized decency that the judge has a right to treat them as non-laws.

The following hypothetical examples may be offered as specimens of legal enactments transcending the bounds of legitimate sovereign power of a state or nation: a law authorizing conviction for crime without opportunity for a hearing in which evidence on behalf of the accused may be presented; a law ordering the extermination [28] or sterilization [29] of an unpopular religious or national minority; a law sanctioning the lynching of persons by mobs; a law—such as the one enacted by King Herod—commanding the killing of innocent children.[30] These would appear to be instances where, as Radbruch says, "the contrast between positive law and justice becomes so unbearable that the positive law, being false law, must yield to justice." [31] It should be noted that in all of the examples given above, certain persons or groups of persons were seriously harmed or likely to be harmed through outrageous disregard of the minimum standards of civilization recognized by reasonable men. There is a fundamental distinction between such laws and statutory enactments in which this element of an unjust affront to the supreme value of life is absent, as, for instance, laws imposing taxes regarded as unduly high by large sections of the population, or laws changing deeply ingrained customs or mores of the people (such as laws abolishing racial or religious segregation). It is not suggested that the principle of invalidity of totally unjust laws could legitimately be applied to the latter categories of laws.

Section 70. *Reason and the Nature of Things*
Reason is the (limited) ability of the human intellect to comprehend and cope with reality. The reasonable man is capable of discerning

[28] See Book of Esther iii: 13.
[29] Memoranda found in Germany after World War II disclosed plans by some Nazi hotheads to sterilize the whole Polish nation.
[30] Matt. ii: 16.
[31] Gustav Radbruch, "Gesetzliches Unrecht und Übergesetzliches Recht," *Süddeutsche Juristenzeitung* 1946, p. 107, reprinted in *Rechtsphilosophie*, 4th ed. by E. Wolf (Stuttgart, 1950), p. 353.

general principles and of grasping certain essential relations of things, between men and things, and between men themselves. It is possible for him to view the world and judge other human beings in an objective and detached fashion. He rests his appraisal of facts, men, and events not on his own unanalyzed impulses, prepossessions, and idiosyncrasies, but on a broad-minded and judicious evaluation of all evidence that can aid in the formation of a considered judgment. He is also unconcerned with the consequences which discernment of the truth will have upon his purely personal, material interests.

Since the relations of men and things are often complex, ambiguous, and subject to appraisal from different points of view, it is by no means possible for human reason, in the majority of cases, to discover one and only one final and correct answer to a problematic situation presented by human social life. The reasonable man will often find that various ways and alternative possibilities are open to him in judging an event or making a determination as to the right course of action to pursue. This is as true for the legislative and judicial processes as it is in other areas of human collective life. Reason alone will often not enable a legislator or judge to make an inescapable and compelling choice between two or more possible solutions of a problem. It was therefore erroneous on the part of some representatives of the classical law-of-nature school to believe that a universally valid and perfect system of law could be devised, in all of its details, by a pure exercise of the human reasoning faculty operating *in abstracto*.[1]

It cannot be denied, on the other hand, that in the administration of a legal system instances occur in which a particular solution of a problem thrusts itself upon the legal decision-maker with a cogent force impervious to dissent. The nature of things itself (*natura rerum*, in the terminology of the Roman jurists) in these cases dictates the result to a legislating or adjudicating organ. Since we are concerned here with a description and evaluation of judicial source materials, we shall confine our discussion to the judicial process.

The *natura rerum* which furnishes a standard of decision in some cases may be divided into several categories: (1) It may be derived from some fixed and necessary condition of human nature; (2) it may stem from inescapably given properties of a physical nature; (3) it may be rooted in the essential attributes of some institution of human political and social life; and (4) it may be founded on perception of fundamental postulates or premises underlying a particular form of society. Examples of these various manifestations of the nature of things as a normative force will now be given.

[1] See *supra* Secs. 8 and 14.

With respect to the first class of cases mentioned, the legal inability of an infant to enter into binding agreements and prosecute an action in court without proper representation by a guardian unquestionably is anchored in natural fact. Likewise, the more or less universal rule that an insane person cannot make a legally efficacious promise springs from the psychophysical incapacity of such a person to act responsibly for himself.[2] The right of self-defense was traced by the Roman jurists to an innate drive of human beings for self-preservation.[3] An American court concluded from an analysis of the intimate bond existing between parents and children that, except for very grave reasons, no court could transfer a child from its natural parent to some other person.[4]

An example illustrative of the second category of cases can be found in the ancient Roman procedure for the recovery of property. A strict rule governing the proceedings before the praetor required the presence of the litigious *res* in court. When the question came up for the first time of whether this rule was applicable to immovable property, the *natura rerum* furnished the answer with compelling persuasiveness. The conceivable alternative, to hold the trial on the piece of real estate forming the object of the suit—which was perhaps located many miles away from the city—was far too impracticable to be seriously considered.[5] There are also instances in which certain rules of law impressed themselves upon a community as necessary and inevitable in view of certain natural or climatic conditions prevailing in the geographical area in question. For example, the common-law doctrine of equal riparian rights to the flow and use of water was never recognized in the arid states of the American West. It was replaced by the principle that the first appropriator of water acquired a priority with respect to the beneficial use of such water. The geophysical fact of water scarcity dictated this result, because adoption of the common-law doctrine might have prevented a socially profitable use of water by *anybody*. As the Supreme Court of Utah pointed out, "If that [doctrine] had been recognized and applied in this Territory, it would still be a desert." [6] Furthermore, the common-law principle of liability

---

[2] *Dig.* XLIV. 7. 1. 12: "It is clear, by natural law, that the act of an insane person who makes either a stipulation or promise is of no effect." S. P. Scott, *The Civil Law* (Cincinnati, 1932), X, 77.

[3] See Ernst Levy, "Natural Law in the Roman Period," *University of Notre Dame Natural Law Institute Proceedings* (Notre Dame, 1949), II, 52.

[4] *People v. Shepsky*, 113 N.E. 2d 801 (N.Y., 1953). See also Justice Lester A. Wade in *State of Utah in the Interest of L.J.J., Minor Children*, 360 P. 2d 486, at 488 (1961).

[5] I owe this example, as well as some valuable general thoughts on the problem, to Helmut Coing, *Grundzüge der Rechtsphilosophie* (Berlin, 1950), pp. 118-131.

[6] *Stowell v. Johnson*, 7 Utah 215, at 225 (1891).

for trespassing animals was repudiated by the courts of the same area, because the territory was characterized by the existence of large, sparsely settled, and uninclosed lands adjacent to the public domain, and recognition of the common-law principle would "practically deprive the owners of livestock of the right to use the public domain." [7]

In the third category, the essential nature of a man-made institution may be productive of legal norms felt to be necessary and inevitable. The rule, for instance, that a judge who is closely related to one of the parties must disqualify himself from hearing and deciding the cause is inherent in the very nature of the judicial office. This office, in the light of the purposes for which it was created, requires impartiality and personal detachment as conditions for its proper functioning.[8] The general purposes and aims of the universal human institution of government may likewise be a determinative factor in recognizing certain rules or principles relating to the powers residing in the organs of sovereignty. Inasmuch as it is the function of all governments to protect the members of the community committed to their care from serious dangers threatening from within or without, it might be argued that the duty to preserve the community from severe harm must always be capable of being exercised by the government. This consideration would seem to have significant bearing on the scope of the executive powers possessed by the President of the United States. Irrespective of whether a broad or restrictive view of the powers of the chief executive is taken,[9] it should be held that by the very nature of his office he must be able to act in an unprecedented and unanticipated emergency for the purpose of protecting the people of the United States until Congress can be assembled to take the necessary legislative measures to cope with the situation.

The authority of John Locke, who strongly believed in the theory of limited government and the democratic idea of political rule, may be cited in support of the proposition suggested above. He said:

> The legislators not being able to foresee and provide by laws for all that may be useful to the community, the executor of the laws, having the power in his hands, has by common law of Nature a right to make use of it for the good of the society, in many cases where the municipal law has given no

---

[7] *Big Cottonwood Tanner Ditch Co. v. Moyle*, 109 Utah 213, at 220–221 (1946); see also *Buford v. Houty*, 5 Utah 591, at 597 (1888), affirmed in 133 U.S. 320 (1889).

[8] See Coing, p. 121.

[9] Article II of the United States Constitution is somewhat ambiguous and has been the subject of conflicting interpretations. See Edward S. Corwin, *The President: Office and Powers*, 4th ed. (New York, 1957), pp. 3–5, 147–158. The case of *Youngstown Sheet and Tube Co. v. Sawyer*, 343 U.S. 579 (1952) throws little light on the scope of the executive powers of the President.

direction, till the legislative can conveniently be assembled to provide for it . . . Nay, it is fit that the laws themselves should in some cases give way to the executive power, or rather to this fundamental law of Nature and government—viz., that as much as may be all the members of the society are to be preserved.[10]

The "common law of Nature" is invoked in this passage to support the view that there can be no vacuum in the exercise of governmental powers where the good of the community is vitally at stake. There is every reason, of course, to insist that the scope of such residual powers is limited by the occasion for their exercise, and that their use remains subject to all applicable constitutional restraints.[11]

The decision in the case of *McCulloch v. Maryland*,[12] in which the United States Supreme Court held that the federal government of the United States possesses such implied powers of regulation as are reasonably necessary in order to carry out the constitutional prerogatives expressly conferred on it, may be said to rest in part on similar considerations derived from the nature of things. By the same token, the International Court of Justice has taken the position that the United Nations must be deemed to have those powers which, though not expressly provided in its charter, are committed to it by necessary implication as being essential to the performance of its duties.[13]

Finally, in the fourth category, some norms of law may be gained from contemplation and observation of certain basic functional characteristics of social, political, and legal institutions viewed in the historical and sociological context in which they were created or developed. The structure of the ancient Roman family, for example, was such that the *pater familias* was considered the only member of the family capable of possessing legal rights and duties. The other members of the family, including adult sons, were completely subject to his control and, figuratively speaking, were regarded as part of the father's personality.[14] In the light of these conceptions a celebrated Roman jurist, Paul, argued that, although there was no rule of law prohibiting a father from bringing suit for theft against his son, the nature of the matter presented an insuperable obstacle to the suit "because we cannot bring suit against those who are under our control,

---

[10] *Of Civil Government* (Everyman's Library ed., 1924), Bk. II, ch. xiv, sec. 159.
[11] The most important of these, under the American system of government, would appear to be the due-process clause of the Fifth Amendment, which prohibits arbitrary deprivations of life, liberty, and property.
[12] 4 Wheat. 16 (1819).
[13] International Court of Justice, Advisory Opinion, April 11, 1949, 43 *American Journal of International Law* 589 (1949).
[14] See Jolowicz, *Roman Law*, p. 118.

any more than they can bring suit against us." [15] In the same vein, it might be asserted that the prohibition of divorce under the system of the canon law flows directly and immediately from the Roman Catholic conception of marriage as a union for life endowed with the solemn force of a sacrament, and that the prohibition would therefore not necessarily require express recognition in a positive rule of Church law. It might also be mentioned that the once-held notion of the complete unity of husband and wife exercised a strong influence upon the development of the common law of torts and property.

In the case of *Crandall v. Nevada*,[16] the United States Supreme Court deduced the existence of a right of free mobility of persons within the borders of the nation, in the absence of a specific constitutional mandate sanctioning the right, from the basic postulates of a free commonwealth. Likewise, recognition of a general principle of freedom of transaction, subject to certain restraints to be specified by positive law, follows logically from the cardinal premises of a capitalist economy, which derives its strength from a maximum exercise of individual initiative in the operation of private enterprise. In a genuinely feudal society, where the chief political and economic institutions are founded on a personal bond of fidelity between the lord and his vassals, it would be contrary to the fundamental postulates of the social system to permit the free alienation of land by a vassal to a third person, with the consequence that the lord might become saddled with a tenant who is unreliable or a personal enemy of the lord. A socialistic society will consider an antisocial form of the exercise of private rights as incompatible with socialistic ideology and, in cases of legal doubt, will give preference to the concerns of the collective whole over those of the individual.

The German jurist Heinrich Dernburg once made the following observation: "The relations of life, to a greater or less degree, contain in themselves their own measure and their own intrinsic order. This order immanent in such relations is called the 'nature of things.' The thinking jurist must have recourse to this concept in cases where a positive norm is lacking, or where the norm is incomplete or unclear." [17] The examples that have been given here amply demonstrate that courts of law, by relying on the dictates of natural reason or drawing legal consequences from a contemplation and analysis of the essential nature or functional characteristics of human political and

---

[15] *Dig.* XLVII. 2. 16.
[16] 6 Wall. 35 (1868).
[17] *Pandekten*, 3d ed. (Berlin, 1892), I, 87; cf. also Gény, *Méthode d'interprétation et sources en droit privé positif*, II, 82 ff., 89.

social institutions, have confirmed the availability of *natura rerum* as a legitimate source of law-finding.

Section 71. *Individual Equity*

It was pointed out earlier that the notion of justice, which is one of the guiding principles in the administration of a legal system, does not exhaust its meaning in the command of an even-handed application of legal rules and normative standards to all cases coming within their purview. A set of facts may sometimes arise in a lawsuit which exhibits extraordinary features and does not lend itself to adjudication under a pre-existing rule or to a comparison with previously decided cases. In such instances considerations of justice may, within certain narrowly circumscribed limits, call for a departure from or a relaxation of a fixed norm for the purpose of reaching a fair and satisfactory decision in the case.[1] In the words of the English medieval jurist Christopher St. Germain, "In some cases it is necessary to leave the words of the law, and to follow that [which] reason and justice requireth, and to that intent equity is ordained; that is to say, to temper and mitigate the rigour of the law." [2] In his discussion of the same problem Cicero referred to the maxim *summmum ius summa iniuria,* which conveys the idea that a rigorous application of strict and invariable rules of law, untempered by equity, may at times produce undue hardship and great injustice.[3]

In dealing with the problem of individual treatment of unusual fact situations, we are not concerned with the question of whether a court, for the purpose of improving the legal system and bringing it into harmony with justice, may inaugurate new forms of redress or new categories of defenses, or whether it may extend such forms of redress or defenses to cases for which they were not designed at their inception.[4] Here we are interested in finding out whether a court, when confronted with a positive rule laid down by a statute or precedent, may depart from it in a case exhibiting unusual features on the ground that application of the norm in this particular fact situation would result in an outrageous denial of justice.

For the purpose of illustrating the problem, an example given by St. Thomas Aquinas and one drawn from the Roman law will be used

---

[1] See *supra* Secs. 47 and 50.

[2] *The Doctor and Student,* ed. W. Muchall (Cincinnati, 1874), ch. xvi. As was pointed out *supra* Sec. 50, the power of equitable dispensation was termed *epieikeia* by Aristotle.

[3] Cicero, *De Officiis,* transl. W. Miller (Loeb Classical Library ed., 1938), Bk. I, ch. x. 33. See also James Wilson, *Works,* ed. J. D. Andrews (Chicago, 1896), II, 123.

[4] See *supra* Sec. 69 and *infra* Sec. 82.

with slight modifications. Suppose that in a medieval city there was a statute providing that the gates of the city must remain closed during all hours of the night, and that violations of the rule would be punished by imprisonment. One night residents of the city were pursued by the enemy and sought entrance into the gates. If the gatekeepers opened the gates to them, were they liable to punishment because the law permitted no exception from its command? Or should the judge in this case have recognized an equitable exception from the operation of the statute, on the ground that the lawgiver, had he foreseen this contingency, would most certainly have provided that the gates be opened in such an event? To give a further illustration, let us assume the existence of a rule of law stipulating that the vendor of real property is obliged to disclose mortgages and other legal encumbrances to the purchaser, and that the latter can claim punitive damages for failure to supply the required information. A sells his property to B, notifying him of the existence of certain permanent encumbrances. After six months, A buys the property back from B. B does not inform A expressly of the encumbrances, knowing that A without any question is aware of them. A sues for punitive damages. Should he be able to recover on the basis of the aforesaid rule, although he is clearly abusing the letter of the law?

Many legal systems have developed mechanisms to cope with the problem of equitable corrections of strict law. Under the republican constitution of Rome, the popular assembly could exempt an individual from the operation of a law, a power which in the course of time was usurped by the senate.[5] During the period of the principate, this power passed from the senate to the emperor.[6] Under the rules of Roman Catholic canon law, the Pope possesses the power to dispense from compliance with general laws laid down by the Church, excepting, however, certain immutable principles of natural law.[7] The medieval English kings were similarly invested with the dispensing power.[8] Under our own legal system we permit Congress to grant exemptions

---

[5] See Jolowicz, *Roman Law*, p. 32.

[6] *Id.*, p. 333. As the author points out, if the emperor acted in contravention of any rule from which dispensation was possible, he was held to have given himself the necessary dispensation. It was in this sense, and this sense only, that the emperor was held to be *legibus solutus* (absolved from the law) during the period of the principate. Cf. also *Cod.* I. 14. 1, denying the power of dispensation to lower-court judges.

[7] See Matthew Ramstein, *A Manual of Canon Law* (Hoboken, 1948), pp. 109–122; cf. also St. Thomas Aquinas, *Summa Theologica*, transl. Fathers of the English Dominican Province (London, 1913–1925), Pt. II, 1st pt., qu. 97, art. 4.

[8] F. W. Maitland, *The Constitutional History of England* (Cambridge, Eng., 1931), p. 188.

from general laws (such as exemptions from income tax or immigration laws) through "private" statutes. We also tacitly permit our jurors, by their rendering of general verdicts unsupported by technical legal reasoning, to correct rigidities or inadequacies in the positive law by not applying it in a particular case, for example, to correct inequities caused by a strict use of the contributory negligence rule.[9]

In the context of a discussion of the informal sources of the law which may legitimately be resorted to in the decision of legal controversies, our primary focus must be fixed on the power of the judge to apply equitable considerations in the adjudication of law suits. Inasmuch as the traditional Anglo-American system of equity jurisprudence, which in its beginnings was administered as an Aristotelian corrective to the generality and inflexibility of the common law, has gradually evolved into a system of rules which are distinguished from common-law rules or statutory rules only in that they are sometimes phrased in a more elastic form, this historical source of equitable dispensation has to a considerable extent become dried up.[10] We are disinclined to permit our judges to refuse application of a statute on the ground that a serious injustice would thereby be caused under the circumstances of the particular case.[11] Furthermore, upper-court judges are often reluctant today to graft equitable exceptions on to judicial rules, although their latitude in this area is greater than in the realm of statutory law.

As a matter of future policy, it would seem feasible and desirable to reinvest the judge with a limited power to dispense individual equity in unusual hardship cases, regardless of whether the applicable rule of law is a statutory or judicial norm. It is not logical to deny this power to the judge while we grant it to the jury.[12] If juries have a *sub rosa* power to prevent bad law from being applied in a case, there is no reason why the judge should not be able to exercise this power openly in an appropriate situation. This argument becomes particularly impelling in view of the fact that the use of the jury in civil cases seems to be on the decline in the Anglo-American legal system, and that the day may come when it will be entirely abolished in this type of case. There does not appear to be any sound reason for holding that the possibility of reaching an equitable result must depend on the acci-

[9] See Jerome Frank, *Courts on Trial* (Princeton, 1949), pp. 127–131.
[10] See Roscoe Pound, "The Decadence of Equity," 5 *Columbia Law Review* 20 (1905).
[11] Contrast with this attitude the opinion in the *Earl of Oxford's Case*, 1 Rep. in Chanc. 1, at 4–11 (1616), where application of the letter of a statute was rejected because it would lead to an unconscionable result. See *infra* Sec. 79.
[12] Frank, pp. 127 ff.

dental factor of whether the case is to be decided by a judge or a jury.

Strong insistence must be made, however, that if we invest the judge with the power to administer individual equity, care must be taken that this power not be used to an extent which would be destructive of the normative system. First of all, the exercise of equitable discretion by the judge must always be subject to appellate review. It must also be made clear that the judge may use this prerogative only in rare situations where the application of a positive rule would lead to a result which the large majority of thinking men would condemn as wholly unacceptable and unreasonable. And in the case of departure from a statutory rule, the judge must be in a position to conclude, on the basis of a study of the background of the statute, that the lawmaker certainly would have created an exception from the rule if he had foreseen the occurrence of the situation. If the power is in this fashion treated as a highly exceptional one, and if the judge becomes thoroughly imbued with the conviction that mere personal disagreement with the positive rule is under no circumstances sufficient ground for the use of the power, the dangers which a recognition of Aristotelian *epieikeia* does hold for an impartial administration of justice would appear to be reduced to that minimum risk to which the exercise of *any* judicial power is exposed.

One distinction must be kept in mind. The case where the judge dispenses from the application of a general norm may be one which appears unique and unprecedented to him. The uniqueness may, however, consist simply in the fact that a similar case has never in the past been before his court or before any other court in his jurisdiction. The case may not be unique in the sense that the situation is unlikely ever to arise again in this or a similar form in the future. The number of cases falling under this second—and more literal—meaning of the term unique would probably always be relatively small as compared with the first group of cases.

If a judge exercises the equitable power of dispensation in a case which has never arisen in the past but which may arise again in the future, he must be aware of the fact that—at least under a legal system recognizing the force of precedents—he may in fact do more than merely decide an unusual case on its own facts in accordance with considerations of equity. He may actually fashion a new normative standard able to govern identical or similar fact situations in the future. This occurred frequently in the early history of English equity. As was pointed out earlier,[13] when the English Chancellor for the first

---

[13] See *supra* Sec. 50.

time allowed the specific performance of a contract, he did so on the grounds of equity or conscience because he felt that the common-law remedy of damages could not adequately compensate the plaintiff for the harm inflicted on him by the defendant's breach of promise. However, as soon as specific performance was granted as a matter of course in other and similar cases, the original equitable departure from the common-law rule (making damages the exclusive remedy) became transformed into a *rule* of equity jurisprudence. A modern example showing the same course of development is the refusal of some American courts to recognize forfeiture clauses in long-term real estate contracts in situations where the vendor would thereby make an unconscionable profit beyond the damages he suffered. In the course of time, much of what had in its inception been an "anti-legal" [14] exercise of discretion, or "justice without law," [15] later formed into a body of legal rules supplementing those of the common law. It is for the purpose of differentiating the historically developed system of Anglo-American equity from the power of equitable dispensation dealt with above that the term "individual equity" has been used here.

Section 72. *Public Policies, Moral Convictions, and Social Trends*
In the case of *Nashville, C. & St. L. Ry. v Browning*,[1] the United States Supreme Court expressed the view that a systematic practice by the state of Tennessee whereby, for purposes of taxation, the property of railroads and other public utilities was assessed at full cash value and all other kinds of property at less than cash value, should be regarded as the law of the state. This conclusion was reached by the court, although the discriminatory practice had not been incorporated into the statutory law of the state. "It would be a narrow conception of jurisprudence," said Mr. Justice Frankfurter, "to confine the notion of 'laws' to what is found written on the statute books, and to disregard the gloss which life has written upon it. Settled state practice cannot supplant constitutional guaranties, but it can establish what is state law." [2] Thus, the court recognized in this case that a settled and consistent practice by government officials, being a reflection of the "public policy" of the state, may be considered a legitimate source of law. Likewise, in the case of *Kansas v. U.S.*,[3] the court, when faced with the question whether the United States without its consent may be sued by a state of the Union, concluded in the absence of a con-

[14] Pound, p. 20.
[15] *Id.*, p. 22.
[1] 310 U.S. 362 (1940).
[2] *Id.*, at 369.
[3] 204 U.S. 331, at 342 (1907).

trolling constitutional or statutory norm that "public policy" forbade the suit.

In the case of *In re Liberman*,[4] a condition in a trust arrangement to the effect that the beneficiary should lose the right to the trust fund if he should contract a marriage without the consent of the trustees was held contrary to public policy by the New York Court of Appeals. Here again the public policy concept served as an independent source of adjudication without the support of controlling precedent. In *Big Cottonwood Tanner Ditch Co. v. Moyle*,[5] the Supreme Court of Utah made the following statement: "In view of the fact that Utah is an arid state and the conservation of water is of first importance, it is with great hesitancy that we subscribe to any contention which would make it appear to be more difficult to save water. It has always been the public policy of this state to prevent the waste of water."

The term public policy is not used in an entirely uniform and consistent sense in the above cases. In the Nashville case, public policy is equated with an executive or administrative practice followed by state officials, whereas in the Liberman case the public policy envisaged by the court is in effect rooted in a cultural value pattern favoring marriage and discouraging unreasonable restraints upon it. The term "public policy" is being used here primarily to designate government policies and practices not incorporated into the law,[6] while the mores and ethical standards of the community are being discussed under the headings of moral convictions, social trends, and standards of justice.

For purposes of semantic clarity, it is also necessary to differentiate public policy from what might be called legal policy or the policy of the law. In the field of conflict of laws, for example, it is held that a foreign statute should not be applied by a court if its enforcement would offend against a strong public policy of the forum.[7] In many—though not necessarily all—conflicts cases, the public policy contemplated is the policy of the law, that is, an important normative pronouncement which has been enunciated in a constitutional provision, statute, or precedent and which reflects a strongly held community view as to what is socially good.[8] Pronouncements are found in Eng-

---

[4] 18 N.E. 2d 658 (1939).

[5] 109 Utah 197, at 203 (1945).

[6] In accord: Edwin W. Patterson, *Jurisprudence* (Brooklyn, 1953), p. 282, who points out that "policy" in its etymological signification refers to plans for governmental action rather than to moral or ethical principles.

[7] See *Loucks v. Standard Oil Co.*, 120 N.E. 198 (N.Y., 1918); *Mertz v. Mertz*, 3 N.E. 2d 597 (N.Y., 1936).

[8] It should be noted, however, that in determining whether or not a given domestic policy embodied in the law is so vital to the maintenance and protection of our legal institutions as to exclude the possibility of recognizing a foreign legal

lish legal literature and court decisions to the effect that in all branches of the law the only type of public policy relevant for purposes of adjudication is the policy of the law, and that the judicial formation of new rules of law founded on considerations of public good should be considered a closed chapter in English legal history.[9] Such views are anchored in a narrow positivism which reserves the fashioning of public policy ideas in the broader sense exclusively to the legislature; they cannot be said to be representative of the current judicial climate in the United States.

Even though it should be held that public policy constitutes a nonformal source of law which may properly be resorted to by the judge where the positive law is ambiguous or silent, the judge should have a veto power against the enforcement of a public policy which is in conflict with fundamental standards of justice.[10] This follows from the general theory advocated here, that justice is an essential ingredient of the idea of law as such, while a public policy sponsored by a government organ does not occupy this exalted status. Although the judge, for the sake of the important value of legal security, must make many compromises and adjustments between justice and the provisions of the positive law, the necessity for such compromises is reduced when we are confronted with a nonformal source of the law which, like public and administrative policy and practice, maintains a secondary place in the hierarchy of legal sources. Public policy, as understood here, chiefly embodies certain axioms of political or social expediency. Expediency, however, represents a value inferior to legal security and justice in the value hierarchy of the legal order.

It is true that in some instances the promptings of expediency become so imperative that they cannot be ignored by the makers or administrators of the law. Thus war, famine, civil strife, shortage of labor, or primitiveness of the productive system may require the tak-

---

rule inconsistent with it, the judges must necessarily have recourse to considerations of public good, concerning which the positive law may offer little direct aid and guidance.

[9] For a discussion of this view see George W. Paton, *A Textbook of Jurisprudence*, 2d ed. (Oxford, 1951), p. 114; W. S. M. Knight, "Public Policy in English Law," 38 *L. Q. Rev.* 207 (1922); Percy H. Winfield, "Public Policy in the English Law," 42 *Harv. L. Rev.* 761 (1929); Dennis Lloyd, *Public Policy* (London, 1953), p. 112.

[10] See in this connection *McCarthy v. Speed*, 77 N.W. 590 (S.D., 1898). In this case the court, after laying down the rule that one of the co-tenants of a mining claim may not relocate the claim as against the other co-tenant, made the following comment: "It is contended that the rule herein announced is contrary to public policy, and will result in endless embarrassment and confusion to a class of rights already sufficiently uncertain. We reply that a sound public policy always requires honesty and fair dealing."

ing of expedient or even drastic measures which may be questionable
from the point of view of justice. But in such instances the organs of
the law should be guided by the determination to carry out the mandates of expediency with the least possible detriment to justice. They
should carefully balance the conflicting interests at stake and should
not without a critical examination accept the solution which appears
to be the easiest and most obvious one.[11]

In the light of these considerations, issue might be taken with the
way in which the United States Supreme Court disposed of the case
of *Nashville, C. & St. L. Ry. v. Browning*.[12] In this case the court,
though recognizing as law an administrative practice under which railroad and utility property was assessed at full cash value, did not discuss the question of whether this discriminatory tax practice was in
consonance with basic tenets of justice. While there may have been
good reasons for justifying this discrimination, the court accepted the
administrative practice without raising the issue of its essential fairness.

The part played by the moral convictions of the community in the
development of the law has been discussed in an earlier section.[13] In
American law, the ascertainment of moral convictions becomes particularly important in those instances in which good moral character
is made the prerequisite for the acquisition of a right or privilege, or
where moral turpitude causes a forfeiture of a right or privilege.[14]
As a United States district court has observed, "In deciding the issue
of good moral character the Court's individual attitude is not the criterion. The test applied, with its acknowledged shortcomings and variables, depending upon time and place, is the norm of conduct accepted
by the community at large." [15] It might be observed that, although
a court must be careful to avoid substituting its own judgment for that
of the community, there may occur exceptional situations where the
community norm is totally without rational basis and may for this
reason be questioned by a court. Where the judge, for example, becomes persuaded that a popular conviction was produced by misinfor-

---

[11] The problem is treated in somewhat greater detail in the author's article on
"Law as Order and Justice," 6 *Journal of Public Law* 194, at 215–218 (1957). See
also Carleton K. Allen, "Justice and Expediency," in *Interpretations of Modern
Legal Philosophies*, ed. P. Sayre (New York, 1947), p. 15.

[12] 310 U.S. 362 (1940).

[13] See *supra* Sec. 57.

[14] See, for example, 8 U.S.C. Secs. 1251(a) and 1427(a).

[15] *Petition for Naturalization of Suey Chin*, 173 F. Supp. 510, at 514 (1959).
See also *Repouille v. United States*, 165 F. 2d 152, at 153 (1947); Benjamin N.
Cardozo, *The Paradoxes of Legal Science* (New York, 1928), p. 37.

A method for ascertaining the moral sense of the community is presented by
J. Cohen, R. A. H. Robson, and A. Bates, *Parental Authority: The Community
and the Law* (New Brunswick, N.J., 1958).

mation, untruthful propaganda, or irrational emotional appeals, he should be conceded the right to adopt a nonconformist attitude toward the community standard.[16]

Community moral patterns cannot always be distinguished with facility from social trends which exert an impact upon the administration of the law. Taking social trends to mean currents of public opinion which cannot be said to have fully ripened into a well-ascertained standard of justice or fixed moral conviction, we find that such trends have often influenced the judiciary. In a celebrated case,[17] Justice Story took the position that a strong international trend against the slave trade, evidenced by numerous international declarations as well as by some municipal statutes directed against its legality, might justify the judicial recognition of a rule of international law condemning such trade even though the institution of slavery itself had not been outlawed as unjust by some of the leading nations of the world. He made the reservation, however, that the municipal courts of a country should enforce the rule only against those nations shown to be in sympathy with the trend. In the interpretation of most-favored-nations clauses in international agreements, the courts have been inclined to follow world commercial trends away from discriminatory practices toward equality of treatment of all nations affected.[18] In the case of *Woods v. Lancet*,[19] the New York Court of Appeals specifically referred to a trend favoring extension of personal injury liability to prenatal injuries caused by negligent acts, and this trend, in conjunction with considerations of justice, caused the court to abandon earlier decisions denying liability in such instances. In *Universal Camera Co. v. N.L.R.B.*,[20] the United States Supreme Court took notice of a trend in litigation away from the battle-of-wits theory of law suits toward the conception of a rational inquiry into truth, in which the tribunal considers relevant everything probative of the matter under investigation. "The direction in which the law moves," said Mr. Justice Frankfurter, "is often a guide for the decision of particular cases." [21] If the same court, in the famous Dred Scott decision,[22] had recognized the

---

[16] A somewhat different approach to the problem is taken by Edmond Cahn, *The Moral Decision* (Bloomington, Ind., 1955), pp. 301–310.

[17] *U.S. v. The Schooner La Jeune Eugénie*, 2 Mason 409 (1st Circ., 1822).

[18] Compare *Whitney v. Robertson*, 124 U.S. 190 (1888) with *John T. Bill Co. v. U.S.*, 104 F. 2d 67 (1939).

[19] 102 N.E. 2d 691 (1951); see *supra* Sec. 69.

[20] 340 U.S. 474 (1950).

[21] *Id.*, p. 497. See also Justice Felix Frankfurter, in *National City Bank v. Republic of China*, 348 U.S. 356, at 360 (1954): "A steady legislative trend, presumably manifesting a strong social policy, properly makes demands on the judicial process."

[22] *Dred Scott v. Sanford*, 19 How. 393 (1857).

strength of antislavery sentiments in many parts of the country instead of taking the extreme view that the institution of slavery was sacrosanct, the Civil War might conceivably have been avoided.

It should be insisted that the social trend, in order to serve as a proper gauge in the adjudication of legal problems, should be a strong and dominant trend. If it is balanced by a countertrend, and if the social principle mirrored in the trend is in a state of flux and great uncertainty, courts should be very reluctant to elevate the trend to the status of a controlling rule of judicial action. Furthermore, as in the case of public policies, a court may feel that a prevailing trend is incompatible with fundamental ideas of justice. If a strong and convincing case is made out in favor of such a position, the court is justified in preferring the maxim of justice to the trend. A court, it is true, should make a large allowance for discrepancies of opinion as to what constitutes elementary justice, and it should not resist social progress by stubbornly clinging to notions of justice which may be those of a dying epoch. Nevertheless, some latitude should be granted to the judiciary in balancing fundamental notions of fairness and decency against social tendencies which, although they may be highly conspicuous and pronounced at a particular time, may be no more than ephemeral opinion lacking a solid rational foundation.

Section 73. *Customary Law*

The general criteria which may be used to distinguish law from social custom were treated earlier.[1] The conclusion was reached there that the lines of demarcation between these two agencies of social control are fluid, and that a practice which in one period of history has been viewed as nonlegal in nature may subsequently become elevated to the rank of a legal rule. At this point in our discussion, it becomes necessary to consider the conditions under which such a transformation of custom into law takes place.

A simplified view of the problem of customary law was taken by John Austin. To him a customary practice is to be regarded as a rule of positive morality unless and until the legislature or a judge has given it the force of law.[2] According to this view, habitual observance of a custom, even though accompanied by a firm conviction of its legally binding character, does not suffice to convert the custom into law; it is the recognition and sanction of the sovereign which impresses upon the custom the dignity of law. This position is, of course, necessitated by the Austinian theory of positive law, according to which

---

[1] See *supra* Sec. 58.
[2] *Lectures on Jurisprudence*, I, 36, 199.

law arises from establishment by political superiors, and never from spontaneous adoption of normative standards by the governed. The historical doctrine of law sponsored the opposite view, namely, that law was primarily the expression of the legal convictions and practices of the community.[3]

If we assume with Austin that customary laws are positive laws fashioned by political or judicial legislation upon pre-existing customs, there would be some doubt as to whether a custom could be made the basis for an adjudication of rights and liabilities in an arbitration proceeding conducted by nongovernment arbiters; government approval would be lacking in such a case, except under some far-fetched doctrine of government acquiescence. Furthermore, in a case where the parties merely wish to be informed of their rights, status, and duties under some customary arrangement without litigation, no lawyer could in good faith give such advice except to tell the parties that no legal rights and duties could come from custom in the absence of an authoritative court pronouncement. And when a regular court of law gives its approval to a pre-existing custom and adjudges a person liable to damages because he has violated the custom, the court, in Austin's view, creates new law and applies it with retroactive force to a situation ungoverned by that law at the time when the facts of the case occurred. In all three of these situations the opposite result is often more closely in accord with reality, justice, and convenience. Unless there exists a compelling necessity for bowing to the consequences entailed by the Austinian theory, there would seem to be good reason for establishing a more satisfactory theoretical basis for the recognition of customary law.

The solution of this problem is, however, attended by some serious difficulties, which stem primarily from the fact that members of a community or group practicing a certain custom do it unconsciously, in the sense that they are not engaged in a deliberate attempt to make law. Since the leading systems of law take the position that a custom is not necessarily law simply because it is observed by a community or group of men, there is always some doubt as to whether a custom represents a social usage, a rule of courtesy, or a depository of moral convictions rather than a rule of law. In other words, the legal efficacy of a custom is often uncertain until a legislature or court puts the stamp of legal approval on it.[4]

---

[3] See *supra* Secs. 18 and 58.

[4] A similar observation was made by Justice Cardozo with respect to international law, a branch of the law in which the customary element is particularly strong. These are his words: "International law . . . has at times, like the Common Law

Under the Civil Law system, the chief source of uncertainty in the legal recognition of custom is the requirement, found in a number of Civil Law countries, that a custom must be accompanied by the *opinio juris* or *opinio necessitatis* before a court can carry it into effect as a rule of law. This requirement means that a custom cannot be recognized as a rule of law in the absence of a firm conviction on the part of the members of the community that the custom is legally binding and the source of enforceable rights and obligations. Customs which flow merely from feelings of sympathy or propriety or from habit are not capable of generating law.[5] Quite obviously the nature of the custom often remains in doubt until a court has determined that community conviction as to its legally binding force does in fact exist.

In the area of the Common Law, the uncertainty surrounding the legal enforceability of a custom prior to legislative or judicial recognition is chiefly caused by the assumption of power on the part of the courts of law to deny legal efficacy to a custom on the ground that it is unreasonable. As the New York Court of Appeals has pointed out, "Reasonableness is one of the requisites of a valid usage, and an unreasonable or absurd custom cannot be set up to affect the legal rights of parties." [6] Thus, when Lord Mansfield in the eighteenth century undertook the task of incorporating the customary rules of the continental law merchant into the English common law, he rejected those mercantile and commercial usages which he considered unreasonable or unsuited to the conditions of his time or country. The English and American courts have generally preserved this selective approach to custom.[7] They have, however, been inclined to put the burden of proving unreasonableness on the party disputing the custom and have thereby attached a presumption of reasonableness to customs.[8]

The fact that customs, prior to sovereign confirmation, abide in a condition of uncertainty with regard to their ultimate recognition does not compel us to accept the Austinian position. As we concluded

---

. . . a twilight existence during which it is hardly distinguishable from morality or justice, until at length the *imprimatur* of a court attests its jural quality." *New Jersey v. Delaware*, 291 U.S. 361, at 383 (1934).

[5] See, for example, L. Enneccerus and H. C. Nipperdey, *Allgemeiner Teil des Bürgerlichen Rechts*, 14th ed. (Tübingen, 1952), pt. I, p. 160; Alf Ross, *Theorie der Rechtsquellen* (Leipzig, 1929), pp. 133 ff., 430–431; Gény, *Méthode d'interprétation et sources en droit privé positif*, I, 356 ff.

[6] *Fuller v. Robinson*, 86 N.Y. 306, 40 Am. Rep. 540 (1881).

[7] See *Wigglesworth v. Dallison*, 99 Eng. Rep. 132 (1779); *Wolstanton Ltd. and Duchy of Lancaster v. Newcastle-under-Lynn Co.* (1940), A. C. 860; *Swift v. Gifford*, 23 Fed. Cas. 558, No. 16,696 (1872); *Ghen v. Rich*, 8 Fed. 159 (1881). See also John R. Commons, "Law and Economics," 34 *Yale L. J.* 371, at 372 (1925).

[8] See Carleton K. Allen, *Law in the Making*, 6th ed. (London, 1958), p. 136.

earlier,[9] law can arise in a community by processes other than government command. Once this is conceded, there is every reason for ascribing legal character to a custom as long as its practice is accompanied by an intent to create relations which are definite, circumscribed, and important enough to produce obligatory rights and duties. We have to realize that an element of doubt and uncertainty attends the existence of many legal relations: we can never be sure how a certain constitutional or statutory rule establishing rights or obligations will be interpreted by a court, or whether a once-adopted interpretation will be overruled or subsequently modified. If we made perfect clarity and infallible certainty conditions for the recognition of a normative standard or arrangement as a source of law, the volume of law in our society would be reduced to an unjustifiably narrow margin.

Some interesting historical instances in which customs practiced as law in a certain field of activity eventually became incorporated into the positive law are found in American mining and water law. To give a few examples, the custom among miners on the public lands of the American West of holding that discovery and appropriation created legal rights to mining claims, and that subsequent development of a claim was the condition for the continuation of the right to the mine, was ultimately recognized by the United States Supreme Court.[10] Mining partnerships, evolved as a special type of partnership peculiarly adapted to serve the mining industry, took the form of customary arrangements in their inception and later received the approval of the courts.[11] In 1866 Congress gave the local customs of the miners on the public lands of the United States the force and effect of law.[12] In the arid states of the West, the acquisition of water rights on the basis of prior appropriation and beneficial use of the water rather than on occupancy of riparian property also had its origin in custom and was subsequently sanctioned by courts and legislatures.[13]

As C. K. Allen points out, "The scope of custom diminishes as the formulation of legal rules becomes more explicit and as a more elaborate machinery is set up for the making and administering of law." [14] Having become absorbed into legislative or judicial law to a far-reach-

---

[9] See *supra* Sec. 52.

[10] *O'Reilly v. Campbell*, 116 US. 418 (1885).

[11] See *Mud Control Laboratories v. Covey*, 2 Utah 2d 85 (1954). For another case of judicial adoption of a mining custom, see *U.S. Mining Co. v. Lawson*, 134 Fed. 769 (1904)

[12] 30 U.S.C. 51; *McCormick v. Varnes*, 2 Utah 355 (1879); *Chambers v. Harrington*, 111 U.S. 350 (1884); C. O. Martz, *Cases and Materials on the Law of Natural Resources* (St. Paul, Minn., 1951), p. 467.

[13] *The American Law of Property*, ed. J. Casner (Boston, 1954), vol. VIa, p. 170.

[14] *Law in the Making*, p. 126.

ing extent, custom plays a reduced role as a source of law in civilized society today. This does not mean, however, that its law-producing force is exhausted or spent. Vocational or business customs or even customs of a more general character may be found to govern human conduct on a nonlitigious basis, and such customs may also find their way into the courts of law. Customs of a local character are sometimes asserted in court as derogating from and displacing a general rule of law. The English courts have developed certain tests for dealing with such local variations of the general law.[15] It is held that they cannot be set up against a positive rule of the statutory law. They may not violate a basic principle of the Common Law, and they must have existed for a long time.[16] They must have been practiced continuously and peaceably, and the public must regard the custom as obligatory. And lastly, the custom must not be unreasonable, that is, it must not violate fundamental principles of right and wrong or injure the interests of outsiders to the custom. The courts in the United States have not strictly followed the English tests and have been inclined to ignore particularly the test of antiquity.[17]

A court would be justified (at least according to the view advocated here) in disregarding a custom that violates a basic standard of justice. Furthermore, if a custom runs contrary to a clearly established public policy or a strong social trend, and if the sole basis for the continuance of the custom is habit or inertia, there would be no reason for denying the court the power to repudiate the custom under the traditional test of reasonableness.

In spite of the fact that the significance of customary law as a direct and immediate source of law is not very large today, custom often enters the arena of the law in an indirect way. In determining whether an act was negligent, for instance, a court may have to ascertain the customary standards of care observed by men of average reasonableness. In suits for professional misconduct or incompetence, attention may have to be given to the accustomed ways of proper professional behavior. Business usages prevailing in a certain branch of business may have to be ascertained in order to determine rights, duties, and responsibilities in the field of commercial law. They are particularly pertinent

[15] *Id.*, pp. 126 ff.; John Salmond, *Jurisprudence*, 11th ed. by G. Williams (London, 1957), pp. 241–246.

[16] It is often stated by the English courts that no local custom can be regarded as legally valid unless its practice reaches back to the beginnings of the reign of Richard I in 1189 A.D. However, if the party alleging the custom can prove that it has existed for a substantial period, such as the time of actual human memory, this will raise a presumption of immemorial antiquity. See Salmond, pp. 245–246; Allen, *Law in the Making*, pp. 130–131.

[17] See Patterson, *Jurisprudence*, p. 227.

to banks and banking, and they may play a significant role generally in the interpretation of commercial contracts and other documents. Customs are also often resorted to in determining the terms of agreements between landlords and tenants.

The last problem to be discussed here is the relation between statute and custom in cases where an antiquated and obsolete statute has given way to a new living law which finds expression in community custom. Suppose, for example, an attempt is made to reactivate, after long nonuse, an old criminal statute which penalizes baseball-playing on Sundays, after general public opinion regarding Sunday activity has undergone a sharp change and it has become quite customary to engage in sports on Sunday. Some Civil Law countries, like Germany, apply the doctrine of *desuetudo* in such circumstances and give the judge the power to ignore the statute on the ground that it has not been used for a long time and has been displaced by a countervailing custom recognizing the propriety of recreational activities on Sunday.[18] In present-day Anglo-American law, the doctrine of desuetude is not as a general rule applied to statutes, and it is held that a statute lives on in full force despite nonuse and cessation of the original *ratio legis*. There would seem to be much reason, however, in favor of a plea for receiving the desuetude doctrine into our legal system.[19] It would appear contrary to fundamental notions of justice and due process to subject a person to criminal liability or civil deprivations under a law which has not been enforced for a substantial period of time and which is obviously at variance with a new and solidly established community opinion. If the enforcement of an antiquated law is thoroughly incompatible with the public interest and the dominating concept of justice, there must be some way of declaring the continued validity of the statute repugnant to the notion of due process of law. However, such cases of *desuetudo* should be rare and unusual, and the conviction as

[18] See Enneccerus and Nipperdey, p. 165; Max Rümelin, *Die Bindende Kraft des Gewohnheitsrechts* (Tübingen, 1929), pp. 27, 30–31. See also Justinian's *Digest* I. 3. 32. 1, stating that laws shall be abrogated not only by the vote of the legislature, but also through disuse by the silent consent of all.

[19] See *John R. Thompson Co. v. District of Columbia*, 203 Fed. 2d 579 (C.A.D.C., 1953), where the court wished to recognize certain exceptions from the Anglo-American theory. The decision was reversed by the United States Supreme Court. Speaking for the court Mr. Justice Douglas said: "There remains for consideration . . . whether the Acts of 1872 and 1873 were abandoned or repealed as a result of nonuse and administrative practice. There was one view in the Court of Appeals that these laws are presently unenforceable for that reason. We do not agree. The failure of the executive branch to enforce a law does not result in its modification or repeal . . . The repeal of laws is as much a legislative function as their enactment." *District of Columbia v. John R. Thompson Co.*, 346 U.S. 100, at 113–114 (1953). See Note, "The Elimination of Obsolete Statutes," 43 *Harv. L. Rev.* 1302 (1930)

to the impropriety of reviving the disused law should be general, palpable, and strong.[20] Where a law has simply been in abeyance for a
substantial number of years, although the policy reasons for its existence remain unchanged, a re-enactment of the law by the legislature
should not be required; a reactivation of the measure by notice to the
public that enforcement will henceforth be resumed would appear to
be sufficient in this situation.[21]

[20] On the question of *desuetudo* see also *infra* Sec. 79.
[21] An example would be a city ordinance requiring the leashing of dogs which
the city officials have not enforced for many years.

XVII

LAW AND
SCIENTIFIC METHOD

Section 74. *The Formation of Concepts*

We have seen that it is one of the essential functions of the law to reduce the multitude, variety, and diversity of human actions and relations to a reasonable degree of order and to promulgate rules or standards of conduct applicable to certain circumscribed types of action or
behavior. In order to accomplish this task successfully, the legal order
must undertake the formation of technical notions and concepts designed to aid in classifying the multifarious phenomena and events of
social life. It thereby lays the basis for subjecting equal or essentially
similar phenomena to a unified and consistent regulation or treatment.
Legal concepts may thus be viewed as working tools used for the purpose of identifying, by a shorthand description, typical situations
which are characterized by identical or common elements. For instance, the often-recurring fact that one person out of anger, spite, or
revenge strikes another person or inflicts bodily harm on him is made
by the law the referent of the term "battery" and is subjected to
certain legal consequences. When one individual promises to another

an act in return for some commitment on the part of the other individual, this is designated legally by the term "contract" and is subjected to an extensive system of norms. If one man intentionally takes away personal property belonging to another, the law applies the concept of "larceny" and decrees punishment for the offender.

Inasmuch as the concepts of the law are products of human language rather than physical objects, the relation of these concepts to the referents which they purport to denote has always attracted the attention of writers. This relation formed the central subject, for instance, of the famous medieval dispute about universals.[1] According to the realist school of medieval thought, there is a parallelism between the general concepts formed by man and the classes of objects in the outer world to which they relate: every generic notion or idea formed by the minds of human beings was believed to have an exact counterpart outside the human mind, that is, in objective reality. The nominalists, on the other hand, argued that nature knows only individual things, and that the generalizations and classifications which are used in describing the world which surrounds us are merely names (*nomina*), convenient symbols of language which cannot be regarded as faithful copies of things existing in reality. The world of the human mind, in other words, must be clearly divorced from the world of objects. In the words of a modern British nominalist, the opposing school of thought has "tended to mistake the structure of discourse for the structure of the universe."[2]

This celebrated dispute, in the sharp and antithetical form which the contentions of the opponents assumed, substantially clarified the epistemological issues involved, but impeded the possibilities of reconciliation. It is undoubtedly true, as the nominalists asserted, that the term "mountain" is an abstraction, a symbol produced by the human mind to designate masses of rock or earth which rise conspicuously above the surface of the earth. In reality, every mountain looks different from every other mountain, and we have therefore with good reason fallen into the habit of identifying almost every individual mountain by a different name. On the other hand, we cannot ignore that there exist in nature large numbers of objects which possess common characteristics and exhibit striking similarities. Let us consider, for example, the term "mankind." This is an abstraction used by us to designate the totality of all human beings. There is, of course, no single physical ob-

---

[1] See *supra* Sec. 7

[2] Glanville Williams, "Language and the Law," 61 *Law Quarterly Review* 71, at 72 (1945). Williams gives a good description of the medieval universals controversy on pp. 81–82.

ject corresponding to the concept. Nevertheless, the term is not wholly linguistic, mental, or symbolic in character, since it refers to the undeniable fact that a determinate number of living beings exist on this earth who are identifiable by a number of common traits and can be distinguished from other living things.

It was the merit of medieval realism to recognize that nature, in a significant sense, operates through patterns and on a large scale produces classes of nearly identical or at least very similar objects. Philosophy cannot ignore this basic truth. Realism oversimplified the problem, on the other hand, by assuming that the uniformities and differences created by nature coincide completely with the generalizations and distinctions created by the human mind for the purpose of describing nature. The fact was overlooked that our language is not rich and subtle enough to reflect the infinite variety of natural phenomena, the combinations and mutations of elements, and the gradual transitions from one thing to another which are characteristic of objective reality as we apprehend it. In the words of Huntington Cairns, "there are more things in the world than there are words to describe them." [3] Although a sea in most instances can be easily differentiated from a lake, or a mountain from a hill, there occur borderline situations causing difficulty to linguistic classification; for instance, the propriety of calling the Black Sea a sea rather than a lake has sometimes been questioned by geographers. However thorough and discriminating our vocabulary may be, there will always exist in reality shadings and atypical instances which defy sharp and unambiguous linguistic classification. Although many concepts may be viewed as mental images of relations and uniformities existing in the natural world, such mental reproductions of reality are often imprecise, oversimplified, and incomplete.

These general considerations have a significant bearing on the utility of concepts in legal science. This bearing is a twofold one: it relates to the *need* for legal concepts as well as to the *limitations* to which their use is subject.

Concepts are necessary and indispensable instruments for the solution of legal problems. Without circumscribed technical notions, we could not think clearly and rationally about legal questions.[4] Without concepts, we could not put our thoughts on the law into words and

---

[3] "The Language of Jurisprudence," in *Language: An Enquiry into Its Meaning and Function*, ed. R. N. Anshen (New York, 1957), p. 243.

[4] Max Rheinstein, "Education for Legal Craftsmanship," 30 *Iowa Law Review* 408, at 415 (1945): "The advice to discard concepts in thinking is as meaningless as advice to make music without tones, to talk without sounds, or to see without images."

communicate them to others in an intelligible fashion. The entire edifice of the law would crumble if we tried to dispense entirely with concepts. Since it is one of the first purposes of the law to render human actions and behavior subject to certain normative standards,[5] and since normative standards cannot be established without classifying the types of conduct to which a particular standard shall apply, the close relation between law and concept becomes at once apparent. As was said above, concepts are tools for identifying and classifying the characteristic phenomena of social reality; in the words of Morris Cohen, they enable us "to arrange in order and hold together diverse phenomena because of some real unity of process or relation which constitutes an element of identity between them."[6] No recognizable patterns for judgment and action could be created by the legal system without the accomplishment of this preliminary task of categorization. Not even the faintest approximation to the ideal of legal certainty and predictability of decision could be achieved if we decided to abandon the use of conceptual generalizations in the administration of justice. A system of law resting on subjective reactions alone and repudiating the need for a rational apparatus of analysis would be an absurdity.[7]

It is in the nature of a concept, however, that while it may be clear and definite in its core, it tends to become blurred and indistinct as we move away from its center. Using a somewhat different metaphor, Wurzel likens a concept to a "photograph with vague and gradually vanishing outlines."[8] The relative extent of the focal region on the one hand and the penumbral zone on the other varies considerably with different concepts. As a general rule it might be stated that the more general and abstract a term is, the wider the penumbral zone around the core. However, as a decision of the United States Supreme Court shows, even a term like "candy," which at first sight appears to be quite concrete and definite, may become the source of interpretative difficulties in terms of core and penumbral meaning.[9]

[5] See *supra* Sec. 42.
[6] *A Preface to Logic* (New York, 1944), p. 70.
[7] See in this connection Alexander Pekelis, "The Case for a Jurisprudence of Welfare," 11 *Social Research* 312, at 332–333 (1944).
[8] K. G. Wurzel, "Methods of Juridical Thinking," in *Science of Legal Method* (Boston, 1917), p. 342.
[9] *McCaughn v. Hershey Chocolate Co.*, 283 U.S. 488 (1931). On the problem of the conceptual penumbra generally see Cohen, p. 67; Arthur Nussbaum, *Principles of Private International Law* (New York, 1943), p. 188; Williams, 61 *L. Q. Rev.* 179, at 191 (1945), and *id.*, 293, at 302; H. L. A. Hart, "Positivism and the Separation of Law and Morals," 71 *Harvard Law Review* 593, at 607 ff. (1958). Fuller, in his reply to Professor Hart's article, questions the usefulness of the "core-penumbra" dichotomy on the ground that problems of interpretation do not usually turn on the meaning of individual words. Lon L. Fuller, "Positivism and Fidelity to Law," 71 *Harv. L. Rev.* 630, at 662–663 (1958). This may be true in

When legal concepts are formed and defined, the most typical cases exemplifying the particular concept are usually taken into account, while the boundary cases are not clearly envisioned. The legal concept of domicile, for example, purports to apply to situations where a person is permanently or for a definite time settled at a particular place. But cases may arise where the home of a person is of less permanent character, where good reasons may exist for recognizing it nevertheless as the person's domicile. It is clear that throwing an object upon another's premises falls within the purview of the legal term "trespass." It may be a matter for legitimate doubt, on the other hand, whether the precipitation of artificial rain upon a piece of land against the owner's will is a trespass or whether this act should be subsumed under a different head of Anglo-American tort liability, such as the concept of nuisance. The line to be drawn between a servant and an independent contractor rests on the infinitely variable matter of control, and the line therefore often becomes unsharp and hazy. In all areas of the law we find the hard borderline case, the peripheral situation where the extent of the bounds of a technical concept is problematic, or where two or more different concepts shading into one another may be equally applicable to the facts from a purely logical point of view. Although, as Nussbaum points out, uncertainty of decision within the penumbral region is often diminished by patterns of inherited legal attitudes and techniques,[10] the problems posed by the fringe meaning of concepts are nevertheless frequent and serious.

An important attempt to undertake a systematic and logical classification and arrangement of some fundamental concepts in legal science was undertaken by the American jurist Wesley N. Hohfeld.[11] His aim was to analyze what he called "the lowest common denominators of the law," including concepts such as legal relation, right, duty, power, privilege, liability, and immunity, as well as to expound the logical relations between these notions.[12] Some of Hohfeld's determinations of fundamental concepts became incorporated into the American Restatement of Property.[13] However, Hohfeld's hope that his conceptions might produce a uniform terminology applicable to the most divergent branches of the law [14] fell short of realization. American

---

many instances, but legal problems may arise in which the proper solution hinges primarily on the interpretation of one particular term or concept.

[10] Nussbaum, p. 188.

[11] Hohfeld was a professor of law at Yale University who died in 1917 at the premature age of 38.

[12] See Hohfeld, *Fundamental Legal Conceptions* (New Haven, 1923); Arthur H. Corbin, "Legal Analysis and Terminology," 29 *Yale Law Journal* 163 (1919).

[13] Secs. 1–4.

[14] See Hohfeld, p. 64.

courts failed to adopt the classifications which he had propounded and continued to use concepts of right, duty, privilege, and immunity in nonuniform and inconsistent senses.[15] Hohfeld's scheme of concepts must therefore be described as one which to this day has remained in the realm of an unrealized attempt at terminological reform.[16]

It is, of course, theoretically possible to make concrete and clarify legal concepts by elaborate definitions framed by the legislatures, the judiciary, or the community of legal scholars. It was the ideal of a movement in jurisprudence known as the jurisprudence of conceptions to create—mainly through the dogmatic labors of legal scholars—a comprehensive system of legal concepts reified into absolute entities and serving as solid, unvarying pillars for deductive reasoning in a rigid normative structure. This movement was quite influential in continental Europe around the turn of this century, especially in Germany. The most absolutist representatives of the conceptualist school went so far as to assert that the legal concepts were given to the human mind a priori and that they existed in a subconscious form before the legal order was called into being. In other words it was not the legal order which created concepts useful for its purposes, but it was the concepts which created the legal order and engendered the rules of the law.[17] An example of the conversion of a legal concept into a taut normative strait jacket was reported by Max Rümelin.[18] In a well-known German textbook on the law of contracts, the author drew a distinction between sales in which delivery of the goods coincides with the making of the contract (sale over the counter) and sales in which the contract consists of an exchange of promises to deliver and pay. From this classification the author dogmatically drew the conclusion that in a sale over the counter the seller of stolen goods cannot be liable for damages

---

[15] Examples are given by Edgar Bodenheimer, "Modern Analytical Jurisprudence and the Limits of Its Usefulness," 104 *University of Pennsylvania Law Review* 1080, at 1082 (1956). See also W. W. Cook, "The Utility of Jurisprudence in the Solution of Legal Problems," in *Lectures on Legal Topics* (New York, 1928), V, 338.

[16] For a criticism of the Hohfeldian concepts see Roscoe Pound, "Fifty Years of Jurisprudence," 50 *Harv. L. Rev.* 557, at 573-576 (1937); Albert Kocourek, "The Hohfeld System of Fundamental Legal Conceptions," 15 *Illinois Law Review* 24 (1920); cf. also Julius Stone, *The Province and Function of Law* (Cambridge, Mass., 1961), pp. 115-134.

[17] See Philipp Heck, "The Jurisprudence of Interests: An Outline," in *The Jurisprudence of Interests*, ed. M. Schoch (Cambridge, Mass., 1948), pp. 34, 156. Rümelin, quoting Stammler, says that conceptual jurisprudence "treated concepts which are nothing but reproductions of historically given material, as pure concepts such as the concepts of mathematics." Max Rümelin, "Developments in Legal Theory and Teaching," *id.*, p. 9.

[18] *Id.*, p. 13. Other examples of conceptual jurisprudence are found in Pound, *Interpretations of Legal History* (Cambridge, Mass., 1930), pp. 120-124.

to the buyer for inability to transfer title, since he did not enter into an obligation to deliver the goods.

In our own day, conceptual jurisprudence—at least in its more doctrinaire manifestations—does not enjoy much favor. A large number of judges and jurists would today endorse Mr. Justice Cardozo's observation that the tyranny of concepts is "a fruitful parent of injustice." Concepts are tyrants rather than servants, he said, "when treated as real existences and developed with merciless disregard of consequences to the limit of their logic. For the most part we should deal with them as provisional hypotheses to be reformulated and restrained when they have an outcome in oppression or injustice." [19] But he also recognized that "concepts are useful, indeed indispensable, if kept within their place . . . [They] are values deeply imbedded in our law and its philosophy." [20] If we realize that concepts are valuable instruments of judicial reasoning in whose absence judicial activity could not be accurately executed, and if we avoid at the same time the error of ascribing to them an absolute, eternal reality unrelated to any social purpose they might be designed to serve, we shall have gained the proper perspective in our effort to appraise the utility of conceptual tools in the administration of justice.[21]

Section 75. *Law and Logical Method*
The role that should properly be assigned to logic in the solution of legal controversies has in recent times been the subject of a vigorous and lively debate in this country and others. On one side of the controversy the assertion is made that law is eminently a logical science, that aptitude in rigid logical thinking is the most essential prerequisite of competence for a good lawyer or judge, and that the reasoning processes of the law are characterized by a precision and inexorable cogency of argumentation which find their closest parallel in the deductions of the mathematician. On the other side of the debate, the position is often taken that the method of logic plays a secondary and subordinate part in the administration of the law, that law is concerned with the making of just and socially desirable decisions rather than with an exercise of logical acumen, and that the proficient lawyer or judge should attempt to emulate the skills of the statesman or administrator rather than those of the logician or mathematician.

[19] Benjamin N. Cardozo, *The Paradoxes of Legal Science* (New York, 1928), p. 61; *Selected Writings,* ed. M. E. Hall (New York, 1947), p. 287. See also Pound, "Mechanical Jurisprudence," 8 *Columbia Law Review* 605 (1908).

[20] Cardozo, *Paradoxes,* p. 62.

[21] Cf. Josef Esser, *Grundsatz und Norm* (Tübingen, 1956), pp. 6–7, 324; George W. Paton, *A Textbook of Jurisprudence,* 2d ed. (Oxford, 1951), p. 178.

No informed judgment on the merits of this controversy can be made without a realization that the very subject matter and scope of the science of logic is a highly disputed question.[1] The most widely current view holds that logic is the science of the necessary laws of thought, something that might perhaps be described as an algebra of the relations that exist between statements and propositions. The chief purpose of logic, according to this view, is to teach us how to distinguish valid from invalid inferences, proper from improper conclusions. This conception of the subject implies that logic is a purely formal science: it is not concerned with the substantive truth of our assumptions and conclusions, but merely with the task of drawing unimpeachable inferences from given premises, that is, premises which are not in themselves questioned for their correctness. In the words of Eaton, logic is "the science that exhibits all the relationships permitting valid inferences that hold between various propositions *considered merely with respect to their form.*" [2]

The chief conceptual tool which formal logic uses in elucidating the proper relations between premises and conclusions is the syllogism. Aristotle, the progenitor of the science of formal logic, defines the syllogism as "discourse in which, certain things being stated, something other than what is stated follows of necessity from their being so." [3] The following would be an example of a simple Aristotelian syllogism:

> All organisms are mortal.
> Man is an organism.
> Man is mortal.

In this syllogism, the first line represents the *major premise*, the second line the *minor premise*, and the third line the *conclusion*. The predicate of the conclusion ("mortal") is referred to as the *major term*, the subject of the conclusion ("man") is called the *minor term*, and "organism" (the word which appears in both premises but not in the conclusion) is designated as the *middle term*. This example of a syllogism is unassailable from the point of view of formal logic, even though the material correctness of the major premise depends upon the breadth of meaning of the term "organism," and the equation of the term with

---

[1] See Edwin W. Patterson, "Logic in the Law," 90 *U. Pa. L. Rev.* 875, at 876 (1942).

[2] R. M. Eaton, *General Logic* (New York, 1931), p. 8 (italics mine). An attempt to develop a juristic logic resting on the foundations of modern symbolic logic—considered by its protagonists as a refined and improved form of classical formal logic—was made by Ulrich Klug, *Juristische Logik*, 2d ed. (Berlin, 1958).

[3] "Analytica Priora," in *The Basic Works of Aristotle*, ed. R. McKeon (New York, 1941), p. 66.

"living organism" might be the subject of legitimate scientific doubt and controversy.[4]

A second and broader conception of the subject matter of logic has been developed by a number of modern philosophers, particularly by John Dewey.[5] According to Dewey, logic is not solely or even primarily concerned with relations between propositions and the laws governing valid inferences. It is a method of inquiry that can be of help to human beings in arriving at sound, reasonable solutions of problems. Logic is "concerned with control of inquiry so that it may yield warranted assertions." [6] It is a discipline which enables us to subject problematic situations to an incisive analysis designed to expose and bring into focus all relevant aspects of a problem and thereby to facilitate the finding of a pragmatically satisfying solution. As Patterson has pointed out, an instrumental logic of this kind will necessarily embrace subject matter which formal logicians would wish to assign to the domain of other sciences, such as psychology or sociology.[7] Furthermore, since the methods of inquiry which will provide guidance for the attainment of satisfactory results may be different for the various branches of the natural and social sciences, the methodology and ratiocination processes of instrumental logic may take on a different color depending on the particular discipline to which they are applied.

What significance do these conflicting views regarding the subject matter of logic have for the theory and methodology of the law? Generally speaking, syllogistic reasoning in law is a type of reasoning in which a certain factual situation or occurrence is subsumed under a general rule or principle of law, and a conclusion is then derived concerning the applicability or nonapplicability of the rule to the facts of the case. We must ask ourselves to what extent and within what limits this type of logic can serve as a useful tool for the solution of legal problems. We might choose as a starting point for this discussion a simple syllogism which, according to some writers, represents a typical instance of a mental operation involving legal reasoning:

A person who appropriates a movable thing belonging to another is
    guilty of larceny.
A has appropriated a movable thing belonging to another.
Therefore A is guilty of larceny.

    [4] On the syllogism in general see H. W. B. Joseph, *An Introduction to Logic,* 2d ed. (Oxford, 1916), pp. 249–334; Paul E. Treusch, "The Syllogism," in Jerome Hall, ed., *Readings in Jurisprudence* (Indianapolis, 1938), pp. 539–560.
    [5] See his *Logic: The Theory of Inquiry* (New York, 1938).
    [6] *Id.,* p. 4. On Dewey's conception of logic see also Jerome Frank, "Modern and Ancient Legal Pragmatism," 25 *Notre Dame Lawyer* 460, at 463 ff. (1950).
    [7] Patterson, p. 890.

The formal validity of this syllogism is beyond question. It is clear, however, that this statement of a major and minor premise, followed by a logically ineluctable conclusion, leaves unanswered the question of whether the judge responsible for the construction of this syllogism in fact has reached a correct decision in the case before him. Suppose, for instance, that the object appropriated by A was electrical current produced by a power station. Is it proper to hold that electrical energy falls within the meaning of the term "thing" as used in the major premise of our syllogism? Or let us assume that A, under the actual facts of the case, took an automobile from B solely for the purpose of stealing a ride to the next town and abandoned the vehicle after having accomplished his purpose. Assuming that no special statute governing this case is in existence, does this act come within the purview of the term "appropriate," which appears in the major premise of our syllogism, or was this term meant to exclude instances of a merely temporary use of an object? Certainly, the syllogism itself throws no light on whether the judge gave the proper and intended meaning to the technical terms used in the syllogistic statement. Whenever such terms are ambiguous, equivocal, or susceptible of being broadly or narrowly interpreted, the logical compulsion of the syllogism is seriously impaired. As long as formal logic gives to the judge any degree of discretion in the application of a normative prescription, it cannot guarantee logical infallibility in the reaching of a conclusion. Aristotle himself was aware of this difficulty, for the syllogism as he conceived it required the use of terms which he called univocal, that is, words which retain the same meaning each time they are used.[8]

Even assuming that the meanings of the terms "thing" and "appropriate" were univocal (perhaps because they had been defined in another section of the statute in a manner leaving no doubt as to their applicability to the facts of the case), the soundness of our syllogism is not as yet proven. The syllogistic conclusion drawn by the judge is correct only if A actually committed the act for which he was held responsible under the criminal statute. In other words, unless the minor premise in our syllogism represented a true finding of the facts by the judge, his conclusion was substantively erroneous.

Syllogistic reasoning guarantees an adequate result impervious to challenge only in instances where the meaning of the legal norm embodied in the major premise is clear in relation to the facts of the case, where the minor premise represents a true determination of the facts by the judge, and where no considerations not reflected in the syllogistic propositions (such as a defense available against the application

[8] See editor's Introduction, *Basic Works of Aristotle*, p. xvi.

of the legal norm) are pertinent to the disposition of the matter. Thus, in the example chosen above, if A stole a car from B for the purpose of keeping it indefinitely, and a confession of his act was supported by uncontested testimony by various other persons, the judge's conclusion that A committed a larceny would appear to be correct and unassailable.

In the above example, a major premise was readily available to the judge in the form of a precept of the criminal law. We found that even in this situation the process of reaching a legally correct result by employing the technique of syllogistic deduction was beset with pitfalls and difficulties. These difficulties become substantially increased when a case arises in which no major premise for the decision is readily available to the judge, or where he faces a choice between several norms under which the facts of the case may be subsumed.

The first situation arises frequently and easily under a system such as the Anglo-American common-law system, which develops on a case-to-case basis rather than upon the foundation of codes or statutes. Under such a system, as Edward H. Levi says, concepts are often created "out of particular instances," and the direction of the system "appears to be from particular to general." [9] Reasoning proceeds "by example" rather than by the application of authoritatively formulated rules of law.[10]

Under the common-law system, the judge called upon to decide a litigated case will set out to find and examine precedents which bear a close or reasonably close similarity to the facts of the case before him. If the facts of the two cases are in all essential respects identical, he may simply declare that a certain precedent controls the disposition of the case at bar. But in a large number of instances, the precedent is similar to the case at bar in some important respects, but dissimilar in others. The judge will be unable to determine the applicability or non-applicability of the earlier case without first identifying the general principle or rationale underlying the first case and then proceeding to decide whether this principle or rationale furnishes a suitable ground for supporting a judgment in the new case. Quite often the discovery of the underlying principle is more than a simple inductive operation because the principle has remained unarticulated in the earlier decision and the judge is in doubt which one of several possible grounds actually induced the decision.[11] Thus, when the Court of Appeals of New York

[9] Levi, *An Introduction to Legal Reasoning* (Chicago, 1949), p. 19. See also A. G. Guest, "Logic in the Law," in *Oxford Essays in Jurisprudence*, ed. A. G. Guest (Oxford, 1960), p. 176.

[10] Levi, p. 1.

[11] On the question of determining the *ratio decidendi* of a case see *infra* Sec. 81.

decided that the distributor of a poisonous substance which had been mislabeled as a harmless medicine was liable to a remote purchaser, the court in later years was unsure and split on the question whether the underlying principle of liability was limited to "inherently dangerous substances" such as poisons and explosives, or whether it was broad enough to cover all articles likely to cause danger if defectively and negligently made.[12] All the court can do in such a situation is to reconstruct the controlling principle upon considerations of reason, justice, and sound social policy. Once the court has settled the question in an authoritative decision, the principle can, of course, be applied henceforth by a process of deductive logic to all cases clearly falling within its scope.

Situations may also arise in which, without the violation of any laws of formal logic, the facts of the case can be subsumed by the judge under two contradictory principles of law. Take the case cited before, for instance, where a person to whom a bequest was made in a will subsequently murders his testator in order to obtain possession of the property. Should he be permitted to take under the will? The principle of law that would perhaps be invoked by the legatee is the principle of the binding force of a property disposition made in a legally valid will; it could be argued that the binding force of the disposition remains unaffected by any subsequent events, especially if the legatee seems entitled to the property under the terms of a statute. On the other hand, recovery by the legatee might be held to be defeated by the equitable principle that a person should not be permitted to derive a benefit from his own wrong, especially if this wrong was committed intentionally. Which of these conflicting principles would prevail in the disposition of the case? Although the courts have differed on the question,[13] the better and probably more widely held view supports the conclusion that the equitable principle should override a statute or judicial rule commanding strict enforcement of the terms of a will. The paramount major premise determining the solution of the problem would seem to be the recognition that the protection of life is superior in social importance to a protection of a property disposition, and that the value of life might be judicially imperiled if the property benefits derived from murdering one's testator received full legal sanction. Once such an overriding major premise (which may be a nonformal rather than a formal source of the law) has been established, the last step in the process of judging would again be the syllogistic

---

[12] See Levi, pp. 10–18.

[13] For one view, see *Riggs v. Palmer*, 22 N.E. 188 (N.Y., 1889); for the other, see *McAllister v. Fair*, 84 Pac. 112 (Kan., 1906).

application of this major premise to the facts of the case. Compared with the importance of discerning the correct norm applicable to the situation, and of making the appropriate findings of fact, this last step would appear to be a secondary one in the chain of mental operations leading to the final decision.

These considerations demonstrate the relatively limited role which formal syllogistic logic plays in the solution of legal problems. It might be said that the less articulate, precise, and narrowly drawn the norms of the law are, the less use can be made of the syllogistic method. In other words, the usefulness of logic as a legal tool is dependent upon the clarity, definiteness, and fixity of the legal norms. But even where a deliberate attempt is made to maximize the scope of deductive reasoning in judicial administration through the adoption of an inclusive code regulating innumerable detailed situations, the area of vacant spots and ambiguities in the positive legal system will still be comprehensive enough to place a limiting barrier on the operative scope of syllogistic logic. We do no longer believe in the possibility of a jurisprudence of conceptions designed to set up a system of tightly and uniformly defined legal concepts capable of furnishing infallible and mechanically operating yardsticks for the decision of any and all cases coming before the courts. "The law . . . never succeeds in becoming a completely deductive system." [14]

Recognition that syllogistic logic plays a relatively subordinate role in the adjudicatory process should not mislead us into attributing an exaggerated weight to what Alf Ross calls the "emotive-volitive" activity of the judicial decision-maker.[15] As Dennis Lloyd has aptly pointed out, a choice made by the judge "is not *logical* in the sense of being deductively inferred from given premises, but it has a kind of logic of its own, being based on rational considerations which differentiate it sharply from mere arbitrary assertion." [16] Legal rulings are usually regarded as right if they are based upon "cumulative reasons which are found to be acceptable." [17] A competent judge, in most instances and wherever possible, will use criteria which are not the product of his uncontrolled will or subjective predilections, but have their basis in the legal order as a whole and in the source materials which tra-

[14] Morris R. Cohen, "The Place of Logic in the Law," in *Law and the Social Order* (New York, 1933), p. 167; see also Frede Castberg, *Problems of Legal Philosophy* (Oslo, 1957), pp. 52–88, and *supra* Sec. 74.

According to the Swiss jurist Eugen Huber, the chief value of the use of legal logic lies in freeing the judge from subjective, irrational psychological influences. Huber, *Recht und Rechtsverwirklichung*, 2d ed. (Basel, 1925), pp. 56–57.

[15] *On Law and Justice* (Berkeley, 1959), p. 140.

[16] *Introduction to Jurisprudence* (London, 1959), p. 399.

[17] *Ibid.*

dition, usage, and the positive law have handed down to the judge to enable him to cement a rational foundation for his judgments. In the absence of a more definite direction, it may be a firmly established value norm of his culture, a general principle pervading the legal system, the obvious necessities of the situation, or persuasive considerations of justice and equity which will supply to him the reason for his judgment.[18] He will not always be able to exclude completely his own emotional reactions from entering into his decision, but every worthwhile legal system will attempt to reduce this nonrational element to a minimum.

When we turn to the second and broader conception of logic discussed above and attempt to analyze the role of logical method in the law in the light of John Dewey's instrumental logic rather than in terms of Aristotle's formal science of logic, we approach the problem from an entirely different perspective. Dewey expressed the hope that application of his method of logical inquiry to the problems of the law might be of service to us in "reaching intelligent decisions in concrete situations" and in "adjusting disputed issues in behalf of the public and enduring interest." [19] His approach then entails the use of a teleological logic, that is, a logic making the choice of a proper principle of decision dependent on the consequences which the decision would bring about, whereas the classical logic of the syllogism operates with fixed, antecedent principles "anterior to and independent of concrete subject matters." [20] As Dewey pointed out, in employing instrumental logic to dispose of a legal controversy, "We generally begin with some vague anticipation of a conclusion (or at least of alternative conclusions), and then we look around for principles and data which will substantiate it or which will enable us to choose intelligently between rival conclusions." [21] In this conception of logical method, logical thinking becomes so deeply intertwined and fused with problems of evaluation and policy selection that the appraisal of this method falls properly within the subject matter of other sections of our discussion.[22]

[18] See also Lon L. Fuller, "Reason and Fiat in Case Law," 59 *Harv. L. Rev.* 376, at 379 (1946): "There are external criteria, found in the conditions required for successful group living, that furnish some standard against which the rightness of his [the judge's] decisions should be measured." Further observations on this problem will be found *infra* Sec. 82.

[19] "Logical Method and Law," in *Philosophy and Civilization* (New York, 1931), p. 132.

[20] *Ibid.*

[21] *Id.*, p. 134. See also p. 138, where Dewey states that legal logic must be "a logic relative to consequences rather than to antecedents."

[22] See *infra* Secs. 76, 80–82. There would seem to be considerable merit in the suggestion made by Klug, p. 2, that the term logic, in order to keep it within manageable bounds, should be restricted to formal logic.

Section 76. *The Role of Value Judgments in the Law*
Values are essential ingredients of the mental activity of human beings and might properly be described as facts of mental life. Throughout our lives, we are constantly engaged in evaluating ourselves, other
human beings and their actions, the merits and effectiveness of institutions, the course of past and present events. The passing of judgments
as to whether a person is right or wrong, whether an action is good or
bad, whether an institution is useful or useless, occupies such a pervasive role in human existence that the proclivity to evaluate may be
said to be one of the most characteristic traits of human beings beyond
the purely mechanistic functions of their nature.

In the area of law, the role of valuation is particularly conspicuous.
The institution of law is devoted to the accomplishment of certain social ends. Determining whether the values to be served by the legal
order are actually realized by its institutions involves a constant evaluation and reappraisal of the normative structure, machinery, and effectiveness of the law. "Every idea of ought-to-be, of normativity, is based
on a judgment, that is, on an appreciation of values." [1] Specific legal
norms are similarly directed to the attainment of certain goals. Thus,
the First Amendment to the United States Constitution is designed to
promote freedom as a value; the legal rules against trespassing are designed to safeguard the security of property; the provisions of the
United Nations Charter are intended to serve the cause of peace. When
we ask ourselves whether these normative prescriptions are adequate to
the task which they purport to accomplish, or whether they should be
replaced by other and better prescriptions, we are appraising the efficacy of the means chosen by the legal order to realize certain social
ends. The ends or goals themselves, however, are also an object of our
evaluative activities. Should all possible individual freedom be made the
highest goal of the legal order? Or should security against the hazards
and risks of life constitute the principal aim of legal institutions? Or is
the creation and maintenance of a rich and abundant civilization the
supreme objective of social control through law? Wherever we are
concerned with the deliberate direction of human conduct, personal or
collective, we are "influenced, if not controlled, by estimates of value
or worth of ends to be attained." [2]

[1] Luis Recaséns Siches, "Human Life, Society, and Law" in *Latin-American
Legal Philosophy* (Cambridge, Mass., 1948), p. 22.
[2] John Dewey, "Theory of Valuation," *International Encyclopedia of Unified
Science*, vol. II, no. 4 (Chicago, 1939), p. 2. See also Bronislaw Malinowski,
Freedom and Civilization (Bloomington, Ind., 1960), p. 137: "Value is the prime
mover in human existence."

The interrelation between the philosophy of values and the science of jurisprudence, and the question of whether the expression of value judgments regarding the ultimate aims of legal control is within the proper scope of scientific inquiry, have already been discussed.[3] Our objectives here are more narrowly circumscribed. Inasmuch as we are presently concerned with an exposition of the techniques and methodology employed by the legal order in the adjudication of controversies, our investigation must be confined to an examination of the general role which evaluation plays in the judicial administration of the law.

It will be of considerable help in discussing the role of evaluation in the judicial process if we recognize a basic distinction between judicial *discernment* of value patterns and judicial *imposition* (or creation) of value judgments. A case discussed by John Dickinson may serve as an illustrative example of judicial discernment.[4] A married women's property act provides that a married woman shall have the right to own, acquire, and enjoy separate property as if she were unmarried; and further, that she shall have the right to contract for such separate property. Let us suppose that under such a statute the question arises of whether a married woman having no separate property and contracting to purchase such property can be held on her contract. From the point of view of formal logic, it could be argued that, since a married woman can contract only for her separate property, she must already own such property at the time of the contract, and that therefore a contract for the acquisition of property is not binding if she owned no other property when the contract was made. On the other hand, it would be equally logical to assert that, by the statute, a married woman is given power to acquire property, that a contract of purchase was an appropriate means of exercising this power, and that therefore the statute when limiting the married woman's contractual capacity to contracts made for her separate property includes the case of property acquired by the contract itself. As Dickinson points out, a decision of the question one way or the other depends upon whether the court thinks that the statute should be given a broad or narrow construction; this in turn depends upon whether or not the court regards the contractual capacity of a married woman as something that should be extended to the utmost bounds permitted by the statute, or as something which should be limited to the narrowest possible range. Let us assume that the court, in the absence of any guidance furnished by the legislative history of the statute or by prior decisions, decides in

---

[3] See *supra* Sec. 38.
[4] Dickinson, "The Problem of the Unprovided Case," *Recueil d'études sur les sources du droit en l'honneur de F. Gény* (Paris, 1935), II, 512 ff.

favor of a liberal interpretation of the act. It rests this decision primarily on the consideration that the entire trend of legislative and social development in the last few decades has favored the emancipation of women from the legal restrictions which the earlier common law placed upon them, citing numerous statutory provisions, judicial decisions, and sociological data in support of the trend. If the court adopts this line of reasoning,[5] it does in fact discern and detect a value judgment disfavoring inequality of the sexes and frowning upon the maintenance of ancient contractual disabilities of women in the structure of the legal and social order; the court does not by its own action or on its own initiative impose or create such a value judgment.

It may be maintained with good reason that a discovery by a court of a social valuation supporting a decision not clearly derivable from a positive source of the law is in fact a logical process within a broader meaning of logical theory.[6] It is a type of logic which reconstructs the basic valuations implicit in the nature of social institutions or consistent with the spirit of an aggregate of norms, and utilizes such basic valuations in the solution of legal controversies. This logic carries the logic of the syllogism to a higher and more complex form, often necessitating the construction of a scale of major premises culminating in certain ultimate value premises of the particular social order or of social order in general. When Holmes framed his famous apothegm, "The life of the law has not been logic, it has been experience," [7] he had in mind the formal logic of the syllogism, operating by way of deduction from the formalized norms of the positive legal system. When he added the words "the felt necessities of the time, the prevalent moral and political theories, intuitions of public policy, avowed or unconscious, even the prejudices which judges share with their fellow men have had a good deal more to do than the syllogism in determining the rules by which men should be governed," he failed perhaps to observe that a mode of judicial operation which takes account of social traditions, views of public policy, and articulated or subconscious collective value preferences [8] does not necessarily discard logic as an instrument of decision.

The discernment of basic valuations furnishing a standard of adjudication is a process of discovery only in situations where the pertinent social value patterns are clear. Where sharp disagreement or uncertainty exists in a social order with respect to these patterns, this

---

[5] The case of *King v. City of Owensboro*, 218 S.W. 297 (Ky., 1920) is indicative of this type of "trend" reasoning. See also *supra* Sec. 72.

[6] See *supra* Sec. 75.

[7] Oliver W. Holmes, *The Common Law* (Boston, 1923), p. 1.

[8] See *id.*, pp. 35–36.

process inevitably transcends discovery and becomes a matter of choice between conflicting standards of value. Thus in the case of *Dennis v. U.S.*,[9] the United States Supreme Court, in upholding the Smith Act of 1940 outlawing the advocacy of revolutionary overthrow of the government, gave preference to the value of national security over the value of freedom of speech and expression. It would be difficult to maintain that, in reaching this result, the court simply gave effect to an unequivocally fundamental idea embodied in our constitutional structure. In fact, the principle of free speech, which had to yield priority in this case, is specifically recognized by the terms of the First Amendment to the Constitution, whereas the notion of national security, which in the opinion of the court overrode the First Amendment freedoms in the context of this case, is not mentioned in the operative clauses of the Constitution and must be derived from nonpositive constitutional sources, that is, the inherent right of self-defense of governments against revolutionary action aimed at their overthrow. The point might possibly be raised that the court, in seeking to guard the government against communist subversion, was at the same time protecting the institution of free speech, inasmuch as this institution would seriously suffer and perhaps die in the case of a communist revolution, and that the court therefore was acting in consonance with the inherent "logic" of our political and constitutional ideals, aiming at the preservation of a free society. However, the logical conclusions arrived at by this mode of ratiocination become so involved and so much exposed to counter-arguments that it might be preferable to concede that the court in this case made a deliberate choice between two conflicting constitutional value standards.

It may also happen that a legal principle firmly embedded in the fabric of the law is held by a court to be incompatible with a major postulate of sound economic policy as conceived by the court. This was apparently the situation in the English case of *Priestly v. Fowler*,[10] even though the court was careful not to spell out the basic policy consideration ultimately responsible for the outcome. In this case, the Court of Exchequer held that an employee cannot recover from his employer for injuries received by him in the course of his employment through the negligence of a fellow employee. At the time of this decision, the principle of *respondeat superior*, rendering a principal liable for torts committed by his agent or servant in the course of employment, was firmly recognized in English law. Logically, this principle is obviously capable of being applied to the facts of the case. The court

[9] 341 U.S. 494 (1951).
[10] 150 Eng. Rep. 1030 (1837).

felt, however, that extension of the principle to a situation where the wrongdoer and the injured person were engaged in common employment in the same enterprise was undesirable, since it might entail heavy financial burdens for the employer. The controlling rationale of the decision must probably be found in the consideration that the imposition upon an employer of comprehensive liability for tortious acts of employees might discourage industrial activity, which at the time of the decision was in an early and vigorous stage of development. The court felt that it was economically and socially desirable to make the burden on the budding commercial and industrial establishments of England as light as possible. On the other hand, the decision made a deep incision into the well-established rules of vicarious liability and ignored the hardships which this exception created for employees injured in the course of their work. Even under the conditions of a laissez-faire philosophy of the economic life, the choice which the court made was hardly thrust upon it by the prevailing social conceptions. The case therefore might be cited as an instance where the court imposed a principle of policy which could not necessarily be derived from the existing structure or spirit of the legal system.

Section 77. *The Aims of Legal Education*

The functions which the law performs for society must necessarily control the ways and means by which lawyers are trained for their chosen vocation. If the chief purpose of the legal system is to ensure and preserve the health of the social body so that people may lead worthwhile and productive lives, then the lawyer must be viewed as a "social physician" [1] whose services should contribute toward the achievement of the law's ultimate goal. That the lawyer engaged in an activity of a legislative character (either as a legislator or as an adviser to lawmakers) is or should be devoting his energies to the promotion of the social good goes without saying. But the existence of unresolved controversies between individuals or groups must also be regarded as a problem of social health, since the perpetuation of unnecessary and wasteful animosities and frictions is not conducive to harmonious and productive living in a community. It may be said, therefore, that judges and lawyers who by their joint efforts bring about a fair and reasonable adjustment of a controversy are performing the task of social physicians. If the dispute were not solved at all, a festering wound on the social body would be created; if it were solved in an inadequate and unjust manner, a scar would be left on this body, and a multiplication

[1] This term was used by Abraham Flexner in his book *A Modern College and a Modern School* (Garden City, 1923), p. 21.

of such scars might seriously endanger the preservation of a satisfactory order of society.

One must fully agree with the conclusions reached by Professor Ralph Fuchs to the effect that "today's major need in training lawyers lies in the development of understanding of the institutions and problems of contemporary society, of the lawyer's part in their operation, and of the techniques required for professional participation in solving the major problems with which lawyers deal." [2] Some of the educational tasks which must be taken on in connection with this training must, of course, be delegated to the nonlegal part of the lawyer's academic career. Without a thorough acquaintance with his country's history, the student of the law will be unable to understand the evolution of its legal system and the dependence of its legal institutions on the surrounding historical conditions. Without some knowledge of world history and the cultural contributions of civilizations, he will be at a disadvantage in comprehending major international events that may exert an influence on the law. Without some proficiency in general political theory and insight into the structure and operation of governments he will be handicapped in apprehending and approaching problems of constitutional and public law. If he lacks training in economics, he will fail to see the close relations between legal and economic questions which exist in many areas of the law. Without grounding in philosophy, he will find it hard to deal with the general problems of jurisprudence and legal theory which are apt to exercise a decisive influence on judicial and other legal processes.

But even during the more strictly specialized phase of the lawyer's education for professional competence, the student must always be reminded that the law is a part of the total life of a society, and that it never exists in a vacuum. It is not a self-sufficient compartment of social science that can be sealed off or divorced from other branches of human endeavor. Many decisions of courts cannot be understood and properly analyzed unless the teacher makes clear the political and social setting in which they were rendered. Many of the older statutes or rules of law may seem strange or even absurd unless we realize that the ideals of justice prevailing at the time of their origin were different from our own.

If this is true, a man cannot be a first-class lawyer if he is merely a legal technician, knowing the machinery of trial procedure and thoroughly versed in the technical rules of the positive law. Justice Brandeis once said: "A lawyer who has not studied economics and sociology

---

[2] "Legal Education and the Public Interest," 1 *Journal of Legal Education* 155, at 162 (1948).

is very apt to become a public enemy." [3] And David Paul Brown, a Philadelphia attorney who lived in the early nineteenth century, is reported to have observed: "The mere lawyer is a mere blockhead."

A lawyer who wishes to predict the behavior of judges and other public officials correctly must be able to discern current trends and to see the direction in which his society is moving. The positive rules of the law may always be looked up in textbooks, digests, or encyclopedias if they pass out of the lawyer's memory. But a knowledge of the political, social, economic, and moral forces which are operative in the legal order and determine its course cannot be easily acquired and must be slowly gained by a prolonged and acute observation of social reality. A lawyer, in order to be a truly useful public servant, must be a person of culture and breadth of understanding.

The institutions of legal learning, in addition to giving their students a thorough grounding in the positive precepts and procedures of the law, must teach men to think like lawyers and to master the complex art of legal argumentation and reasoning.[4] But legal education ought to go beyond these immediate objectives and open up to the students the broadest horizons which can be reached in an encompassing view of the profession. These horizons include the place of the law in a general philosophy of life and society, its ethical aims and their limitations, and the nature and range of the benefits which a society can expect from a legal system impregnated with the spirit of justice. Abraham Flexner once raised the question: "Is it not possible that tensions would be reduced and social evolution achieved with less friction, if our lawyers and judges were not only learned in precedents, but were thoroughly versed in history, ethics, economics, and political science?" [5] The esteem and prestige which a legal system commands in the eyes of general opinion depends to a large extent on the breadth of the perspectives of its functionaries and the character and strength of their sense of responsibility toward the society they serve.

This brief discussion of the aims of legal education may be properly concluded with a quotation from a famous article by Justice Holmes:

Happiness, I am sure from having known many successful men, cannot be won simply by being counsel for great corporations and having an income of fifty thousand dollars. An intellect great enough to win the prize needs

[3] Quoted by Arthur L. Goodhart, *Five Jewish Lawyers of the Common Law* (London, 1949), p. 31.
[4] See Lon L. Fuller, "What the Law Schools Can Contribute to the Making of Lawyers," 1 *J. Leg. Ed.* 189 (1948); Fuller, "The Place and Uses of Jurisprudence in the Law School Curriculum." 1 *J. Leg. Ed.* 495 (1949).
[5] Flexner, p. 31.

other food besides success. The remoter and more general aspects of the law are those which give it universal interest. It is through them that you not only become a great master in your calling, but connect your subject with the universe and catch an echo of the infinite, a glimpse of its unfathomable process, a hint of the universal law.[6]

[6] Oliver W. Holmes, "The Path of the Law," in *Collected Papers* (New York, 1920), p. 202.

XVIII

THE TECHNIQUES OF
THE JUDICIAL PROCESS

Section 78. *The Interpretation of Constitutions*

Constitutions are destined by their authors to form a fundamental law for the governance of a politically organized group of human beings. A constitutional document sets forth the principles upon which the government of the state is founded. It regulates the division and distribution of the governmental powers among the various organs exercising the sovereignty of the state; it directs the manner in which these powers are to be exercised; and it often contains a chart of the basic rights (and perhaps also the basic duties) which attach to membership in the community for which the constitution is the governing law.

In those countries where the interpretation of the meaning of constitutional precepts is entrusted to an independent judiciary, an exalted task is imposed upon this department of the government. Inasmuch as decisions involving the application of constitutional norms to the problems of government and its relation to the citizens are often fraught with momentous consequences for the well-being and happiness of the polity, the responsibility thrust upon the organs of justice in this area of judicial administration cannot be discharged without a deep concern for the political, social, and economic impact which a constitutional decision may exert upon the lives of the people and the public weal. What help can general jurisprudence give to the authorities charged with this duty?

There are two cardinal problems in the realm of interpreting constitutional precepts which cannot be solved without some reflection on the ultimate ends of legal ordering. The first is the question of whether uncertainties regarding the meaning of a constitutional provision should be resolved by recourse to the understanding of the provision which was prevalent at the time of its adoption or whether a constitutional provision should be interpreted in the light of the knowledge, needs, and experience existing at the time when the interpretative decision is rendered. The second problem pertains to the recognition or nonrecognition of nonformal sources of constitutional adjudication. It is concerned with the issue of whether the meaning and scope of a positive constitutional command may be interpreted in the light of important principles of policy which have found no direct and immediate acknowledgment in the formal text of the constitution. Our discussion will be limited to these two major problems of constitutional exegesis.

With respect to the first question, the authorities on American constitutional law are sharply divided into two camps. For purposes of convenient terminology, we may describe the view propounded by the members of the first group as the theory of *historical interpretation,* while the second view may be identified as the theory of *contemporaneous interpretation.*

The theory of historical interpretation of constitutional clauses was enunciated with uncompromising frankness by Chief Justice Roger Taney in the case of *Dred Scott v. Sanford.*[1] In that case the United States Supreme Court held that at the time when the Constitution of the United States was adopted, Negroes were regarded as persons of inferior status, not as citizens; that the Constitution did not include them in the term citizens; and therefore that Negroes can have no right to sue in the federal courts under the clause which gives to these courts jurisdiction in suits between citizens of different states.[2] In the course of his opinion, Chief Justice Taney laid down his philosophy of constitutional interpretation in the following words:

[1] 60 U.S. (19 How.) 393 (1857).
[2] On this case see Carl B. Swisher, *American Constitutional Development,* 2d ed. (Boston, 1954), p. 247.

No one, we presume, supposes that any change in public opinion or feeling, in relation to this unfortunate race, in the civilized nations of Europe or in this country, should induce the court to give to the words of the Constitution a more liberal construction in their favor than they were intended to bear when the instrument was framed and adopted. Such an argument would be altogether inadmissible in any tribunal called on to interpret it. If any of its provisions are deemed unjust, there is a mode prescribed in the instrument itself by which it may be amended; but while it remains unaltered, it must be construed now as it was understood at the time of its adoption. It is not only the same in words, but the same in meaning, and delegates the same powers to the Government, and reserves and secures the same rights and privileges to the citizen; and as long as it continues to exist in its present form, it speaks not only in the same words, but with the same meaning and intent with which it spoke when it came from the hands of its framers, and was voted on and adopted by the people of the United States. Any other rule of construction would abrogate the judicial character of this court, and make it the mere reflex of the popular opinion or passion of the day.[3]

More recently the same theory of interpretation was advanced by Mr. Justice Sutherland in *Home Building and Loan Assn. v. Blaisdell*.[4] In this case the United States Supreme Court upheld the constitutionality of the Minnesota Mortgage Moratorium Act of 1933, which granted relief to mortgage debtors, on the ground that the severe economic emergency existing in the state when the legislation was passed rendered this exercise of the state's police power reasonable under the circumstances and immune from attack under Article I, section 10 of the Constitution, prohibiting an impairment of the obligation of contracts. In a dissenting opinion, Justice Sutherland pointed out that the contract clause was inserted into the Constitution at a time of emergency for the very purpose of preventing the type of legislation that was passed in Minnesota in 1933. He considered the view of the framers, that *any* relief of debtors was unconstitutional regardless of the existence or nonexistence of an economic depression, as strictly binding upon the court.[5] In another case, Justice Sutherland formulated his theory of constitutional interpretation as follows:

The meaning of the Constitution does not change with the ebb and flow of economic events. We frequently are told in more general words that the Constitution must be construed in the light of the present. If by that it is meant that the Constitution is made up of living words that apply to every new condition which they include, the statement is quite true. But to say, if

[3] *Dred Scott v. Sanford*, 60 U.S. (19 How.) 393, at 426 (1857).
[4] 290 U.S. 398 (1934).
[5] *Id.*, at 453–455.

that be intended, that the words of the Constitution mean today what they did not mean when written—that is, that they do not apply to a situation now to which they would have applied then—is to rob that instrument of the essential element which continues it in force as the people have made it until they, and not their official agents, have made it otherwise.[6]

The opposite theory, the theory of contemporaneous interpretation, was advocated by Chief Justice Marshall in the celebrated case of *McCulloch v. Maryland*. In this case, Marshall declared that the American Constitution was "intended to endure for ages to come and, consequently, to be adapted to the various *crises* of human affairs." [7] The trend of this thought was taken up by Chief Justice Hughes in the Blaisdell case already referred to above, where Hughes repudiated Justice Sutherland's theory of historical interpretation in the following words: "It is no answer to say that this public need [for a moratorium on mortgage foreclosures] was not apprehended a century ago, or to insist that what the provision of the Constitution meant to the vision of that day it must mean to the vision of our time. If by the statement that what the Constitution meant at the time of its adoption it means today, it is intended to say that the great clauses of the Constitution must be confined to the interpretation which the framers, with the conditions and outlook of their time, would have placed upon them, the statement carries its own refutation." [8] Seconding the views of Justice Hughes, the Supreme Court of Washington once pointed out that "constitutional provisions should be interpreted to meet and cover changing conditions of social and economic life." [9]

In forming a considered judgment on the merits of these opposing arguments, it is well to keep in mind a distinction which Justice Brandeis drew in a dissenting opinion in *Burnet v. Coronado Oil and Gas Co.*[10] In this case Justice Brandeis considered it necessary to distinguish between *interpretation* and *application* of a constitutional provision. The judges of the Supreme Court, including Mr. Justice Sutherland,[11]

[6] *West Coast Hotel Co. v. Parrish*, 300 U.S. 379, at 402–403 (1937). The same position is taken by Thomas M. Cooley, *Constitutional Limitations*, 8th ed. by W. Carrington (Boston, 1927), I, 123–124.

[7] 17 U.S. (4 Wheat.) 316, at 415 (1819). For an interesting study in constitutional interpretation see James B. Thayer, "Legal Tender," in *Legal Essays* (Cambridge, Mass., 1927), pp. 60–90.

[8] *Home Building & Loan Assn. v. Blaisdell*, 290 U.S. 398, at 442–443 (1934).

[9] *State v. Superior Court*, 146 P. 2d 543, at 547 (1944). See also Justice Holmes in *Gompers v. U.S.*, 233 U.S. 604, at 610 (1914), to the effect that the meaning of constitutional terms is to be gleaned "from their origin and the line of their growth."

[10] 285 U.S. 393, at 410 (1932).

[11] See the quotation above from his opinion in *West Coast Hotel Co. v. Parrish*, supra n. 6.

have usually agreed that a constitutional clause, as interpreted in consonance with its original understanding, must often be applied to new conditions and new fact situations which would have been unfamiliar to its framers. Thus, after it has been determined by an authoritative interpretation that the equal protection clause of the Constitution prohibits classifications and discriminations devoid of reasonableness, the question of whether or not a certain discriminatory law violates the clause must be decided in the light of the conceptions of reasonableness prevailing at the time of the decision. After the commerce clause has been construed to preclude the imposition of substantial burdens upon interstate commerce, the question of whether a particular burden on such commerce is substantial enough to warrant judicial interposition must be appraised against the background of the conditions of commerce existing at the time of the dispute. Even on questions involving application rather than interpretation of constitutional provisions, however, the judges may disagree on whether they should feel bound by earlier precedents dealing with substantially identical fact situations.

The chief point of such controversy centers around the area of judicial *interpretation* of the meaning of constitutional precepts. If the framers of the contract clause of the Constitution had intended to bar *any and all* impairments of contracts, may the judges of the Supreme Court later take the position that, for strong and convincing reasons of public order and morality, certain types of impairments may be countenanced? If the framers of the Constitution desired to impose on Congress an absolute incapacity to tamper with freedom of speech and assembly, may the Supreme Court subsequently sanction certain congressional restrictions on free speech and assembly deemed imperative in the interest of national security and self-preservation? Here we are confronted with an issue of clear-cut scope and utmost gravity.

In trying to find a solution for this problem, one may reasonably start from the presupposition that a generation of men intent upon setting up a durable framework of government and societal organization are necessarily handicapped by certain limitations of experience and shortcomings of vision which will be made manifest by long-range operation and functioning of the constitutional system created by them. Such inability to foresee certain consequences and concomitants of a new institutional order is a limitation of perception which even the most gifted and ingenious men are heir to. It would be unwise to assume that the writers of a constitution, even if they represent an august body of experienced men, are unaware of these confining limits of their judgment and desirous of forcing their time-bound interpretation of the Constitution, in every detail and particularity, upon future generations. It should, on the contrary, be assumed that they would not want to foreclose the people of a later time from solving their problems in their own way, as long as such a solution remains consistent with the general spirit and basic objectives of the constitutional system they fashioned. Inasmuch as they sought to establish an enduring pattern for societal living in the knowledge that social conditions are always in a state of flux and subject to unpredictable contingencies, it would be unreasonable to assume that they regarded the fundamental law they established as a complete petrification of the *status quo* as it existed at the time of the adoption of the law. When Mr. Justice Cardozo declared that "a constitution states or ought to state not rules for the passing hour, but principles for an expanding future," [12] his words may be interpreted as reflecting not only his own views but also those of every broadminded and judicious constitution-maker. It must therefore be concluded that, in situations where a material and substantial change of conditions has occurred, no injustice is done to the founding fathers of the American commonwealth, or of any other commonwealth, if the courts of a later day, instead of ascertaining the intent which these men voiced with respect to the meaning of a constitutional clause in their own day, attempt to determine the intent which these men would presumably have held had they foreseen what our present conditions would be.[13]

This view of constitutional interpretation should, however, be tempered by a qualifying consideration. Even though the enactment of a constitution may properly be construed as a delegation of a mandate to its future interpreters to treat it as a living instrument designed to meet the varying exigencies of later times, this mandate cannot be held to extend to changes which would totally subvert the spirit of the document and transform its precepts into the opposite of what they were originally meant to be.[14] The difference between modification and subversion of a constitutional provision through the process of interpretation may be illustrated by some examples. A constitutional clause guaranteeing freedom of speech and press might be held, under a permissible latitude of interpretation, not to sanction utterances posing a serious threat to the safety of the nation, such as publication of troop ship sailings in wartime, or statements apt to divide the nation into

[12] Benjamin N. Cardozo, *The Nature of the Judicial Process* (New Haven, 1921), p. 83.

[13] *Id.*, p. 84; Josef Kohler, "Judicial Interpretation of Enacted Law," in *Science of Legal Method* (New York, 1921), pp. 192–193; Lorenz Brütt, *Die Kunst der Rechtsanwendung* (Berlin, 1907), pp. 62–65.

[14] See in this connection the dissenting opinion of Mr. Justice Frankfurter in *National Mutual Ins. Co. v. Tidewater Transfer Co.*, 337 U.S. 582, at 646–647 (1949).

hostile and warring camps, such as incitements to racial or religious hatred and strife. It can be reasonably assumed that the purpose of guaranteeing freedom of expression was to ensure full and even hotheaded debate of all matters of public concern; but the intent to permit disclosure of information likely to benefit an enemy or the dissemination of propaganda apt to engender riots or civil strife need not be imputed to the framers of the guaranty. On the other hand, interpretations of the free-speech guaranty which would enable the legislature to suspend it on slight pretexts or by simple reference to the public interest would clearly violate the spirit and purpose of the guaranty, even though the prevailing views regarding the value of free speech might have undergone a marked change. Only a new constitution or a far-reaching amendment could legalize the new attitude toward free speech under these circumstances. In the same vein, under a constitution based on the general principle of separation of powers, a court's approval of legislation which merges or blends certain governmental powers in a limited field for persuasive reasons and under proper safeguards against abuse may not necessarily transcend the bounds of the judicial interpretative power. On the other hand, an approval of a fusion of powers which would seriously jeopardize the basic principle and undermine its foundations in a broad area of public life would appear to be violative of an essential command of such a constitution. The result of these considerations is that the elasticity and pliability of a constitutional philosophy which permits the agents of interpretation to take account of the changing needs of the time and enables them to cope with new and unprecedented problems must find the ends of its bounds in the necessity for preserving the core and essential integrity of a constitution. Truly fundamental changes must be effected by amending a constitution, not by interpreting it.

The second question to be discussed here is related to the first. It is the question of whether the courts have power to read exceptions or qualifications into unambiguously worded constitutional provisions for the purpose of accommodating such provisions with opposing or at least partially conflicting constitutional principles which are not directly embodied in the text. This has happened frequently in the interpretation of the United States Constitution. For example, Article IV, section 1 of the Constitution requires states to give full faith and credit to the public acts, records, and judicial proceedings of other states. In construing the meaning of this clause, the United States Supreme Court has held that the command of full faith and credit—although enunciated in unequivocal terms in the text of the Constitution—was not all-embracing, so that there may be exceptional cases where a state confronted with the enforcement of public acts or judgments of another state may prefer its own laws or policies to those of the sister state.[15] The court in these cases has taken the position that the idea of state sovereignty must be held to balance, to a restricted extent, the constitutional command of full faith and credit, although such an interpretation requires a gloss on the Constitution which cannot find its justification in the text of the Constitution itself. In the same way, the Supreme Court has taken the view that the guaranties of freedom of speech, press, and assembly, which are set forth in absolute and unqualified terms in the First Amendment, are subject to the regulatory power of Congress to the extent that a restriction of free expression is necessary to forestall a grave danger threatening some other interest which it is within the constitutional power of Congress to protect. Thus in *Dennis v. U.S.*,[16] it was held that advocation of revolution by communists could be prohibited by congressional statute in order to preserve the national security. The protection of national security is not, however, entrusted to Congress by the constitutive provisions of the fundamental law, and the recognition of this power must be largely derived from nonpositive sources of constitutional law.[17]

Some judges of the United States Supreme Court, notably Justices Black and Douglas, have taken issue with the practice of the court's majority to balance conflicting public interests even in the face of an unambiguously worded command of the Constitution protecting a particular public interest in unmistakable terms. Thus, Mr. Justice Black has taken the stand that individuals, under the First Amendment, "are guaranteed an undiluted and unequivocal right to express themselves on questions of current public interest," [18] and that the court "has injected compromise into a field where the First Amendment forbids compromise." [19] Mr. Justice Douglas declared in 1953 that the command of the First Amendment is "that there shall be *no* law which abridges . . . civil rights. The matter is beyond the power of the legislature to regulate, control, or condition." [20]

---

[15] See, for example, *Fall v. Eastin*, 215 U.S. 1 (1909); *Magnolia Petroleum Co. v. Hunt*, 320 U.S. 430, at 438 (1943); *Williams v. North Carolina*, 325 U.S. 226 (1945); *Alaska Packers Assn. v. Industrial Accident Commission*, 294 U.S. 532, at 547 (1935); *Huntington v. Attrill*, 146 U.S. 657 (1892).

[16] 341 U.S. 494 (1951). See the discussion of the case by Bernard Schwartz, *The Supreme Court* (New York, 1957), pp. 307-319.

[17] The principle finds *indirect* support in Article I, section 8, which gives Congress power to suppress insurrection by the use of the militia, and in the Preamble to the Constitution ("to insure domestic tranquillity").

[18] *Wieman v. Updegraff*, 344 U.S. 183, at 194 (1952).

[19] *American Communications Assn. v. Douds*, 339 U.S. 382, at 448 (1950).

[20] Dissenting in *Poulos v. New Hampshire*, 345 U.S. 395, at 423 (1953). See also William O. Douglas, *We the Judges* (Garden City, 1956), p. 307: "The mandate

The advocates of libertarian absolutism would seem to be oblivious to the fact, however, that "the First Amendment freedoms are vital, but their exercise must be compatible with the preservation of other rights essential in a democracy and guaranteed by our Constitution." [21] Thus, practically everybody will agree that the right to a fair trial by an unbiased and unintimidated judiciary is essential to a free society worthy of its name, although the right is not explicitly phrased in these terms in the text of the Constitution. Experience has shown that this right can easily come into conflict with the freedoms protected by the First Amendment in cases where public pressure of severe proportions is exercised, through the medium of the press or otherwise, in order to make the judiciary amenable to the will of a certain community group. As Mr. Justice Frankfurter remarked in *Pennekamp v. Florida:* [22]

Without a free press there can be no free society. Freedom of the press, however, is not an end in itself but a means to the end of a free society. The scope and nature of the constitutional protection of freedom of speech must be viewed in that light and in that light applied. The independence of the judiciary is no less a means to the end of a free society, and the proper functioning of an independent judiciary puts the freedom of the press in its proper perspective. For the judiciary cannot function properly if what the press does is reasonably calculated to disturb the judicial judgment in its duty and capacity to act solely on the basis of what is before the court. A judiciary is not independent unless courts of justice are enabled to administer law by absence of pressure from without, whether exerted through the blandishments of reward or the menace of disfavor.

Thus two conflicting values, both of which are embedded in the structure of our constitutional life, are in need of a reasonable adjustment and reconciliation by the judiciary in cases of this type. Similarly, the right of a government to preserve its existence against active attempts to overthrow it by force is one that, in view of the reactions of human nature when faced with a threat to survival, must be recognized, as a matter of general principle, as an inherent right, whether or not it is expressly sanctioned in the Constitution; it might not, however, be unreasonable to regard the right as forfeited where the government has violated its trust by letting its power degenerate into unmitigated tyranny or anarchical disorder. Where the constitutional system involved is that of a free society resolved to preserve the freedom of vigorously criticizing the government, it is axiomatic that the right

---

is in terms of the absolute . . . the provision is all-inclusive and complete. The word 'no' has a finality in all languages that few other words enjoy."
[21] Schwartz, p. 232.
[22] 328 U.S. 331, at 354–355 (1946).

to suppress revolutionary activities must be confined to conduct which poses a very grave threat to the security of the nation.

In order to form a well-considered opinion on such momentous questions, it is necessary to keep in mind that the positively formulated law of a society can never embrace the "living-law" structure of that society in its totality. A society will always operate on principles which flow from the spirit and character of its institutions and are indispensable to its effective functioning, even though these principles have not received adequate formal expression at the hands of a legislature or constitutional assembly. Although the positive law of the society, in the interests of legal clarity and stability, must normally be given a preferred position as compared with the nonformal sources of the law, there are situations where a mutual adjustment between formal and nonformal sources becomes inevitable. This is especially true in the area of constitutional law, where the entire organized way of life of a nation is affected by court decisions on significant problems and where constitutional values unrecognized in their particular manifestations by the framers of a constitution may be in urgent need of judicial protection at a later stage of the life of the nation. To put it briefly, a written constitution will always be incomplete. It must nevertheless be insisted that a positive rule of constitutional law must be given a very high degree of priority, and that it may be held to yield to an unwritten principle (such as national security, self-preservation, or inexorable necessity) only where the force with which the unarticulated principle makes its claim for recognition in a given situation is exceedingly strong.

Section 79. *The Interpretation of Statutes*

As Roscoe Pound has shown, four different ways may be conceived in which courts may deal with an innovation in the law brought about by means of a statute:

(1) They might receive it fully into the body of the law as affording not only a rule to be applied but a principle from which to reason, and hold it, as a later and more direct expression of the general will, of superior authority to judge-made rules on the same general subject; and so reason from it by analogy in preference to them. (2) They might receive it fully into the body of the law to be reasoned from by analogy the same as any other rule of law, regarding it, however, as of equal or coordinate authority in this respect with judge-made rules upon the same general subject. (3) They might refuse to receive it fully into the body of the law and give effect to it directly only; refusing to reason from it by analogy but giving it, nevertheless, a liberal interpretation to cover the whole field it was intended to cover. (4)

They might not only refuse to reason from it by analogy and apply it directly only, but also give to it a strict and narrow interpretation, holding it down rigidly to those cases which it covers expressly.[1]

The position of the Roman law as reflected in Justinian's Corpus Juris Civilis generally accords with the first method described by Pound. "Not all special cases can be contained in the laws and resolutions of the Senate," said the Roman jurist Julianus, "but where their meaning is manifest in some case, the one who exercises jurisdiction must apply the provision analogously and in this way administer justice."[2] Ulpianus, another celebrated Roman jurisconsult, spoke in the same vein: "For, as Pedius says, whenever anything has been introduced by law, there is good opportunity to extend it by interpretation or at least adjudication to other cases involving the same social purpose."[3] Celsus added the following admonition to these general principles of interpretation: "The laws should be liberally interpreted, in order that their intent be preserved."[4]

The attitude which the Roman law, after attaining maturity, observed toward statutes was carried over into the modern systems of the Civil Law. As a general rule, the Civil Law rejects a theory of interpretation according to which the *words* of a statute, as such, should furnish the sole basis for determining the content of the enactment. It prefers the view according to which the chief aim of interpretation is the ascertainment of the *intent* or *purpose* underlying the enactment in question.[5] The Civil Law is, on the whole, not favorably disposed toward the plain-meaning rule, according to which the words of a statute, if they appear to be plain and unambiguous, must be applied without regard to the sense which their authors intended to convey and without recourse to any exterior aids that might help elucidate their meaning. Furthermore, the Civil Law is much predisposed toward permitting extension of statutory provisions to situations which, although they do not fall within the broadest possible meaning of the statutory language, do fall within the general principle or social

---

[1] Pound, "Common Law and Legislation," 21 *Harvard Law Review* 383, at 385 (1908).

[2] *Dig.* I. 3. 12.

[3] *Dig.* I. 3. 13.

[4] *Dig.* I. 3. 18. See also Celsus, *Dig.* I. 3. 17: "To know the laws does not mean to be familiar with their words, but with their sense and significance."

[5] There are differences of opinion, however, as to the best means by which such intent or purpose should be discovered. See Arthur Lenhoff, "On Interpretative Theories: A Comparative Study in Legislation," 27 *Texas Law Review* 312, at 326 (1949); L. Enneccerus and H. C. Nipperdey, *Allgemeiner Teil des Bürgerlichen Rechts*, 14th ed. (Tübingen, 1952), p. 199; François Gény, *Méthode d'interprétation et sources en droit privé positif*, 2d rev. ed. (Paris, 1954), I, 253 ff.

purpose envisaged by the statute. This method is known as the method of *analogy*. Thus, if a certain kind of action is given by the law to executors of a will, the same action will probably be allowed to administrators of an estate, although not mentioned in the act, if the general purpose of the act is applicable to the latter and no reasonable ground can be discerned for limiting the action to executors. If the law contains no general provisions dealing with liability for negligent performance of obligations, but imposes such liability on vendors, purchasers, landlords, tenants, bailors, and bailees, the principle might be extended to other obligors in the absence of cogent arguments favoring the limitation of the principle to the enumerated categories.

Samuel Thorne has shown that, during certain periods of English medieval history, the position of the Common Law toward the construction of statutes was similar to the general attitude of the Roman and Civil Law.[6] Statutes were frequently extended to situations not expressly covered by them. Conversely, if the application of a broadly phrased statute to a particular complex of facts led to a hardship or injustice, a judge was under no constraint to follow the words of the statute. In the early fourteenth century, the freedom with which statutes were treated by common-law judges was so great that a substantial rewriting of statutory law by the judiciary was not at all uncommon. In the words of Thorne, statutes were viewed as "suggestions of policy to be treated with an easy unconcern as to their precise content."[7] While this freedom of interpretation was gradually curbed and farreaching extensions of statutory norms came to be looked upon as improper, the emerging doctrine of the equity of the statute still permitted a liberal interpretation of legislation according to its purpose and the use of analogy within moderate limits. The reporter Plowden stated in 1573 that "the intent of statutes is more to be regarded and pursued than the precise letter of them, for oftentimes things which are within the words of statutes, are out of the purview of them, which purview extends no further than the intent of the makers of the Act, and the best way to construe an Act of Parliament is according to the intent rather than according to the words."[8] By also pointing out that "when the words of a statute enact one thing, they enact all other

[6] Samuel E. Thorne, *A Discourse upon the Exposicion and Understandinge of Statutes* (San Marino, Calif., 1942), Introduction.

[7] *Id.*, p. 42.

[8] *Eyston v. Studd*, 75 Eng. Rep. 688, at 694 (1573). See also *id.*, p. 695: "Our law (like all others) consists of two parts, viz. of body and soul, the letter of the law is the body of the law, and the sense and reason of the law is the soul of the law . . . And it often happens that when you know the letter, you know not the sense, for sometimes the sense is more confined and contracted than the letter, and sometimes it is more large and extensive."

things which are in the like degree," [9] Plowden demonstrated that a statutory remedy at that time was deemed to be merely illustrative of other analogous cases that deserved to be governed by the same principle.[10]

In the eighteenth century Blackstone, in his *Commentaries on the Laws of England*, still recognized the doctrine of the equity of the statute in a restricted and cautiously worded form.

If the Parliament will positively enact a thing to be done which is unreasonable, I know of no power in the ordinary forms of the constitution that is vested with authority to control it: and the examples usually alleged in support of this sense of the rule do none of them prove that, where the main object of a statute is unreasonable, the judges are at liberty to reject it; for that were to set the judicial power above that of the legislature, which would be subversive of all government.

He then added an important qualification to this acknowledgment of parliamentary supremacy: "Where some collateral matter arises out of the general words, and happens to be unreasonable; there the judges are in decency to conclude that this consequence was not foreseen by the parliament, and therefore they are at liberty to expound the statute by equity and only *quoad hoc* to disregard it." [11] The following example is given by Blackstone as an illustration of the judicial power with respect to equitable correction of a statute: "If an act of parliament gives a man power to try all causes that arise within his manor of Dale; yet, if a cause should arise in which he himself is a party, the act is construed not to extend to that, because it is unreasonable that any man should determine his own quarrel." [12] Blackstone observes, however, that the opposite result should obtain if an intent on the part of Parliament to confer the right without exceptions may be properly inferred.

During the nineteenth century, the remaining force of the equity of the statute doctrine was destroyed in England. It is held today that the function of the judge is merely to determine what Parliament has said in its enactment and to apply the words of the statute to the case at hand. It is considered beyond his power to supply omitted particulars (unless, perhaps, the statute would be completely senseless without the addition) or to write equitable exceptions into the statute in hardship cases. The position is taken that the true meaning of the statute

[9] *Id.*, p. 698.
[10] See James M. Landis, "Statutes and the Sources of Law," in *Harvard Legal Essays* (Cambridge, Mass., 1934), pp. 215–216.
[11] Ed. W. D. Lewis (Philadelphia, 1898), Bk. I.91.
[12] *Ibid.*

coincides with whatever the plain meaning of the words conveys to the judicial mind, and that the judge should give full force wherever possible to the literal meaning of the words employed.[13] The judge is directed to gather the intent of the legislature from the words used, even if the consequences of such an interpretation may be mischievous.[14] The duty of the courts is "not to make the law reasonable, but to expound it as it stands." [15] Even recourse to the parliamentary history of an enactment as an aid to the ascertainment of its meaning is, as a general rule, not permitted.[16]

In the United States, the law of statutory interpretation is in a state of flux. Conflicting tendencies are at work in the courts which make it difficult to formulate any general statements as to what should be considered the prevalent American attitude towards statutes. Karl Llewellyn has shown that the array of interpretative maxims available to American courts contains sets of contraries and contradictories, and that some rule of statutory construction can be found to support practically any result a court might wish to reach.[17] Nevertheless, despite the large amount of uncertainty and confusion presently existing in this branch of the law, certain trends and directions of development are noticeable which may warrant a cautious prediction as to what the future of statutory interpretation law in this country is likely to be.

There was a time in United States legal history when the courts conceived of statutes in the fourth way described by Pound, as set forth at the beginning of this section. Whenever a statute contained a legislative innovation departing from the Common Law, the courts not only refused to reason from it by analogy, but they also interpreted the terms of the statute in the most narrow and restrictive fashion. Their attitude in this respect was similar to that of the English courts

[13] See E. R. Hopkins, "The Literal Canon and the Golden Rule," 15 *Canadian Bar Review* 689–690 (1937). As Professor Hopkins points out, the case of *Altrincham Electric Supply Co. v. Sale Urban District Council* 154 L.T.R. 379 (1936), seems to suggest that, in the recent opinion of the House of Lords, a court has no jurisdiction to alter the plain meaning of statutory words even when they lead to an absurd result.

[14] See P. B. Maxwell, *The Interpretation of Statutes*, 8th ed. by G. H. B. Jackson (London, 1937), p. 4. English courts have, however, at times applied the *Golden Rule*, according to which words need not be given their ordinary signification when such use of the words would produce a great inconsistency, absurdity, or inconvenience. See *River Wear Commissioners v. Adamson*, 2 App. Cas. 742, at 746 (1877).

[15] Maxwell, p. 4.

[16] *Id.*, p. 25.

[17] "Remarks on the Theory of Appellate Decision and the Rules or Canons about How Statutes Are To Be Construed," 3 *Vanderbilt Law Review* 395 (1950).

as described by Sir Frederick Pollock in 1882, an attitude which, according to Pollock, "cannot well be accounted for except upon the theory that Parliament generally changes the law for the worse, and that the business of the judge is to keep the mischief of its interference within the narrowest possible bounds." [18]

Today, statute law is on the whole received with less hostility by the courts of the United States and of the several states than was the case in the last century.[19] Remedial statutes conferring rights unknown at the Common Law (such as minimum wage, social security, or workmen's compensation statutes) are often accorded a liberal and broadminded treatment by the courts, and particularly by the United States Supreme Court.[20] This seems to indicate that the courts have tended to accept the third approach toward statutory construction listed by Pound. It is also the practice of American courts to make free use of committee reports and other materials which might throw light on the legislative history of an enactment.[21] But there is judicial vacillation on the question of whether resort to extrinsic aids helpful in determining legislative intent is permissible in situations where the wording of a statutory provision appears to be plain. Many of the state courts take the position that when a legislative act is clear and, when standing alone it is fairly susceptible of but one construction, this construction must be given to it without an inquiry into legislative history.

United States Supreme Court adjudications involving the plain-meaning rule have not always followed a consistent line. Perhaps the most striking instance of a decision setting legislative intent above the statutory letter is the celebrated Trinity Church case.[22] Congress in 1885 forbade the encouragement of the importation of aliens by means of contract for labor and services entered into prior to immigration. A proviso excluded professional artists, lecturers, singers, and domestic servants, but made no mention of ministers of the gospel. A church made a contract with an English clergyman to come over and serve as rector and pastor of the church. After he had arrived in this country

[18] *Essays in Jurisprudence and Ethics* (London, 1882), p. 85.
[19] See J. B. Fordham and J. R. Leach, "Interpretation of Statutes in Derogation of the Common Law," 3 *Vand. L. Rev.* 438 (1950).
[20] *Fleischmann Co. v. U.S.*, 270 U.S. 349, at 360 (1925); *Jackson v. Northwest Airlines*, 70 F. Supp. 501, at 504–505 (1947); *Judd v. Landin*, 1 N.W. 2d 861, at 863–864 (Minn., 1942); *Hasson v. City of Chester*, 67 S.E. 731, at 733 (Va., 1910).
[21] See Notes, 3 *Vand. L. Rev.* 586 (1950); 52 *Columbia Law Review* 125 (1952).
[22] *Church of the Holy Trinity v. United States*, 143 U.S. 457 (1892). For a criticism of the plain-meaning rule see Harry W. Jones, "The Plain Meaning Rule and Extrinsic Aids in the Interpretation of Federal Statutes," 25 *Washington University Law Quarterly* 2 (1939).

and assumed his duties, the government sought to recover the penalty provided by the act. The court refused to interpret the statute literally. Looking to the title (referring only to "labor") and the purpose of the act rather than to its words, the court concluded that all available data pointed to an intent to control only the influx of cheap and unskilled labor from abroad.

In *Chung Fook v. White*,[23] on the other hand, the same court took an extremely narrow and literal position in the interpretation of a legislative enactment. A statute provided that where a naturalized citizen was sending for his wife or minor children to join him in this country, a wife to whom he was married or a minor child born to him after his naturalization, if afflicted with a contagious disease, should be admitted to this country without detention for treatment in a hospital. The court held that the privilege was not applicable to a native-born citizen, since the act (undoubtedly by oversight) mentioned only naturalized citizens. The court said: "The words of the statute being clear, if it unjustly discriminates against the native-born citizen, or is cruel and inhuman in its result, as forcefully contended, the remedy lies with Congress and not with the courts." Notwithstanding such illiberal decisions, it may be stated that the trend in present-day Supreme Court decisions moves in the direction of a purpose-oriented policy of statutory interpretation. In *United States v. American Trucking Association*,[24] the court launched an attack on the plain-meaning rule in its orthodox form in the following words:

When [the plain] meaning has led to absurd or futile results . . . this Court has looked beyond the words to the purpose of the Act. Frequently, however, even when the plain meaning did not produce absurd results but merely an unreasonable one "plainly at variance with the policy of the legislation as a whole" this Court has followed that purpose, rather than the literal words. When aid to construction of the meaning of words, as used in the statute, is available, there can certainly be no "rule of law" which forbids its use, however clear the words may be on "superficial examination."

Roscoe Pound has ventured to predict that "the course of legal development upon which we have entered already must lead us to adopt the method of the second and eventually the method of the first hypothesis" (as set forth at the beginning of this section).[25] The likelihood of such a development stems from the fact that codified law is coming to play an increasingly prominent part in our legal system, and

[23] 264 U.S. 443 (1924). See also *Caminetti v. United States*, 242 U.S. 470 (1917).
[24] 310 U.S. 534, at 543–544 (1940); see also *Boston Sand & Gravel Co. v. United States*, 278 U.S. 41 (1928).
[25] See Pound, *op. cit. supra* n. 1, p. 386.

that the suspicion which the common-law judges exhibited toward legislative innovations at an earlier period of our history is on the way to being replaced by a more affirmative attitude toward statutes.

In dealing with codified and statutory law, we know from universal experience that the words of an enactment frequently reflect the intentions and aims of its framers incompletely or inaccurately. When legislators endeavor to express their thoughts in concise yet general terms, situations are almost invariably omitted that were within the over-all intention of the measure; on the other hand, cases are frequently covered by the statutory language for which the lawmakers, had they been aware of the problem, would have provided an exception. Is it necessary or desirable to bind the judges to the words of a statute, even though a literal interpretation might result in an unfair decision which the legislator himself would never have sanctioned if he had been conversant with the facts of the case?

One possible argument in favor of a literal interpretation of statutes is based on the consideration that such a theory of interpretation leads to certainty and clarity of the law. A person who reads a statute in order to acquaint himself with his rights and duties or those of other persons should be able to rely on the text without being compelled to undertake laborious investigations into what was actually in the minds of the lawmakers when they passed the act. This argument would, on first sight, seem to have particular force when applied to a private citizen or businessman who does not have at his disposal facilities for delving into the legislative history of statutes which are of concern to him. But there are answers to this argument. First of all, laymen rarely read statutes; if the content of a statute is vitally pertinent to their private or business affairs, they will usually consult an attorney or some other person acquainted with the problem. Second, even if such laymen read the statute, the import of the language will in a large number of cases either not be clear or, conversely, deceptively clear to them. Many enactments contain technical legal terms which are not necessarily self-explanatory. Even where words of ordinary language are used, such words can often be understood in a broad as well as a narrow sense. It would, under these circumstances, be an oversimplified solution of the problem if statutory interpretation were to be subjected to the test of the ordinary and natural meaning of language as understood by the man of average intelligence.

It might be asserted, on the other hand, that while the interest of the layman in a plain-meaning approach to legislative language cannot justify recourse to a literal theory of interpretation, the interest of the lawyer demands the adoption of this method. Some highly competent observers have pointed out that inquiry into legislative purpose through the use of the preparatory materials is an endeavor beset with traps and pitfalls, that the discovery of a unified legislative intent is for the most part an illusory and futile undertaking, and that it is therefore preferable, as a general rule, to let the judges find their own solution of an interpretative problem by means of a reasonable construction of the statutory text.[26]

There is a core of truth in the doctrine which counsels restraint in the use of legislative background sources, but its cautioning admonitions have sometimes overshot the mark. It is quite clear that the numerous members of a lawmaking body, or even the members of a legislative committee, frequently do not have a common understanding with respect to the range or purpose of a legislative act, and they may differ substantially on the scope of applicability of a statutory clause or provision. As Harry W. Jones has pointed out, "if 'legislative intention' is supposed to signify a construction placed upon statutory language by every individual member of the two enacting houses, it is, obviously, a concept of purely fictional status." [27] But Jones also demonstrates that by the examination of committee reports and the history of proposed amendments accepted or rejected during the course of the legislative debates it is often possible to discover that at some stage of the process committee members or other interested legislators had in fact come to an understanding on the essential meaning of a given provision or group of provisions.[28] Furthermore, a study of the preparatory materials will often throw light on the general climate of opinion from which the legislative enactment arose, the general social conditions responsible for its passage, and the particular "mischief" which the legislature sought to redress. By disclosing the political, social, or economic purpose which was the driving force behind the bill, such materials will significantly aid in the ascertainment of general legislative intent. It may, however, be conceded that the judge might be justified in refusing to enforce the legislative intent, as discerned by

---

[26] See Max Radin, "Statutory Interpretation," 43 *Harv. L. Rev.* 863 (1930); Radin, "A Short Way with Statutes," 56 *Harv. L. Rev.* 388 (1942); Ernest Bruncken, "Interpretation of Written Law," 25 *Yale Law Journal* 129 (1915).

For an excellent analysis of this view and a discussion of various other problems of statutory interpretation see Joseph P. Witherspoon, "Administrative Discretion to Determine Statutory Meaning," 35 *Tex. L. Rev.* 63 (1956); 38 *Tex. L. Rev.* 392, 572 (1960).

[27] "Statutory Doubts and Legislative Intention," 40 *Col. L. Rev.* 957, at 968 (1940).

[28] *Id.*, p. 969. Cf. also Felix Frankfurter, "Some Reflection on the Reading of Statutes," 47 *Col. L. Rev.* 527 (1947).

recourse to extrinsic aids, where such intent has remained entirely un-enacted, that is, where it is simply not reflected in the statutory lan-guage chosen to effectuate it.

Assuming that the judge, if he is in doubt as to the purported mean-ing of a legislative regulation, will consult the preparatory work as a clue to the ascertainment of its intent, the question arises of whether he is bound by the views which the legislators held with respect to the enactment at the time of its passage. Must the judge follow the his-torical understanding of the statute, or is he empowered to decide the case in accordance with the views which the lawmakers would pre-sumably have expressed had they been present at the time of the deci-sion? The latter position was taken by Plowden in 1573:

> In order to form a right judgment when the letter of a statute is restrained, and when enlarged, by equity, it is a good way, when you peruse a statute, to suppose that the law-maker is present, and that you have asked him the question you want to know touching the equity; then you must give yourself such an answer as you imagine he would have done, if he had been present . . . And if the law-maker would have followed the equity, notwithstanding the words of the law, . . . you may safely do the like, for while you do no more than the law-maker would have done, you do not act contrary to the law, but in conformity to it.[29]

The drawback of this approach lies in the fact that a determination of the position the lawmakers would presumably have taken toward the statute at the time of the decision, as distinguished from their views at the time of its passage, is a hazardous undertaking, whose outcome must frequently remain in the realm of guesswork. Furthermore, dif-ferent legislators might have expressed different reactions if it had been possible to solicit their views concerning the interpretation of the statute at the time of the decision. Should the work of statutory con-struction be predicated on such uncertain and elusive criteria?

In cases where doubt arises as to the meaning and scope of statutory language, the judges should, as a general rule, ascertain the legislative purpose through the use of all aids and resources at their disposal and give effect to the purpose of the legislation as so found. This rule should prevail even though the social conditions obtaining at the time of the adoption of the statute may have changed somewhat since and the mischief or evil at which it was directed may not be present to quite the same degree at the time the decision involving a construction of the statute is handed down. This may result in a decision which is

[29] *Eyston v. Studd*, 75 Eng. Rep. 688, at 699 (1573).

potentially objectionable from the point of view of fairness and justice, but this approach will tend to prevent excessive subjectivity in speculating on legislative intent projected into the future.

Where, on the other hand, the social conditions, mores, and general attitudes which conditioned a certain piece of legislation have undergone a *pronounced, substantial,* and *unmistakable* change since the time when the statute was passed, a different result should be reached. In this situation, the judge should be able to assume with a high degree of probability that this conspicuous and striking change of conditions would not have remained without influence on the makers of the law. Thus, if a statute differentiating between the civil status of men and women was enacted in a period when the legal inequality of men and women was regarded as a necessary and beneficial postulate of the social order, the legislators responsible for its passage were presumably inclined to allow a broad scope to the statute. After the social attitudes favoring inequality of the sexes have given way to the idea of the essential equality of men and women, there would exist good reasons for holding the same statute to the narrowest possible scope of application. If this technique leads to the creation of artificial and discriminatory distinctions, a possible way out of the difficulty—apart from repeal of the statute—would in some situations be to deny it continued validity under the due-process clause on the ground of total obsolescence.[30]

A good case can also be made for restoring the right of judges to supply omitted particulars and to correct obvious instances of excessive breadth in the formulation of statutory rules in situations where such corrective action is essential to produce a fair and sane result in a legal controversy. Thus, it is hard to see why a statute granting a certain civil cause of action to trustees, fiduciaries, and executors cannot be extended to administrators, where no reason for their exclusion from the statutory terms except inadvertence on the part of the legislature can be discovered, and where no unfair result is accomplished by the extension.[31] Conversely, where an application of the strict words of a statute would lead to a totally unreasonable or absurd result, the courts should be allowed to graft an equitable exception upon the statutory rule. Let us assume, for example, that a statute provides that no person may enter the United States without a permit obtained in the country of departure. A woman who has secured the requisite permit lands in the United States with a child born on the voyage.

---

[30] See also *supra* Sec. 73 on the desirability of recognizing a limited doctrine of *desuetudo*.

[31] Such an extension of a statute by analogy cannot be carried into the criminal field, where fair notice of scope is essential to due process and justice.

Should the immigration authorities be required, in consonance with the unambiguous words of the statute, to admit the mother, but deny entry to the baby? While the answer in this case ought to be clear, it should be insisted that the power of judges to depart from the literal sense of statutes in the interest of fundamental justice must be restricted to strong cases demanding equitable relief, and that misuse of discretion by the judge in writing an equitable exception into a statute should be a ground for appeal.[32]

The position here taken might be criticized for countenancing an undue degree of judicial interference with, and encroachment upon, the powers of legislative bodies. It might be argued that, while the improvement of judge-made law might well be regarded as being within the legitimate prerogatives of the judiciary, the taking of liberties with statutes must be held to constitute an improper arrogation of legislative power by a body of men not endowed with such power.

This line of argument falls short of being persuasive. A reasonable lawmaker is aware of the deficiencies inherent in the products of his legislative efforts. He knows that statutory rules can almost never be phrased with such perfection that all cases falling within the legislative policy are included in the textual formulation while all situations not within the purview of the statute remain outside of its linguistic ambit. Furthermore, a legislative body composed of reasonable men cannot be presumed to insist on retaining an exclusive right to correct minor errors and inadequacies. If such an exclusive right were claimed and granted, the legislature would forever be busy amending its own laws, often in small particulars, which is impractical, since other and more immediate political demands press down upon harassed modern legislators. Even if the necessary amendments are ultimately made, the injustices done in the meantime by judges tied down to a literal interpretation of statutes will remain without redress.

In the light of these considerations, it must be said that a legislature implicitly delegates to the judiciary the power to make certain rectifications in the literal language of statutes, provided that such rectifications are necessary to guarantee essential fairness and justice. As long as this power is exercised judiciously and with restraint, and as long as substantial judicial rewriting of statutes (which was characteristic for certain periods of the English medieval law) is avoided, conferring limited power of equitable correction upon the courts does not entail the destruction of the normative system or of substantial portions of it. When we realize at the same time that the era of literalness in statutory construction was by no means productive of that measure of

---

[32] See the more detailed discussion of this problem *supra* Sec. 71.

legal security which the advocates of a plain-meaning interpretation had hoped to be able to accomplish, this realization increases the persuasiveness of arguments favoring the reintroduction of considerations of justice into the law of statutory interpretation.

Section 80. *The Doctrine of* Stare Decisis

In an earlier section,[1] the conclusion was reached that judicial precedents, under the Anglo-American system of law, are today regarded as formal sources of law. It was pointed out, on the other hand, that in view of the free manner of courts in dealing with legal rules laid down in earlier decisions (by rephrasing, qualifying, broadening, narrowing, or changing such rules), a precedent must be regarded as a weaker and less authoritative source of law than a statute. We do not empower our judges to rewrite or amend the text of a statute in the same sense in which we permit them to restate or revamp a judge-made legal precept. In this section, the treatment and degree of authority accorded to judicial precedents under our system of law will be subjected to a more detailed analysis. This analysis will be concerned principally with two basic subjects: (1) the meaning and limitations of the doctrine of *stare decisis*, and (2) the effect of the overruling of precedents. The closely related question of how the *ratio decidendi* of a case is to be determined will be reserved for discussion in the following section.

Stare decisis is the most commonly used term for designating the Anglo-American doctrine of precedent. This term is an abbreviation of the Latin phrase *stare decisis et non quieta movere* (to stand by precedents and not to disturb settled points). Stated in a general form, *stare decisis* signifies that when a point of law has been once settled by a judicial decision, it forms a precedent which is not to be departed from afterward. Differently expressed, a prior case, being directly in point, must be followed in a subsequent case.

In a legal system where the rule of *stare decisis* is strictly and consistently applied, a precedent must not be disregarded or set aside, even though the rule or principle for which it is authority may seem archaic and wholly unreasonable to the judge called upon to apply it in a lawsuit. This element of the doctrine has frequently evoked criticism from laymen as well as from lawyers. A famous instance of lay criticism of the doctrine is an often-quoted passage from *Gulliver's Travels* by Jonathan Swift. "It is a maxim among . . . lawyers," says Gulliver, "that whatever hath been done before may legally be done again: and therefore they take special care to record all the decisions

---

[1] See *supra* Sec. 67.

formerly made against common justice and the general reason of mankind. These, under the name of precedents, they produce as authorities to justify the most iniquitous opinions; and the judges never fail of directing accordingly." [2] Some jurists and judges have likewise charged that the doctrine of precedent produces excessive conservatism.

Since adherence to the doctrine of precedent obviously tends to freeze the law and to preserve the *status quo,* it must be asked what the advantages and meritorious features of the doctrine are. We may list the following five positive factors in support of the *stare decisis* principle:

(1) The doctrine introduces a modicum of certainty and calculability into the planning of private and business activities. It enables people to engage in trade and arrange their personal affairs with a certain amount of confidence that they will not become entangled in litigation. It gives them some basis for predicting how other members of the community are likely to act toward them (assuming that such other members of the community comply with the law). Without this element of calculability, people would be uncertain of their rights, duties, and obligations, and they would be unable to ascertain what they might do without fear of coercive sanctions. Men would never know whether to settle or litigate a dispute if every established rule was liable to be overthrown from one day to the next, and litigation would be increased a thousandfold under such a state of affairs.

(2) *Stare decisis* provides attorneys counseling private parties with some settled basis for legal reasoning and the rendering of legal advice. A lawyer who does not have available to him the benefit of certain tools which are helpful to him in forecasting the probable outcome of litigation is of little use to his clients. In the words of Sir William Jones, "No man who is not a lawyer would ever know how to act and no lawyer would, in many instances, know how to advise, unless courts are bound by authority." [3]

(3) The doctrine of *stare decisis* tends to operate as a curb on the arbitrariness of judges. It serves as a prop for the weak and unstable judge who is inclined to be partial and prejudiced. By forcing him to follow (as a rule) established precedents, it reduces his temptation to render decisions colored by favor and bias. "If the doctrine of precedent were to be abolished in this country (where statutes have a relatively limited scope), the judges would be free to operate according to their individual whims and their private notions of right and wrong

[2] Pt. IV, ch. 5.
[3] *Essay on Bailments,* 4th ed. (London, 1836), p. 46.

throughout the entire area of human relations not covered by statute." [4]
Such a condition would not be conducive to the maintenance of respect
for the law and the preservation of public confidence in the integrity
of the judiciary. One important reason why people are willing to accept judicial decisions as binding is that they are supposed to be based
on an objective body of law and on impersonal reasoning free from
subjective predilections—even though this condition may not always
be fully realized in the practical operation of the legal system.

(4) The practice of following prior decisions facilitates dispatch
of judicial business and thereby promotes efficient judicial administration. Following precedents saves the time and conserves the energy
of judges and at the same time reduces the costs of litigation for the
parties. It makes it unnecessary for the court to examine a legal problem de novo each time the problem is presented again. "The labor of
judges," said Mr. Justice Cardozo, "would be increased almost to the
breaking point if every past decision could be reopened in every case,
and one could not lay one's own course of bricks on the secure foundation of the courses laid by others who had gone before him." [5]

(5) The doctrine of precedent also receives support from the human sense of justice. The force of precedent in the law is heightened,
in the words of Karl Llewellyn, by "that curious, almost universal
sense of justice which urges that all men are properly to be treated
alike in like circumstances." [6] If A was granted relief last month against
an unwarranted interference with his privacy, it would be unjust to
deny such relief to B this month if the facts shown by B are essentially
the same as those that were presented by A a month ago. [7]

In its relation to justice, however, the doctrine of precedent exhibits
a weakness which has often been noted. A precedent controlling the
decision of a court may be considered antiquated at the time when the
problem arises again for decision. The prevailing notions of justice
may have undergone a marked change in the interval between the
earlier and the later decision. The first decision, reflecting perhaps the
views of an earlier epoch of history, may have denied an action based
on an invasion of the right to privacy. The decision may appear iniquitous to a modern judge, since our notions regarding infringement of

[4] Delmar Karlen, Primer of Procedure (Madison, Wis., 1950), p. 119.
[5] Cardozo, Nature of the Judicial Process, p. 149.
[6] "Case Law," Encyclopedia of the Social Sciences, III, 249.
[7] Hocking points out that the principle of stare decisis is an ethical principle.
Since it is always wrong to disappoint an aroused expectation, ethics demands
that authoritative decisions shall be reached and that law shall be stable in its
operation. William E. Hocking, "Ways of Thinking about Rights," in Law: A
Century of Progress (New York, 1937), II, 259.

personal privacy may in the meantime have become more sensitive and refined.

Assuming that there is a close relation between equality and justice, it must be realized that the equality contemplated by *stare decisis* is that between a *past* and a *present* decision. Justice, on the other hand, may require a modification of the standards of equality because of a change in social outlook. While *stare decisis* promotes equality in *time*, that is, equal treatment as between A litigating his case in 1760 and B obtaining a decision in a lawsuit occurring in 1960, justice may be more properly concerned with equality in *space*, with an equal treatment of two persons or two situations measured in terms of contemporary value judgments. Furthermore, the earlier decision may have been rendered by a weak or inept judge, so that considerations of justice and reasonableness might be adduced in favor of its overthrow on this ground.

What can the judge confronted with an outdated or unreasonable precedent do? May he disregard or set aside the precedent on the ground that it is repugnant to our contemporary notions of right and wrong? Or is he compelled to sacrifice justice to stability and adhere to the unwelcome precedent? With respect to this question, the highest courts of England and the United States take conflicting positions.

The British House of Lords, which is the highest appellate tribunal for the United Kingdom, decided in 1898 that it was absolutely bound by its own decisions. This principle was established in the case of *London Street Tramways Co. v. London County Council*,[8] in which the House of Lords ruled that "a decision of this House upon a question of law is conclusive, and . . . nothing but an act of Parliament can set right that which is alleged to be wrong in a judgment of this House." In endeavoring to justify the rule, the Earl of Halsbury, who wrote the opinion in this case, made the following comments: "I do not deny that cases of individual hardship may arise, and there may be a current of opinion in the profession that such and such a judgment was erroneous; but what is that occasional interference with what is perhaps abstract justice as compared with the inconvenience—the disastrous inconvenience—of having each question subject to being reargued and the dealings of mankind rendered doubtful by reason of different decisions, so that in truth and in fact there would be no real final Court of Appeal?"[9] The Court of Appeals—subject to a few exceptions—likewise feels bound by its own decisions. The rule of the binding force of precedents does not, however, apply to the Judicial

[8] [1898] A.C. 375.
[9] *Id.*, p. 380.

Committee of the Privy Council, which is free to disregard a prior decision.[10]

In the United States, the courts take a more liberal position toward the doctrine of precedent. *Stare decisis* is not considered an inexorable command, and the duty to follow precedent is held to be qualified by the right to overrule prior decisions. Although the inferior courts within a certain precinct of jurisdiction are considered bound by the decisions of the intermediate or highest appellate courts, the highest courts of the states, as well as the supreme federal court, reserve to themselves the right to depart from a rule previously established by them. In the interest of legal security, however, they will not lightly make use of this prerogative. "Adherence to precedent should be the rule and not the exception," said Mr. Justice Cardozo.[11] Mr. Justice Brandeis observed: "*Stare decisis* is usually the wise policy, because in most matters it is more important that the applicable rule be settled than that it be settled right." [12] Nevertheless, the court will sometimes overrule its own decisions when it is necessary to avoid the perpetuation of pernicious error or where an earlier decision is wholly out of step with the exigencies of the time. On the whole, the United States Supreme Court will be less inclined to set aside a precedent which has become a well-established rule of property or commercial law than to overrule a case involving the validity of legislation under the federal Constitution. In the words of Chief Justice Stone, "The doctrine of *stare decisis*, however appropriate or even necessary at times, has only a limited application in the field of constitutional law." [13] In this area, it is particularly important to keep the law in accord with the dynamic flow of the social order, since correction of constitutional decisions by means of legislation is practically impossible.[14]

It would seem that the American attitude toward precedents is preferable to the policy followed by the English House of Lords. Since the maintenance of stability is not the only goal of the legal order, the judges should be given authority to set aside former decisions which

---

[10] See C. M. Schmitthoff, "The Growing Ambit of the Common Law," 30 *Can. B. Rev.* 48, at 59–60 (1952); G. R. Y. Radcliffe and G. Cross, *The English Legal System*, 3d ed. (London, 1954), p. 358. That the earlier position of the English courts was different is shown by Percy H. Winfield, *The Chief Sources of English Legal History* (Cambridge, Mass., 1925), p. 149; T. E. Lewis, "The History of Judicial Precedents," 46 *Law Quarterly Review* 207, at 210, 215 (1930); 47 *L. Q. Rev.* 411, at 422 (1931).

[11] Cardozo, p. 149. See also Note, 59 *Col. L. Rev.* 504 (1959).

[12] *Burnet v. Coronado Oil and Gas Co.*, 285 U.S. 393, at 406 (1932).

[13] *St. Joseph Stock Yards Co. v. United States*, 298 U.S. 38, at 94 (1935).

[14] See William O. Douglas, "Stare Decisis," 49 *Col. L. Rev.* 735 (1949); Brandeis, J. in *Burnet v. Coronado Oil and Gas Co.*, 285 U.S 393, at 407 (1932).

are hopelessly obsolete or thoroughly ill-advised and contrary to the social welfare. "If judges have woefully misinterpreted the mores of their day or if the mores of their day are no longer those of ours, they ought not to tie, in helpless submission, the hands of their successors." [15] The same elasticity should be allowed to the judges with respect to precedents which represent an anomaly, do not fit into the structure of the legal system as a whole, or are at odds with some of its guiding principles. This last point was emphasized by Justice Frankfurter in *Helvering v. Hallock*,[16] where he wrote: "We recognize that *stare decisis* embodies an important social policy. It represents an element of continuity in law and is rooted in the psychological need to satisfy reasonable expectations. But *stare decisis* is a principle of policy and not a mechanical formula of adherence to the latest decision, however recent and questionable, when such adherence involves collision with a prior doctrine more embracing in its scope, intrinsically sounder, and verified by experience." In granting courts the right to overrule their decisions, it should be made clear, however, that in exercising this right they should make certain that less harm will be done by rejecting a previous rule than by retaining it, even though the rule may be a questionable one. In every case involving the abandonment of an established precedent, the interest in a stable and continuous order of law must be carefully balanced against the advantages of improvement and innovation.

An unfortunate consequence of discarding a precedent under the still-prevailing doctrine is the retroactive effect of an overruling decision. The problem is well illustrated by the decision in the case of *People v. Graves*.[17] In 1928 the United States Supreme Court decided that a state had no right to tax income from copyright royalties. In 1932 this decision was overruled on the ground that it was erroneous. During the three intervening years Elmer Rice, a dramatist living in New York, had received large royalties from his plays on which he had paid no New York income tax. After the overruling of the 1928 decision, the New York authorities demanded three years' back taxes from Mr. Rice on these royalties. The New York courts, supporting the tax authorities, made Mr. Rice liable not only for the back taxes but also for the payment of interest at six per cent for being late.

The Appellate Division grounded its judgment on the theory that, when a precedent is overthrown, the overruling decision must be

[15] Cardozo, p. 152. On the doctrine of precedent see also R. A. Wasserstrom, *The Judicial Decision* (Stanford, 1961), chs. 3 and 4.
[16] 309 U.S. 106, at 119 (1940).
[17] 273 N.Y.S. 582 (Sup. Ct. App. Div., 1934).

viewed as enunciating the law as it always had been, and that the discarded decision must be treated as a nullity. "A judicial decision is but evidence of the law. An overruling decision does not change law, but impeaches the overruled decision as evidence of law. Adopting the theory that courts merely declare pre-existing law, it logically follows that an overruling decision operates retroactively." [18]

Such rulings may lead to hardship and injustice in cases where parties who have been relying upon an earlier decision suddenly find out that the law they had regarded as controlling has been overturned. The courts have tried to avoid such injustices in some instances. In the case of an interpretation of statutes, for example, it has often been held that the construction of the terms of a statute by a court must be read into the text of the statute and becomes in effect an integral part of it; consequently this construction cannot be changed by the court with retroactive effect so as to invalidate or impair contracts made and rights acquired in reliance upon such construction.[19] The principle embodied in such holdings would appear to be capable of broad application, and the United States Supreme Court has expressly given constitutional authorization to the courts of the states to deny a retroactive effect to their overruling decisions, whether or not a statute or a rule of the common law was involved.[20] Regardless of the answer to the theoretical question as to whether a judicial decision is law until such time as it is changed, or merely rebuttable evidence of the law, it would seem to be perfectly sound practice for a court to overturn a precedent but refuse to apply, on grounds of equitable estoppel, the new principle to the facts of the case at hand. This is justifiable at least in those cases where definite proof of reliance by one of the parties upon the old and discarded principle is submitted to the court, and the manner and degree of reliance has been such as to convince the court that the new rule should not be applied in the pending case.[21] In the absence of a type of reliance worthy of being protected, on the other hand, there

---

[18] *Id.*, p. 587.

[19] *Payne v. City of Covington*, 123 S.W. 2d 1045 (1938); see 21 *Corpus Juris Secundum* 329, with citations.

[20] *Great Northern Railway Co. v. Sunburst Oil and Refining Co.*, 287 U.S. 358 (1932). See also *Warring v. Colpoys*, 122 F. 2d 642, at 645–646 (1941); *Commissioner of Internal Revenue v. Hall's Estate*, 153 F. 2d 172, at 175 (1946); Roger J. Traynor, "Bad Lands in an Appellate Judge's Realm of Reason," 7 *Utah Law Review* 157, at 167–168 (1960); Note, 60 *Harv. L. Rev.* 437 (1947).

[21] See on this question A. Kocourek and H. Koven, "Renovation of the Common Law through Stare Decisis," 29 *Illinois Law Review* 971 (1935); Orvill C. Snyder, "Retrospective Operation of Overruling Decisions," 35 *Ill. L. Rev.* 121 (1940); Beryl H. Levy, "Realist Jurisprudence and Prospective Overruling," 109 *University of Pennsylvania Law Review* 1 (1960).

would seem to be no good reason for not immediately enforcing the new rule enunciated by the court.

Section 81. *The* Ratio Decidendi *of a Case*

The preceding section dealt with the general meaning of the *stare decisis* principle, the policy arguments sustaining it, and the desirable limits of its application. The question before us here is a narrower and more technical one, which arises from the well-established fact that not every statement made in a judicial decision is an authoritative source to be followed in a later case presenting a similar situation. Only those statements in an earlier decision which may be said to constitute the *ratio decidendi* of that case are held to be binding, as a matter of general principle, in subsequent cases. Propositions not partaking of the character of *ratio decidendi* may be disregarded by the judge deciding the later case. Such nonauthoritative statements are usually referred to as *dicta* or (if they are quite unessential for the determination of the points at issue) *obiter dicta*.

Unfortunately, the question as to what are the constituent elements and the scope of the *ratio decidendi* of a case is far from being settled. In the case of *Northwestern Life Ins. Co. v. Wright*,[1] the Supreme Court of Wisconsin stated its conception of the *ratio decidendi* of a case in the following language: "The key note of an adjudication is the ruling principle. The details showing the particular facts ruled by some particular principle are helpful; but, in the end, it is the principle, not the detail circumstances, commonly evidentiary only, which is the important feature as to whether an existing adjudication is a safe guide to follow in a case." It is widely conceded, however, that not every proposition of law formulated by a court in the course of a judicial opinion—even though it may have been the basis of the decision—possesses the authority belonging to the *ratio decidendi*. The principle of law enunciated by the court may have been much broader than was required for the decision of the case before it; and it is well established that in such situations the surplus not necessary to sustain the judgment must be regarded as a *dictum*. This qualification of the theory which identifies *ratio decidendi* with the ruling principle of a case is aptly brought out in the discussions of the problem by Sir John Salmond and Professor Edmund Morgan. Salmond points out that "a precedent . . . is a judicial decision which contains in itself a principle. The underlying principle which thus forms its authoritative element is often termed the *ratio decidendi*." He then goes on to say:

[1] 140 N.W. 1078, at 1081–1082 (1913).

Although it is the duty of courts of justice to decide questions of fact on principle if they can, they must take care in such formulation of principles to limit themselves to the requirements of the case in hand. That is to say, they must not lay down principles which are not required for the due decision of the particular case, or which are wider than is necessary for this purpose. The only judicial principles which are authoritative are those which are thus relevant in their subject-matter and limited in their scope. All others, at the best, are of merely persuasive efficacy. They are not true *rationes decidendi,* and are distinguished from them under the name of *dicta* or *obiter dicta,* things said by the way.[2]

Morgan defined *ratio decidendi* in a similar fashion as "those portions of the opinion setting forth the rules of law applied by the court, the application of which was *required* for the determination of the issues presented." [3]

A substantially different theory as to what constitutes the *ratio decidendi* of a case was developed in England by Professor Arthur Goodhart.[4] According to him, it is not the principle of law laid down in a decision which is the controlling element under the doctrine of *stare decisis.* In his opinion, the *ratio decidendi* is to be found by taking account of the facts treated as material by the judge who decided the case cited as a precedent, and of his decision as based on these facts.[5] Goodhart submits three main reasons for rejecting the proposition of law theory of the *ratio decidendi.* First, he points out, there may be no rule of law set forth in the opinion of the court. Second, the rule formulated by the judge may be too wide or too narrow. Third, in appellate courts the rules of law set forth by different judges in their separate opinions may have no relation to one another.

Goodhart's theory was, in its basic core, adopted by Professor Glanville Williams.[6] Williams explained that in the light of the actual practice of the courts, however, the phrase "*ratio decidendi* of a case" was slightly ambiguous, because it may mean either the rule that the judge

---

[2] John Salmond, "The Theory of Judicial Precedent," 16 *L. Q. Rev.* 376, at 387–388 (1900). See also Salmond, *Jurisprudence,* ed. G. Williams, 11th ed. (London, 1957), pp. 222–226.

[3] Edmund M. Morgan, *Introduction to the Study of Law,* 2d ed. (Chicago, 1948), p. 155 (italics mine); see also John C. Gray, *The Nature and Sources of the Law,* 2d ed. (New York, 1921), p. 261; Carleton K. Allen, *Law in the Making,* 6th ed. (Oxford, 1958), p. 247.

[4] See Goodhart, "Determining the *Ratio Decidendi* of a Case," 40 *Yale L. J.* 161 (1930). A criticism of Goodhart's article is presented by R. N. Gooderson, "*Ratio Decidendi* and Rules of Law," 30 *Can. B. Rev.* 892 (1952).

[5] Goodhart, p. 182.

[6] Williams, *Learning the Law,* 4th ed. (London, 1953), p. 63: "The *ratio decidendi* of a case can be defined as the material facts of the case plus the decision thereon."

who decided the case intended to lay down and apply to the facts, or the rule that a later court concedes him to have had the power to lay down. This is so because, as Williams rightly emphasizes, "courts do not accord to their predecessors an unlimited power of laying down wide rules." [7] This undeniable fact prompted Dean Edward Levi to take issue with Professor Goodhart on the ground that the later judge may quite legitimately find irrelevant the existence or absence of facts which the prior judge considered important. In the words of Levi, "It is not what the prior judge intended that is of any importance; rather it is what the present judge, attempting to see the law as a fairly consistent whole, thinks should be the determining classification. In arriving at this result he will ignore what the past thought important; he will emphasize facts which prior judges would have thought made no difference." [8]

A more radical point of view was advanced by Professors Sidney Post Simpson [9] and Julius Stone.[10] According to their approach, it is erroneous to assume that each decided case has its distinct *ratio decidendi*. They contend that practically each case has implicit in it a whole congeries of possible principles of decision. When a case is decided, no one can be certain which of the possible principles of decision is destined eventually to become the controlling one. In Stone's opinion, if there are ten facts stated in an opinion, as many general propositions will explain the decision as there are possible combinations of these facts. Only a study of a whole series of decisions on a particular problem of the law will to some extent reveal what the fate of a particular precedent has been in the dynamic process of restricting, expanding, interpreting, reinterpreting, and reformulating a prior body of doctrine in the creative work of the courts.

If we ask ourselves what the presently prevailing attitude of the American courts toward the question of determining the *ratio decidendi* is, we must probably conclude that the views of Salmond and Morgan are accepted by most American judges as representing the most satisfactory approach. In other words, most judges will hold that the *ratio decidendi* of a case is to be found in the general principle governing an earlier decision, as long as the formulation of this general principle was necessary to the decision of the actual issue between the litigants. Nonetheless, even though the majority of today's judges may

---

[7] *Id.*, p. 69.

[8] Edward H. Levi, *An Introduction to Legal Reasoning* (Chicago, 1949), p. 2.

[9] "English Law in the Making," 4 *Modern Law Review* 121 (1940).

[10] "Fallacies of the Logical Form in English Law," in *Interpretations of Modern Legal Philosophies*, ed. P. Sayre (New York, 1947), pp. 709–710; cf. also Stone, "The *Ratio* of the *Ratio Decidendi*," 22 *Mod. L. Rev.* 597 (1959).

theoretically agree on the basic method for finding the *ratio decidendi*, they may come to widely diverging conclusions in concrete cases calling for the application of this method. As Karl Llewellyn has shown,[11] many judges will be disinclined to examine prior decisions alleged to be relevant with razor-blade sharpness and discernment in order to determine whether the principle laid down by the prior court was, in the exact form in which it was phrased, truly necessary for the determination of the case. They will often seize upon some broad language found in a precedent and treat this language as the "rule of the case," without engaging in an incisive search to see whether the scope of the formulated rule was coextensive with the exact issue that had to be decided by the earlier court. Other judges will take quite the opposite attitude toward former decisions alleged to be in point. They will use a sharp knife to cut past opinions down to what they consider to be their proper size and limits, refusing to recognize the authority of the earlier case as going one inch beyond what was indispensable for the disposition of the issues. In the opinion of Llewellyn, these two views of the authority of a precedent—the broad view and the narrow one— exist side by side. The first method is employed for the purpose of capitalizing upon welcome precedents, the second one is used in order to whittle down or immobilize unwelcome precedents. "The same lawyer in the same brief, the same judge in the same opinion, may be using the one doctrine, the technically strict one, to cut down half the older cases he deals with, and using the other doctrine, the loose one, for building with the other half."[12]

It would seem that, in any judicious attempt to find a solution for the presently rather confused state of the *ratio decidendi* doctrine, two dangers must be guarded against. On the one hand, it would not be desirable to invest a statement of principle originating from the bench rather than from a legislative body with the trappings of quasi-statutory force. Judges, under the pressure of their business, usually do not have the time and leisure to work out with great care and particularity a rule of law which will not only fit the case at hand but at the same time accomplish the dual task of covering by its formulation all instances similarly situated while eliminating all situations which should be excluded from the scope of the rule. The legislator, on the other hand, perhaps with the aid of committees of experts, can thoroughly ponder over the wording, content, and range of a code provision or other statutory enactment and attempt to integrate it into

[11] See *The Bramble Bush*, rev. ed. (New York, 1951), pp. 67–69.
[12] *Id.*, p. 68.

the whole fabric of the positive law. As St. Thomas Aquinas perceptively observed: "Those who make laws consider long beforehand what laws to make; whereas judgment on each single case has to be pronounced as soon as it arises." [13] It is inadvisable under these conditions to ascribe to rules formulated by judges in response to the stimulus of a specific fact situation the same authority and permanence that is usually accorded legislative norms. We must also take account of the fact that judges, although they cannot avoid laying down rules and principles in order to fill the interstices in the positive legal system, are not in the first place appointed for a legislative task, while the making of rules of law on behalf of the public is the special function entrusted to a legislature. For these reasons it is a sound command of wisdom to attribute to judicial rules a weaker formal authority than is customarily imparted to legislative norms, and to permit their revision, reformulation, expansion, or contraction in instances where they have been found to be ill-conceived, awkwardly phrased, overbroad, or unduly restrictive.

The second danger confronting the *ratio decidendi* doctrine points its threat from a different direction. While the investment of judicial rules with quasi-statutory force would result in an unduly tight and overrigid structure of the precedent system, the adoption of a nominalistic philosophy toward the *ratio decidendi* problem would give rise to the opposite peril of engendering a hyperflexible and semianarchical condition of the legal order. According to what we have found to be the preponderant view, only that part of a legal proposition stated by a court is *ratio decidendi* which was necessary for the decision of the point at issue. If the word "necessary" is construed in a radically restrictive sense as being synonymous with "absolutely necessary," and if a court is always justified in carving down a rule of law found in a judicial precedent to the narrowest range consistent with the fact situation in that case, judicial nominalism will have won the field. An extreme example is offered by Llewellyn.[14] The defendant, a redheaded man named Walpole, riding in a Buick automobile painted pale magenta, caused his car to swerve on the road, and a collision with another car occurred. The plaintiff, Atkinson, was injured in the accident. The court's award of damages to Atkinson was upheld by the appellate court which, in the course of its opinion, laid down a broad rule of law for the guidance of courts in automobile accident cases. If a later court should narrow down the *ratio decidendi* of this

---

[13] *Summa Theologica*, transl. Fathers of the English Dominican Province (London, 1913–1925), pt. II, 1st pt., qu. 95, art. 1.　　　　[14] *Bramble Bush*, p. 48.

case to its particular facts by holding that "this rule holds only of red-headed Walpoles in pale magenta Buick cars," [15] an example of an improper and dangerous application of the prevailing *ratio decidendi* doctrine is presented. Another instance of a situation illustrative of this inadmissible technique would be one in which a former court had laid down the rule that overhanging branches of a tree may be cut off by a neighbor if they interfere with growth on his land or otherwise cause an inconvenience to him. A later court in a case involving the cutting off of branches of a rosebush by an adjoining landowner rejects the controlling force of the former decision on the ground that, since the former case involved a tree and not a rosebush, and since all that was necessary was the laying down of a rule applicable to trees, the *ratio decidendi* of the tree case did not cover rosebushes.

Under Goodhart's theory, such results would be avoided as long as the first judge had made it clear in his opinion that he regarded facts such as the make or color of a car involved in an accident or the kind of branch overhanging into another's land as immaterial to the decision of the case. But Goodhart's theory of the *ratio decidendi* is subject to two weaknesses which furnish arguments against its adoption. First, judges do not always tell us in so many words what specific facts set out in their opinions they view as material or immaterial. The reconstruction of the facts deemed material by the previous judge is often a matter of conjecture and guesswork, and perhaps the best and safest clue to be used in determining what facts were regarded by the judge as material is his formulation of the proposition of law controlling the case, if one can be found in his opinion.[16] Second, it would seem impracticable to vest the first judge with absolute power to appraise the materiality of facts and bind the second judge by such an appraisal. The first judge may have treated certain facts as relevant which, on a second and closer scrutiny of the situation, and perhaps against the background of a different constellation of facts, may be found to be quite subordinate and secondary in importance.

The correct view of the nature and scope of the *ratio decidendi* must proceed from the premise that it is neither the material facts of the case nor the rule of law as formulated by the court which form the authoritative element in a decision. The controlling question to be asked in determining the weight of a prior decision is whether the rationale of public policy underlying the first decision (which the first court tried to cast into the form of a proposition of law) is equally applicable in the second case. *A later case involving facts similar to*

---

[15] *Id.*, pp. 66–67.
[16] See in this connection the comments by Gooderson, pp. 893, 899 ff.

those present in an earlier case should, as a general rule, be decided in consonance with the earlier case where both cases fall under the principle of public policy or justice which lay at the bottom of the earlier decision. It is possible, however, that the policy rationale of the earlier case was inadequately or awkwardly stated by the judge, or that the verbal formalization chosen by him in spelling out the principle was either too broad or too narrow. The principle enunciated in the decision should not be broader than necessary to dispose of the legal problem before the court, but broad enough to include situations that cannot on any reasonable ground be distinguished from the facts at hand.

It is the principle in its essential core and properly delimited scope rather than the formalized rule of law into which the principle was cast by the first judge that should be accorded precedential force. Thus, where a court has decided that a legatee who murdered his testator cannot take under the testator's will because "no one may take advantage of his own wrong," a court in a later case involving a negligent killing of a testator by the legatee may hold that the principle contemplated by the court in the earlier case was not in truth as broad as it would appear to be from the verbal statement of the principle. The second court may conjecture that what prompted the first court to decide the case as it did was the consideration that the legatee who had *wilfully* killed his testator should not be permitted to take under the terms of the will. The second court need not assume that the first court meant to prejudge the case of negligent killing or that it had the power to bind future judges by its overbroad formulation of the principle of policy underlying the decision.

According to this view, a case is not controlling as a precedent for the sole reason that similarities and parallels between the facts of the earlier and later cases can be discerned. The *ratio decidendi* must be discovered by relating the facts of the two cases to a principle of legal policy which reasonably covers both situations. In many instances, this principle of policy will not spring into existence as a finished creature the first time it is expressed by a court. It will often have been stated by the court in a tentative and groping fashion, and its true import and scope will not be capable of being ascertained until other courts have had a chance to correct the inadequacies of the first formulation and to graft exceptions, qualifications, and caveats upon the principle. In this way the *ratio decidendi* of a case often develops its true and full meaning slowly and haltingly, and it may take a whole series of decisions involving variations of the situation presented in the first case until a full-blown rule of law, surrounded perhaps by a cluster of exceptions, replaces the tentatively and inadequately formulated generalization found in the initial decision. In short, a whole course of decisions will gradually mark out the outer limits of a legal principle left indeterminate by the first decision attempting to give form to it.

Section 82. *Discovery and Creation in the Judicial Process*

It was pointed out in an earlier section [1] that the role which the judge plays in the processes of adjudication is the subject of disagreement and debate. Many famous figures in the history of English law, such as Coke, Hale, Bacon, and Blackstone, were convinced that the office of the judge was to declare and interpret the law, but not to make it. Justice Cardozo said, "The theory of the older writers was that judges did not legislate at all. A pre-existing rule was there, embedded, if concealed, in the body of the customary law. All that the judges did, was to throw off the wrappings and expose the statue to our view." [2] The newer theory, initiated by Bentham and carried to a radical conclusion by John Chipman Gray, asserted that judges produce law just as much as legislators do; in the view of Gray, they even make it more decisively and authoritatively than legislators, since statutes are construed by the courts and such construction determines the true meaning of the enactment more significantly than its original text. [3] In our own day the creative theory of law must be regarded as the most widely accepted view of the judicial process, although disagreement may exist with respect to the volume and scope of judicial lawmaking.

In trying to find an answer to the question of whether judges are the makers or discoverers of the law we must, as a first step in the argument, deny that the question can be propounded in this form at all. There are many different types of judicial decisions, and it is impossible to measure all of them with the same yardstick. In order to give a well-considered answer to this question, a number of different situations must be distinguished.

(1) Where there is a well-established common-law rule or an unambiguous statutory rule clearly applicable to the facts of the case, the creative activity of the judge is obviously at a minimum. The judge, finding that no practical alternatives are available under the circumstances, simply applies the rule to the facts of the case. This is so at least where no thought occurs to the judge, or no good reason exists, in favor of changing or overturning the common-law rule or to declare the statute unconstitutional.

---

[1] See *supra* Sec. 67.
[2] Cardozo, *Nature of the Judicial Process*, pp. 124–125.
[3] Gray, *Nature and Sources of the Law*, pp. 84, 95, 170–172. On Gray see also *supra* Sec. 25.

It is true that judges sometimes recognize exceptions to the applicability and operation of statutes. Thus, equity courts have traditionally enforced some agreements technically violative of the Statute of Frauds when there had been substantial part performance, and the court considered it unfair under the circumstances to permit one party to renege on its obligations on the sole ground that the contract was not in writing. It would seem to be largely a matter of verbal disputation whether one argues, in consonance with the newer theory, that the judge in such an instance "makes" new law or whether, in accord with the older view, he is held to "discover" the exception in the true intent of the legislator or in overriding considerations of equity and justice.

(2) There are situations where no precedent or statutory rule is directly in point, but where the court, in trying to arrive at a reasonable solution of the issue at hand, can find indirect guidance from the mass of reported decisions. There are in existence decisions which bear a certain similarity to the case before the court, and which are based on some principle of law which lends itself well to extension to the case under consideration. In such cases, it may be said, the judge discovers the proper law in an analogy which rests on a common social policy connecting the earlier cases with the case at bar. *Ubi eadem legis ratio, ibi eadem dispositio* (where the reason for the law is the same, the disposition must be the same).

(3) Suppose in a western state of the United States, after it has been accepted into the Union, the courts are called upon to decide for the first time what type of water law should prevail in the state. The common-law doctrine of riparian rights regards all riparian proprietors as being on an equal footing; it allows to each a reasonable use of the stream for his own land at any time. The opposing doctrine of prior appropriation, on the other hand, gives priority rights to the first appropriator of the water if he puts the commodity to a beneficial use.

If the court, after carefully weighing the implications and effect of both rules, decides in favor of adopting the prior appropriation doctrine, it might be said that the court fashions new law. If the state is an arid state, however, with few and small streams and little annual rainfall, the "natural law" of the physical conditions of the state makes it practically imperative for the court to prefer the prior-appropriation doctrine to the common-law doctrine. If all persons have equal rights to the streams, nobody will be in a position to do anything useful with the water. It would therefore not be entirely amiss to say that the court in such a case finds the law in the pressing social and economic needs of the region.

(4) There are cases where the judicial choice between two competing lines of authority, or between two persuasive principles of public policy, is a difficult one to make. In constitutional cases, for example, two public interests (such as the right of a free press and the right to a fair trial) may have to be weighed against each other, or a valuable private interest may have to be accommodated with a vital public interest. The courts, in making their decision in such situations, must consider the whole fabric of the social order, its prevailing value structure, and the ideals of justice governing the society in question in order to find the correct answer to a problem involving clashes between conflicting principles or social interests. Frequently a balance sheet of the arguments on both sides of the question will, in the light of a careful analysis of the positive and nonpositive elements of judgment, result in a lopsided preponderance of arguments on one side of the ledger. It could then be said that the judge finds the law in the more cogent or persuasive line of argumentation, but here we are clearly reaching the borderline area between discovery and judicial creativeness.

(5) There are situations where the courts cannot find any guidance in the reported decisions and where an attempt to feel the moral pulse of the community yields no tangible result. The court may have to come to a decision on a technical point of procedure, of bankruptcy law, or of administrative law, without being able to discover the proper answer in the purpose of a statute, in considerations of justice, or in the articulate or inarticulate premises of the social order. Reason would permit the adoption of several valid solutions, and the Gordian knot must be cut somehow by the judges confronted with the problem. In such situations, rare as they may be, the creative or lawmaking ingredient in judicial adjudication is undeniably present.[4]

Our modern legal systems are usually disinclined to give to the judiciary a far-reaching power to make large-scale alterations in the law. The basic rules of procedure, for example, have been largely codified, although the courts through delegation of rule-making (legislative) powers may have had a hand in such a codification. New departments of the law, such as those dealing with workmen's compensation, social insurance, and atomic energy, have usually been launched into existence through legislative rather than judicial initiative. We do not give our judges the power to fix minimum wages and maximum hours for workers and employees; we do not permit them to set up pension systems or to change the rate of income taxation, or to introduce com-

---

[4] See in this connection Lon L. Fuller, "Reason and Fiat in Case Law," 59 *Harv. L. Rev.* 376 (1946).

pulsory arbitration of labor disputes. As Mr. Justice Holmes once pointed out,

> I recognize without hesitation that judges do and must legislate, but they can do so only interstitially; they are confined from molar to molecular motions. A common-law judge could not say "I think the doctrine of consideration a bit of historical nonsense and I shall not enforce it in my court." No more could a judge exercising the limited jurisdiction of admiralty say "I think well of the common-law rules of master and servant and propose to introduce them here *en bloc*." Certainly he could not in that way enlarge the exclusive jurisdiction of the District Courts and cut down the power of the states.[5]

Mr. Justice Cardozo summarized the situation in these words: "Insignificant is the power of innovation of any judge when compared with the bulk and pressure of the rules that hedge him on every side." [6]

Since the chief function of the judge is to decide disputes which have their roots in the past, we cannot, as a matter of general principle, assign to him a full-fledged share in the task of building the legal order of the future. He must, by and large, remain within the framework of the existing social structure and work with the materials which the past and the present have furnished him. This is so because he must take into consideration the reasonable anticipations of attorneys and their clients who cannot be expected to divine the intentions of judges bent on major revisions and reforms of the law. The judge may, within the limits suggested in earlier sections, make alterations and repairs necessary to protect the edifice of the law, or parts of it, from decay or disintegration. He may extend or constrict existing remedies and occasionally invent a new remedy or defense where the demands of justice make this step imperative. For fundamental structural changes in the legal system, however, the judge must usually rely on outside assistance. He cannot himself tear down the edifice of the law, or substantial portions of it, and replace these parts with new ones.

Thus a judge, in making a decision, will in most cases undertake to shape the existing materials at his command rather than to manufacture something entirely novel.[7] In discharging his functions, he will rely on technical legal sources, the general spirit of the legal system, certain basic premises or clearly discernible trends of the social and economic order, received ideals of justice, and certain moral conceptions of his

---

[5] *Southern Pacific Co. v. Jensen,* 244 U.S. 205, at 221 (1916).
[6] Cardozo, pp. 136–137. See also Edwin W. Patterson, *Jurisprudence* (Brooklyn, 1953), p. 573: "Courts make law but they do not make it out of whole cloth."
[7] See Allen, *Law in the Making,* pp. 292–295.

society.[8] This, in the majority of cases, is for him a natural way of dealing with legal problems, for he is a member of his society and a product of its cultural synthesis. There are always contemporary social forces at work to which the judge will respond in his opinions, and the social and cultural framework of his age will often supply him with standards and rationales of decision. Finding the law, in this sense, does not mean automatic discernment of its true content or the absence of choice.[9] It merely means that judging is generally and essentially not an act of unfettered judicial will, but a conscientious attempt to rest a decision on formal and nonformal source materials that are regarded as legitimate tools of adjudicatory activity.

In taking the position that the judge, in the light of the functions which he performs for society, should not as a general rule be regarded as an architect of a new and better order, we do not by any means wish to deprecate the work and accomplishments of those few and rare judges whom history regards as revolutionaries and trailblazers of social progress. Lord Mansfield belongs to this group of select men, and perhaps Chief Justice Marshall in some aspects of his work may also be included among them. There may be times or historical contingencies where bold and unconventional action on the part of a judge becomes wholesome and beneficial for society. There may be situations where stagnation or decay can be overcome only by a judicial decision-maker who, being convinced that the preponderant values of the community are wholly obsolete or unreasonable, is willing to take risks and is determined to chart a new course into the future. Progress often depends on the courageous, decisive, and antitraditional action of great men. And although we should insist that the major tasks of law reform should be reserved to the action of men or bodies entrusted with the business of legislating, we would be taking a narrow and perhaps philistine viewpoint if we did not, at times, concede to the judiciary the right to lead the moral sentiment of society and to inaugurate, in a judicial decision, a new conception of justice in accord with the highest knowledge and truest insight perceptible to the human mind.

[8] By treating these nonformal sources as genuine sources of law, we are enlarging the range of the area in which the judge is able to "discover" law, as compared with the positivist approach, which regards every judicial act not directly referable to a formal source as an act of lawmaking.

[9] "Notwithstanding all the apparatus of authority, the judge has nearly always some degree of choice." Lord Wright, *Legal Essays and Addresses* (Cambridge, Eng., 1939), p. xxv. See also Wallace Mendelson, "The Judge's Art," 109 *U. Pa. L. Rev.* 524 (1961).

TABLE

OF CASES

INDEX

OF AUTHORS

INDEX